Queer BDSM Intimacies

Queer BDSM Intimacies

Critical Consent and Pushing Boundaries

Robin Bauer

University of Hamburg, Germany

First published 2014 by
PALGRAVE MACMILLAN

Palgrave Macmillan in the UK is an imprint of Macmillan Publishers Limited,
registered in England, company number 785998, of Houndmills, Basingstoke,
Hampshire RG21 6XS.

Palgrave Macmillan in the US is a division of St Martin's Press LLC,
175 Fifth Avenue, New York, NY 10010.

Palgrave Macmillan is the global academic imprint of the above companies
and has companies and representatives throughout the world.

Palgrave® and Macmillan® are registered trademarks in the United States,
the United Kingdom, Europe and other countries.

ISBN 978–1–137–43501–9

This book is printed on paper suitable for recycling and made from fully
managed and sustained forest sources. Logging, pulping and manufacturing
processes are expected to conform to the environmental regulations of the
country of origin.

A catalogue record for this book is available from the British Library.

A catalog record for this book is available from the Library of Congress.

Contents

Acknowledgments

The first time in my life I entered a space of strangers who immediately recognized me for what I was – a boy in a woman's body at that particular time – changed my life forever. It ultimately gave me the strength to live my gender and sexuality according to my own rules. The space I am talking about was one of the European WALP/Berlin Easter-Conference dyke+ BDSM community events. I am deeply indebted to this community as an individual, an activist and a researcher. Therefore, my first thanks go to the community, my interview partners, who trusted me with the most intimate details of their lives, those who passed on my request for interviews to others, those who let me stay at their places when I was on the road to conduct interviews on a low budget (Kate Huh; Lynnee Breedlove; Hida Viloria; Ken Rowe; the Tuntenhaus, especially Rocky, Andre and Tarek; Justus Eisfeld; Sebastian De Line and others) and those who paved the way in community-building in Europe: among many others, most prominently Tania and Denya from WALP and Birgit and Eva from the Osterkonferenz. For providing me and others with a space to celebrate our trans* identities at a time of severe exclusions, I thank, among many others, ratz and Jasco for building a queer BDSM community and claiming FTM presence within the gay men's community in Europe. I am also grateful to Martin Inane and John Weiss for getting me to the Leather Leadership Conference in New York to speak about trans* inclusion in the leather community with inspiring community organizers.

In terms of my academic journey, I am indebted to many peers and superiors. First of all, this study could not have been imagined, let alone finished, without the support of, and the intriguing theoretical debates with, Marianne Pieper. I also owe a great deal to the opportunities provided to me during my time at the project 'Degendering Science'. My heartfelt thanks go to my dream team co-worker Helene Götschel, and the head of the project, Christine Mayer, who also supported my research all the way. Special thanks also to all those who read versions of early drafts of the chapters and articles I have worked on in the past, leading up to this. Their comments were invaluable and inspiring: Volker Woltersdorff, Larry Ianotti, Anja Paulsen, Christian Klesse, Gesa Mayer, Andrea Rick and Margot Weiss. I am also indebted for feedback to Lisa Conradi, Camel Gupta, Jin Haritaworn, Meg Barker, David Savran, Susan Stryker, Vassilis Tsianos, Josch Hoenes, Eva Hayward, Dossie Easton, Maisha Eggers, Lüder Tietz, Elisabeth Tuider, Julia Hammerschmidt and all those whose names unfortunately have slipped my mind, but who have surely left an imprint. I am also thankful to all those who have invited me to give lectures on the subject and the countless exciting questions and conversations that have emerged from these events. Thank you also for interesting discussions to all my students in Hamburg, Göttingen and Stuttgart.

Thanks also go to Meg Barker for her advice, to Merryl Sloane for being the most competent proof-reader a queer and trans* theorist could wish for, and to the Palgrave staff, who always found the time to answer all my questions.

I am also lucky and happy to have various families of origin and choice that have been invaluable sources of strength and support and even refrained from asking me how the book was going, but nonetheless never gave up on me: my parents, the SISC family, the dreamers circle and especially Manda Scott and my guides, the Rattenbar community, both Wuschels and the Knuffels, Florian and various extended poly-families throughout these years, and finally many, many dear friends in various places. I am especially grateful to Christina and Claude for doing what they are doing for our communities and to Omar for giving me shelter in the desert when a working retreat was much needed, as well as Hilal for sharing her 'Lieblinge'. Finally there is Emmanuel, through whom it all fell into place.

This work is dedicated to all the friendly spirits, embodied and out of bounds, and to those queer and trans* warriors and ancestors who did not survive or live to read this, but were paving the way.

1
Introduction

At the end of the 19th century, a scientific culture dedicated to the study of sexualities emerged simultaneously with a new concept of sexual identities and minorities within Western European and US cultures. Over time, the meaning of certain acts changed, and they were reframed as sexuality. Moreover, sexual practices were no longer seen simply as singular events or as series of acts, but as constitutive of a coherent sexual identity, thus effectively producing a distinct minority in the population (Foucault 1978; D'Emilio 1983a; 1983b; Halperin 1990; Katz 1996). Within a Euro-American tradition of binary thinking, sexual subjectivities were not simply differentiated, but were constructed as exclusive either–or categories in a social hierarchy that was later analyzed as systems of heterosexism and heteronormativity by lesbian, gay, bisexual, trans*[1] and queer activists and scholars (Rich 1980; Butler 1990; Warner 1993). One example of binary thinking is that sexual preference was reduced to whether one's sexual partners were exclusively cismen[2] or ciswomen. The homosexual served as the constitutive other[3] for the *white*[4] heterosexual norm (Katz 1996), while other options, like bisexuality (Tucker 1995; Firestein 1996) or fluid identities, were dismissed.

These material-discursive processes were repressive, oppressive and productive at the same time. They singled out certain individuals such as homosexuals, trans* people and sadomasochists to label them as deviants and subjected them to various disciplining and oppressive technologies, from electro-shock therapy through criminalization to hate crimes. Simultaneously, the production of sexual identities created new pleasures, desires, intimacies, types of relationships, whole subcultures and finally political movements, like gay liberation or lesbian feminism, and academic fields, like lesbian and gay studies, queer theory and transgender studies, resignifying these acts and identities. The subject of this study, dyke + queer BDSM, also emerged under these contradictory yet productive conditions. Here, I differentiate between the scientific construction of these practices as individual pathology (which I call sadomasochism) and the popular construction of those practices and the meanings they hold for consensual participants within their community contexts (which I call BDSM). The acronym BDSM has increasingly replaced the formerly common SM, S/M or S&M within the community, because it does not carry the baggage of the pathological associations and because it stands for a broader range of practices: bondage, discipline, dominance/submission and sadism/masochism.

Heteronormativity and the ideal of harmonic sex

This research is situated within a queer and trans* theoretical context. Crucial to my employment of queer theory is the specific yet broad notion of critiquing heteronormativity as a guiding analytical tool. Heteronormativity is a concept and a structure of power that permeates society. It naturalizes the notion of opposite-sex sexual object choice; celebrates and privileges specific forms of heterosexual relationships, identities and practices and posits the heterosexual couple as the primary social unit of society (Warner 1993; Bell & Binnie 2000; Phelan 2001; Monro & Warren 2004; Langdridge 2006). Heteronormativity has been used historically and continues to pathologize, criminalize, morally condemn and discriminate against non-heteronormative ways of being, such as homo- and bisexuality, BDSM, promiscuity and public and commercial sex (Rubin 1992a: 282), and it can be extended to include 'interracial' sexual interactions and relationships (Steinbugler 2005) and those that involve disabled bodies (Luczak 1993; Tremain 1996; Clare 1999; McRuer & Wilkerson 2003; Guter & Killacky 2004; McRuer 2006). Racialization intervenes when certain heterosexuals are not awarded the benefits of heteronormativity because their sexuality is constructed as deviant (in comparison to the unstated *white* heterosexual norm), such as single Black mothers in the US (Cohen 2005) or Thai women in European contexts (Haritaworn 2007). A queer perspective that does not take into account the interweaving and the simultaneities (Erel et al. 2007) of sexual object choice and gendered identities and bodies with other categories of social stratification fails to generate analyses that adequately address the complex social realities it tries to describe. Therefore, I am working with an expansive definition of anti-heteronormative critique in three regards: including all social hierarchies and norms that privilege one kind of sexual and intimate relating over others; including a simultaneity analysis; and paying attention to how heteronormativity is part of the weaving of the social fabric in general and is not restricted to the sexual, domestic or private sphere. This research is also part of the evolving field of transgender studies (Stryker 2006a) because it is concerned with the lives of trans* people from a non-pathological perspective and emphasizes the material aspects of gender. For instance, trans* theorists have critiqued queer theory's erasure of trans* materialities (Namaste 2000) and have made productive use of phenomenology as a way of focusing on the body in theorizing (Prosser 1998; Henry Rubin 2003).

Queer theory has worked successfully with the concept of heteronormativity as an analytical tool. Yet the term has also been utilized in reductionist ways, restricting analysis to the homo/hetero binary despite the fact that sexual hierarchies and norms often include other dimensions as well. One of the elements of heteronormativity, which has not yet been awarded much attention, is what I call the *ideal of harmonic sex*. The ideal sexual interaction has been increasingly constructed as occurring between egalitarian partners whose intimate bodily interactions are devoid of power dynamics and anything that may be thought of as unpleasant emotions or sensations, such as pain, humiliation, shame or discomfort. The ideal of harmonic sex is closely related to the liberal construction of the sexual as a subset of the construction of the private sphere (Hausen 1976; Leap 1999) as a space remote from socio-political life. Therefore, the ideal of harmonic sex serves to obscure the fact that the sexual, constructed as the most intimate and private sphere of interaction, is not distinct from socio-political contexts, but is infused with power dynamics just like every other area of life (Foucault 1976; 1982; Weiss 2011). The ideal of harmonic sex therefore aids in rendering invisible the pervasiveness of domestic violence and sexual abuse in the nuclear family and in romantic relationships, as well as ongoing economic dependencies, especially between heterosexual partners (Jamieson 1999; Klesse 2007). The ideal of harmonic sex also serves to perpetuate racist and classist ideologies of social progress and civilization, claiming that only 'civilized', *white* and middle-class heterosexuals practice egalitarian sex in a way that is considerate of each partner's needs (Carter 2007). It fuses discourses of sexual moralities based on monotheistic ideals of purity and innocence with contemporary emancipatory discourses, which pay lip service to feminist visions of sexual equality, into a depoliticized, privatized and sanitized ideal of the pure relationship (see Giddens 1992; for a critical view see Jamieson 1999).

Klesse points out that power has been neglected in some queer discourses and in gay and lesbian studies, and research on same-sex partnerships tends to present them as, in principle, egalitarian (2007: 2; 6). Referring to Gidden's equation of his concept of 'the pure relationship' with gay lives, Klesse sees that view as 'utterly romanticising the reality' and working with a one-dimensional (gendered) concept of power (Klesse 2007: 7). The narrative of harmonic and synchronized sex (as in the ideal of the 'simultaneous orgasm') feeds into the illusion that, in *white* middle-class Euro-American contexts of monogamous, mono-racial couplehood, this ideal of the egalitarian relationship or the companionate marriage is not only achievable, but has also already been established. Harmonic sex is taken as the moral and political gold standard against which other cultures, such as Islamic and Mormon polygamy, are constructed, measured and evaluated. The discursive construction of the ideal of harmonic sex can be traced back to the 19th century in the US, when the conflation of heterosexual marriage with citizenship helped to construct *whiteness* as synonymous with American concepts of just relationships (Carter 2007: 78) and marriage as sexual democracy was imagined as the foundation of state democracy (107). This was expressed in the ideal of simultaneous orgasm (96–7) and the mystical experience of unity across difference (106).

Dyke + queer BDSM practices and identities violate the ideal of harmonic sex and a variety of other, related social norms: heterosexual partner choice, fixed sexual preference, sex as natural, reproductively derived sex which centers on (vaginal) penetration and by extension genital stimulation, the sexual context as private and within a monogamous romantic dyad, and the moderateness of sex. Dyke + queer BDSM might, therefore, be understood as creating *alternative intimacies* and, more specifically, *exuberant intimacies*, intimacies that reject reason, moderation, mediocrity, harmony and equality as well as reproduction and usefulness. Instead, alternative intimacies celebrate difference, tension, intensity, risk, excess, ecstasy, wastefulness, perversity, campy extravagance, fluidity and insanity, as well as becoming something beyond the human. Yet, since all this occurs in a space that is partially contained through the negotiating of consent, exuberant intimacies present an alternative sexual ethics rather than transgressiveness per se.

The part played by the ideal of harmonic sex in heteronormative structures and processes, and how BDSM engages with these structures and processes, has not been adequately addressed in queer studies, which tends to focus on the issue of partner choice alone. This book seeks to address some of these and other gaps in queer studies, including the lack of empirical studies to confront and disrupt theorizing by analyzing in-depth interviews. I do not consider BDSM as pathology, perversion, paraphilia or deviance for the purpose of this study, mainly for two reasons. First, my data do not suggest that any of these is a suitable characterization of BDSM practices, identities or relationships. Second, from a queer theoretical perspective, I question the validity and usefulness of the social construction of a normal/deviant binary. Rather, I argue from a perspective of human difference, which views the idea of classifying certain consensual sexual behaviors as normal and others as deviant, sick or criminal as a modern form of social regulation, part of what Foucault calls biopolitics. Rather than taking the normal/perverse binary for granted, we should interrogate its function in establishing and maintaining social hierarchies and norms. In this study I am, therefore, taking a close and intimate look at how dyke, trans* and queer BDSM practitioners experience and interpret their own BDSM practices in the context of various interwoven social contexts. Specifically, I reconstruct how they (re)negotiate their genders, sexualities and intimate relationships within dyke + queer subcultures that are embedded in structures of power and social hierarchy. I examine how dyke + queer BDSM practices and identities intervene in heteronormative realities and what dyke + queer BDSM perspectives as situated knowledges may contribute to the contested fields of queer theory, politics and practices.

From de Sade to F65 – The social construction of sadomasochism

Through the construction of BDSMers as 'perverse' and distinct from the sexually 'normal' population, the power dynamics and the elements of sensation play and immobilization in non-BDSM encounters have been obscured. This has led to the idea that BDSM and non-BDSM sexuality are two sharply distinct sets of behaviors, and that individuals are either 'into BDSM' or not. Many of the BDSM practitioners I interviewed share this assumption and position themselves as part of a sexual minority, which contradicts both the fact that they stress the fluidity of their actual practices and the fact that there are many elements of BDSM in 'vanilla' practices. Mandy, a US-based queer/dyke high femme bottom in her 60s, presented a slightly different view:

> It's not just what I think, but observed experience. That given access to BDSM in a safe, sane and consensual way almost everybody will want to [do it]. I don't think we're a minority at all. When I was with [a local sex education network] before BDSM opened up, we ran a community sex education switchboard. And we were very bi, we were doing group sex and very far out people. When SM came along, 80 per cent of us – given some kind of cultural community support for doing it – became SM people. Those few who didn't felt very left out and kinda lost.

So Mandy's argument is twofold in dismantling the idea of a distinct sexual minority of BDSMers. First, a majority, rather than a minority, of people have the potential to gain pleasure from BDSM practices. Second, the social context often determines whether people end up practicing BDSM. Studies not specifically designed to assess BDSM participation, but conducting broad surveys of a nation's sexual behaviors, estimate that between 5 and 14 per cent of the general population have had SM experiences (Reinisch 1990; Janus & Janus 1993) and enjoy pain in a sexual context, a number which quickly climbs up to as much as 50 per cent if one includes items like 'love bites' (Kolmes et al. 2006: 302). These numbers seem to support Mandy's observations that larger numbers of people have the basic capacity to include BDSM elements in their sex life and that there is no clear boundary between a BDSM minority and a 'harmonic' sexual majority. Yet, since the 19th century, sadomasochism has been constructed discursively as a distinct entity, for example, as part of a psychopathological personality or as a subcultural identity. I will briefly trace this social construction of sadomasochism based on the available research literature in this field.

The history of the social construction of sadomasochism as a social and sexual pathology started in the 19th century with the work of the German-Austrian physician and psychiatrist Richard von Krafft-Ebing. In his influential work *Psychopathia Sexualis* (first published in 1886) he invented the terms 'sadism' (after the French author Marquis de Sade) and 'masochism' (after the Austrian author Leopold von Sacher-Masoch) and introduced the concepts to the medical sciences. The use of pain or dominance/submission for sexual arousal thus did not attract any special interest until Krafft-Ebing named and classified these practices. Bullough and Bullough point out: 'Sadomasochism is a good example of the way a pathological condition is established by the medical community, for until it became a diagnosis it received little attention and was not even classified as a sin' (1977b: 210). Krafft-Ebing's diagnoses were not based on broad empirical data, but were derived solely from clinical case studies from his own practice, from historical and anecdotal illustrations and from literary figures. Furthermore, as a forensic psychiatrist, his samples consisted of criminal offenders and were thus strongly biased, since they only referred to harmful non-consensual acts that attracted the attention of state institutions. Since then, sexological research has generally made a priori assumptions based on purely theoretical or fictional grounds or on broad generalizations based on forensic or clinical case studies without critically reflecting on these sample biases. Until recently, the discourses about BDSM constructed it in various ways as the 'other' to such cultural ideals as reason, sanity, enlightenment, the law, democracy, equality, reproductive heterosexuality and the ideal of harmonic sex.

The term 'sadomasochism', which links the (for Krafft-Ebing, two separate) phenomena of sadism and masochism, was first used in 1913 by the Austrian psychoanalyst Isidor Sadger (Passig & Deunan 2002: 36). Sigmund Freud placed the concept of sadism into the average male psychoanalytic subject. According to him, each individual went through a stage of sadism as part of his sexual development, and sadism in the adult became one of the arrested developments. Later, Freud expanded the term 'sadism' to include non-sexual aggression, unifying various previously disconnected phenomena under the concept of the death drive (Moore 2009: 498). Since then, there have been various psychoanalytical and psychological theories that have tried to explain BDSM as pathological or deviant behavior. Sadomasochism has been theorized as an intimacy issue; as anxiety around dependency, autonomy and control; as a compulsive re-enactment of trauma (Taylor 1997: 113) and as a result of brain pathologies (115). Sexual deviation was first introduced as an official psychiatric diagnosis in the International Classification of Diseases (ICD)-6 in 1948 and differentiated into subcategories in the ICD-8 in 1965. The diagnostic system has barely changed since, despite the growth of research implying its inadequacy (Reiersøl & Skeid 2006: 244). The current version of the ICD-10 by the World Health

Organization groups various BDSM and related practices under the header F65 'Disorders of sexual preference' (World Health Organization 2010), which includes sadomasochism, fetishism, fetishistic transvestism, exhibitionism and voyeurism. Many sexual behaviors that do not have genital interaction between partners as their primary focus are thus pathologized. Moreover, acts for which consent is never possible, such as pedophilia and various kinds of sexual harassment, are grouped together with consensual ones like fetishism and BDSM.[5] But, even beyond the therapeutic profession, the social construction of BDSM as pathology remains one of the dominant paradigms today. In the media, BDSM is constructed as a disorder that needs explaining (how one 'became this way'); it is generally psychologized (Wilkinson 2009) and represented in stereotypes, such as the sadistic psychopath and the self-harming masochist (Barrett 2007).

Within colonialist[6] discourse, BDSM practices are perceived as reflecting an earlier stage of the colonizing countries' own history, the 'primitive' or 'savage' past (Hoople 1996: 217; Moore 2009: 487). In the UK 'Spanner case', for instance, the gay BDSM activities that were subject to trial and conviction were characterized as breeding cruelty, as increasing barbarity, as lacking control, as a logic of violence, as unruly escalation (Moran 1995: 226), as disorder and irrational, as the law's (and civilization's) other, whereas the law was seen as providing order, predictability, reason, control and limit (227). In this cultural progress narrative, which goes back to Norbert Elias (1976), throughout *white* European history, humanity has supposedly become less violent and more 'civilized'. Within this logic, Wetzstein et al. see the function of SM fantasies as suspending the normative and moral boundaries of civilized society, paving the way for transgressive, dangerous and immoral acts (1993: 105). This reasoning takes for granted that there is a 'precivilized nature' of humans that is prone to violence and rape. Moreover, the equation of controlled violence with 'civilization' has a racist undertone, implying that 'non-civilized' cultures are destructive and amoral (or at least less self-controlled than Western culture), which is not grounded in historical and global reality, obscuring the actual violence perpetrated by the colonizers. Some subsets of the BDSM community itself understand BDSM as a counterbalance to the downsides of 'civilization' (Mains 2002). These accounts do not posit 'Western civilization' as superior; on the contrary, they point out deficiencies in its culture and they honor the wisdom of other cultural traditions, yet they remain caught in a discursive frame of othering (the 'civilized West' vs. 'primitive cultures').

Sadomasochism is also understood as the other in relation to democratic and progressive agendas. It has been constructed as the ultimate cause and/or expression of patriarchy by many lesbian feminists (see Chapter 2) and as inherently fascist (Reti 1993). There are two main arguments rendered as proof by those accusing BDSMers of being fascist: one is that the post-World War II gay leatherman look supposedly resembles the SS uniforms (Sontag

1975),[7] and the other is that Nazi scenarios are sometimes reproduced in role play.[8] Moore attributes this framing of the Holocaust in sadomasochistic terms to the linguistic void the unspeakable horrors produced (2005: 166). This void is then filled with the taboo nature of sexual perversion. More broadly, sadomasochism is often understood as violence. In the 1980s, gay BDSM in particular was presented in mainstream media as dangerous and even lethal, often in order to discredit the gay community as a whole (Gayle Rubin 2003: 274ff).

While all these constructions of BDSM still prevail today, alternative representations of BDSM are slowly finding their way into the hegemonic culture. BDSM can be liberating for the individual, but remains the other to heteronormative harmonic sexuality (Khan 2009: 90). In her study of non-BDSMers' perceptions of the representation of BDSM in the film *Secretary*, Weiss finds that the audience makes sense of this sexual minority through the mechanisms of *acceptance via normalization* and *understanding via pathologizing*. Both mechanisms ultimately serve to reinforce the boundaries between socially acceptable and stigmatized sexualities. Representations of BDSM allow the mainstream audience to flirt with danger and the other while remaining in the protected position of normalcy, thus utilizing a mode of distanced consumption (2006a: 105). The public image of the BDSM practitioner as an exotic other, as depicted in advertisements and films, can be understood within the logic of multiculturalism that Žižek analyzed as one of the more subtle forms of oppressing the other (2001: 299). Despite the current logic of flexible normalism described by Link (1999: 30), BDSM as a whole has certainly not been awarded the status of 'the normal'. While a certain discursive normalization is evident, it is still BDSM that makes subjects *not* normal, while *other* properties render them normal, like being *white* and in a monogamous marriage (see Khan 2009). Therefore, BDSM may (yet) be one of those instances that actually mark a moment of proto-normalism.

In contrast, various recent studies (Alison et al. 2001; Cross & Matheson 2006) and some community activists aim to prove that BDSM practitioners are just like everybody else and are well-adjusted, law-abiding citizens, which I interpret as a reaction to the long history of pathologization and criminalization. Langdridge and Butt identify two different discourses in BDSM communities, one that seeks inclusion within sexual citizenship (like the 'National Coalition for Sexual Freedom' (NCSF), a US BDSM rights organization) and one that is about transgressing norms and positioning BDSM as an oppositional identity (2004: 44). The former constructs practitioners as responsible members of society, facilitating self-surveillance and therefore embodying a neoliberal form of governing through citizenship (Rose 1996); the latter is positioned within a context of danger and dissidence (Langdridge & Butt 2004: 45). In a fusion of BDSM community discourse and some sociological and ethnographic research (Weinberg 1995; Beckmann

2001), BDSM has also been constructed as a sexual identity and as a sexual minority analogous to homosexuality.

All of the social constructions of BDSM practices and identities I have described remain in force today in scientific, popular and community discourses. Traces of them also appear in the interviews: some people distance themselves from BDSM as violent, patriarchal and pathological, while others posit certain practices within a tribal context, as the other of modern society. Some of my interview partners also attest to having internalized some of the negative stereotypes, and some openly embrace the stigma of insanity in a dissident move, rejecting classification as good, responsible neoliberal citizens.

Methods and methodology: Situating knowledges[9]

This study is based on a qualitative empirical research design, utilizing 'grounded theory' (following Strauss & Corbin 1990) for data analysis. All of the results presented in the following chapters are based on this analysis.

Through interviewing dyke+queer BDSMers, I have given subjugated subjects and the knowledges they embody center stage. Therefore, my work can be positioned methodologically within a Foucauldian framework of insurrecting subjugated knowledges, which Susan Stryker (2006a: 12) has appropriated for the project of transgender studies. More specifically, this study seeks to desubjugate previously marginalized forms of knowledge about gendered embodiments and sexual practices (13). I agree with Stephenson and Papadopoulos that empirical methods may serve as both a rupture in and an expansion of theorizing (2006). Since the data – like life itself – never stand still and always offer more than one possible interpretation, I call my approach *grounding theories* rather than grounded theory: it presents an active, constant renegotiation of meanings and a stuttering translation of data into a simultaneous multiplicity of theories.

Methodologically, I am following the epistemological concept of situated knowledges proposed by the feminist science studies scholar Donna Haraway (1991), combining standpoint theory with poststructuralist approaches. She points out how some bodies are marked as other, while the unmarked position of the *white* (and, I add, straight, non-disabled, cis) man holds the power to see without being seen, to represent without being represented. From this perspective, he may supposedly see everything from nowhere. But, according to Haraway, 'that view of infinite vision is an illusion, a god-trick' (1991: 189). In social reality, each vision is an embodied one; each social actor, including scientists, is embodied and positioned within social power relations. Each perspective is therefore particular and specific; none may claim epistemological, moral, political or scientific neutrality or detachment. Therefore, Haraway holds that only a partial perspective that makes itself accountable for its situatedness may claim objectivity (190). She also argues that the standpoints of the subjugated are not 'innocent'; rather, they are valuable because they are the least prone to denying the critical and interpretative core of all knowledge claims, since they are structurally denied the authority to speak 'the truth' (191). Knowledge production is always about interpretation, translation, stuttering and partial understanding. Situatedness is about vulnerability and resists a politics of closure and finality. The knowing self is always partial, stitched together imperfectly, and therefore able to see together with heteromorphic others; objectivity is partial connection, generating a conversation between situated perspectives, generating situated knowledges (193). While Haraway is not concerned with empirical social sciences, her epistemological framework translates well into a useful methodological approach. Each person I interviewed may be seen to have contributed their own situated knowledge(s). It was my task to critically situate myself and my interview partners and to engage the situated and partial knowledges they produced in a critical, polyphonic and power-sensitive conversation. No one truth will emerge in this book, but instead we will see non-dissolvable contradictions as well as unexpected connections across difference. The categories I developed in my research should not be mistaken for fixed terms, but, rather, should be seen as open-ended concepts with fluid boundaries, just like the genders and sexualities of my interview partners. If scientific commitment is about reconstructing social life and recapturing it in a way that is 'fair'[10] to those studied and represented, then the theories we generate have to become as fluid, simultaneous, interwoven and contradictory as the social worlds we inhabit.

To situate the knowledges I produce, I position myself and my interview partners (according to their own descriptions of self[11]) in regard to structural power relations[12] in order to enable the critically engaged reader to assess the investments that these knowledges carry with them. I consider these to be strategic–political positionings, not essentialist categories or identities (Minh-ha 1986/7). On all levels, my academic work (research questions, field access, manner of conducting interviews, analysis, presenting results and so on) is informed by and simultaneously renegotiates my positioning as a *white* German with a Polish grandfather, as a queer/gay, polyamorous, BDSM top and transman with a mixed lower-class background and a precarious economic situation.

At the beginning of this study in 2003, I conducted my first interviews as a non-hormone-taking, non-operative transboy, and my main home base for these topics was the international dyke + queer BDSM community, even though my primary partner was a gay cisman. In 2008, my last interviews were conducted after I had transitioned physically and legally to male, and the gay male BDSM community had become my main point of reference and activism. In 2012, I became the manager of a gay men's BDSM camp in Denmark, probably the first transman in Europe to be in such a position of relative community authority, which shows that my academic and my grassroots organizing work are interwoven.

If ethnography is understood as immersive, long-term, multi-sited, full participant observation (Newmahr 2011: 5), then my study can also be considered ethnographic in nature. Since I was an active member of the community studied at the beginning of my research and my knowledge of dyke + queer BDSM is not merely intellectual, but embodied, this work might also be considered an auto-ethnography in part (Ellis & Bochner 2000). But my analysis is crucially focused on the interview data I generated and is not based mainly on my personal experiences or observations. For instance, I have tried to read between the lines of my interviews and confront some of the conclusions with outsider perspectives, such as critical *whiteness* studies (Morrison 1992; Frankenberg 1993; Delgado & Stefancic 1997; Dyer 1997; Bérubé 2001; Wollrad 2005; Riggs 2006; Carter 2007), to produce self-critical knowledges and to foster dialogue within the community studied. My research can therefore be described as community-intrinsic observation. This position gave me access to resources that outsiders would not have been granted.

Between 2003 and 2008 I conducted 49 qualitative, semi-structured interviews (Fontana & Frey 2000) in person with self-identified dykes, bi/pansexual ciswomen, trans* people and queers from the US (18) and Western Europe (31) who practice BDSM. The majority of the European interviews took place in Germany. The rest of the interviews were conducted at an international radical queer gathering and at the Women at Amsterdam Leather Pride (WALP) in Amsterdam and included respondents from other Western and Northern European countries. Although I received responses from *white* people with a working-class background or limited economic resources,[13] and my sample includes people between 20 and 60 years of age, people of color are underrepresented in my sample, which might have to do with the fact that I am *white* myself and that I did not mention discussing race and class as a focus of my study when searching for interview partners. The low participation of dykes + queers of color in my sample might also be 'representative' of the organized mixed-race dyke + queer BDSM community, which is predominantly *white*.

Nine of my interview partners self-identified primarily as women, five as male-to-female (MTF), five as female-to-male (FTM), one as a transboy and one as transmasculine, 15 as femme, one as lesbian (as gender), one as uni-sexual/alien, three as butch, four as transgender butch, two as genderqueer, two as transgender in the sense of in-between genders and two refused any gender label. Two were also born intersex. Twenty-seven identified (roughly) as the gender they were assigned at birth, thus as women, while 22 used primary identity labels departing from the gender assigned at birth. Twenty-two interview partners mostly presented as feminine in everyday life, 16 mostly as masculine and 11 were not fixed at all, were decidedly non-binary or were emotionally indifferent to their gender presentation. This confirms that this community departs significantly from the regular population and from previous empirical studies on BDSM and other women-only or lesbian spaces, with almost half of the sample not primarily identifying with their gender of birth.

In terms of primary sexual preference or identity, 16 interview partners identified as queer, an additional four as queer dyke, 12 as dyke or lesbian, five as bisexual, an additional three as pansexual and one as polysexual.[14] Six identified as gay male, and two refused any label. Those identifying more within the gender binary (as women or men) tended to use sexual identity labels that depend on the gender binary to make sense, such as lesbian, bisexual or gay male, while those strongly rejecting the gender binary tended to reject these labels and identify as queer. While the term 'queer' is used in countless ways, in the context of my interviews it was mostly used to express genders and sexualities that moved beyond the dichotomies of man/woman, homo/heterosexual and the hegemonic model of sexual orientation.

When it came to BDSM roles, 14 interview partners identified primarily as tops, 25 as switches and ten as bottoms.

Overall, my sample stands out from previous research on BDSM communities, especially in regard to the gender and sexual identity composition, but also in regard to class, health and political convictions. For instance, an overwhelming majority (36 interview partners) identified in various ways as left-wing. These included subdivisions such as anti-capitalist, anarchist, sex work activist, anti-racist and fat activist. Twenty interview partners were involved in BDSM community organizing, public education and activism in some way. Dyke, trans* and queer BDSMers seem to be a less privileged and more politically radical subset of the overall BDSM communities.

Addressing interview partners as experts on their own practices, I chose not to document their individual biographies as a whole, but to hone the focus in regard to their status as representatives of certain dyke + queer BDSM practices, identities and communities. I asked interview partners to position themselves in terms of gender identity, sexual preferences and practices and discussed their personal experiences with BDSM in regard to such issues as power, healing, politics, spirituality, social marginalization, intimate relationships, gender and so on. Another set of questions addressed the standards and norms of the BDSM communities they were familiar with and their own positioning in relation to these. Interview partners were given the opportunity to pick their own aliases. Because the community is rather small, cities and other references were also neutralized to protect the privacy of interview partners.

It is important to remember that the interviews represent a snapshot of a moment in the lives of the research participants, including how they recapitulated and reconstructed certain events of their biographies and social contexts in the interactive situation of the interview. To stress this, I will use the past tense when referring to their stories and reflections. I also prefer the term 'interview partner' to emphasize the interactive nature of the process of knowledge production in general and the active role those interviewed played in particular (while terms like 'interviewee' imply that the researcher is active and the research participants are passive and simply sources the interviewer taps into).

Chapter outline

This book is divided into nine chapters. Each addresses a theme, but some empirical and theoretical concepts also travel through these themes, and therefore the chapters are interwoven as well.

Chapter 2, 'The Culture of Dyke + Queer BDSM', introduces the reader to the social context of this study. It starts with a history of the BDSM communities and goes on to describe the dyke + queer BDSM communities in the USA and Western Europe, with a special focus on questions of difference, community boundaries and norms, especially in regard to trans*. It also discusses how this community relates to other social and political contexts, including the impact of anti-BDSM feminism.

Chapter 3, 'Renegotiating Dyke + Queer BDSM', traces how my interview partners negotiated the meanings that their erotic, sexual and BDSM practices held for them. The intent of this chapter is not to provide a definition of BDSM, because these practices mean different things to different people. But I do introduce various concepts of desire and sexuality as well as views of BDSM as a social space and as an alternative reality. These apply in various situations for different actors, depending on the specific practices and contexts in question. I suggest that BDSM can be understood as intimate theater, stressing that this entails the production of its own specific kind of reality and social space.

Chapter 4, 'Negotiating Critical Consent', discusses the one feature that all interview partners agreed was crucial for an activity to count as BDSM: consent. While, in the general BDSM community discourse, consent tends to be treated as an uncomplicated given, my interview partners situated their consent-making processes and power dynamics within a society of hierarchy and abuse. I therefore offer an analysis that complicates liberal notions of consent as a contract between equal individuals, and instead shows the difficulties of distinguishing valid from pseudo-consent. I also offer suggestions for how a working practice of critical consent can be established.

Chapter 5, 'Exploring Exuberant Intimacies', starts with a definition of intimacy as access, which entails both positive experiences of boundary transgression, which I conceptualize as touch, and negative experiences of boundary violation. I discuss my interview partners' engagement with BDSM in 'public' as one example of creating intimacy through transgressing the private/public boundary. The chapter then investigates why non-monogamous relationship practices are the norm in the dyke + queer BDSM communities, connecting the BDSM culture of negotiating consent with the negotiating of non-normative relationship styles. Further, I discuss BDSM-specific kinds of relationships and intimacies, such as the fulltime ownership relationship or sharing intimacy in play party spaces, which lead to synergetic effects.

Chapter 6, 'Exploring and Pushing Boundaries', discusses BDSM as voluntary risk-taking, by creating intense experiences through facing vulnerabilities, which stresses the significance of establishing trust. My interview partners used BDSM for exploring, pushing and transgressing their own and cultural boundaries. This helped them to encounter the limits of their bodies and to experience bodies as boundary projects that can be opened up to transformational processes. The dyke + queer BDSM space holds potentials for constructing a Deleuzian 'body without organs' and for experiences of becoming.

Chapter 7, 'Exploring Intimate Power Dynamics', describes how my interview partners understood power as intrinsic to sexuality. I reassess various power theories in the light of dyke + queer BDSM perspectives on power on two levels. On one level, my interview partners stressed the transparency of the power dynamics within BDSM in contrast with everyday life contexts. On the second level, I trace how social hierarchy is constructed through technologies of power, and how my interview partners were erotically invested in power, domination and subversion. This chapter also discusses how not all social hierarchies are equally addressed in dyke + queer BDSM. Especially, race is evaded, which I discuss from a critical *whiteness* perspective.

Chapter 8, 'Exploring Intimate Difference Through Gender', discusses the various ways in which dyke + queer BDSM practices are transgressive or transformative in regard to engaging with categories of social difference, which I conceptualize as intimate. I analyze how gender specifically held erotic as well as transformative potentials for my interview partners. I show how the community has come up with specific subcultural skills for creating alternative genders and how gender labor includes erotic benefits and the strategy to go on strike. I describe various ways of becoming other; show how concepts of identity are expanded through integration rather than exclusion when constituting a self and how embodiment is reinvented to include artifacts and non-material entities within the body image. I also utilize recent transgender theorizing that draws on phenomenological approaches.

Based on all of this, Chapter 9, 'The Sexual Politics of Exuberant Intimacy', presents my attempt to think through dyke + queer BDSM in terms of a theoretical concept of excess, abundance and exuberance, critically reassessing Bataille's theory of economy. I also ask what potentials dyke + queer BDSM holds in terms of transformative, rather than just transgressive, micropolitics, stressing its power-sensitive, socially situated character. Finally, I summarize my findings in the Conclusion.

2
The Culture of Dyke + Queer BDSM

In the US and Western Europe, most BDSM communities are organized around sexual preference (along the normative lines of heterosexual, gay male and lesbian) and are rather segregated. While the gay male and straight communities have grown, differentiated and become increasingly commercialized in the last decades, a phenomenon Weiss describes for what she calls the 'New Guard' in the Bay Area (Weiss 2011), the dyke + queer BDSM community is so small that it hardly exists on local levels and remains largely non-profit. My interview partners were often part of informal communities rather than established groups or organizations. Only in some metropolitan areas do specific 'women/trans only' organizations or play parties exist. Lesbian-only spaces in general are rare and usually non-permanent (Valentine 1995), which is especially true for women-only spaces with a sexual purpose. If they exist at all, they are usually dependent upon using gay men's or heterosexual spaces periodically. Moreover, most women's spaces tend to be described in scholarship as asexual (Hammers 2008). Therefore, the even smaller community of dykes + queers with a BDSM interest manifests itself transnationally at annual or biannual gatherings, such as the now defunct 'Women at Amsterdam Leather Pride' (WALP), as well as through individual friendships and play partner networks.

My interview partners were critical of the fact that the commercialization of BDSM excluded people with lower incomes. In most dyke + queer BDSM communities, dress codes were much less restrictive and entrance fees were lower than in the straight and gay male spaces, which makes the community more accessible. My interview partners had limited resources for their BDSM. They boycotted events and specialty stores that were too expensive and sought out alternative play spaces in both private homes and the public sphere. They went naked to circumvent dress codes or used thrift-store clothing, made their own toys, borrowed toys and so on. This 'do-it-yourself' (DIY) culture shows that the image of BDSM as a middle/upper-class leisure or paradigmatically consumerist sexuality (Weiss 2011: 15; 104ff) is biased because of its focus on certain community subsets and the more visually sensational aspects (the fetish scene). One take on BDSM that may be specific to my sample is that many of my interview partners rejected the necessary association of BDSM with toys, costumes and fetishes, what queer-straight femme Teresa called 'accessorized sex'. While many of them appreciated certain implements, they insisted that body and mind were sufficient to practice BDSM. In contrast, based on her study, Weiss claims that toys are an integral part of contemporary BDSM (2011: 102). Based on my research, the generalization of this finding has to be restricted to specific segments of the community. Rather than depend on expensive implements and costumes, my interview partners considered dyke + queer BDSM to be a creative endeavor and an art form.

In this chapter, I will introduce the community context of this study by providing a retelling of its history and a description of the dyke + queer BDSM community culture based on my interviews, focusing on the issue of difference and on community boundaries. Special attention will be given to the question of trans* individuals within a gender-segregated community. Finally, I will situate the community in its geopolitical contexts, with a specific focus on the vexed relationship of my interview partners to anti-BDSM strands of feminism.

I chose the signifier *dyke + queer* for the following reasons. The community that is the focus of my empirical research started out as a women's community with the emphasis on same-sex BDSM interactions, but has become ever more heterogeneous through the inclusion of various other groups of people, such as trans* people, as well as bisexual, pansexual and heteroflexible women. Therefore, I use the term *dyke*[1] to acknowledge its history and celebration of woman-to-woman encounters, but add the ' + ' to indicate that there are genders that move beyond the signifier 'woman'. The ' + ' also implies that this change is indeed a plus, that it adds something that my interview partners described as a valuable contribution to these communities, namely, gendered difference. Moreover, while I was conducting my research, various queer BDSM networks and spaces began to emerge, which deliberately worked at defying the gender binary and included more genders, such as gay and queer cismen. Many interview partners were part of building these spaces, and the boundaries were fuzzy, not only in terms of social spaces, but also in terms of identities and practices. In addition, many interview partners identified as queer, not as women or lesbians. Some dykes had fag sex with each other. Therefore, to me, the most appropriate term to classify the practices and identities discussed here without fencing them in seems to be dyke + queer. Throughout this book, whenever I refer specifically to women's spaces that do not include any male-identified cismen (instead of referring to the virtual community of the whole sample), I will use dyke+ to make this clear.

A critical brief history of the dyke + queer BDSM communities

To situate the communities I researched, I will present a brief overview of the history of the BDSM communities with a special focus on the women's, queer and trans* segments of the US and Europe.

While the use of pain to enhance sexual arousal seems to have existed throughout human history (Taylor 1997: 108), it was not until modern times that a distinct BDSM identity and community evolved. Their roots seem to lie in flagellation bordellos in the UK (Passig & Deunan 2002: 14). The first women-only BDSM space may have been a flagellation club of women who took turns beating each other in the 1790s in London (13). Today's overall BDSM community in the US and Western Europe has its roots in gay male biker clubs, mostly composed of World War II veterans whose experiences in the war and whose homosexuality prevented them from going 'back home'; instead, they stayed in the San Francisco area or in New York City and fashioned themselves as outcasts in all-male friendship networks. The first gay motorcycle club was founded in Los Angeles in 1954 (DeBlase n.d.: 19). This so-called 'Old Guard' based many of their social interactions on the discipline, hierarchy and homosocial/sexual camaraderie they were familiar with from the military. They were a small, secretive community and novices were introduced to BDSM practices through personal mentors and had to undergo certain initiations. Safety was ensured through social control. A larger, mixed BDSM scene emerged after the 'sexual revolution' in the 1970s, marked by the founding of 'The Eulenspiegel Society' (TES) in New York City in 1971 and 'The Society of Janus' (SOJ) in San Francisco in 1974 (Sisson 2007: 18), but the community quickly split into heterosexual and gay male segments (22).

People of color were at the time, and remain today, largely underrepresented in subcultural discourses and images, but they have always been part of the community, and separate Black or people-of-color-only structures exist. For instance, the first organizations for Black leathermen were founded in the 1980s (Dark Connections n.d.), and since 1995 an annual Black leathermen's BDSM conference, 'BlackOut', has taken place, called into life by Mufasa Ali (Dark Connections n.d.). Despite instances of racism and pervasive *white* ignorance, many people of color have self-confidently claimed their positions in the community and made significant contributions to community-building and activism, such as the Asian American fetish diva Midori and the Black Cuban Mama Reinhard, who is a fundraising legend in the Bay Area with her leather family.

The history of the women's and lesbian BDSM communities starts in 1976, when some women of SOJ started a women's group called 'Cardea' in San Francisco, which was mostly composed of bisexual and straight women, but provided a context in which BDSM dykes gathered. They eventually formed 'Samois', the first lesbian BDSM organization, in 1978. Before then,

BDSM dykes in the US were usually part of gay male communities, and therefore elements of that sexual culture found their way into the emerging women's BDSM community. Dyke femme Mandy recalled that 'in 78 the first women's – that we know of – leather party happened at my house, right when Pat [Califia] was founding Samois'. In 1979, Samois published its first pamphlet, 'What Color is Your Handkerchief?', and marched in Gay Pride, thus giving BDSM dykes new public visibility. In the same year, 'Werkgroep Vrouwen en SM', the first women's BDSM group in Europe, was founded in the Netherlands (Passig & Deunan 2002: 72). In 1980 'Coming to Power', the first lesbian BDSM anthology ever, was published by Samois. Samois split up two years later because of internal conflicts. Yet the foundations for the development of a separate dyke BDSM community and subculture had been laid. The feminist sex wars, which had BDSM as one of the main issues of conflict, gained full force in the 1980s. This clash affected, for instance, Krista Beinstein, the first artist in Austria and Germany in the 1980s to present transgressive dyke BDSM photography and performance art. All of her early exhibitions were destroyed by anti-SM feminists (Beinstein n.d.). In 1981 the first known meeting of BDSM lesbians with the goal of organizing nationally took place in Germany (Passig & Deunan 2002: 74) and the 'Lesbian Sex Mafia' (LSM) was founded in New York City. In 1984 in San Francisco the lesbian BDSM group 'Outcasts' formed; it included bisexual and transgender women. In contrast to Samois, the Outcasts self-defined as a support and educational, rather than political, organization (Fish 1993). In 1987 the first 'International Ms. Leather' contest took place. The first titleholder was the Native American Judy Tallwing-McCarthey. The first 'international' lesbian BDSM conference, 'Powersurge', took place in Seattle in 1992, with 300 lesbians attending from the US and Canada.

There are no separate groups for Black leatherwomen to my knowledge, but Black women have been outstanding activists in the community, among them Viola Johnson and her partner Jill Carter, who was the first Black woman to become International Ms. Leather (1996) and who started the 'Ms. World Leather' contest in 2001 (Dark Connections 2004). Stacey, an African American woman, was 'Ms. NLA Leather' in 1996 and has become an international 'Ambassador of Leather' (Leatherweb n.d.).

The cultural visibility of the BDSM community generally grew in the 1980s, for instance through events such as the 'Folsom Street Fair' in San Francisco, which was launched in 1984 by a gay leatherman of color, Michael Valerio, and Kathleen Connell, a lesbian, who met each other through social anti-poverty activism in the South of Market district; it has not only become a local annual event, but has also spread to the East Coast and Europe. In 1989 the gay leatherman Tony DeBlase designed the leather flag, and in the 1990s more organizations and activism emerged. In 1992, the first demonstration for BDSM rights took place in London as a reaction to the

Spanner case (Passig & Deunan 2002: 102). This development also led to more lesbian BDSM organizing. 'SchMacht', a German lesbian network, emerged in the 1990s (133) and continues to be the main national organization for dyke+ BDSM there. In the Netherlands, WALP was founded in 1996 by Tania Oudemans and Denya Cascio, a co-founder of the LSM, 'to create a social and educational network for leatherwomen within Europe and to encourage connections between leatherwomen in Europe and other continents'. From 1997 until 2002 WALP was an annual event; it then became biannual, but was officially terminated by the organizers because their long-term relationship ended (personal communication). WALP was a central space for dyke+ BDSM community development in Europe and set a precedent for the most inclusive gender policy for a women's event: it welcomed all 'straight, bisexual, and transsexual women' and 'XX-transgender boys/men and FTM transsexuals in transition, who felt they had a place in the women's community' (WALP 2009). In 1999, the first 'Women's Easter Conference' took place in Berlin, organized by Birgit Scheuch and Eva, with approximately 50 participants (BDSM Berlin n.d.). It has since been organized annually and presents one of the main contexts in which many of my European interview partners move. I have found most of my European interview partners via the SchMacht, WALP and Easter meeting networks. In 1997, there was for the first time a BDSM space at the German annual 'Lesbian Spring Meeting' (Lesbenfrühlingstreffen) (Passig & Deunan 2002: 138), marking a growing acceptance of lesbian BDSM in the women's communities despite the feminist sex wars.

Also in 1997, the 'National Coalition for Sexual Freedom' (NCSF) was founded as a US organization to protect the rights of BDSM practitioners through a system of legal support, education and lobbying. Earlier, in 1994, US BDSM activists associated with the gay leatherman and psychotherapist Race Bannon had achieved a major success with the removal of BDSM as a psychopathology from the fourth edition of the *Diagnostic and Statistic Manual of Mental Disorders* (DSM) of the American Psychiatric Association. In 1997, 'Revise F65', a group campaigning for the removal of the paraphilia from the ICD, was founded in Norway by gay, lesbian and transgender groups (Reiersøl & Skeid 2006: 256). It turned into an international project. The first country to officially remove the diagnosis of sadomasochism from its ICD was Denmark in 1996 (258); Sweden followed in 2008, Norway in 2010, and Finland in 2011.

While transwomen were often included in the women's BDSM communities, transmen are still fighting their way into the gay men's BDSM communities. In 1998, Billy Lane was the first transman to take part in the 'International Mr. Leather' (IML) contest (Rüster 2010). In the 2000s, some of my interview partners in San Francisco were involved in organizing 'trans* and friends' BDSM events. Since 2002 the queer play party 'Experiment' has taken place in Berlin, establishing a trans*-friendly space for the gay male and dyke+ BDSM communities to connect (The Experiment n.d.). In 2006, the Norwegian lesbian, gay, BDSM and trans* activist Tore Barstad/Eric Jåsund died at 32 from complications related to diabetes. Eric was a leading member of the Revise F65 project (Revise F65 n.d.). He was also interviewed for my research during WALP 2004 in Amsterdam and insisted on using not an alias, but his real name, as a reflection of his personal principle of being visibly out in all regards and 'being yourself'. In 2010, Tyler McCormick was the first transman, and the first wheelchair-user, to win the IML contest. His selection once more fueled the discussion over transmen in the gay men's community and deeply divided the community (Rüster 2010). In 2011, I became the manager of an annual international gay men's SM camp in Denmark, and therefore the first known transman in a leadership position in the European context. In 2012, the 'Chicago Hellfire Club' (CHC) officially opened up 'Inferno', the most famous gay men's annual BDSM gathering, to transmen.[2]

Today, the social organization of the Old Guard has mostly been replaced by a community that is open to anyone interested in joining, that educates its members through handbooks, workshops and so on and that forms broad national and transnational alliances to fight for social acceptance and public recognition. The main foci of BDSM activism in the last decade have been the depathologization of consensual sexual practices and the fight against the legal prosecution of BDSM practitioners. Some dyke, trans* and queer BDSM practitioners organize within the mixed BDSM community, while most prefer dyke+ and queer BDSM communities.

This brief history of various BDSM communities shows that, in all of the supposedly straight organizations and events, queers have played and continue to play major roles, remaining overrepresented in numbers and effort. Yet they are often not given credit for their contributions to community-building and their activism in support of the overarching BDSM community and movement. If authors simply leave out the explicitly gay and lesbian organizations and events and queer people's contributions to mixed structures, or do not make explicit the sexual preferences of major actors, this does not amount to writing 'heterosexual', but *heteronormative*, BDSM history. This is especially critical to address, given the fact that a lot of the original gay community elders were lost through AIDS in the 1980s. Furthermore, it is evident that, at least in the US, a separate Black BDSM community exists (see also Weiss 2011: 193) and that people of color have made significant contributions to racially mixed communities as well. These facts are also ignored by most *white* historians and activists, which serves to uphold the falsity that the community is *white* or that BDSM is a *white* thing (see Weiss 2011: 192–3 for racist reasons given by *white* BDSM practitioners for the lack of people of color in the organized community).

The dyke + queer BDSM communities in Western Europe and the US

What started out as the women's BDSM community at this point usually includes self-defined dykes/lesbians, bi/pansexual and queer women, femmes, butches, genderqueers (who do not necessarily consider themselves women), the whole FTM spectrum, transwomen (but not cismale transvestites or cross-dressers) and intersex people, all of whom are represented in my sample.

Some interview partners used the term 'pansexual' as an alternative to 'bisexual'; this acknowledged that there are more than two genders and that they were open to all genders sexually.[3] 'Femme' is a self-definition with a long lesbian/queer tradition, which denotes a lesbian, pan/bisexual or queer woman with a feminine self-expression, and 'butch' denotes a lesbian, pan/bisexual or queer woman or transmasculine person with a masculine self-expression. Butch–femme as a subcultural and visible expression of lesbian and queer sexuality dates back to the 1920s at least, as has been documented for parts of the US and Western Europe (Bullough & Bullough 1977a; Nestle 1992; Lapovsky Kennedy & Davis 1993). The butch identity was perceived to be dying out by some interview partners, partly because it has been replaced by the concepts of transgender butch, boy and FTM (female-to-male trans* identities and expressions). This corresponds with Henry Rubin's research on the genealogy of the emergence of FTM as a gender identity in distinction from lesbian as a sexual identity (Rubin 2003). As lesbian feminism became predominant and as a lesbian was redefined as a 'woman-loving woman', those community members who were masculine-identified lost their previous cultural niche, and some of them substituted one of the alternatives, the transsexual choice (Henry Rubin 2003: 64). Yet, in my sample, the lines between butches and FTMs were not as clearly drawn as in Rubin's. Some interview partners located butches and femmes firmly within the women's or lesbian community. Others considered the concept of butch as expanding beyond the category of woman, and the butch–femme community as queer rather than as a women's community. So, while some femmes identified as lesbians and considered female homosexuality to be crucial to the concept of the femme, other femmes identified as queer. Some butches identified as androgynous or as masculine women, others as transgender. But, as Gayle Rubin points out, the butch–FTM distinction cannot be drawn by objective criteria, such as degree of masculinity, but is mainly a matter of self-definition (Rubin 1992b) and, I would add, community regulations. Furthermore, the FTM inclusiveness of the dyke + queer BDSM communities lessens the necessity to disidentify lesbian experiences from FTM experiences, which is so essential in the FTM community Henry Rubin refers to (2003: 89–92), because it creates a space to co-exist and to live in the border zones between identity categories.

According to my US interview partners, the term 'genderqueer' was originally invented to express a queered gender position. While genderqueers do not identify full-time as either men or women, they do not conceive of themselves as being in the middle of a spectrum, or as androgynous either. Their gender can be fluid or shifting, and multiple at the same time, which means that their positioning within a variety of genders depends on the context. Today, genderqueer is sometimes also used as an umbrella term for all kinds of queer genders, including trans*, butch and femme individuals (see Nestle et al. 2002). My interview partners used it in both ways. Within the context of this study, MTF refers to individuals who were assigned male at birth and who live as women, independent of their legal, hormonal or post-/pre-operative status. Their most common self-description is 'transwoman'. The FTM spectrum refers to all individuals assigned female at birth with a masculine gender expression and/or identity, regardless of medical and/or legal transition, which includes transsexual men/transmen, transboys, some drag kings and some butches. 'Intersex' is the medical term for those whose sex is neither clearly male nor female according to medical and social heteronormative standards at birth or starting with puberty. Those who claim this identity use it for lack of a non-pathological term, while some also have reappropriated the derogatory term 'hermaphrodite'. My interview partners who were born intersex were subjected to non-consensual sex-conforming surgeries in early childhood or puberty (Fausto-Sterling 1993; 2000; Chase 1998; Reiter 1998) and used the term intersex as an adjective in their gender positions, in combination with identities such as trans*.

My interview partners were confronted with various limits to their self-descriptions as queers and trans* individuals in heteronormative discourse: 'I mean, to use masculine and feminine, it's just [makes a sound resembling vomiting], but I don't know what else to say about it.' This quote by queer femme Emma was typical. My interview partners struggled with language and faced a lack of appropriate terms for what they wanted to express. Language about gender is binary, for instance in terms of pronouns, when their gendered experiences, bodies and affects were not. They were often at a loss for the words to adequately communicate their practices and identities, yet at the same time they were inventive, filling in the gaps and creating new non-binary language. Many interview partners tried to rupture gender-binary language by making these norms explicit, for example calling women-born-women *biological women* or *ciswomen* instead of simply *women*, thus disconnecting sex from gender. The dyke + queer and trans* communities take great care to develop validating and inclusive language. It is common for individuals to choose their personal pronouns independent of their anatomy, and, furthermore, some prefer gender-neutral pronouns, using *ze* instead of *she/he* and *hir* instead of *his/him/hers/her*.[4] In this book, all of the gender assignments and pronouns are those put forth by the inter-view partners themselves, regardless of their ability to be accepted in their gender of choice according to heteronormative standards.

Community as shared and embodied social space

The notion of community remains a contested issue. Is it real or illusionary (Anderson 1983)? Can it be accommodating to difference, or is it by defini-tion exclusionary (Gamson 1995)? Are exclusions a problem per se, or are there necessary/good versus unintended/bad kinds of exclusion? How do communities relate to each other? How do visions of community work to center certain groups of people and marginalize others (Cohen 2005)? What are community boundaries based on: self-definitions or imposed criteria? Commentary on community by my interview partners shows that a commu-nity entails constant renegotiations and change. Yet, a community may also be quite resistant to change in certain regards, especially when it comes to social hierarchies and norms that are also supported by the society at large. For my interview partners, community has at least two faces: a very con-crete and embodied one that they are part of and interact with on a regular basis, and a more virtual idea of a community of all potentially like-minded (anonymous, disconnected) individuals under an umbrella term. The first face, the concept of a lived and interconnected community, transcends the public/private dichotomy because it builds collectives that operate in con-tained as well as open social spaces. In this sense, community is very alive: it produces embodied experiences, and my interview partners saw themselves as members who actively participate in this social structure. Community can be understood as a shared social space with shared as well as different knowledges and practices. This community concept includes an openness to critique of the particular social space; it does not presuppose that referring to and building community always already implies a misguided romanticizing of a 'liberated' refuge from the harsh neoliberal socio-political realities, as Weiss holds (2011: 120). Instead, it is possible to read the renegotiations of community in dyke + queer BDSM spaces as critical engagement with difference (Duncan 1996) in social contexts that are often structured by dominations and normativities, and as a quest for alternative social practices and ways of belonging and collectivity.

For many interview partners, the dyke + queer BDSM community was of great significance, and some felt they had found a place where they could feel appreciated for the first time in their lives. Mandy said: 'Before that, everybody just thought I was crazy.' The community provided her with a context where her identities and practices were intelligible and accepted, as opposed to mainstream society, where she was met with cultural incom-prehension and marginalized as deviant. Many interview partners reported being marginalized in various communities due to their BDSM interests or gender identities. Therefore, their circle of friends over time often ended up being entirely composed of other dyke + queer BDSM practitioners. But, despite the great significance of BDSM to many of their lives, my interview partners reported community affiliations of varying degrees of involvement and commitment, from feeling at home to being a complete outsider or solitary personality. Thus, the notion of community was conflicted and not romanticized. It was also multi-dimensional; BDSM was not the only point of affiliation. Some interview partners sought out communities according to cultural or political affinities rather than those based on sexual or gender identity. Genderqueer Firesong generally questioned the concept of identity-based communities: 'I do have a resistance to identity-based community in those kinds of ways. I don't know if kink is the same thing to you as it is to me.' A certain identity may hold different meanings for individuals, and for Firesong the solution was to 'build a coalition and solidarity. I don't wanna make assumptions about what we have in common, unless I know that that's true'. To use Haraway's useful distinction, Firesong was advocating a politics of affinity rather than identity (Haraway 1991: 155).

Difference and community boundaries

In general, members of the dyke + queer BDSM community were rather critical of social hierarchy, and they valued difference. They fostered a self-image of being highly self-reflective in their dealings with their sexuality and in engaging with social status in role play. Mandy said: 'Because we do a lot of psychological role play, we are accept[ing] of playing outside the box and challenging roles and questioning roles, including gender roles.' To her it was in the nature of BDSM to challenge social roles and thus to be more self-critical. Mostly, my interview partners promoted an approach of being non-judgmental of others' practices within the ethos of consensuality.

Yet, as in any community, there is the issue of boundaries. Many interview partners preferred women's spaces, while some preferred queer spaces that are open to all trans* people and to queer cismen as well. Only a few did not care about the gender composition of their play spaces. Even though they did not really like the idea of excluding any group of people per se, such as straight cismen in queer play spaces, they also acknowledged the necessity of excluding individuals who are acting sexist or transphobic (out of ignorance or intentionally) in order to create safer spaces. Those who were excluded were mostly individuals with male and straight privileges. Other social inequalities, such as racial or class hierarchies, were not discussed in a similar way, indicating a privileging of awareness about sexuality and gender above other categories of social stratification.

Following the convention of HIV prevention, I therefore use the term 'safer' instead of 'safe' for separatist spaces to indicate that absolute safety from discrimination and violations is not guaranteed and likely impossible to achieve, especially if one considers all possible forms of discrimination. Rather, setting up alternative spaces may be understood as an attempt to reduce the risks and probabilities of encountering certain forms of discrimination. Such spaces are, therefore, safer or more power-sensitive in comparison to hegemonic or other alternative social spaces, but usually only in regard to one or two social hierarchies (for instance, gender and sexuality but not race, able-bodiedness or class), and various kinds of violations still take place.

My interview partners described various experiences and observations of how social difference was approached and struggled with in their communities of reference, and how community boundaries were policed and (re)negotiated. First of all, there were structural exclusions, which were often experienced as unintentional. My interview partners described the dyke + queer BDSM communities as predominantly *white* and middle class, and were critical of the fact that certain kinds of queer culture in general are based on *white* youth cultures, such as DIY or punk, a fact that may serve to alienate and exclude queers of color. They also found that there was a lack of action in regard to working to eliminate racism, classism and ableism. Ellen, a *white* queer femme with a Jewish background, observed:

> A lot of genderqueer sex positive people are doing work predominantly around their own identity issues, around their own transness, around their own kinkiness or whatever. But people of color are doing more work around racism and things like that, and there is not enough coalition building going on between the two groups.

Thus, there is a tendency for *white* queers to center on issues of their own oppression as *white* queers, while for queers of color anti-racism may assume a higher priority, or they are forced to choose between various single-issue movements or spaces (see also Duncan 1996: 93), with few options to integrate their identities and political issues as queers of color besides creating their own spaces, which is a matter of resources. This problem is, of course, not unique to the dyke + queer BDSM community, but is a common phenomenon (see Conerly 1996; Goldman 1996; Lee 1996; Eng & Hom 1998; Constantine-Simms 2000; Anzaldúa & Keating 2002; Haritaworn 2005; Johnson & Henderson 2005). But, because this community has grown out of pre-existing *white*-dominated lesbian/women-only and BDSM contexts, rather than out of pre-existing people of color or anti-racist contexts, it therefore shares most of the flaws of the former. Interview partners who came out of anti-racist community affiliations into the world of BDSM, such as *white* Jewish queer transgender stone butch Terry,[5] or Teresa, a *white* queer-straight femme and sex worker, were the minority in my sample.

My interview partners were often at loss for satisfying explanations of why the communities they interacted with were so monochromatic. They assumed it was partly for economic reasons, citing the mediation of racial exclusion through socio-economic status.[6] Other authors have also suggested that non-conformist lifestyles such as BDSM are more accessible to those with race and class privilege, since privilege may be able to buffer some of the negative consequences of violating social norms (Sheff & Hammers 2011: 13; Weiss 2011: 9). Some interview partners had witnessed racist situations; *white* queer trans/genderqueer/butch dyke Scout recalled 'this incident where I was bottoming and one of my Sir's acquaintances started saying some really racist shit, but I wasn't allowed to speak, and I wasn't yet devout enough in my boyness and my bottomness to find a language to speak respectfully about things when I needed to'. So Scout experienced a conflict between his anti-racist politics and BDSM protocol. This situation made him question the loyalties in BDSM spaces and reconsider his understanding of protocol in a way that would not compromise his politics. More often, though, it was less overt racism than the centrality of the *white* experience in combination with ignorance about various people of color's realities that resulted in a monochromatic, exclusionary culture.

Furthermore, communities tended to only be aware of certain exclusions, while others remained largely unacknowledged, as Teresa pointed out: 'Disability is an issue. Many people won't acknowledge it. At the last "Queeruption" in [this town] they were gonna have a sex party that wasn't going to be accessible, when the rest of the conference was. That was like: "What the fuck is that about?"' In this case, a DIY queer gathering excluded disabled queers specifically from the sharing of sexuality, reproducing the hegemonic discursive production of the disabled as asexual and not attractive (Galler 1992; Tremain 1996: 15). This highlights that, even in a community that prides itself on possessing a high degree of reflection about sexual norms, this only applies to certain groups of people, while others remain sexualized or desexualized according to hegemonic discourse and are not given spaces to reinvent their sexuality on their own terms. Sometimes the marginalization of the community itself produces unintended exclusions. Since dyke + queer BDSM communities do not have the resources to finance their own play spaces, and those available to them on a temporary basis (from gay male and straight organizations) are often not wheelchair-accessible, the only option left for community organizers might be to lobby for making other spaces more accessible in the long run.

While mixed and pansexual BDSM spaces and organizations are open to dykes + queers in theory, they were overwhelmingly experienced as heteronormative and exclusionary by my interview partners, as queer femme Katharina summarized: 'Hetero-dominated with a few freaks at the margins about whom one is able to boast a bit that one is so great and that one can talk so wonderfully about make-up with them [laughs].' Mixed-gender spaces tended to remain trans- and homophobic as well as ignorant of queer practices and communities. The straight community was characterized as pseudo-inclusive and lacking understanding and respect for the need of dykes + queers for their own spaces, such as separate play parties or gay pride events, which have been increasingly adopted by straight BDSMers as venues and platforms for their own agendas. Therefore, conflicts abounded when interview partners entered straight BDSM spaces; various anecdotes attested to straight cismales assuming that their needs and wants took precedence over those of dyke + queers and objectifying them sexually. This problem put a limit to the queer ideal of inclusiveness and highlighted the need for criteria for respectful interactions in shared spaces. Most interview partners did not feel comfortable being sexual in front of straight cismen or sharing play spaces with them, since male privilege often expresses itself through habitual claims to space. In other words, separatist women's, queer and trans* spaces remained valuable alternatives.

Trans* intelligibility and the policing of gender boundaries in BDSM communities

One of the main issues of the feminist sex wars besides BDSM was and remains the trans* question in women's spaces. A thorough discussion of this aspect is beyond the scope of this work, and the debates have been well documented elsewhere. But one of the starting points was the conflict around 'Olivia Records' in the late 1970s. A transsexual woman, Sandy Stone, was part of this women's collective, which sparked a lot of protest that forced her out of this group eventually (Riddell 2006: 150). Another historically significant event occurred in 1991, when Nancy Burkholder was escorted off the land at the 'Michigan Womyn's Music Festival' after coming out as a post-operative transwoman (Prosser 1998: 171). Her exclusion led to the establishment of 'Camp Trans', a protest camp by trans* activists, which is run each year outside the festival grounds. My interview partners have participated in both the festival and the protesting camp. In light of this history, one central issue for interview partners was the question of how the gender boundary of the dyke+ BDSM communities is negotiated and drawn. The criteria for defining womanhood and women's spaces were highly contested. Some dykes + queers criticized women's spaces' construction of men or penises as 'not safe' or, correspondingly, women as innocent and needing childlike protection. Femme bottom Lisa rejected the notion of 'safe spaces' because they infantilize women. She wanted to foster a discussion that would consider the actual specific limits of individuals rather than restricting any practices out of principle, while others equated the presence of biological men or penises with a threat of sexual violence.

The existence of trans* people who do not neatly fit into the gender binary has challenged the boundaries of women's communities. Many cis interview partners had come to include trans* people in their personal, sexual and political lives over the years and wanted this development to be reflected in their communities as well. Queer cisfemme Emma, genderqueer Femmeboy and others were, therefore, actively working toward increasing trans* acceptance and participation in the dyke+ BDSM communities. They considered this an ongoing political and educational process. More generally, Emma questioned the usefulness of the category 'woman': 'And I also go to Kate Bornstein's[7] place about "What's a woman? Are you one?" – "I don't know",' which echoes the critiques by various feminists and queer theorists of the exclusionary effects of trying to define the term 'woman' (for instance, Minh-ha 1986/87: 30[8]; Bornstein 1994). Therefore, one strategy has been to broaden the definition of women's spaces to include certain trans* people as a reflection of the fluid boundaries of that category. The criteria for inclusion in women's spaces have extended beyond the binary logic, adopting a situational notion of gender: 'Other places I know, their phrasing said: "if you are now or ever have been a woman" ' (Emma). But many women's spaces included trans* people only with reservations. Often it remained a statement of tolerance, granted from ciswomen who have the authority over these spaces, rather than full acceptance. Also, for some, there was a distinction between social and sexual inclusion.

Therefore, today, varying degrees of acceptance of gendered difference and of trans* people co-exist. Inclusiveness remains a struggle, with the power to grant admission in the hands of ciswomen, which dyke cisfemme Mistress Mean Mommy defended: 'I realize it is exclusionary to have only one of something, but everyone has a chance to create their own spaces, and if one space is not welcoming or open to someone, they are free to create their own and invite anyone they want.' She held that every person or group has the right to create spaces according to their own criteria. The problem with this reasoning is that (a) like other marginalized groups, for the most part trans* people do not have the resources to create their own spaces if they are facing exclusion, and (b) regarding transwomen in women's spaces, the majority of MTFs want and need to be acknowledged in their gender identity as women, not as a third category. Not being admitted to women's spaces does not only mean a lack of social and political support systems, but potentially robs them of their gender identity and sense of self. It has also been argued that trans* individuals face gender-based violence as well and should therefore be given the relative safety of women's spaces (see also Kaldera 2009: 222ff). This seems especially pressing when considering the extent to which transwomen especially are subject to hate crimes and discrimination (Balzer 2009; FRA 2009; Grant et al. 2011).

One barrier to the full inclusion of trans* people is what I call the issue of *trans* intelligibility*, which is distinct from the issue of passing. Passing means that a trans* person is perceived as a member of a certain sex according to hegemonic, binary thinking. That is, trans* are judged according to binary gender system rules, and hegemonic ways of reading and assigning sex/gender are perpetuated.[9] In contrast, trans* intelligibility is about understanding and accepting the genders of trans* persons *on their own terms*. It requires an active effort to learn how to read unconventional genders, and therefore challenges the hegemonic logic of sex/gender assignment. It requires gender-conforming members of society to learn to read alternative genders and/or not to make any assumptions, but to create a social climate in which gender becomes self-defined, in which everyone is asked how they identify instead of being classified by others, and gender is therefore co-constructed in a power-sensitive way. It requires learning trans* etiquette, such as using the pronouns of choice, and may (paradoxically) include refraining from calling someone trans* if they reject that label and refraining from outing someone as trans* or as having a trans* biography without their consent. Gender policing is related to the issue of trans* intelligibility; gender police relate to the world with a sense of entitlement when it comes to sorting individuals into male and female. Some people feel it is their right to interrogate and hassle people whose gender is questionable to them, rather than learning how to interact respectfully. Therefore, the question of trans* intelligibility is crucial when it comes to acceptance and recognition of trans*.

The meaning of genitals in assigning gender is contested within the dyke + queer BDSM community. A woman with a penis is not intelligible as a woman to most people, while in trans* communities biological sex has mostly been detached from gender and its symbolic inscriptions, such as equating the penis as part of an individual human body with the phallus as patriarchal power. Rather, a penis can be reassigned as a large clitoris. At times, this emphasis on trans* genitalia seems displaced, as most trans* individuals are reluctant to present their (pre-op/non-op) genitals in public spaces anyway because of their body dysphoria (see also Kaldera 2009: 244). As Kaldera points out, BDSM spaces that do not include genital sex and nudity may be more comfortable for trans* people (2009: 112). Lesbian ciswoman top Nico reported perceiving MTFs as masculine, which caused a crisis for her because she was resisting disrespectful comments toward transwomen by third parties. Thus, some dykes + queers were struggling to adjust their perceptions of gender to their political stance, which demonstrates that gender intelligibility has to be learned. For lack of space, I will only be able to discuss the admittance and acceptance of trans* in the dyke+ BDSM community in detail, but first I will briefly acknowledge the experiences of interview partners in other communities.

Often, the issue of trans* acceptance is discussed in terms of gender-segregated communities, which are criticized for their door policies. Yet, mixed-gender spaces are not necessarily trans*-friendly simply because they do not bar entry based on gender. My interview partners found that mixed straight/pansexual spaces were transphobic, in particular toward MTFs. Some interview partners, though, had encountered pansexual communities that were accepting of trans* individuals, which gay transman Mik attributed to their history of having cross-dressers in their midst, who helped to introduce trans* etiquette.

Most FTM and genderqueer interview partners faced strong resistance from the gay male BDSM communities. They were denied entrance or removed violently if they were recognized as biologically female or as in between sexes, which happened to gay transboy Björn in a dark room. Queer transgender stone butch Terry had managed to find allies in the gay men's community, partly by teaching novice fag friends about BDSM. This was typical of FTM inclusion in men's communities; mostly, personal connections served as a way of entry for individual FTMs, who then had to work hard to earn respect and acceptance. Political arguments usually were not successful in gay men's spaces.[10] The downside to these individualistic strategies is evident: FTMs are evaluated on a case-by-case basis. They have to prove themselves as men first, which establishes a double standard between them and cismen.

Trans* acceptance in dyke+ BDSM communities

According to my interview partners, the various local dyke+ BDSM communities differed significantly in their degree of trans* admittance. Some found that acceptance was not genuine or that trans* people were subtly excluded even if organizations had adopted trans*-friendly policies officially. Terry felt that women's spaces tended to remain women's spaces with exceptions: 'It felt a lot like women's space has felt to me. They were just making exceptions for particular people.' Generally, though, from interview partners' reports, it seems that a development toward increasing trans* acceptance was the trend at the time.

There were various ways that this inclusion took place, and there were different dynamics for MTFs and FTMs, the former usually having to seek entry into a new context and the latter usually negotiating under what circumstances they would be allowed to remain in their communities of origin. One process of inclusion for MTFs was through precedents within a 'case law' logic. Often, a space harbored reservations about trans* people based on an experience with a particular trans* person who had been deemed problematic.[11] This might be reversed by encounters with an individual trans* person who adjusts well to the space. Even if no negative examples from the past were cited, however, some discomfort with trans* individuals had to be overcome in personal interactions. Dyke Michaela, who identified as a ciswoman, described her own development: 'But I also found to accept that and to accept those women as women, as part of the community, I had to meet them and interact with them, because otherwise all I was thinking was "men in women's privy". But now I get it.' Since gender is constructed in everyday interactions to a certain degree, it is not surprising that this kind of personal interaction helps to foster the intelligibility of MTFs as women. Sometimes, acceptance of individual transwomen eventually led to a general acceptance of MTFs as a group, especially if key organizers in a given community came to support trans* presence; a paving-of-the-way effect occurred. Michaela's comment also fits the findings of studies about discrimination that have shown that prejudices against trans* people tend to be highest in those individuals who are never in actual touch with them (FRA 2009; Franzen & Sauer 2010).

An important factor in gaining access to women's spaces was trans* solidarity and appreciation by the ciswomen who possess the authority in those spaces. Cis interview partners did not only value gender difference; many actively worked toward it, for instance, boycotting women's events that excluded trans* people. Partners of trans* individuals have historically been of great support (Califia 1997), and this was also evident in the dyke + queer BDSM communities. The erotic appreciation of trans* people was a powerful incentive to work toward their social acceptance and recognition.

Cis interview partners had developed various technologies of recognition. A significant one is to take great care in gender-appropriate interactions with trans* individuals. Emma mentioned the significance of the respectful and inclusive labeling of spaces for making trans* people feel truly welcome. Bisexual butch Erika explained that one has to learn to use the correct pronouns and other etiquette, such as asking for the preferred gender and gender pronouns of the day, not touching certain body parts without permission and refraining from using gender humiliation during play. Furthermore, they made efforts to validate their trans* play partners' identities (see Chapter 8). These can be considered examples of gender labor, which Ward defines as affective and bodily efforts in 'giving' gender to someone (Ward 2010: 237). Producing and confirming genders, therefore, is collective work (239), which is one of the ways gender is social rather than 'biological'.

Trans* people themselves also had developed technologies of resistance against their exclusions from various communities. One strategy was to refuse to be defined as a problem or to be marginalized: 'There are individual people who suddenly have a major problem with me after the outing. Their problem.' Transwoman switch Daphne thus reversed the logic of who is the problem: not her as a transwoman, but transphobic cispeople. They have to deal with their own gender issues. Daphne's strategy of resistance can be considered a strike in the arena of gender labor: she refused to accept the uneven distribution of work that gender non-conformers are burdened with. She refused to do the work of making cispeople comfortable when encountering limits to their binary gender worldview. Thus, I would expand Ward's concept of gender labor to include the work that trans* individuals and genderqueers are expected to perform to make gender-conformers comfortable with trans* and genderqueer presence.

FTMs in dyke+ BDSM communities

Gay transman Jonas described his post-transition relationship to the dyke+ BDSM community: 'Well, I feel definitively somehow [laughs] affiliated with the lesbian SM scene. Simply from the historical background. And because

I don't feel like giving up the relationships, now in the broadest sense of the term relationships.' This held true for a lot of FTMs; they retained biographical, social and sometimes erotic ties to the community, which was the main reason why for the most part they were still welcome at women-only events, turning them into women's and trans* events. But some FTMs also withdrew themselves in order to respect women's spaces or because they found new communities elsewhere where they felt more at home, such as gay men's communities.

There were various criteria for including FTMs in women's communities. Their inclusion may have been based on having been labeled a woman at/for some time of their life, independent of self-definition, or on a political affinity with women's communities, as lesbian femme top Frl. R. came up with for her events: 'My wording that we have agreed on at some point then, is that transboys are invited if they feel somehow in solidarity with the women's community.' Both approaches were based on the implicit assumption that being treated by society as women had generated a shared experience of being in the world and relating to each other. At the same time it left behind the gender binary, since a women's community in this case was not based on a shared biological sex or gender identity; rather, it was about cultural and political affinity.

Yet, in many spaces, the choice for trans* individuals remained within a binary logic, for instance when a legally female identity document was the criterion for admittance. This door policy is problematic, since it does not take into consideration the complex choices trans* people have to make when it comes to transitioning physically and legally, let alone the lack of access to these resources for some. Especially in the US, where trans*-specific medical care is often not covered by health insurance, and many people do not have health insurance in the first place, the post-operative criterion effectively becomes a class issue (see also Kaldera 2009: 230). Lesbian butch transwoman Kay also criticized the dyke+ BDSM community for being more welcoming to FTMs than to MTFs, which meant that a women's community was being more supportive of some men than some women. It might also mean that this women's community was still more attached to the concept of women as born female or socialized as women, and thus felt more connected to FTMs than MTFs.

Finally, there was a sense of loss in the lesbian community when it came to the transitioning of FTMs. This was evident in Frl. R's remark that including transboys in the women's community might prevent them from having to transition. This sense of loss was not without a cause, since, for some FTMs, adopting a masculine identity did result in distancing themselves from the dyke+ BDSM community. Some members of the dyke+ BDSM community wanted to address this alienation of FTMs from the women's community through broadening it to include them, while others wanted to preserve it as a women's community and demanded that FTMs accept the consequences of transitioning. Mistress Mean Mommy explained: 'But if a woman chooses to be male/masculine, s/he is choosing to identify with that gender community and has to make the choice to fully embrace it while leaving behind the familiarity and security of the women's community.'

MTFs in dyke+ BDSM communities

For the MTFs in my sample, women's spaces were of great importance in living fully in their gender identity. However, even though they had given up their privileges as men, they still faced exclusion from many women's communities, especially if they had not had bottom surgery. In some dyke+ BDSM spaces, genitals were still taken to be the major criterion for womanhood. Ciswoman Michaela rejected this door policy:

> I had explained to me about how many more ways there are of being a woman than what your body is like. And that defining transpeople as pre- and post-operative is not really very helpful, because some people choose not to or can't for medical reasons or whatever to modify their body. And that has absolutely no bearing on their personality.

This kind of trans* intelligibility (understanding the meanings that trans* individuals themselves assign to their identities and bodies) was paving the way for different gender policies that did not create a two-class system of pre- or non-versus post-medical intervention MTFs. Another criterion for inclusion was passing as a woman, which is closely related to the status of the body, but also to gender performance. This usually amounted to a double standard for transwomen, who had to present as much more conventionally feminine than ciswomen to be acknowledged and included as women (see also Kaldera 2009: 117).[12] Passing as a criterion also puts the burden of making choices about disclosure of their trans* status on the trans* individual.[13] Another common criterion, the legal status of one's sex as female, equated community acceptance with state approval, which reproduced the binary logic of gender and was a problematic choice for a community that otherwise tended to be critical of hegemonic notions of gender. In contrast, the German Supreme Court (BVerfG) has declared various parts of the German law on transsexuality unconstitutional recently. As a result, trans* people are now able to change their legal sex without any body modification, which makes the law in this context more trans*-accepting than are many gay and lesbian communities, which still base acceptance on anatomy or on sex assignment at birth.

The most accepting policy for entry into BDSM spaces was the criterion of lived gender identity or self-definition, because it empowered transwomen by placing the authority over their gender identity in their own hands and it questioned both hegemonic biologically determinist and legal notions of sex and gender. It also opened up a space for self-defining as in between, as both or as more than one gender, and therefore acknowledged that, for some trans* individuals, being able to move between differently gendered spaces might be essential to their self-definition (see also Kaldera 2009: 219). This was certainly the case for some multi-gendered interview partners, for instance if they had femme and gay male partial identities (see Chapter 8).

When it comes to gender policing in women's spaces, there are often two lines of reasoning pitched against each other. The first holds that organizations that run a space have a right to define themselves and therefore to exclude whomever they want. The counter-logic is popular in queer politics and holds that all exclusions are bad. Both have in common that they are more or less power-insensitive. The first neglects social hierarchies, such as racist group dynamics. The fact that some people invest energy in creating a group or a space should clearly not exempt them from examining their own racism, transphobia and so on. The second reasoning ignores social hierarchies that still make separate spaces necessary for groups of people who face discrimination, such as women in the context of the trans* debates. Thus, it seems necessary to adopt a power-sensitive position that acknowledges the need of certain groups of people for their own spaces and the necessity for these to be accessible to all who are in need of such spaces. As the social and political contexts keep changing, these spaces keep changing. As long as they do, it seems imperative that organizers be really clear about the intent of a space and communicate that accordingly.

Between fetishizing and erotically appreciating trans*

There are two main images of trans* sexuality: (a) oversexualization through pornographic discourses that fetishize predominantly MTFs, which goes hand in hand with the sexological definition of sexually motivated transvestitism,[14] and (b) asexualization in the sexological discourse about the body dysphoria of transsexuals.[15] Many theories today still hold that sexuality is only available to those who have acquired a minimum basic security in their body/skin, which is often not the case for trans* individuals, especially pre-transition transsexuals (Salamon 2010: 26). Trans* interview partners contrasted this with the lived reality of their sexual trans* experience. To them, dyke + queer BDSM offered options to be sexual outside the usual genitally focused binary gender script: it is not necessarily dependent on genital sex, the intense stimulation of non-genital regions of the body creates non-genital sensations and sexual chastity as part of a slave role may reduce stress about the issue of sexuality for some trans* people (see also Kaldera 2009).

Finding partners is also difficult for trans* individuals in a social context that is not only transphobic, but bases sexuality on binary concepts of gender (Kaldera 2009: 114ff); moreover, transitioning often breaks up existing relationships (135). The dyke + queer BDSM community is one of only a few spaces where trans* people can find other trans* people as partners, and also can find cispartners (if that is what they want) who appreciate them without fetishizing them. Cis interview partners were highly critical of the fetishization of trans* people and sometimes struggled to come to terms with their own attractions and how to live and communicate them while leaving the identities of trans* individuals intact. Queer-straight cisfemme Teresa identified differing motivations for straight cismen seeking transwomen as partners and for queer cisfemmes seeking FTMs:

> If I was to generalize, I'd say a lot of straight boys are doing it because they can fuck someone who's way more disempowered than they are. That's speaking from my outsider perspective. And non-trans women who are involved with transmen, there's more often a dynamic of wanting to have sex with someone who understands your oppression as opposed to wanting to fuck someone who's way more oppressed than you. So I'm pretty scared of straight boys who often date transwomen or often have sex with transwomen. I'm scared of them, unfortunately. I fear they might be abusive.

Thus, one may differentiate between fetishizing trans* people in a way that reinforces gender hierarchies and appreciating trans* as a strategy to balance gender hierarchies. Teresa attributed this to the better understanding most FTMs possess of gendered power dynamics. Yet even respectful erotic appreciations of trans* people may be experienced as inappropriate by some, as gay transman Mik explained: 'Because I don't really identify that way, I identify as a man. So if I say "I'm a transman", that is a description of the condition, but it is not my identity.' Any reference to being different from cismen was a conflict with Mik's identity as a man and therefore did not feel like a celebration to him, but like an invalidation of his own sense of self. Trans* people who actually identify as trans* in some affirmative way and not only out of necessity were much more likely to welcome partners who seek them out specifically.

Community norms

My interview partners discussed various kinds of standards of behavior or norms specific to the dyke + queer BDSM communities they encountered.

For instance, protocol is a standard of behavior that is particular to BDSM culture. It is a complex, normative set of behaviors for the interaction between tops and bottoms, but also for addressing other tops and other bottoms. Traditionally, the concept of protocol implied that certain rules applied across the board, underlying all community interactions; therefore, any bottom had to address any top in a certain manner, independent of their individual relationship and also outside specifically negotiated sessions.

Protocol was a community norm; once you entered the community, you automatically were expected to behave according to these rules. Today, protocol is more often only considered appropriate if it has been previously negotiated between individual play partners. Therefore, culture clashes have occurred between the Old Guard and the New Guard around these differing takes on protocol.

In the dyke + queer BDSM community, experience was valued above age, but experience was (falsely) associated with older age, which resulted in ageism directed at young people as a BDSM-specific norm. Younger age was associated with inexperience and 'cuteness', and some young tops experienced belittling and ridicule; Scout, for instance, was not accepted in his role as a daddy at age 20.

Between lookism and queering beauty standards

Outer appearances and body norms play a major role in Euro-American societies, ranking people according to their ability to achieve certain (often unrealistic) ideals. This kind of lookism comes in various forms and impacts groups of people and individuals differently (Atkins 1998). Besides such bodily markers as sex and race, weight has become a major marker of social status (Rice 2007: 158). People of size are constructed discursively as unattractive, incapable and downwardly mobile; as not physically or emotionally healthy and as overindulgent and lacking in restraint or willpower (LeBesco 2004). Big female bodies, specifically, are seen as uncared for, unmanaged, excessive, holding unchecked desires and out of control (Murray 2004: 241). Sexual subjectivity is closely linked to body image. Thus, 'fat' women are constructed as asexual and unattractive, since sexual desire is culturally understood as a reaction to outer appearance (Murray 2004: 237–9).

My interview partners were very aware of the significance that their bodies had as currency in the sexual market. Looks were important for fetishes and in the context of voyeurism. Many enjoyed the specific erotic atmosphere that was created by dress codes, including being surrounded by people in sexually charged outfits. But the fact that there were different tastes and fetishes made dress codes problematic. Quite a few interview partners rejected the stereotypical BDSM look in this sense and preferred a diversity of appearances and creativity in outfits. As opposed to the straight and gay male communities, dress codes in dyke + queer BDSM communities tended to be less normative and less strictly enforced.

Beauty standards and lookism still existed, but they worked differently in the dyke + queer BDSM communities. Generally, interview partners observed a large range of difference in body types, and particularly an acceptance of women of size. My interview partners contrasted this lack of body conformity with heteronormative beauty standards for women in the straight BDSM communities and for men in the gay communities, while segments of the non-BDSM lesbian community also have developed a culture of valorizing fat bodies (LeBesco 2004). The sample was divided on the issue of body norms; some uncritically reproduced conventional beauty norms and did not value the existing body diversity in the community:

> Well, I'll say the SM scene is from, now according to my feeling, bodily close to the limit of the aesthetical to super beautiful. So there is every-thing, [for instance] a person is I'll say fat, not big, but really fat, where you don't know anymore is it still wearing a slip or not?

Bisexual top Franka's usage of 'it' instead of the female pronoun illustrates how fat women are often not actually seen as women, but as something gen-derless or less than woman (Rice 2007: 168[16]; Hole 2003: 318). While such openly anti-fat comments illustrated the uncritical reproduction of main-stream beauty ideals, other interview partners had to deal with the affective limit to their own pro-fat political ideals. Firesong, for instance, described how she had not been socialized to eroticize fat femmes and was working on broadening her own desires in that regard. Yet fat-positivity was not only a political goal among most interview partners, but also a reality. Some, like Terry and Kay, had a stated preference for partners of size.

The fat woman is also constructed as ultra-feminine because of her accen-tuated breasts and hips, emphasizing the maternal and radiating mature femaleness and, therefore, matriarchal power (Hole 2003: 318). So it might not be surprising that fat femmes also encountered sexual appreciation in dyke + queer BDSM communities. Most interview partners of size and the self-defined fat brats (SM dykes of size) in a discussion in the dyke BDSM fanzine *Brat Attack* experienced the dyke+ BDSM community as valuing their bodies more than other communities did (*Brat Attack* #1: 18). They attributed this to the facts that this community valued powerful women and size was associated with power, that difference was valued and that one's spe-cific BDSM preferences were as important as one's looks (19). This was also evident in the fact that most interview partners found that conventional notions of beauty hardly played a role in their partner choices or played no role at all, as polysexual transwoman Anna stated: 'I think these standard model types are nice, are yes, OK; somehow like that. They sometimes also look chic, but personally I find them rather boring.'

Overall, notions of beauty were extended and questioned. In the inter-views this happened on two levels: the decentering of the significance of conventional beauty ideals and the decentering of the significance of beauty (and related categories such as age) per se. One alternative notion of beauty and attractiveness in the community was self-expression:

> We're not necessarily looking for skinny girls with blonde hair, we're look-ing for how do you carry your weight, what do you do with your hips,

how do you play with the way that scar goes next to your ear? What are you doing with who you are and how you're expressing yourself through your body?

As queer high femme Zoe described, expressing oneself as a real, individual person was valued above abstract, conventional beauty ideals. Yet what Zoe described also amounted to a high standard in terms of a successful performance. Presenting yourself as a confident top, for instance, requires labors and self-disciplines that not everybody is able to accomplish. The embodied work expected of individuals in order to count as attractive has shifted here, which opens up new niches in the market, so to speak.

According to Emma and others, play parties may function as empowering for women in terms of body image and as sexual beings:

It's very helpful to them to go to sex parties and see how gorgeous and fabulous women look, no matter what their size or shape, when they're having good sex. To see other people and appreciate how fabulous they look while being sexual helps them realize that they look that good even if they think they've got too much weight on them or whatever.

Perceiving other women as beautiful even if they cannot adhere to normative standards of beauty may provide a reality check about one's own body issues and thus be empowering. For many interview partners of all sizes, but especially those who self-identified as fat or of bigger size, practicing BDSM, and being part of the dyke + queer BDSM community in particular, made them more comfortable with their own bodies.

Rice found in her study that, by framing fat girls as unfit, anti-fat discourses actually may produce fat girls' presumed lack of physical ability, strength and skill, eroding their sense of agency (Rice 2007: 165ff; 170–1). For a girl, not expressing dissatisfaction with your body may even put you at risk of accusations of arrogance (Bell & McNaughton 2007: 120). Rice concludes her study with a suggestion to move 'away from cultural practices of enforcing body norms and toward more creative endeavors of exploring physical abilities and possibilities unique to different bodies' (2007: 171). Dyke + queer BDSM seems to have provided interview partners with such a venue in the erotic field, for instance, when those with fat bodies found they could embody certain powerful roles, or they could offer a top more canvas to play on (see also Newmahr 2011: 101) or they encountered a sex-positive environment where indulgence was associated with sensuality and hedonism – and thus activity and agency – instead of a lack of willpower.

Geopolitical contexts

Self-defined BDSM practitioners constitute a marginalized and partially criminalized sexual minority in the US and Western Europe. This has historically resulted in driving BDSM underground. Many interview partners were completely out as gay, trans* or queer, but not as BDSM practitioners. This situation has created a coming-out discourse akin to coming out as gay. BDSM practitioners, especially dyke + queer ones, face social marginalization and everyday discrimination (Wright 2008) of various kinds. Many commentators on the legal situation in Anglo-American contexts have concluded that BDSM practitioners are currently excluded from full citizenship (Langdridge 2006). For instance, since *People vs. Samuels* in 1967 in US case law, and since the convictions of gay male BDSMers in the Spanner trial in the UK, consent has been denied as a defense in BDSM-related trials (Pa 2001; White 2006), creating a double standard between sexual and other practices, such as sports. Furthermore, several critics have pointed out that the law is more lenient toward heterosexual, married, monogamous, *white* BDSM practitioners, regardless of the severity or risk of their acts (Khan 2009: 109; Houlihan 2011).

Specific forms of discrimination further affect the dyke + queer BDSM community. During the sex wars, a pattern of violence by lesbian feminists against BDSM women emerged and was documented in a survey by 'Female Trouble', a Philadelphia-based women's BDSM group (Keres 1994). Over half of the women had experienced some kind of violence within the women's community due to being into BDSM (8). Women of color were more often victims of violence than were their *white* counterparts (10).

My interview partners had had anti-BDSM experiences, too. Roommates, partners and friends had been lost due to the interview partner being into BDSM. Common justifications of anti-BDSM attitudes were leftist, feminist or psychiatric frameworks. Pathologization remains one of the main narratives about BDSM. Their therapists had pathologized Daphne's and Terry's BDSM interests, but Daphne resisted the logic of what Deleuze and Guattari (2004) call interpretosis in psychoanalytic reasoning:

> Then he stated I would compensate for psychological pain with physical pain. So that would be a question or a point that is still open in my case. That I have not clarified yet. I still have to find an explanation for that somehow. But so far, even if I don't find it, I can live with it. I don't have to know everything and question everything.

Daphne did not share her therapist's assumption that she needs to understand her intrinsic motivations for all of her inclinations and actions. This dismissal of the relevance of pathologization and the psychologization of life in general may be a powerful form of resistance, foregrounding a type of subjectivity that has no origin and refuses explanation and usefulness.

My interview partners often experienced the social marginalization of BDSM in contrast to individual normalization: 'I consider it normal, I don't consider it not normal. I am sometimes really confused if someone says, like, "SM, oh my God."' Thus, non-defining[17] queer switch Petra resisted discourses of pathologization that led to social irritations with outsiders who took for granted that BDSM was deviant, or at least extraordinary. Petra therefore normalized BDSM in such encounters through analogies to socially accepted behaviors, such as sports: 'I mean, there are sports that are much more violent than SM. Then I say: "Aikido, isn't that violence?" [laughs]', exposing the double standard. This kind of normalization, however, was distinct from assimilationist notions of normalization. Interview partners like Petra radically rejected the dominant norms and redrew the boundaries of normality, based not on the hegemonic discourse of pathology and perversion, but on their own ethics of negotiated consent, trying to change the very definition of normality. Others rejected the distinction between normal and deviant, while still others rejected the value of being normal. For some, embracing an outsider status was empowering. For queer transwoman Leslie, 'the reason I also find [BDSM] sexy is because it's not allowed in society. Being into SM, it's so much more exciting and so much more sexually arousing because it's actually sort of a forbidden fruit you're touching'. Thus, for some practitioners, the normalization of BDSM would decrease its attraction and its erotic and subversive gratification.

The fact that for some people part of the allure of BDSM was its outlaw status resulted in a split in my sample into self-defined BDSM outsiders/rebels and those seeking state and social recognition, following the (neo)liberal notion of a right to privacy. The latter is a political strategy followed by the US-based BDSM rights organization NCSF, which positions BDSM practitioners as 'private individuals (not groups) who should have access to normal/good citizenship on the basis of their similarity to the norm' (Weiss 2008: 94–5). Scout felt alienated from this NCSF-style rights agenda

> because I've been fighting for my right to be queer on the street with my hands, in my job, for years, for so many years, that to stand up and start yelling about a guy who gets fired because he likes to beat his wife because they're kinky is just so not my battle, so not my struggle.

For Scout, a poor, working-class genderqueer who had been homeless for a year, the liberal agenda of fighting for rights within the system was a privileged kind of politics that was beyond his immediate needs for survival. He had to use his energy to deal with daily harassments on the street.

For many interview partners, the political value of BDSM was to be found exactly in its countercultural aspects. In Teresa's view, for example, being a pervert[18] was about rejecting mainstream culture's pretenses and lies:

> No, we're not going to be part of straight culture, because straight culture is all about lies. It's all about pretending that everything is OK. But there's so much abuse and we get attacked by more people that we know than people we don't, and attacks by people we know are way, way, way more

serious than attacks by people who we don't know. Stuff like that, so much hidden violence.

Thus, (re)negotiating power and violence within BDSM holds the potential to uncover the hidden violence in society, such as domestic violence and sexual abuse in relationships and nuclear families. One of the main reasons interview partners considered their BDSM practices to be politically relevant was the way they address gender stereotypes, gendered power relations (see Chapter 8) and social power in general (see Chapter 7). Therefore, for some dyke + queer BDSMers, their practices were part of a general radical critique of society.

Victim vs. agentic feminism: The feminist BDSM controversy

The controversy over BDSM among feminists dates back at least as early as 1976, when it was first documented (Linden 1982: 3), and continues today (see Bauer 2008a). In 1980, the 'National Organization for Women' (NOW) passed a resolution stating that NOW rejected BDSM because it violates feminist principles (Wright 2006: 219). In 1996, BDSM members of NOW launched a campaign to revise its anti-SM policy, resulting in its being revoked in 1999 (223). The controversy over BDSM was part of a larger conflict in feminist contexts about women and sexuality, known as the 'sex wars' (Vance 1992a; Duggan & Hunter 1995). The feminist sex wars are continuing today, and anti-SM feminism in particular affected my interview partners and their communities and how they related to feminism as a consequence.

Feminist anti-BDSM positions

I will briefly summarize the most common feminist anti-BDSM arguments, but I will refrain from a thorough discussion, since they are characteristically purely theoretical and not based on the actual experiences of BDSM dykes + queers (even though they are sometimes presented as facts, for example, in Linden et al. 1982).[19] Feminists critical of BDSM fail to take into account the perspectives of the women who have positive experiences with BDSM, or they find ways to discount the validity of their testimonies, saying they are caused by mental illness or false consciousness (Linden et al. 1982). When I reviewed the literature on the feminist debates pro and contra BDSM, the two positions seemed to present incommensurable paradigms (Kuhn 1962). This holds true for other anti-BDSM discourses as well. If one considers BDSM to be a pathology (mental, moral or social), anything that BDSM practitioners will say or that research will reveal about their practices will be interpreted within this frame of reference. This brings us to the issue of the cultural intelligibility of BDSM, since certain terms have different meanings in BDSM contexts, and these differences seem to foreclose any common references with which to build a shared discourse. For example, the term 'submissive' in the BDSM world implies a chosen role, not a personality trait that makes it impossible to act with a sense of agency or to resist domination.

Lesbian feminists argue that lesbian sadomasochism[20] is rooted in patriarchal sexual ideology and reflects the power asymmetries embedded in most social relationships (Linden 1982: 4) and, moreover, that the social and historical conditions that shape human relationships and erotic desires render the notion of consent meaningless (7). The lesbian feminist position does not consider sadomasochism as deviant but as normal: it is the basis for all social relations in patriarchy (Roesch Wagner 1982: 28). Therefore, although it is the norm, it is still pathological behavior because patriarchal society as a whole is sick. Gay and lesbian relationships are exempt from this, however, because partners possess 'the same access to gender power' (33), a position that fails to take into account the social hierarchies among women, created by differences in class, race, age, education and so on. From this *white* middle-class perspective, lesbian sadomasochism shatters the lesbian feminist illusion of egalitarian relationships among women and sullies the image of the pure, politically correct lesbian, as Lisa states: 'Because lesbians are not nicer, they are not friendlier, they have as many fantasies of violence or they are maybe even violent or whatever else, just like other people as well. So why shouldn't that be visible? It is there anyways. And we are not the ideal world somehow.' Hart (1998) also holds that the lesbian became the sign of purity within feminism and that this lesbian feminist identity has had to be guarded from any patriarchal contamination ever since (52). Lesbian BDSM may thus serve to politicize relations among women, which may explain some of the negative reactions toward it by a feminism invested in notions of women as non-violent and of the women's community as free of hierarchies and the abuse of power.

Anti-SM feminists oppose liberalism, arguing that no behavior is purely individual, and every action has a social impact. While I would agree with this, they falsely conclude that, if dominating a person is deemed acceptable in a BDSM situation, it endorses the idea that domination is acceptable under any circumstances in general (for example, Hein 1982: 87). Thus, they ignore context, and the social becomes oversimplified, as if actions had the same social meaning in any given situation, equating the negotiated, partially denaturalized domination in BDSM with real-life domination. But these are not merely theoretical discussions. As stated above, my interview partners experienced various kinds of discrimination in feminist contexts. I will briefly discuss some of the most significant effects of the debates on the communities involved.

Effects of the sex wars on the dyke + queer BDSM communities

Feminism and gay liberation had significant meaning in the biographies of most interview partners. Yet, because of their BDSM sexuality, they faced exclusion from women's communities. One way of community policing was the barring of BDSM dykes from women's spaces, and one of the major sites of the sex wars in this regard were large lesbian gatherings like the 'Michigan Womyn's Music Festival' in the US or the 'Lesbenfrühlingstreffen' in Germany. Today, the equation of BDSM with violence remains an issue in feminist communities, and many women's institutions that my interview partners encountered were anti-BDSM, including women's shelters, therapists who specialized in work with sexual abuse survivors, affirmative action programs and cultural events.

My interview partners attributed a general, pervasive sex-negativity as well as specific sexual norms in the lesbian community to the sex wars. In addition to a policing of behavior, this established a good lesbians/bad queers discourse, as dyke/queer butch switch Lola pointed out:

> People think I'm dirty a lot. I definitely [have] encountered people critiquing me that I'm too sexual and employing that in a very negative way. [...] So I definitely feel I have to censor myself quite often. Or just sort of pick and choose who I'm willing to talk to about what and where.

Thus, a consequence of this kind of policing is self-censorship, one variety of self-governance. The sex wars also had an impact on censorship policies in general, restricting access to information on sex and BDSM for women and queers. Lack of information on how to do BDSM safely may have severe consequences, such as physical injuries or falling prey to partners who lack integrity. Echols summarizes the position of the anti-pornography movement as considering all sex to be reactionary and that having no sex at all is better than sex under the existing circumstances (1992: 57). In her analysis of various strands of feminism, she finds that radical feminists subordinated sexuality to politics (58), and that lesbian feminists went back to romantic love as the ideal for women (59). Some feminists actually claim that women need sex less than men do and that abstinence does them no psychological harm (60), thus reproducing stereotypical notions about gender and sexuality. Finally, Echols asks us not to confuse feminism with female moral outrage (65).

'I think I like feminism better than feminism likes me'

One major function of the sex wars was to police the boundaries of (lesbian) feminism. The fact that some BDSM dykes claimed BDSM as a lesbian feminist practice or as compatible with feminism enraged many lesbian feminists (for example, Nichols et al. 1982: 145; Sims et al. 1982: 100). This highlights that what is at stake is what may count as feminist politics and who gets to be included under this label. Accordingly, many interview partners had a sense of not fitting into certain strands of feminism, especially lesbian feminism or '1970s feminism':

> The lesbian community had gone in the [direction of] politically correct feminism, more about rigidity and laws and exclusion: 'We're only safe if we close out all these other people'. And I didn't fit in there either, even though I worked at the battered women shelter. I invented a women's self-defense course back in '71. But I didn't fit into feminism.

As this quote by Mandy illustrates, it was not any lack of political and social work to further self-determination in women's lives that marginalized her within the feminist community, but the norms for what was appropriate (sexual) behavior.

As a consequence of these exclusions, many interview partners felt alienated from feminism, even if they shared a radical critique of heterosexism and were doing activist work. Still, a great majority of my interview partners (39) were self-defined feminists of different varieties, with many qualifying the specific branch of their feminism, such as gender activism, queer feminism, trans-feminism and sex-positive feminism. Only four rejected this label, and six did not explicitly discuss feminism. The quote from Katharina used as the subheading for this section, therefore, highlights a dilemma some interview partners faced: they strongly believed that gender is still a category of social stratification, but they were not accepted as part of the feminist movement. My interview partners observed a huge overlap between feminist and BDSM communities nonetheless. Many had come up with their own varieties of feminism, which did not pose a contradiction between practicing BDSM and being a feminist (see also Ritchie & Barker 2005). Their approaches may be characterized broadly as sex-positive feminism and as *agentic feminism* (see also Chapter 4 on sexual agency). A woman owning her sexuality was considered to be a revolutionary act by Emma, and exploring sexuality and BDSM was a feminist endeavor for many because it is empowering and offers new options for behavior. Agentic feminism stresses the power women already have to make choices among the limited options available to them in a heterosexist environment. My interview partners rejected victimizing discourses. Therefore, Vance's suggestion to use both pleasure *and* danger as a framework for doing research on women's sexuality (Vance 1992a; 1992b: xvii) proves useful. Feminism has too often focused on the dangers of sexuality, but Vance demands: 'Feminism must speak to sexual pleasure as a fundamental right, which cannot be put off to a better or easier time' (Vance 1992a: 24). She holds that feminism must insist that women are sexual subjects, sexual actors and sexual agents. This is a position that interview partners claimed for themselves when engaging in dyke + queer BDSM, and the necessity to simultaneously engage with danger and with potentials for pleasure also applies to trans* people.

Katharina considered it part of her feminism to deal with power in a way that moved from her own status as a victim to an intersectional analysis that also interrogated her own privileges:

> I am also not always only a victim. That is a bit easy to always only take a look at that, because it is so comfortable as well. And now I have to start engaging with where I also exercise non-consensual power in everyday life or at least have that potential to do so.

Analyzing social power relations, for many interview partners, was what connected their BDSM with their feminist practices. Thus, agentic feminism may be conceptualized as claiming one's own agency as a woman both to empower oneself and to interrogate one's own positions of power. It may also entail 'living as if' one already is in a position of power in order to explore new strategies of action. This approach could be characterized as performative and is connected to the performative character of the BDSM space. In their BDSM, each of my interview partners learned to consciously construct their own realities, for instance as a powerful dominant woman. In a second step, this experience of self-determination may be, at least partially, taken out of the space of dyke + queer BDSM into other social spaces, where she might perform as if she had the same access to powerful positions. Constructing one's own reality in this performative way may actually have real-life effects, such as taking one's competence in a professional context for granted and in return being treated with more respect by male co-workers. While this political strategy of performative agency clearly has its structural limits, it may serve to claim more space in public spheres for women.

Chapter conclusion

Dyke + queer BDSMers' access to civil society is limited due to discrimination, exclusion and heteronormative standards of behavior. Moreover, dyke + queer BDSMers also face anti-BDSM sentiments within women's spaces and lesbian feminism. As a result of the feminist sex wars, many dyke + queer BDSMers have been alienated from feminism. Rejecting victimizing feminist discourses, some have redefined feminism as agentic feminism. Finally, certain groups are marginalized within the overall BDSM community, even though queers and people of color have made significant contributions to it. Its history, therefore, needs to be rewritten to acknowledge this and to further the acceptance of difference within.

The dyke + queer BDSM communities value difference and negotiate their shared spaces accordingly. They fail in some regards, remaining a rather monochromatic, class-biased and ableist constituency, but have developed trans*-appreciative gender-segregated spaces. This demonstrates the power of desire, since it is the erotic appreciation of trans* people that has pushed the community's boundaries to include them. Yet trans* acceptance remains connected to trans* intelligibility. Trans* people should not have to pass to be accepted in their gender of choice, but their gender performances have to be understood on their own terms for full participation in public and collective spaces. Dyke + queer BDSM communities have their own norms and standards of behavior. They decenter the significance of heteronormative beauty standards and in part replace them with their own alternative notions of beauty.

3
Renegotiating Dyke + Queer BDSM

Definitions commonly try to freeze fluid situations that refuse to be contained, reducing complex phenomena to manageable units of knowledge. In contrast, from the perspectives of the dyke + queer BDSM practitioners I interviewed, no general definition of BDSM can be offered, not even of dyke + queer BDSM, since people make very different connections to that term, assign diverse meanings to it and are emotionally invested in it in different ways. My interview partners defined their own BDSM practices, identities and relationships in varying, sometimes contradictory, ways. Often, the same practices had different meanings to the same person over time, with different partners or in various contexts. Therefore, research that tries to find a generalized definition of BDSM has to fail, or has to prioritize specific views and experiences over others. In this chapter, the meanings that interview partners assigned to their BDSM identities and practices will be reconstructed in an attempt to delineate the ongoing renegotiations of what dyke + queer BDSM is to various individuals engaged in it.

I will start with an argument that dyke + queer BDSM can be understood as an alternative approach to sexuality. In the second part I will take a closer look at the specific social space of dyke + queer BDSM. Dyke + queer BDSM may be usefully understood as a particular social space, which is partially contained, creating an alternative reality for interview partners, and more specifically as intimate theater and as an out-of-the-ordinary space enabling experiences of bodies as boundary projects and spiritual experiences. In the following chapter, the criterion of consent, which distinguishes BDSM from violence and is a defining element of dyke + queer BDSM, is critically discussed.

Renegotiating sexuality through dyke + queer BDSM

Engaging in dyke + queer BDSM practices and communities often led my interview partners to question heteronormative assumptions and categorizations about sexuality:

I think it's mainly to recognize all forms of new types of sexuality. There's always new ones you're learning about and seeing, and things you're hearing about. And it makes me recognize just how limited terms like straight, gay, lesbian, bisexual are. How those just recognize a few forms of sexuality, and there are so many more that exist. There's so many things that people get off on.

As queer femme bottom Ellen's experience shows, new forms of sexuality are constantly invented. The dyke + queer BDSM perspective has thus prompted her to question the usefulness of categorizing people solely along the lines of the anatomical or birth sex of their partners, when there are many more points of reference for sexual preferences. This corresponds with the queer theorist Sedgwick's (1990: 8) observation that it is amazing that the gender of one's object choice is the qualifier for sexual orientation instead of countless other possibilities.

A sexual experience includes the specific bodily state of arousal and is highly subjective, since there are various ways to enter this embodied state. Therefore, I have left it to my interview partners to define what counts as sexual for them. And, since there is a great deal of variation in this, I speak of sexualities in the plural. Moreover, in the BDSM context, interview partners experienced many erotic practices not directly as sexual, but as creating an erotic atmosphere. The sharing of these BDSM-specific erotic situations was one way of creating alternative intimacies.

To start with, many interview partners stressed that they were highly sexual and enjoyed sex outside romantic discourse: 'I thought that was super, that I had that for the first time with a woman. So with my current girlfriend, who also practices SM, it's simply about sex for the sake of sex, and not sex for the sake of love.' Butch-loving, non-monogamous femme bottom Lisa and others therefore valued sex in itself, contradicting the stereotype that women only enjoy sex as an expression of love. Studies point to the persistence of sexual double standards (Dunn 1998; Klesse 2005). Today, women are interpellated by increasingly complex and contradictory normative standards as being both sexually active and virtuous (Dunn 1998: 499–502); thus, being *moderate* in one's sexuality can be said to be a recent norm for women. Dyke + queer BDSM practices presented a social context in which women and trans* interview partners were able to expand their sexual subjectivity beyond these norms. Practicing BDSM became a way toward sexual ownership of themselves, which some, like polyamorous queer femme Emma, considered to be of political value: 'If somebody can be labeled a whore or a slut because she is openly sexual, not for money, but because she chooses her sexuality, she is a woman who knows that it's her right to have this access to her own body, this is a revolutionary act in society still.' Using their bodies for their own pleasures was an act of reclaiming self-determination over women's and trans* bodies and sexualities in particular.

For many interview partners, BDSM was part of their identity; for others, it was merely a sexual practice they enjoyed. In the dyke + queer BDSM community as a whole, the range of BDSM practices engaged in was broad. Individual interview partners were diverse in their tastes and simultaneously aware of their ethical and personal limits. As ethical limits, they cited permanent damage to themselves or to play partners and interactions with real-life animals and children. Some interview partners had limits related to their personal history, like needle play for a former intravenous drug user or incest play for an abuse survivor, or just totally random personal aversions, like being licked on the face.

Desires and pleasures as situational

Terms connected to the sexual realm, like pleasure and desire, are not defined precisely in everyday usage or in research. My interview partners and various theorists use them differently. The dominant Western tradition of thought, starting with Plato (2006), has conceived of desire as based in lack, which, according to Hegel (1993), necessarily has to remain unfulfilled. Freud (1991) attributes the origin of desire to the loss of the unity of the mother–infant dyad. Since it is not possible to re-create that unity, desire necessarily is directed toward substitute objects, which locates desire in a deficient subject. In the interviews, in some instances, desire seemed to appear as an embodied force that can be experienced as a longing that is directed at something, that has an orientation in space and time. It may be goal-oriented, about wanting something, and it may be potentially complicit in categorizing that something in order to obtain it, as, for example, when a 'tranny-chaser' is trying to define what it is that is attractive about trans* people to her/him. But my interviews also show that not all desire is rooted in a perceived lack, or need or fixed orientations; quite the opposite. New sexual desires have, for instance, been created in my interview partners through their encounters with dyke + queer BDSM spaces. Desire was, therefore, presented as a productive force in my interviews. This resonates more with how Deleuze understands desire. Following Spinoza, Deleuze (1996) rethinks desire as a force that seeks to maximize the affective potentials of the body, and therefore as a productive, creative and transformative energy (see also Pieper & Bauer 2014). Thus, desire is not located in a subject, but is a presubjective intensity, circulating between bodies and creating connections between heterogeneous elements, effectively pervading the whole social body.

From a phenomenological perspective, one may also understand desire as reaching out toward the world with one's body. Following Merleau-Ponty, Gayle Salamon describes the movements of desire as a decentering of the self in turning toward another, but also as a recentering because the other grounds one through touch (2010: 53), therefore de- and reterritorializing in a Deleuzian sense. The body becomes active and alive when it opens itself to others and makes itself vulnerable (63). Merleau-Ponty's and Salamon's theorizing of desire is another useful starting point for under-standing dyke+queer BDSM, but I would add a distinction between desire and pleasure. While desires incite bodies to move, pleasures are experi-enced exactly when bodies are opened to touch through lingering. A body experiencing pleasure is lost in a moment of enduring intensities, defying categories, accepting what is rather than how things might be. Pleasure is not directed at something and, rather than being associated with motion, it is about stillness: it is being in the moment without an intentional direct-edness. Like desire and affect in the Deleuzian understanding, pleasures happen to bodies and are therefore excesses beyond a subject's control. While desires are about reaching out, stretching out to touch, pleasures are about allowing oneself to be touched. This kind of openness to touch and vulnerability is not passive in the stereotypical sense of the 'active versus passive' dichotomy, though. Rather, pleasure in this sense actively opens up undefined spaces for new ways of being and experiencing, and constructs new kinds of subjectivities. This is why bottoms describe such seeming paradoxes as feeling liberated or empowered when in bondage or when sur-rendering to a top. The question is whether one can seek out pleasures like desires, since it is necessary to remain open and waiting to be touched. But, at least, one may want to revisit past pleasures or one may have a desire for experiencing certain pleasures, which might be accessible through certain techniques, such as bondage or service (a state of being in the moment can-not always be entered into at will, but one may learn to access it more easily with techniques like meditation).

My concept of pleasure is therefore different from Deleuze (1996) and Deleuze and Guattari (2004: 173), insofar as they interpret pleasures as affectations that make persons find themselves, and pleasures are therefore limited to reterritorializing functions. But in my understanding, especially in bottom space, pleasure can produce precisely a state of losing oneself, of letting go and therefore opening up the embodied subject to transfor-mations and reinventions, becoming a deterritorializing force. So, I prefer a more differentiated and contextual analysis of desire and pleasure, one that highlights how they join hands with power to become sometimes inventive, sometimes reproductive, but always productive forces. Moreover, I would like to add the concept of pleasure as being touched to the Deleuzian con-cept of desire, which seems too focused on movement and expansion, and particularly the expansion of power. This view is possibly privileging mas-culine perspectives on sexuality as active or initiating, while neglecting the potentialities of being open to touch and lingering in the moment, which are also active engagements with one's surroundings, since it takes a lot of strength to be vulnerable in this world, as queer femme bottom Teresa put it.

In dyke+queer BDSM practices and spaces, both pleasure and desire are significant, and they join forces with power to experiment and cre-ate new embodied experiences of intensities and connections beyond the

heteronormative, genital-focused and pseudo-harmonic. Based on my interviews, I would agree with Deleuze and Grosz that pleasures and desires travel.
Yet they do not travel only across the surfaces of bodies. Following Deleuze,
Grosz explains that there are no predesignated erogenous zones. Rather, the
coming together of two surfaces produces a tracing that imbues certain parts
of bodies with erotic meaning, making them throb and intensifying sensation (1994: 78). This way of theorizing desire is well suited to making sense
of dyke + queer BDSM with its fluid, non-genital and non-heteronormative
sexual interactions. Desire, pleasure and which body parts are erotic then
become a matter of imprint, in biographical and, I would add, social and
historical processes: as the case of BDSM shows, social histories like those
of sexism and racism also shape bodies and desires. Individual biographies
shape desire (Salamon 2010: 45, referring to Merleau-Ponty), and collective
histories shape desires as well. Thus, the sexuality of an individual is shaped
by bodily and social encounters and is not predetermined. Yet my interviews
reveal that understanding desires as merely a product of surfaces, in terms
of touch to the skin, misses dimensions of their experience. Being touched
intensely, be it with fleshly body parts, extended body parts or implements
such as whips, reverberates beneath the surface, exciting parts of the interior body, causing a quickening of the breath, the heart to beat faster and
stronger, weakening the knees, causing the head to spin, generating body
heat and so on. Therefore, desires and pleasures do not simply travel *across*
bodies: they *enter* bodies, they travel *through* bodies. Moreover, the skin, the
surface of the body, does not hermetically seal the body. Rather, it is semi permeable; the surface is not closed, but is a gateway to the interior fluids and
materials of the body. Touching practically always includes some exchange
of bodily fluids, microbes and so on.

The descriptions of my interview partners make especially clear that
desires and pleasures in the world of dyke + queer BDSM depend not only
on bodily surfaces, but also on head games, 'mindfucks', power play, that
which is beneath the surface, and the symbolic meanings behind them. For
instance, if a bottom blacks the boots of her top, the act is not only about
sensuality. It is at least as much about the symbolic power inherent in the
boot as a marker of authority, and the whole situation of someone kneeling in front of another and servicing them. Finally, trans* sexuality is often
also not about the surface, but about what is felt inside the body, since the
body image is often not congruent with the body surface (see Chapter 8).
So, by allowing desires and pleasures to travel not only across, but also
through, bodies, we arrive at a much more useful theory for understanding
the experiences of dyke + queer BDSMers.

Sexual desires were situational for my interview partners. They tended to
fluctuate. Not all interview partners practiced BDSM all the time, so for some
BDSM did not represent a sexual need, but an option. The majority of my
interview partners switched, as gay transman switch BJ described: 'For me,

it's not whether today I'm a top or a bottom. I'm a top and a bottom all the time. So I can walk down the street and go: "God, I'd like to bottom for him. Boy, I'd love to top him". I'm equally both at all times.' BJ's desires could not be contained by one particular role or type of partner, but instead enabled all kinds of different connections. Switches did not necessarily distribute their sessions evenly between the roles of top and bottom; rather, their desire for each role fluctuated. BJ, for instance, did not have a preference for the top or bottom role, but decided which to take according to the dynamic with the individual in question; others went through periods of preferring one role over the other. For some, switching did not work with the same partner, while others switched constantly within a relationship. Therefore, desires were not fixed, as in a sexual orientation model, but context-dependent.

My interview partners described desires as interpersonal dynamics, which became evident in the theme of responsiveness that emerged like a red thread in the interviews. My interview partners stressed the significance of receiving pleasure from evoking a response in their partners. For instance, queer transgender stone butch top Terry defined stone[1] (butch) in this way: 'I get sexual pleasure from other people's sexual pleasure, from invoking that in other people. And so that's what stone means to me in terms of sexual preference.' This was also typical more generally for the top role for many interview partners. Emma explained what she gained from service bottoms: 'What is sexy to me is watching the expression on that person's face, because they're turned on by doing it.' This kind of responsiveness[2] in sexuality becomes circular: the partner's arousal becomes one's own arousal. There is no point of origin in the directionality of desire in this circular dynamic, as implied by the hegemonic understanding of sexual desire through the concept of sexual orientation. The desire is not directed toward a certain goal, and the aim of the sexual interaction is not fixed or closed, but left open to a becoming, emerging in the situation as intra-action. Therefore, the whole situation involving certain embodied actors turns into a site of pleasure. Thus, dyke + queer BDSM desires and pleasures are best understood as situational, as responsive to interpersonal dynamics in a given situation.

Sexualities as cultural phenomena

The kinds of sexual desires and pleasures that were common among interview partners largely did not follow the hegemonic model of sexual orientation. Sexual self-definitions were neither exclusively based on the biological sex of potential partners nor understood as inborn or fixed throughout time. Rather, gender and sexuality as expressed in the interviews may be best understood as cultural in various ways: they were no longer based on biological sex alone, and (sub)cultural contexts played a significant role. Yet there were also situations where the gender binary was reproduced. This presents no contradiction to the notion of sexuality and gender as cultural, but may, rather, be taken as traces of the impact of hegemonic culture in dyke + queer

BDSM spaces, stressing the fact that culture is infused with social power relations and that dykes + queers move in various social contexts simultaneously
and are interpellated as subjects in different and contradictory ways.

To some interview partners, their lesbian identity signified that their
sexual interests were exclusively directed at women, while others simply
preferred women as partners. The definition of 'woman' varied, though.
Most lesbian- or dyke-identified interview partners included transwomen in
their range of (potential) partners. Many dyke interview partners included
transmen in their sexual desires. To some, lesbian was an open-ended category; they focused on women, but were open to trans* individuals and men
for playing and/or having sex. Since BDSM does not necessarily involve genital sex, it is possible that a lesbian-identified person could involve (cis)men
in her BDSM practices (Sahra in Elb 2006: 221–2; interview partners such
as lesbian/queer transgender Kelvin), which might lead to a renegotiation
of her sexual identity (Ritchie & Barker 2005: 231). Thus, BDSM provides a
space for engaging with open-ended pleasures and desires rather than fixed
sexual orientations. One example of a sexual interest or preference beyond
the gender binary that remains in flux is the desire for expressions of female
and/or trans* masculinities.

Desiring female/trans masculinities and disidentifying with heterosexualities*

A common pattern among interview partners, especially femmes and FTMs,
was being attracted to masculine or queer masculine gender expressions
regardless of body anatomy, as gay transman BJ explained:

> I identify as queer on the spectrum that I'm attracted to people with mas-
> culine energy. So I do consider myself gay male, but – and that's the harder
> thing about identity, for me at least – I've never even based my identity
> on a body type. I've always based it on the energy that has run between
> the person and I. But as long as there's some masculinity in their energy,
> in the way they present, I'm very attracted to that. So there are some
> dykes, some other tranny queers that I'm attracted to, because they run
> male energy.

This was the definition of gay male sexuality for many interview partners,
which transformed the conventional notion of gay as cisman-on-cisman
interactions to masculine-on-masculine gender expression or energy.

Although interview partners detached masculinity from biological sex,
many queers excluded cismen, especially heterosexual ones, from their
range of masculine partners. Sometimes this was an indication of how
the significance of sexed body parts remains virulent. For instance, queer
genderqueer Femmeboy was reluctant to deal with biological penises, while
Teresa rejected the pathologization of 'having issues with bioboys'. She did

not want to consider lesbian or queer sexual preferences to be an individual incapacity to be sexual with cismen due to bad or traumatic autobiographical experiences. Instead, for Teresa, a preference for transmen over cismen was a complex negotiation of sexual pleasures and dangers in a sexist and heteronormative environment (Vance 1992a). The issue of where to draw the line in their desire for masculinity was of great significance to femme interview partners in particular. Mostly, the preference for FTMs over cismen was attributed to FTMs' higher level of insight into gendered power dynamics: 'With transboys I'm happy to be a straight femme type person. Because they get that it's queer and chosen and consensual. And there aren't the same sort of non-consensual power dynamics that exist for me in relationships between me and non-trans boys.' Thus, for Teresa and others it was about a certain culture of perspectives on gender, which transmen were more likely to share than were cismen. For queer women, choosing masculine partners who share the experience of being the object of sexism becomes a strategy to address gendered power imbalances in intimate relationships. Rather than disempowering transmen through fetishization, queer femme desires decenter cismen in feminine sexuality. The structure of femme desire can be split roughly into two versions: one that is primarily or exclusively directed at the butch as female masculinity, and one that eroticizes masculine gender expressions by people assigned female at birth or identifying as women.[3] The latter pattern of desire had led some to redefine their femmeness: the term 'lesbian' did not make sense to them (any more), since only some of their partners identified as women. Therefore, many interview partners identified as queer femmes because it better represented whom they were attracted to.

Butch–femme dynamics played with references to straight culture in the erotic setting, for instance in role play interactions. Queer transgender butch Tony understood a queer hetero dynamic (as in butch–femme interactions) to be a praising of difference. Queer femmes desired masculinity outside heteronormative frameworks; they may be said to disidentify with heteronormative desires within the concept of disidentification discussed by José Esteban Muñoz (1999). Poststructuralist theorizing starts on the premise that there is no getting outside of reason, the text, hegemonic culture, but that shifts within are possible, and are simultaneously minor and radical (Derrida 1976; 1991). But Derrida's strategy of reading between the lines of hegemonic texts to trace what has been excluded from culture has too often led to naïve celebrations of ambivalence as subversion, especially if social contexts are not considered (Namaste 2000: 22). Therefore, McClintock questions the sufficiency of locating agency in the fissure of discourse (McClintock 1995: 63). She points out that the more one insists on the transhistorical ubiquity of ambivalence, the less powerful a concept it becomes. If ambivalence is everywhere, at what point does it become subversive (65)? Even worse, history has shown that ambivalence is too easily foreclosed by (colonial and other) violence (66). It is therefore necessary to move beyond the mere detection and celebration of ambivalences in hegemonic cultures to find out whether and how they can be put to use for changing the status quo. Muñoz offers a promising theoretical input with his concept of disidentification as a survival strategy of the minority subject in order to negotiate a phobic majoritarian public sphere (Muñoz 1999: 4). He draws on Pêcheux, who differentiates between three modes in which a subject is constructed by ideological practices. Besides identification with the dominant culture, there are counteridentifications, which continue to validate the dominant ideology by reinforcing its supremacy through the controlled symmetry of counterdetermination. The third modus is disidentifications, which work on and against the dominant ideology, trying to transform cultural logic from within (11). Disidentificatory practices do not dispel ideologically contradictory elements. Rather, the disidentifying subject holds on to these objects and invests them with new life (12). Disidentification is ambivalent in its recycling of encoded meanings (31), but it does not simply celebrate ambiguity. Rather, it uses the dominant code actively as raw material for representing a disempowered politics or positionality that has been rendered unthinkable by the dominant culture (31). One advantage of the strategy of disidentification, to me, seems to consist in the use of affective attachments to dominant as well as countercultural codes to construct a subversive agency. This is something that dyke + queer BDSM draws on as well, infusing those codes of domination with not only affective, but also erotic value. For dyke + queer BDSMers as marginalized subjects, some BDSM practices entailed at least a partial identification and eroticization of their own oppressors. This was evident when interview partners enjoyed playing with sexism, homophobia and transphobia (see Chapter 8) or military roles while being the victim of and/or opposing these institutions in real life. In this sense, one could understand femme–butch culture and dyke + queer BDSM as disidentificatory practices. They take up themes of cultural hegemony, infuse them with erotic value, use them for their own desires and pleasures, appropriate them without necessarily endorsing the ideology behind the institutions and 'pervert' their meanings in ways that work against the original logics and rationalizations of the inequalities behind them.

Decentering biological sex

Especially for some bi- and pansexual interview partners, the biological sex of their partners was irrelevant. Some bisexuals prefer one sex, while others are equally attracted to men and women or any sex/gender. Being bisexual does not necessarily imply that one needs to be involved with people of both sexes simultaneously (Rust 1996); bisexual woman top Vito was sexually attracted to men and women, but was happy being in a monogamous lesbian relationship with her wife. For transwoman Daphne, gender was not a high priority in choosing sexual partners at all: 'In this regard I say most important is the person first of all. The person comes first and then gender. The person comes first, then SM, and then gender' [laughs]. This is congruent with other findings in research that, for some, BDSM is the main sexual preference, overriding gender and other factors (Spengler 1979: 92; Mitra 2005: 274). This is one of the ways in which dyke + queer BDSM transformed common understandings of sexual partner choice. It decentered the focus of sexual desires from sex/gender orientation toward BDSM-related shared interests and dynamics. For instance, one alternative to focusing on the biological sex of partners was to eroticize difference. This was not restricted to the polarity in gender expressions, as in the butch–femme straightness described above. Emma described her desire in general as tension-based, which found its expression in various power dynamics through the construction of difference in social status.

Those interview partners whose gender identities were outside the gender binary (see Chapter 8) dissolved hegemonic sexual orientations such as straight, gay, lesbian and bisexual altogether, because these are based on two distinct and stable sexes (or, at least, genders). Queer transguy Matt explained:

> I think that gay, straight, bi are all terms that are really working within a gender binary, so granted that I don't identify with the gender binary, and neither does my partner, I guess we just identify as queer. Especially also because I think queer speaks to a certain cultural thing, to a certain community and identifying as being a part of that, of being of fluid gender and of fluid sexuality.

Since Matt and his partner were both trans* individuals living their daily lives outside the gender binary, they related to queer as a concept that expressed an affinity with fluid boundaries in terms of gender and sexuality. Queer in this sense moves away from anatomy as the reference for sexual identity and categorization, and replaces it with a (sub)cultural context. Matt identified with a specific gender and sexual culture rather than with an absolute signifier based on biology. His sexual identity as queer was context-sensitive and questioned hegemonic categories.

Significance of the sexual (sub)culture context

Identities and labels refer to certain contexts or communities: switch, for example, is an identity in the BDSM community, or queer can be used as shorthand to communicate complex statements about unconventional desires in certain communities. Labels can also express belonging, an individual's connection and emotional attachment to certain histories and communities. Sometimes, a subculture is a precondition for being able to claim and live a certain identity. Queer/dyke high femme Mandy was only able to really identify as a BDSM dyke when she finally found others to build a community with after years of relating to mostly gay men.

There were various ways in which interview partners' sexual identities related to queer subcultural contexts and only made sense within them. There were examples of cultural transfer between the gay men's and the dyke + BDSM communities; for instance, Mandy used her drag queen friends as role models for acquiring a powerful femininity as a femme. This can be considered a strategy of disidentification that utilizes the fact that the drag queens were used to claiming privileges and power as men in a way that had been denied to Mandy growing up as a woman in the 1950s and 1960s. Mandy used their reconstructions of femininity as a way to refuse hegemonic notions of femininity as powerlessness without eschewing femininity altogether. My interview partners also imported aspects of gay male sexual culture, such as cruising, and certain icons, like the leather daddy, into their community (see also Bauer 2007a).

One version of a subcultural sexual self was about claiming a counter-hegemonic or disidentificatory identity. For instance, dyke + queer BDSM was positioned as outside heteronormative and romantic culture, as Emma put it: 'This isn't hearts and flowers, mythological heterosexuality; it's not any of that.' Thus, queer identities may incorporate a rejection of hetero- and mono-normative standards of intimacy and sexuality. Queer, then, stands for being unlike the others, as challenging the mainstream and male privilege and inventing new sexual variations. To my interview partners, straight people were different culturally, and they identified with queer, dyke or trans* cultures instead. In this sense, queer as a formerly derogatory term was embraced and seen as perverse, sexy, strange, eccentric, deviant. Non-conformity and political subversion were sexually attractive to some interview partners. It was not homosexuality as a sexual orientation, but queer culture that became the material of queer resistance, much as Foucault postulated (1996). Overall, sexual preference as cultural rather than directed at a certain biological sex of a partner represents an alternative kind of intimacy; it introduces a different kind of circulation of desires. Desires do not stick to specific bodies constructed within a normative binary, but travel through various bodies and assemblages of organic and artificial body parts, and are invested in cultural affinities like sharing a non-heteronormative or disidentificatory perspective on life.

Beyond sex as natural: Dyke + queer BDSM as continued learning

Hart points out how BDSM sex is discursively linked to the theatrical, as performing or *doing* scenes, while regular intercourse is seen as *having* sex. Thus, heteronormative sex is seen as preperformative compared with BDSM

(Hart 1998: 148). From their dyke + queer BDSM perspective, my interview partners understood all sex as not simply given, but as cultural and as something that involves continued learning. One has to acquire skills and expertise to practice BDSM sex safely and with a certain amount of quality. Newmahr's and Weiss's informants also emphasized this process of learning to play for both tops and bottoms (Newmahr 2010: 319–22; 2011: 84–9; Weiss 2011, especially Chapter 2). Yet my interviews showed that there are also individual properties or capacities that present limits to learning. While it may be possible to increase one's personal pain tolerance, individuals bring their own capacity to deal with pain to begin with.

Tops carefully plan, arrange and orchestrate sessions, although there are also spontaneous encounters. With its emphasis on planning beforehand, BDSM further violates the mystification of sexuality, which in the romantic imagination simply happens (Hart 1998: 151–2). But even highly structured scenes develop self-dynamics, and tops need to remain flexible. Sessions go through phases, according to my interview partners, such as a ritualized entry into the roles (for instance, the collaring of the bottom), a building up of tension and a cool-down. To achieve the finesse of leading a bottom through a session and balancing her on the edge, the top had to learn how to read a bottom's reactions. Overall, the manifold skills one needs to acquire and manage to practice BDSM successfully may be usefully understood as Foucauldian techniques of the self (Foucault 1990: 27): they require work on the self beyond the mere replication of technical skills or knowledge, for instance, the focus and self-control a top needs to run a session without losing herself. Weiss also understands the becoming of a BDSM practitioner in this way and emphasizes the significance of the transformation of the self in the process of interpreting and individualizing the community rules (2011: 64–5; 79). In regard to my sample, I would stress that dealing with community standards is an active and *critical* acquisition, in the course of which the rules themselves are also subject to renegotiation and do change over time (see Chapter 6 on community guidelines).

Dyke + queer BDSM as an alternative approach to sexuality

Even recent sexology often still defines sexuality first and foremost via genital stimulation (Rye & Meaney 2007: 29). In contrast, my interview partners' definitions of what constitutes a sexual act varied greatly. Some equated sex with penetration. Others included all genital contact in their definition, while others defined it independent of any genital involvement. Some took orgasm as the criterion, no matter how it was achieved, for instance through being spanked. Other interview partners did not consider orgasm a necessary ingredient of sex, especially since it may be part of playing with power to be denied (or to deny) climax. Instead, they defined anything as sex that was sexually arousing to them, as gay transmasculine switch Craig discussed:

But sometimes sex is kicking the crap out of somebody. I don't know if it's sex, yeah it is, because I get off on it. So it's sex. If I get a really good bootlicking, and most people wouldn't consider somebody lying at your feet licking your boots as sex, but I would say it's sex, because it's like [roars]. I don't know how I should define it. I would say anything that gets me hot and bothered, not necessarily getting off.

So, for Craig and others, a variety of non-genital or even non-physical BDSM activities may qualify as sex. This sabotages any universal definition of sex, since individuals are aroused in very different ways. Therefore, sex becomes self-defined and may not even be mutual, as dyke switch Michaela pointed out: 'And that encounter can possibly be sexual for one person and not for the other, based on their definition.' If an individual's level of arousal is the qualification for a situation to be deemed sexual, then arousal is also dependent on context, since the same activity may be sexually charged in one circumstance and not in another, such as within a private as opposed to a sex work context, as lesbian Lilly, who worked as a professional top but also played privately, pointed out.

For almost all interview partners, BDSM had broadened the definition of the sexual and/or erotic, creating new ways of being intimate. For some, it sexualized the entire body and everyday behaviors and artifacts, as lesbian bottom Cara recapitulated: 'So I believe I never used to find the view of a rose with its thorns so unbelievably erotic [laughs] as is the case now with new connotations.' Many interview partners described experiences of non-genital sexuality within BDSM. My interview partners may get aroused and even orgasm through strap-on or packy[4] sex, bondage, sensation play or dominance/submission (DS) situations, like being led on a leash. For instance, dyke femme lifestyle submissive Tanya was able to orgasm from being ordered to. And Mandy recalled: 'But in SM, because we do so much sex that has very little to do with genitals, it's amazing to me. I mean, one time I had three orgasms when someone was flogging me. Not only that one time, but three contraction kind of orgasms. I was amazed.' Sensation play is one way that BDSM sexualizes the whole body instead of just the genitals, for instance the back or buttocks when being flogged or spanked. My interview partners concluded that their sex life had become less genitally focused through BDSM. The interviews in many regards prove Foucault's thesis that BDSM creates new pleasures (and desires):

We know very well that what all these people are doing is not aggressive; they are inventing new possibilities of pleasure with strange parts of their body – through the eroticization of the body. I think it's a kind of creation, a creative enterprise, which has as one of its main features what I call the desexualization of pleasure.

(Foucault 1996: 384)

Foucault calls for building relationships with the self that are about differentiation and creation, rather than identity, to strive toward a desexualization, a general economy of pleasure that would not be normatively sexed (1996: 213), an intensification and an ethics of pleasure (380). All these aspects were apparent in the interviews: creating new pleasures, eroticizing the whole body (even entities that are not part of the organic body), desexualizing or decentering pleasure through disconnecting it from its genital or penetrative focus, intensifying pleasure, generating multiple sexual selves and therefore intrinsic difference rather than sameness and, finally, an ethics of pleasure, since the criterion of consent had replaced traditional moralities about sexual acts. Therefore, dyke + queer BDSM can be seen as redefining sex and can be characterized as an alternative approach to sexuality.

I understand sexualities to be embodied interactions that are not limited to the organic body, but, rather, involve cyborg bodies including such extensions as fetish artifacts and sex toys, and that generate a state of embodied arousal that individuals have culturally learned to associate with specific out-of-the-ordinary, transgressive social spheres (the erotic, the intimate). In my research, I leave it to the self-definition of interview partners which interactions and experiences they make sense of within a sexual framework and which BDSM interactions they might, rather, frame as something else, such as a spiritual experience, or most likely as carrying different meanings simultaneously, such as spiritual and erotic and relaxing.

The social space of dyke + queer BDSM as alternative realities

In the interviews, dyke + queer BDSM emerged as a specific kind of social space with its own rules and regulations, creating alternative realities. Some interview partners considered their BDSM to be mainly a sexual experience, while others were more interested in the power dynamics and specific BDSM energy than the sexual aspects of it. Some interview partners also enjoyed non-BDSM sexual interactions, while others solely practiced BDSM sexuality. But all interview partners described BDSM within an erotic framework, even those who refrained from combining it with genital sexual activities.

Sexual arousal or the pursuit of sexual fantasies was the main motivation to engage in BDSM, even though it might include other dimensions, such as spiritual or therapeutic. Therefore, my sample repudiates Newmahr's argument that BDSM is not sex (2010; 2011). Her claim that BDSM is not sex, but, rather, a serious leisure activity stems from various problems with her study and theoretical approach. First, the community she studied defined itself by excluding those BDSMers who played sexually (2010: 329; 2011: 66–8). The argument that BDSM is not sexual is circular, if one precludes sexual BDSM in the first place. Furthermore, her study was limited to public play in the US. But public play tends to be less sexual than private play, in many US regions sex is not allowed in BDSM spaces for legal reasons, and public play is not the whole of BDSM. Second, she understands sex as private (rather than social) and criticizes the oversimplification of BDSM as sex. But the real problem seems to be her oversimplification of sex as something that stands outside the social realm, which neglects how social and power relations permeate what is constructed as private or intimate as well. She also remains within a heteronormative understanding of sex as genital contact, and sex as pure in that it cannot have any social functions.

Yet there is no reason why sex should not be a serious leisure activity itself; in fact, there are phenomena like tantra workshops, swinger clubs and so on which could be understood in this way. Contrary to Newmahr's efforts to 'clean up' the image of BDSM by downplaying the sexual aspects, my interview partners followed a strategy of imbuing sexual BDSM with social value and questioned the heteronormative discourses that consider sex per se as something dirty or sinful. But maybe even more significant is that the erotic framework was the only feature besides the criterion of consent that all dyke + queer BDSM practices and identities had in common, and thus it is elemental when trying to define BDSM. Overall, dyke + queer BDSM represented its own distinct form of intimacy, generating emotions, affects and bonding that were experienced as unique by dyke + queer BDSMers and which they often described as a 'special SM energy' or a specific space, such as 'going into bottom space'. My interview partners used the metaphors of energy and space to describe a unique quality of experience that exceeds discourse.

Dyke + queer BDSM as semi-contained space

The dyke + queer BDSM community has developed standards to provide its members with safety frames enabling them to venture into their risk-taking activities (see also Chapter 6). My interview partners described dyke + queer BDSM as a structured space with defined boundaries, a secure setting, a game with a specific set of rules. Therefore, I call it a semi-contained space. Like a game, it has different rules and usually a ritualized beginning and ending, as dyke/queer butch switch Lola explained:

> Say I put a collar on somebody. I know I might tell them that for the period of time that they have the collar on, I'm completely in control of them, but that as soon as the collar comes off, their control is returned to them. So we both know it's play night and that also actually gives the other person the opportunity that if they weren't feeling OK with that, they could just take off the collar themselves at any time. And the power would get evened out again.

A collar was a common symbolic device that facilitated the transition between ordinary reality and BDSM space. Other techniques to mark a beginning were someone entering a room, changing into fetish clothing, the bottom kneeling down or starting to address each other according to their respective roles. The terms 'scene', 'session' or 'play' were used synonymously to denote such a contained BDSM encounter of limited duration.

This semi-contained space opens up possibilities to explore and drop ordinary boundaries one needs in everyday life to go about one's usual business. Emma compared it to 'putting a kid in a playpen' and a 'sonnet. It's got really strict rules, but you can be incredibly creative within those rules'. This semi-contained setting that BDSM provides allows creativity, exploration and improvisation within that structure. This social space has been described via analogies with game, theater and group performance, which will be discussed in the following sections. I will argue that BDSM may be understood as *intimate theater*, even though no single concept is able to represent the great diversity of practices under the umbrella of BDSM. What is important is not to confuse my notion of semi-contained space with the concept of privacy. Dyke + queer BDSM is not a private matter in the sense of being separate from the socio-political; social structures of inequality permeate the so-called 'private sphere' as well. Therefore, I call it semi-contained rather than contained. Yet, within this space, these social structures are engaged with and dealt with under partly different conditions.

BDSM as an out-of-the-ordinary experience or semi-contained space is, therefore, distinct from ordinary life. Most interview partners drew and maintained boundaries between work life, family of origin life and their dyke + queer BDSM identities or practices. For instance, they differentiated between role play and everyday personas. Or they described BDSM as a subset of their lives, restricted to a semi-contained space. But they also experimented with integrating their BDSM into ordinary life through 24/7 ownership dynamics or public play (see Chapter 5). And for some, BDSM was part of their identity in a way that could not be separated from the rest of their life.

Fetishes might also expand one's sexuality into everyday life, as Lola observed: 'Now I get turned on when I'm in hardware stores and stuff. That's crazy. I mean it's crazy how many things I can fetishize. I also have a real fetish for work clothes and work boots and tools and things like that.' Her work fetish produced arousal in hardware stores, because it is a fetish that is derived from everyday items. Therefore, the relationship between BDSM and ordinary life may become circular: Lola gets her inspiration for BDSM from items in the real world; then, in turn, the fetish gets transported back and eroticizes everyday life. The different realities of BDSM and ordinary life are not completely separate; cross-pollination occurs, transporting meanings back and forth and constantly transfiguring them. Thus, these different realities co-exist and can be pictured as overlapping spheres rather than as separate entities with clear demarcations.

Many interview partners described their BDSM not only as a semi-contained space in the social world, but also as an alternative reality. When switching from one type of reality to another, structures of relevance are left behind (Schütz & Luckmann 2003: 182). For instance, when it comes to the reality of dyke + queer BDSM, interview partners were able to leave parts of the hegemonic binary gender system behind. To some, therefore, dyke + queer BDSM served as a retreat from the stress of everyday life, like a vacation or adventure. Role play may function as a liberation from everyday subjectivity through entering a different role or expressing a part of the self that has no space in ordinary life, such as an inner child or the slut within. There seemed to be a need to readdress and rebalance everyday experiences of authority and powerlessness in various ways for interview partners. Dyke + queer BDSM became one tool to do this on a personal level in a social situation where political struggles to redistribute power (symbolically and materially) seem to have become futile and where the individual is increasingly assumed to be responsible for her own emotional and physical health and happiness (Hirsch 1995; Pieper 2003). To use dyke + queer BDSM in this way may be considered a creative individual solution to a social problem. Practicing BDSM may ease interview partners' emotional burdens of living in an unjust world, whether they profit or suffer from these power hierarchies, or more likely both, depending on the situation and circumstances.

Dyke + queer BDSM as intimate theater

The role-playing aspect of many of the BDSM practices of my interview partners was one way in which they considered dyke + queer BDSM to be a different kind of reality. Emma captured this aspect clearly in her definition of dyke + queer BDSM as *intimate theater*. Others also used the analogy to theater to characterize their BDSM. It was described as performance or as staged, sometimes literally before an audience at play parties. People rehearsed scenes in their head beforehand and sometimes anticipated performance anxiety. As in theater, there are various levels of reality in a BDSM session. As Emma pointed out, players suspend their disbelief. BDSM performances are simultaneously real and not real as embodied enactments of fantasies. Bottoms are aware that they are not really being damaged, they are not powerless, yet everyone goes through genuine emotions and – as opposed to theater – the physical effects are genuine as well; sensation play really affects the body.

Dyke + queer BDSM as enacting fantasies

To many, BDSM was first and foremost a means of enacting erotic fantasies. While someone's fantasy life is, in principle, limitless (albeit influenced by socio-historical realities), enactment even in the semi-contained space of dyke + queer BDSM had clear boundaries. For instance, the body presents anatomical limits, and bisexual top Franka contrasted real BDSM with fantasy: 'I am always laughing myself to death about certain SM stories, where anything goes. And then I say: "Oh God, if I was tied up like that for only five minutes, it would be madness." That is absurd.' This again demonstrates the containment of BDSM; techniques are created that accept that there are bodily limits to unlimited fantasies and keep physical harm at bay.

Moreover, there are ethical limits, as BJ explained:

> I know that some of my fantasies really should not be brought into reality, because some of the things that I masturbate to and think upon it's really intense stuff. I said murder is out of the question, but I have fantasized about murdering people. Children and animals are out of the question, but I tell you I read magazines and jack off to the idea of fucking eight-, nine-, ten-year-old boys. Fantasies are one thing, [but] there are certain lines I won't cross.

Although other interview partners did not spell it out so clearly, many expressed that their fantasy life is more 'extreme', intense or transgressive than their actual practices, for various reasons. BJ was discussing ethical boundaries here. In his philosophy, while in fantasy anything goes, in reality valid consent cannot be established with children and animals, and permanent damage is unethical as well. Thus, practicing BDSM does not necessarily lower the inhibition threshold. Instead, interview partners carefully examined their fantasies on the basis of their ethical convictions.[5] To make risk-aware and ethical choices, they had to be able to distinguish between fantasy and reality.

Yet, the distinction between fantasy and reality is not a clean cut. As mentioned above, the social world serves as a resource for dyke + queer BDSM fantasies. For instance, social hierarchies like boss and secretary are a rich cultural resource for BDSM scenarios. Queer transwoman bottom Leslie differentiated between thematic fantasies like doctor–patient and the agents in one's real life:

> I don't have fantasies about my work or job or when I'm with my doctor. I can have a fantasy about playing in medical surroundings, but then I don't think about my doctor, or the room that I'm in when I go to the doctor, to the hospital, or anything. That doesn't come to mind.

Thus, while the real-life social theme of the power dynamic between doctor and patient might serve as a frame for a BDSM role play, the distinction between fantasy and reality was upheld because it was only the archetype or stereotype that was enacted, not the actual social context of one's personal life. It is *the* doctor or *a* doctor, not *my* doctor, who is used in play.

In a similar vein, Hoople argues that BDSM practitioners do not rely on any real master–slave or other social oppressive relationship in their simulation, but they take a *fantasy relation*, for example a fantasy of a sexual master–slave relation, and (attempt to) actualize it (1996: 207). Thus, he considers BDSM to be a genuine performance of a fantasy (not reality), which, I might add, may bear more resemblance to fantasy role-playing or children's role-playing than to theater. Therefore, Hoople suggests adopting Butler's notion of reiteration to dissolve the false opposition of considering BDSM as either replication or simulation (1996: 208ff). While a BDSM master–slave relationship, even if mediated through fantasy, does relate to the original historical model, it also transforms that model through reiteration, a repetition that shifts its meaning, most significantly through introducing the element of negotiated consent: 'historical Master/slave relations were relations of oppression; SM Master/slave relations are relations of power, insofar as the slave is empowered to leave the relationship' (1996: 209). Hoople's point is validated by the interview partners, who stressed that, without consent, scenarios involving rape or domination were not sexually arousing, but abhorrent to them. Furthermore, the polarized roles assumed in BDSM are structural but not essentialized (since, in principle, any role can be chosen by any participant), which sets them apart from oppressive structures such as sexism or racism (209). Following Foucault (1982), historical master/slave relations could then be understood as a structure of violence in which the strategic power game is foreclosed, while the BDSM reiteration utilizes the strategic power game. For instance, the bottom has the power to leave, which could be put to use in negotiations with a top. Negotiations highlight the interdependence of top and bottom; in BDSM the top relies on a willing bottom.

McClintock considers BDSM to be a theater of conversion, transmuting the social meanings it borrows. In BDSM, paradox is paraded, not resolved. It achieves this through its exaggerated performance, demonstrating the scriptedness of social power (McClintock 2004: 237) and thus denaturalizing power relations (239). While this theorizing makes significant points, it fails to acknowledge that the theoretical potential of BDSM practices is not always realized empirically, starting with the fact that only switches are free to actually choose which role they want to take. While those identifying exclusively as tops or bottoms may in principle switch roles, in reality this is not an option if the other role is not erotically charged for them or if they cannot embody or perform it comfortably or convincingly. Furthermore, BDSM only gains erotic currency through emotional attachments to certain forms of power and powerlessness or the subversions they offer. Such affects are sticky and simultaneously enable and limit the transformation of social power relations through BDSM.

In contrast to Hoople, Weiss argues that through using realism, such as historical references to slave auctions, a BDSM scene becomes more credible (2011: 22). Yet this is not always the intention of the players. In my sample, many dyke + queer BDSMers preferred fantastic, unrealistic scenes, because social structures like racism were not sexy to them. Theorists seem to take for granted that real-life social systems of domination and oppression are erotically charged. Yet the opposite may apply as well: one's political convictions and life experiences can make these real-life scenarios abhorrent and disgusting and prevent any erotic affects. No theoretical attention has been paid to this effect, and little has been paid to the eroticization of the subversion of hierarchies or leftist political subcultures.

Fantasies may also represent a part of the self. Mandy understood them as voices from the Jungian shadow (see also Easton 2007) and therefore as clues to real-life issues, although they are not necessarily an accurate representation of real life. This is one reason why BDSM fantasies feel so intimate; in addition to their sexual content, they may stand for a (repressed or hidden) part of one's personality that is disclosed to another in the enactment during play. Some interview partners stressed that they were not interested in being someone else in BDSM, but that they expressed a part of their personality. Thus, to some, BDSM was a part of their everyday reality, not a distinct sphere.

Dyke + queer BDSM as play-acting

Most interview partners found the term 'play' appropriate for their BDSM, since it is associated with the assuming of roles, creativity, improvisation, art, joy, fun, parallel (fantasy) worlds, suspension of consequences, regulations and self-irony. Others only found it useful for describing casual encounters, but felt it did not capture the depth, intensity or all-encompassing nature of their committed BDSM experiences and relationships. Some of Woltersdorff's interview partners rejected the term 'play' as well because it robs BDSM of its sinister and dirty sides, and some preferred to say they do not play, but live their SM (2011a: 5). Yet queer switch Petra pointed out: 'Children also play in a cruel way with each other.' Thus, the play-acting analogy is able to accommodate the sinister parts of dyke + queer BDSM, while simultaneously stressing the fun and physical aspects. My interview partners described instances in role play that made them giggle or laugh. According to Kelly, play is intrinsically motivating and expressive and it is a non-serious, temporary suspension of consequences, creating a world of its own meaning, which is often a shadow of the 'real world' (cited in Williams 2006: 337). Therefore, dyke + queer BDSM as play can be characterized as another reality, and, contra Kelly, it may be serious at times as well. Understanding BDSM as a real or serious game dissolves this seeming contradiction, as lesbian[6] switch Connie pointed out: 'Game does not mean that it is less real. Game stresses the regulative [nature] of the safe, sane, consensual [guidelines]. Games have limits.' Thus, the regulation and containment of the action is a feature that games and BDSM share. Woltersdorff points out how conceptualizing BDSM as play opens up spaces for agency because it emphasizes that one can design one's own rules for this game (2011c: 19). While some rules were community standards and not open to debate (such as consent), my interview partners did indeed make use of the fact that they could negotiate their own dyke + queer versions of BDSM, for example, that everyone could choose a gender for play. Games have rules that are different from real life, but within that frame they may trigger real emotions (watch any sports event to witness an example of real emotions during a game). Likewise, Ahrens rejects the notion of distinguishing between seriousness and play; rather, he considers BDSM to be a serious game, like children's games (2006: 290). Weiss also discusses BDSM as a serious game (using a term by Ortner, cited in Weiss 2006b: 237) or deep play, a concept by Geertz for play with dangerously high stakes (236). Instead of play, the Old Guard called their BDSM 'work' (Magister 1997: 125), which prioritizes the seriousness aspect and resonates with the concept of BDSM as a Foucauldian practice of the self, which requires work. Weiss also theorizes BDSM as 'working at play', since it is conceptualized as a craft in the community she studied, with talk about being an apprentice and a journeyman (2006b: 235), but terms like these were not part of the discourse in my sample. Still, understanding BDSM as a serious leisure activity seems to be a suitable theoretical approach (Williams 2009; Newmahr 2010; 2011), since it may be characterized as a devotion to the pursuit of an activity that requires specialized skills and resources and that provides particular benefits (Newmahr 2010: 318), although the focus on education and resources varies greatly in local communities.

Improvisations on a theme are typical for play-acting, which is another characterization of dyke + queer BDSM by interview partners. For Vito and Cara, the entryway into BDSM was actually fantasy role-playing. Vito's main character in their BDSM play was a male vampire, while her lesbian wife, Cara, embodied a female human victim. In dyke + queer BDSM a lot of role-playing involves gender and age play (see Chapter 8). One especially playful role was being a puppy or dog; Connie cherished the playful/irrational aspect of it. There is the stereotype of doggy submissiveness, while dogs may also stray and receive unconditional love. Animal play in general is a good example of an alternative state of mind, as well. It allowed interview partners to leave behind rationality and intellect, signified through verbal language and social etiquette, and enter a state of complete abandonment. Deleuze and Guattari understand the process of becoming-animal as a desire to expand or becoming-other through what is different and more than oneself. The animal one seeks to embody is not simply a metaphor for some human quality, but another mode of perception or becoming (2004: 262). This was true for my interview partners; they were drawn to the state of becoming-animal in order to enter a completely different mode of being beyond the human experience. This was one of the many pathways to an experience of intensity in dyke + queer BDSM.

Parallel levels of reality and fantasy: Dyke + queer BDSM as illusion and as real

Interview partners took different stances on the realness of their BDSM. Some held that BDSM was an illusion; others considered it a variant of reality. Emma stressed that it was the illusion of slavery, the illusion of danger or risk, that was played out in dyke + queer BDSM. Others insisted it was more than that: BDSM was a material matter, physically as well as emotionally, which became evident to bottom Yosh in the aftereffects of a session: 'And through the aftereffects somehow, say you still got some "ouch" somewhere if you sit down or something like that, it all comes back to you, even days later. That is something I really like, because that's this "yes, it wasn't just a dream, but really happened."' Thus, to the body, dyke + queer BDSM is as real as ordinary life.

Moreover, BDSM was also not so easily separated from real life in the mind:

> Even if I watch a movie, it has a reality unless I do something actively in order to do away with its reality by distancing myself from it. Or if I read a book, it has a reality. The same applies if I embody roles, then it also doesn't matter if that is theater or if it is SM. So SM is even more clearly real than theater. And even theater then at least has a temporary reality, which changes how I feel and how I experience myself perhaps as well in a broader sense.

To queer femme switch Katharina, suspending disbelief was not an active act; she easily slipped into alternative realities as the recipient of books, films and theater and as an actor in BDSM. And, of all those examples, BDSM most closely resembles everyday reality, probably due to its employment of physical sensations and the fact that many roles are embodiments of personal sexual fantasies or partial selves. It is more real (understood as resembling ordinary, everyday social experience) than acting in a drama, even though actors may also go through embodied emotions onstage. I suggest that it feels more real, closer to home, than theater does because of its intimate character; in order for BDSM to be sexually stimulating, one has to enact one's personal erotic fantasies; not every intellectually stimulating or professionally challenging script will work.

The degree of realness, therefore, may fluctuate depending on various factors, for instance the proximity of the roles to one's real-life personality. It is a general question whether BDSM dykes + queers play roles or enact partial identities in their BDSM, and whether this distinction has any bearing on the realness of it: 'If I feel my gender is a role, that doesn't make it not real.' Teresa pointed out how the fact that individuals have to enter certain pre-structured social roles does not preclude them from appropriating those roles as their own realities, embodying them, filling them with their own meanings and producing their own experiences. Thus, social roles in everyday life and BDSM roles can both be experienced as real. Gay transman bottom Mik did not draw any fundamental distinction between his everyday and BDSM persona: 'So I am a slave then, but I am not playing a slave that has such and such a personality or so. But I am myself as a slave.' He did not create a distinct slave role for himself to play, but he expressed his own slave personality, which is a part of his sense of self. To Teresa, dyke + queer BDSM roles may even feel closer to one's real personality than the masks one has to wear to navigate through ordinary life, such as work places (see also Lyng 1990: 881), especially for dykes + queers, something that Weiss also found in her research (2006b: 239).

Dyke + queer BDSM is also more real as a game of make-believe than engaging with a work of fiction, which generates responses that Walton (2004) characterizes as 'quasi-emotions'. According to him, the emotional responses to fictions are distinct from real-life emotions; for instance, if we witness a murder on TV, we are not going to call the police or try to flee. Therefore, we experience quasi-fear: the emotions are real even though the situation is only 'fictionally true'. Quite similarly, dyke + queer BDSM as a semi-contained space establishes a different context for actions, interactions and affects: 'Fear is fun as well, when it's in the context of SM. I'd say fear, like in walking down the street and being scared, that's not really sexy, unless it was part of a scene I'm doing.' As Craig explained, the meaning possessed by certain emotions like fear depends on the context. BDSM provides a space in which it is possible to experience emotions that would not be welcome or safe in other contexts, such as fear or loss of control. But, as opposed to engaging with a work of fiction, the emotional responses in BDSM may involve running away, fighting back or experiencing impacts on the body. These are not quasi-emotions, but may better be understood as *semi-contained emotions*. Moreover, Stear adds the interesting observation that the pleasures in BDSM do not correspond to quasi-emotions, but to the real pleasure one obtains from engaging with works of fiction (2009: 32). I would say that, in dyke + queer BDSM play, one experiences (at least) two levels of emotions simultaneously: the semi-contained emotions *and* the real pleasures these emotions are capable of providing in a safer context, such as the joy of the adrenalin kick in response to semi-contained fear.

Accordingly, the active or automatic suspension of disbelief in BDSM role play leads to an experience of parallel levels of realities. Katharina described how in age play she was simultaneously aware of being in a girl-mind and in a grown-up body. This fits well with Winnicott's thesis that play involves the simultaneous recognition and suspension of the norms of reality (1971).

Emma likewise pointed out how bottoms are aware of the parallel realities of handing over control to the top, yet remaining in control through their veto right. This is why dyke + queer BDSM may be experienced as empowering for a bottom.

Some interview partners encountered problems in suspending disbelief. It is a challenge for tops to create an environment that makes the scenario believable and real. They use techniques like sensory deprivation to keep up the illusion, and they take care of details like light, smells and so on. Lee finds that going slightly beyond the slave's limits adds realism to the scenario (1979: 89). He interprets BDSM according to Goffman as a special version of team performance (91). This stresses the cooperative aspect of BDSM: rather than an active top doing something to a passive bottom, both are active in co-constructing a shared alternative intimate reality that feels authentic to them in the situation. Bisexual femme lifestyle Mistress Mz Dre told me of a scene that showed how real a BDSM session may become through consensually pushing limits: 'In fact, she cracked in the scene at the time Laura was flogging her and I had a knife at her throat, talking shit. And I slid the knife across. And she just lost it' [makes loud, hysterical sound]. In this story, her experienced bottom in an intense scene 'cracked', that is, she was overwhelmed by her very real emotions. These kinds of real effects are common in BDSM encounters. They are not play-acted but are gut reactions to situations experienced as real, although they are prompted by what community members refer to as 'mindfucking'. Mindfucking is a technique of playing with the boundary between reality and illusion by making someone believe they are actually going to be harmed during play, like Mz Dre's sliding the knife across the throat of her bottom. Mindfucking can be considered a practice of shifting the balance of the parallel realities toward the real, as Craig described: 'If you're playing with somebody, they would never actually take the knife and kill you. They'll make you believe they're going to do it, but they actually wouldn't do it. And that makes it all very sexy.' Play-acting refers to theatrical realism in this sense, seeking to create the illusion of non-illusionism (Hart 1998: 8). My interview partners stressed the significance of what they called 'Kopfkino'[7] during a session in order to achieve theatrical realism. Their own imagination added to the realness of a scene by running a film that filled in the gaps, such as inadequate surroundings. While imagination may serve to create a perfect illusion, miscommunication may also arise if partners have different 'Kopfkinos' running.

Weiss understands BDSM as a cultural performance that reflects and produces larger social relations (2011: 189). Because it may be transformational, it may change players and audiences and become a performative intervention into the social world. Cultural performances produce new meanings and relations (Weiss 2007: 14); they enable individuals to understand, criticize and expose hypocrisy and potentially change the world in which they live through dramatization and through moving or discomforting the audience and players (15). But spectacle may similarly function to obscure social relations (16), which Weiss exemplifies through the reading of Abu Ghraib images as BDSM and therefore perversion and fantasy, which enabled US citizens to distance themselves from both torture and imperialism. Effective BDSM produces social relations through affective involvement, while effective torture destroys social relations (Weiss 2011: 227). Weiss concludes that BDSM is not safely performative, since it may 'open up or expose the practitioner and the audience to different modalities of feeling, being, touching and knowing' (2007: 30). This is exactly the terrain through which dyke + queer BDSMers navigate when they use BDSM to explore social power relations.

I agree with Weiss that BDSM is not safely performative in the common usage of that concept, which has neglected the embodied and affective dimensions. Moreover, I share the more general critique that language has been granted too much power (Barad 2003: 801) in poststructuralist theorizing, which neglects the fact that matter is an active participant in the world's becoming (803). Following Barad, Haraway and other feminist science scholars, we need to come up with sociological theories that account for the role of matter as well as language, prioritizing neither to move beyond the body/mind dualism. Therefore, I will propose a related but alternative way to understand performativity in dyke + queer BDSM, drawing on Barad and Haraway.

Barad refers to the quantum physicist Bohr's epistemological positions, starting with the observation that things do not possess inherently determinate boundaries or properties (Barad 1996; 2003: 813). To Bohr, the primary epistemological unit is not independent objects with inherent boundaries and properties, but phenomena (2003: 815). Agencies of observation (such as scientific instruments or human perceptions) are inseparable from the observed object (814), and phenomena are the result of intra-acting components (815). Thus, Bohr brings about a profound conceptual shift: rather than speaking of interaction, which presumes the prior existence of independent entities with clear boundaries, he introduces the notion of the *intra-action* of phenomena. Through specific agential intra-actions, the boundaries and properties of the components of phenomena become determinate; intra-acting matter is constraining and therefore shaping. But the outside boundary remains indeterminate and prevents any permanent closure, since apparatuses of production are themselves open-ended practices and phenomena. Therefore, agency is understood by Barad as an ongoing refiguring of the world (818) and is not aligned with human intentionality or subjectivity. Matter is a stabilizing and destabilizing process of iterative intra-activity (822), and boundaries, therefore, do not sit still (817), a point that Haraway also stresses. Boundaries of bodies materialize in social interactions/intra-actions. Therefore, objects/bodies are boundary projects. But boundaries shift from within; they are tricky, and siting (sighting) boundaries remains a risky practice (Haraway 1991: 201). Thus, for Barad, performativity is not understood as iterative citationality, as it is by Butler and other theorists who privilege language, but as iterative intra-activity (2003: 828), stressing its material-semiotic quality (in Haraway's words). To Haraway, bodies as objects of knowledge are material-semiotic generative nodes (1991: 200).

Intensity in dyke + queer BDSM as out-of-the-ordinary space

Dyke + queer BDSM was characterized as a space of intensity by my interview partners, who looked for 'what scared us the most and what gave us the most delight', as queer high femme Zoe put it. They contrasted the emotional and spiritual depth they experienced in their BDSM with the superficiality of everyday life. Again in Zoe's words:

> Well, I mean as a top I think it's dramatic. It's dramatic. You take people, you find the edge and then you push them just a little bit further. And also as a bottom, you do the same thing. Just you wanna go as deeply as you can go without dying. And then in everyday life there's a lot more finesse and carefulness, and the depth that we're going to is not the same. It's more a social dance, it's more superficial, more baroque.

So dyke + queer BDSM is a social space where one may encounter one's own limits (see Chapter 6) and/or spirituality as out-of-the-ordinary experiences. The consensual enactment of power relations and social roles may unmask the character of normal life as a game in this sense (Beckmann 2007: 104), reversing the notion of what is real or authentic (BDSM fantasy worlds and interactions) and what is fake and a masquerade (ordinary life, such as work and socializing).

Intensity is constituted in various ways, for instance through fulltime DS relationships, through sensation play or through psychological limit experiences, such as humiliation or devotion. Emma encountered the latter in a situation with a bottom on all fours in front of her, serving as her footrest: 'and I said: "How long can you stay there?" And he said: "Forever, Ma'am." ' Likewise, Vito enjoyed making her wife tremble before her. Intensity may be created specifically through the stimulation of seemingly contradictory affects, such as cruelty combined with nurturance and love in dyke + queer BDSM. And this intensity, in turn, created great intimacy for interview partners.

The maximum degree of intensity may result from playing with the fear of death:

> So I have done breath reduction on myself. And I think that I – I don't want to call it a near-death experience, but what I have read about that

in the literature, came rather close to it. And there I trusted my mentor-master 100 per cent and said: 'We are doing this now until the heart stops beating for a single beat. Then, I know.' Just so I know what comes up then, the panic, that you sweat, that you suddenly muster incredible powers to escape this situation, and all that happens. So that I simply know: OK, that is my fantasy, but in reality it's a whole different matter. And that you can also play with fear of death a little bit, rudimentarily.

This limit experience enabled Franka to explore how one reacts in the most existential situation humans ever encounter. This kind of play also makes it clear that the semi-contained space of BDSM needs its own regulations to prevent the participants from potential harm, even if the vast majority of BDSM encounters are taking place on a much lower level of engagement with limits. In fact, the dyke + queer BDSM communities have come up with their own subcultural standards of behavior or ethics, which will be discussed in the following chapters.

Chapter conclusion

The definition of BDSM remains contested. To some interview partners it was sex, to others foreplay or an erotic activity; some combined it with genital sex and others separated the two, but dyke + queer BDSM always took place within an erotic context. What interview partners agreed upon was the significance of consent for a practice to qualify as BDSM (see Chapter 4).

Dyke + queer BDSM creates alternative forms of sexuality and intimacy. The concept of sexuality is detached from genitals, eroticizing the whole body, artificial extensions of the body, objects and mental practices like shared fantasies or power dynamics. Sexual preference is also reinvented, decentering the sexed bodies of partners in favor of a cultural model of sexual attraction. Queerness becomes a matter of a shared (sub)culture. Butch–femme as well as dyke + queer BDSM practices can be considered disidentificatory desires. They take up themes of cultural hegemony, infuse them with erotic value, use them for their own pleasure and appropriate them without endorsing the dominant ideologies. Desire is usefully understood as excessive (rather than as lack), a spilling over of non-contained human bodies, which are always open, always in the process of becoming and stretching out to touch others.

In conclusion, the theater analogy is more accurate than some critics claim. The arguments against understanding BDSM in this way seem in part to be caused by a limited understanding of theater (see Newmahr 2011: 60 for a claim that actors are insincere and distanced from their roles). If we follow those theories that hold that theater is also real to and embodied in the actors, then dyke + queer BDSM may be usefully understood as intimate theater. Actors also tend to immerse themselves fully in the reality of their roles, for example when gaining a hundred pounds for a role or falling in love with their co-actors. A professional British film and theater actress told me that acting has to be real and to be felt in this way, and that on stage she listens to the other characters as if she never before heard what they are saying. It is like entering another dimension, and acting may even be the only time an actress is real, because for the rest of the time she cannot be sure what role she is playing (Liza Goddard, personal conversation, 12 April 2012). All these themes resonate with the descriptions of my interview partners. Theater also has material effects and performative efficacy, as theater scholars have pointed out (Hart 1998; Savran 1998). Other arguments against the theater analogy have more substance, although they can also not be overgeneralized. One such argument is that BDSM is unrehearsed (Newmahr 2011: 61), but there is also improvisational theater. It is also not true across the board that BDSMers are not playing for an audience (62): 'Role plays are partly also stagings. I was thinking once about how stagings always need an audience. Yes, [laughs] so a role play is also like a drama – it's nothing without an audience.' As top MCL, who refuses to self-define in terms of gender and sexuality, explained, one of the interesting aspects of BDSM to hir is having an audience. Finally, Newmahr claims that BDSM is unlike role-playing or theater because real dangers are involved (2011: 86). But, given that both theater/film and BDSM work with risk management, this seems more like another parallel. In this sense, one may compare some risk-taking BDSMers to stuntmen/women.

Thus, one may conceptualize dyke + queer BDSM as *intimate improvisational theater* in the sense of an *alternative serious game reality* and a *semi-contained space*. One danger of using the theater analogy in theorizing about BDSM, however, is focusing too much on the performative effects on the audience (including the observing ethnographer), neglecting the productions of subjectivity for the players themselves. Therefore, it is important to discuss BDSM sessions as intra-actions in which bodies as boundary projects are constantly renegotiated under specific conditions. This view highlights that desire is social but nonetheless experienced as being rooted deep inside the body, rather than just traveling on the surface.

4
Negotiating Critical Consent

Consent is a core concept of BDSM practitioners' self-understanding; it is crucial for an activity to be defined as BDSM (Langdridge & Butt 2004: 40). Often it is presented as an uncomplicated given:

> While nowhere else in this book we will speak directly on behalf of the sadomasochistic community in total, here we will: We have chosen to do these activities, we have chosen the people with whom we share them, we know what we are doing, and what we are doing is consensual. Period.
>
> (Moser & Madeson 1996: 71)

This quote shows how consent has gained the status of a dogma in the BDSM community, the 'period' stating that no discussion is allowed about this. Furthermore, consent is treated as if it were easy to define and establish, but in the work quoted it is not explained at all: it is considered self-evident.

Consent has also been deemed problematic. It was a feminist achievement to bring the issue of sexual consent to public attention in the 1970s, but it was not until the 1990s that it generated interest among other researchers and theorists (Cowling & Reynolds 2004: 1). And sexual consent continues to be discussed in terms of its absence, as in rape law cases, while there is hardly any understanding of what constitutes consent in a positive sense (Cowling & Reynolds 2004: 11) and how it is actively achieved. The dyke + queer BDSM community is, thus, an exception in its explicit negotiation and establishing of consent beforehand and its extensive and sophisticated communication about sex and power in general. This study is the first to take an empirical look at how consent is established among dyke + queer women and trans* people in a BDSM context. In this chapter I analyze the concepts of consent as put forth by my interview partners regarding their actual practices, including how they address the complications of consent through individual and social hierarchies, establishing a notion of critical rather than liberal consent. Sexual agency will also be discussed as it is directly related to questions of negotiating power. Finally, this is also the first empirical study to address abuse within the BDSM community.

The law in the countries involved in this study largely takes a liberal stance toward the concept of consent, understanding it as a sexual contract set up by free individuals. The larger BDSM community seems to employ a similar liberal notion of consent, assuming that contracts between individuals can be entered into of their own accord and free will, as in the quote above. Some lesbian feminists oppose this idea, pointing out that women especially have been socialized into consenting to male dominance in a patriarchal culture. Therefore, even if a woman consents to dominance, this does not mean she does so of her own free will. In this line of reasoning, the giving of consent only proves how effective the internalization of oppression is. Thus, consent does not equal self-determination (Rian 1982: 49). This feminist critique is significant, since real-life power dynamics and hierarchies, be they societal, subcultural or individual relationship based, have an impact on one's ability to negotiate and establish consent. Yet this is the case with all sexual interactions, not just BDSM in particular. Establishing a double standard is dangerous because it criminalizes BDSM practitioners per se while foreclosing discussion about consent in presumably egalitarian relationships. While in BDSM power dynamics are made more explicit, this also makes them more accessible to critical reflection. Finally, the lesbian feminist perspective neglects other structures of social inequality that have an impact on the validity of consent, such as racism, ableism, ageism, classism, lookism or 'sexual market worth' and so on.

It can, therefore, be said that both the liberal notions of consent and lesbian feminism fall prey to what Klesse calls the myth of equality (2007: 116). Sociological narratives, like those following Giddens' claim that same-sex relationships are in principle egalitarian and the prototype of the pure relationship, romanticize the realities of ongoing social hierarchies (Klesse 2007: 7). Rather, all relationships involve power issues and the potential for the abuse of positions of power (Samuels 2010: 213). Much creative energy goes into sustaining a sense of intimacy despite ongoing gender-based inequalities in heterosexual relationships (Jamieson 1999), and despite other inequalities as well, I would add. Possibly, dyke + queer BDSM could be used as a way out of these myths; its open and playful engagement with power dynamics could help to shatter the illusion that same-sex relationships are exempt from inequalities.

Consent as the crucial distinguishing feature

> I feel consent is the base of BDSM, and if there's no consent then it can't happen. So if you don't give your consent to being beaten, how can you be beaten? Then there's no BDSM. I don't see how it can exist without it. Then it's not BDSM, but it's abuse, if you don't give your consent and

someone's beating you. So anyway, for me, it's the framework in which BDSM occurs, it's the roots, the base.

This quote from genderqueer switch Femmeboy is representative of the whole sample. Consent was the defining characteristic of BDSM and distinguished it from violence, abuse, rape, oppression and so on, with which it is often associated in medical, legal, scientific, media or popular perspectives. Consent was more significant to my interview partners than the often-cited other ethical criteria of BDSM, safety and sanity:

> I'm a very hard player, I play with things that look dangerous, very on the edge. No sane person and no normal person who is sane would look at me and say: 'That's a sane way to play.' Nor would they look at me when I hold the knife to somebody's neck and say: 'That's a safe way to play.' It's really not. [But] it is entirely consensual.

Lesbian MTF butch top Kay was not the only interview partner who considered her own practices to be neither safe nor sane, but consensual and thus still BDSM (and not violence or pathology). The knowledge that certain acts were consensual was what made them sexually arousing to my interview partners, as queer transgender stone butch top Terry put it: 'When consent is there, when I actively choose something for myself because I want it, and I know that the person I'm playing with is actively choosing it because they want it – oh god, that's what's really hot.' Thus, sexual fantasies that involve coercion, such as abduction or rape, were only appealing to interview partners if they were acted out within the framework of consensual dyke + queer BDSM. 'Real' abuse was not sexually arousing to them, which underlines the significance of social context for the meaning of actions.

My interview partners considered the issue of consent not as specific to the arena of BDSM, but as a general social issue:

> We live in a society, we live in a culture, with all kinds of non-consensual power dynamics that are enforced on us all the time. I'm not consenting for the government to take my money and use it to kill people. That's the least consensual thing that I can think of. There's so much real violence, real violation, real degradation and disempowerment in the world. Where SM where you respect each other's boundaries is so valuable.

In queer-straight femme bottom Teresa's view, hegemonic culture was characterized by non-consensual power dynamics like warfare, and dyke + queer BDSM was one of the few spaces in which people were actively working toward consensual behavior. Yet she pointed out how dyke + queer BDSM practitioners were also affected by the oppressive societies they live in: 'Consent is I think really not black and white unfortunately, because we're all very complicated people and we live in a world where there's tons of oppression. And we are all suffering from a lot of internalized oppression that we're working on.' The fact that everyone has grown up with and is constantly surrounded by non-consensual power structures complicates what it means to give consent and makes it hard to establish *valid* consent, not only in BDSM interactions but also in general. This resonates with feminist critiques of liberal notions of consent based on free will. On the other hand, giving consent is also an everyday activity, as dyke femme switch Mistress Mean Mommy observed: 'We consent all the time. Going to the dentist, you don't tell the dentist how to do it, or what to use, but you say: "Fix my teeth, because that's your job." ' My interview partners compared the issue of sexual consent to medical consent, an arena where everyone considers the action of giving consent to high-risk interventions into physical and psychological integrity as necessary and possible. So, pragmatically, in everyday life, consent is assumed to be functioning and is only scrutinized if the outcomes are negative or agreements are violated, for instance if the dentist removes a healthy tooth. To understand the complex relationships between consent, abuse and BDSM on various levels, I will first review the existing research on the issue of sexual consent and problematize the liberal notion of consent based on my interview data. I will describe how my interview partners are addressing these problems and how they define and establish working consent in dyke + queer BDSM practices. Finally, I will draw theoretical conclusions from dyke + queer BDSM consent-making processes in regard to the notions of sexual consent and sexual agency.

Negotiated consent in dyke + queer BDSM practices

The liberal approach to consent assumes that it is an easily agreed-upon contract entered into by autonomous subjects with free will. Following the liberal tradition of thought, the individual is the one who knows best what is good for her/him. This presupposes some kind of unmediated access to self-transparency and the means to live accordingly (within the constraints imposed by respecting the liberty of others). It takes neither psychological entanglements nor social power dynamics into account and is therefore not context-sensitive; it treats humans as if they were living in a social vacuum. In reality, for many of my interview partners, it was a long and sometimes stony road to negotiate and establish consent, even though spontaneous encounters were also experienced as capable of attaining valid consent. While consent was crucial for them in that it distinguished BDSM from abuse, they were not naïve about the social contexts in which negotiations take place. Therefore, the interviews revealed a critical engagement with the concept of consent. The notion of consent as put to work in dyke + queer BDSM practices may be characterized best as *negotiated consent*.

Defining consent

There have been various attempts to define consent in different contexts. Pa's take seems to summarize much of the current discussion: consent has to be 'voluntary, knowing, explicit, and with full understanding of the previously agreed to parameters' (Pa 2001: 61; see also Athanassoulis 2002: 144). Yet it remains unclear what voluntary actually means beyond a naïve liberal notion of an individual exercising her free will or autonomy. Some of my interview partners took a more practice-oriented approach. Teresa did not believe in the possibility of absolute consent in the sense that it might erase power imbalances between two individuals, but she did believe in situational mutual agreements: 'Between two people whether or not one person has power over the other, you can try to establish to the best of your ability what interaction between you and the other person is desired by both people the most.' Thus, consent was seen as a mutually beneficial agreement, which might be considered a different kind of contract that does not harbor the illusion of equally empowered or free individuals entering into it and is restricted to finding a common ground or goal in a specific situation, like a provisional alliance. Furthermore, Teresa speaks of desires, which frames consent as affective, rather than rational, choice-making processes.

My interview partners could be seen as constructing themselves as social beings with agency. This agency was limited, but it could be accessed in negotiations. Instead of going along, complying or yielding to another's approaches, which is the prescribed sexual role for (heterosexual) women, an active and collaborative negotiating of consent was stressed, as exemplified in dyke/queer high femme Mandy's definition of consent as 'an active collaboration for the pleasure and well-being of everyone involved'. This property of consent is usually overlooked in heteronormative discourse: consent needs to be cooperative and relational as a social interaction, instead of being considered a unidirectional, disassociated enterprise where the man initiates a sexual encounter and the woman complies or resists (see also Barker 2013). In one of the few empirical studies to date which compared (heterosexual) women's and men's understandings of consent, Humphreys found that women tend to view consent as a process of ongoing negotiation, and men see it as a one-time event (2004: 218). My interview partners also stressed that consent is ongoing, and this is further evidenced in the structure of BDSM encounters, which include pre-negotiations, checking in and veto rights during a session as well as aftercare (see also Newmahr 2011: 76ff).

Some authors are also practice-oriented in their attempt to define what consent actually means. For McCarthy and Thompson, valid consent includes a degree of equality that ensures that each partner has the power to decide to engage in sex without fear of consequences (2004: 234). Yet, refusing to have sex with someone most often has some repercussions, even if they are not severe or are situational, such as causing someone embarrassment through rejection. For instance, Hickman and Muehlenhard found that indirect communication in sexual situations is favored because it enables one to gain sexual access while avoiding explicit rejection and the social awkwardness that goes with it (1999: 270). This problem might be solved in part by a sex-positive approach that accepts sexual rejections as integral to the negotiation process, as in the dyke + queer BDSM community. I remain skeptical, however, about the possibility of measuring equality and making generalizations about the point at which a relationship has sufficient equality for valid consent to happen. Two people might be theoretically completely equal when it comes to social hierarchy, for example two *white*, middle-class, able-bodied, conventionally beautiful ciswomen in their 30s with college degrees and stable jobs. Yet, one may be very outgoing and expressive, the other really shy and fearful of disharmony. Is there equality between them in the sense that neither may fear the consequences of saying yes or no to a sexual/BDSM activity? I would suggest that what may be necessary for valid consent is a position of empowerment that enables one to deal with the material, social and emotional consequences of saying no to sex or BDSM, even if that just means being able to endure a moment of awkwardness. This would resonate with a feminist criterion that all parties involved must have real choices open to them, since real choices depend not only on material but also on emotional realities. This approach also takes into account that the negotiation of consent is relationship-specific (Hickman & Muehlenhard 1999: 271; Humphreys 2004: 222).

Flexible boundaries of consent

There were varying degrees of explicitness of consent, both verbal and non-verbal. Consent could be very formal, even written, as in contracts that detail every aspect of a DS relationship. Or it could be rather informal or implicit. Informal negotiations sometimes took longer, since they usually involved extended exchanges about experiences and fantasies and were much more individualized and less schematic. Some interview partners established consent with certain partners based on slowly building trust instead of negotiating formally. Straight-queer femme bottom Teresa used flirtation and subcultural codes to negotiate:

> But in terms of flirtation, I'll be talking to a butch and she'll be like: 'I totally have a boner for you' and I'll be like: 'Oh, I love dirty old men', and then I'll kind of be setting up what kind of power dynamic we want in terms of 'I want you to treat me like a little girl.'

Certain codes or roles, for example 'dirty old man' or 'drill sergeant', imply certain modes of sexual interaction that facilitate a framework of options without extended negotiations. Sometimes, people slipped into a BDSM situation without prior formal negotiations, as in queer transgender butch switch Jacky's first real-life encounter with his partner-to-be: 'And when we slid into a more or less play situation for the first time, which actually happened in the first night that we saw each other in real life at all, there was nothing at all in terms of agreements. And actually zero, niente, nada, nothing at all.' Consent was still established in this situation, through non-verbal communication and through the fact that, before they met live for the first time, they had been discussing BDSM extensively online, which had functioned as informal pre-negotiations. So the degree of negotiation varied greatly. It depended on the situation, including the familiarity of the partner.

Consent also varied in its degree of specificity. Novices especially might not be aware of the extent and the details of negotiating consent, for example, whether marks are acceptable or not. Sometimes unspoken assumptions collided; for example, bisexual butch switch Erika assumed it was acceptable to cut off a t-shirt during a session if not told otherwise, while her bottom assumed this was out of the question unless explicitly agreed upon. Mistress Mean Mommy explained:

> I think that you have to understand that consent has flexible boundaries. I've been told from the tops I've played with that I could say: 'spank me', but I can't tell them with the right hand or the left hand. I can't say I only want three at a time and not ten. I can't say: 'OK, you can spank me, but after you spank me, you have to rub my ass.' I mean, I'm just saying: 'You can spank me.' That means I'm consenting to this particular action, but not the parameters of that action.

So consent usually means agreeing on a frame of actions, but not on every detail or a precise script. Therefore, consent creates flexible boundaries around a theme. Contrary to many stereotypical notions of BDSM, my interview partners did not refer much to scripted fantasies or sessions at all.[1] Although certain fantasies might serve as an inspiration or basic plan for a session, there was always improvising and no detailed script. Expectations from fantasies might even lead to frustrations in actual play, if the session took on a different dynamic. Thus, negotiated, expressed consent does not preclude the suspense of what comes next or elements of surprise. It also leaves the top enough space to express her dominance and feel that she is in charge.

Most interview partners did not see negotiated dyke + queer BDSM as limiting, but, on the contrary, as collecting information, opening up possibilities and pointing out options, as Femmeboy pointed out:

> There is a lot of spontaneity still. There's even more because you can do a lot more things when you know in advance that someone's open to all of those things. But if you don't know, it can just be trying one little thing

and they might get freaked out, and you might not try all those other ten things that you could have tried if you had known they were open to it. So I think it means a lot of freedom negotiating.

Therefore, negotiations do not eliminate the spontaneity of a session. And the fact that there are negotiations says nothing about the level of specificity in agreements.

Furthermore, besides consent for specific actions in a specific session there is also what gay transman bottom Mik called meta-consent: 'There is also something like meta-consent within an encounter, a relationship, like this famous infamous "do to me what you want." ' Meta-consent in this sense removes the limits within a specific time frame or gives a top the right to initiate a BDSM dynamic without prior negotiation, usually within contexts where trust has already been established. So here the boundaries of consent are even more flexible. Meta-consent is typical for ongoing relationships, where certain standards of interaction have already been established. It may be risky, though, if consent is not negotiated for each situation, but extended to a whole relationship, since this may lead to people engaging in sex/BDSM out of convention or habit rather than active participation. In BDSM contexts, meta-consent within 24/7 (fulltime power exchange) relationships is actively sought out with full awareness of these ambivalences (see Chapter 5). The Old Guard community protocols, mentioned above, resulted in conflicts around the boundaries of consent: did all bottoms have to defer to all tops in social interactions, or was there individually negotiated action only? This issue is not unique to BDSM, since social conventions generally prescribe what kind of interactions are considered appropriate or not in a given cultural context, irrespective of an individual's boundaries, such as greeting rituals that involve bodily contact. Troost (2008: 175ff), therefore, points out how the body is publicly owned and how this plays out in everyday interactions in so-called 'maps of consent' that dictate what body parts can be touched without prior permission. Ze also describes how much irritation and aggression result if one demands explicit verbal consent before being touched in daily life. In a BDSM context, this sense of a lack of body ownership in society may, paradoxically, be experienced by someone who is consensually owned: dyke femme lifestyle submissive Tanya's protocol stated that nobody but her owner was allowed to touch her without prior permission. This was a constant source of conflict with her surroundings, demonstrating the power of the cultural entitlement to assumptive touch, especially toward certain groups of people, such as children, people of color, women and the disabled. In the dyke + queer BDSM community with its emphasis on prior consent, community protocols that installed this kind of assumptive consent were, therefore, deeply contradictory and conflictual.

Consent also has flexible boundaries in another sense, when it comes to the question of the ramifications of actions on a social network or in a specific context. Many interview partners stressed that consent did not only include the participants in a session but also the third parties who might be affected by it, such as a non-BDSM partner or one's children. Most notably, gay transman switch Jonas held that public or semi-public play needed to be conducted in such a way that it did not non-consensually confront anyone with acts they did not wish to witness: 'If you extend safe, sane, and consensual to outsiders, then I believe that also non-SMers have the option to say: "No, I don't want to watch" or "I don't want to see that."' But, even within dyke + queer BDSM spaces, not all practices might be appropriate to impose on others. Examples often cited by interview partners were blood play and Nazi play, since it was common knowledge that these tended to violate the boundaries of many individuals in such a way that the damage might be done before one is able to remove oneself from the situation.

Finally, consent also has indeterminate boundaries from the perspective of time. My interview partners described it as tentative; it holds until further notice. This had to do with the flexibility of desires that some interview partners, such as queer genderqueer switch Firesong, observed: 'But consent is a weird thing, because one thing that I experienced as tricky is when I'm in a scene, sometimes what I want changes. So I find it hard sometimes to negotiate beforehand.' Despite all the self-awareness and the preparation for a scene, psychological dynamics remained unpredictable to a certain extent. Each session developed its own dynamics, and unanticipated desires or limits might arise. Therefore, negotiations might serve as a direction, but were not completely reliable in the actual course of a session. For some, their situational desires were not foreseeable at all, as butch lesbian top Luise explained:

> So I have extreme difficulties, this negotiating is not my thing, because first of all I cannot say beforehand what I want later on. I anyways have incredible difficulties in determining today that I will feel like SM in a week from now or like having sex or no matter what, eating ice cream, whatever.

This stresses that consent is an ongoing as well as a situational process and emphasizes the significance of the communicative process during a session. Furthermore, Luise's comment points to a larger general problem for at least some individuals: the question of whether it is possible at all to consent to something before the deed, or whether consent can actually only be given in the moment of action or even in retrospect, once one can actually feel in the body whether a certain action is desired in this situation or not. This underlines that desires may always escape self-transparency and that consent-making processes are not a matter of rational choice, but remain unpredictable through their affective character.

Veto rights: Maintaining limits

Limits play a crucial role in establishing and maintaining consent. The 'Leather Leadership Conference' (LLC) guidelines on distinguishing abuse from BDSM define consent as 'respecting the limits imposed by each participant' (LLC n.d.), which provides a practice-oriented rather than theoretical approach to consent. Most interview partners echoed this. To them, consent was valid if everyone's limits were respected. So one way to ensure consent in practice was to discuss limits and respect them, although my interview partners also experienced their personal limits as flexible and changing over time. Tanya criticized the community discourse that seemed to neglect that tops have limits as well; everyone has to learn how to acknowledge their own limits and learn to accept and respect them even when this might conflict with issues of personal pride and self-worth (see also Cho 2008). Everyone, therefore, has to learn to enforce their personal limits, but, as queer femme bottom Anastasia observed,

> There is some risk, because sometimes you give your consent beforehand and then you go to this place during a scene that you're not really in charge of yourself anymore and you may not realize you're being hurt, because maybe you go to this place where you really feel this person has control over you and you feel like you can't say stop.

So in certain bottom spaces one might lose the awareness of the possibility to veto, perhaps because the role one was supposed to play became too real or because of some other state of vulnerability.

An important criterion for valid consent, therefore, is the right to veto any actions at any time, even if they have been agreed upon beforehand. Femmeboy said: 'For me the reason why consent works is because it's also coupled with safewords. So you're giving your consent ahead of time: "these are the things that can happen", but in the play when you don't want that to happen, you can just safeword out and say no.' So the veto right may apply in at least three cases: if something arises that has not been part of negotiations, if there was a lack of clarity in the agreements, or if something is experienced differently than expected during a session. Therefore, the validity of consent is dependent on the option to withdraw one's consent at any time. The veto right gives the bottom control over the situation because it ensures ongoing choices even after the negotiations. Therefore, the veto is a technique that stresses the point that consent is an ongoing process, not fixed beforehand, and leaves space for 'irrational', affective changes of mind; this departs from the contract and rational choice model.

For many interview partners, the way a veto right is put into place is through the use of safewords. Safewords are code words that are used to stop the session or slow it down. Safewords create the possibility to play with limits, since they can be seen as an instant feedback system. A safeword does not automatically guarantee adherence to limits, though. Some interview partners had encountered situations in which someone was unable to make use of their safeword. Some bottoms lost the ability to remember to use their safeword once immersed in their inner world, or they did not trust a particular partner to respect their veto. This points to the fact that the safeword is only as good as one's trust in the integrity of one's partner. On the other side of the coin, safewords may be superfluous if the communication during a scene is ongoing and functioning well. With a familiar partner, the limits are often known anyway. If there was no role play, just sensation play, some interview partners did not need safewords, since they were not trying to stay in character, but instead were able to communicate directly.

To queer transwoman bottom Leslie, safewords sabotaged her experience: 'When you don't have a safeword, it's so much more intense and I enjoy it so much more. Because it's sort of the safe aspect kind of disappears a bit, and that's what makes it more intense, and I enjoy it more.' Playing without safewords may thus increase the intensity of the experience. But playing without safewords does not mean that there are no limits or no right to veto. Gay transman switch BJ explained how safety and consent can be established without safewords:

> When I start playing with somebody, I don't wanna play with them just once. I want to develop a play relationship with them, where I get to know them, I get to know their body, I get to know the way they respond to things, what scares them, what turns them on. And I think with repetitive play, you get to go deeper and deeper and deeper. And to me safety is built on trust and clear communication. I don't need a safeword. For if you're telling me 'That scares me!' why do I need to hear a red, yellow or green? You're telling me 'that scares me.'

BJ learned his BDSM skills through Old Guard gay leathermen who did not use safewords, but developed the skills to read body language and to communicate verbally and non-verbally throughout any encounter or relationship. He also stressed the significance of trust and slowly increasing the intensity of play within an ongoing play relationship.

Communicative sexuality

The notion of negotiated consent endorsed by my interview partners relied on communication in sexual encounters, as Tanya summarized: 'Consent is only as good as the open, honest communication between people.' Dyke + queer BDSM can, therefore, be seen as making an argument for communicative sexuality within the broader discussion about sexual consent. For many interview partners, the greatest clarity was achieved through verbal communication, but non-verbal communication also played a significant role. One had to learn to interpret body signals in general and each partner's body language in particular. Non-functioning communication proved to be a source of accidents, boundary violations or a reason to stop a session as a precaution:

> Where nothing at all comes across, I sometimes stop such actions. So when nothing comes across [from the bottom], I simply say: 'Sorry, but that is rather difficult for me now, because if I don't get any reaction at all, I cannot make any assessment about anything. And it is great that you've got your body functions under control, but that doesn't help me to proceed.'

Top MCL described how bottoms who do not show any visible or audible reactions disable both verbal and non-verbal communication. Because the top is in charge of the session, which results in heightened responsibility, it is usually her task to check in during the scene to ensure ongoing consent. This may be done verbally at each step of the way, as queer femme switch Emma described: 'And when I'm in a Dominant[2] place, I am frequently checking in: "I'm gonna touch you now, is that all right with you? I want you on your knees right now, are you gonna do that?"' But a lot of the communication was more subtle, non-verbal and not always apparent to outsiders, as high femme switch Zoe explained:

> I think out of 20 years of playing, twice in my life I've had to stop a scene. Because we communicate. Whether the communication is overt enough that somebody who's not familiar with the scene would understand, I can't say. To teach novices consent, I guess maybe I'd have people playing and I'd have a commentator. I might have the top saying: 'Did you see how she just did this thing?' To sort of translate. Because our culture has ways of communicating that aren't verbal.

As is apparent in this quote, understanding non-verbal and indirect communication is an art one has to learn, and dyke + queer BDSM culture has developed it to such a degree that it functions very well. Complementary to the top's skill of checking in, the bottom has the responsibility to keep the communication going by giving feedback. Some players used safewords (for instance, red, yellow and green if they played with a three-level code system) to give feedback, to prompt checking in, or to fine-tune a session. Some bottoms tried to send non-verbal signs to their tops. I refer to this active non-verbal communication from the bottom side as signaling. The work of signaling reinforces the fact that understanding bottoming as passive behavior is a misconception (based on sexist social constructions of the receiving end in sexual interactions as 'passive'). Rather, negotiated consent is neither a one-time event nor unidirectional, but an *ongoing collaboration*.

Some sexologists generalize communicative sexuality, such as the guidelines institutionalized in the 'Antioch College Code' (Hall 1998), as a new morality of negotiation or consensus, and interpret it as a new variant of rational choice discourse, based on the idea that sexuality can be rationalized (Schmidt 1998). From this perspective, processes of negotiation are understood as artificial, eliminating spontaneity and destroying passion and the eroticism that lie in the transgression of the limits of reason, which are considered to be crucial elements of sexual and romantic relationships. This perspective puts an emphasis on the alleged restrictions that occur through the mutually set-up agreements between partners. In contrast, the perspective of my interview partners was that negotiations were not generally experienced as restrictions or as rigid norms, but as open-ended practices that broaden the options of the encounter by encouraging the partners to share their sexual fantasies. The pre-negotiations may even extend the session itself, since they establish an erotic atmosphere beforehand.

Therefore, I suggest that the resistance to the Antioch College Code and communicative sexuality was largely caused by its implicit attack on heteronormative ideas about sexuality, namely, that sex is natural and not something that is learned and that the male in heterosexual encounters orchestrates the encounter, which is geared toward his desires and a heteronormative script. The whole public, legal and academic debate on sexual consent remains heteronormative, since it operates within a logic of an initiating or pressuring male and a complying or resisting female (Corinna 2008), thus reproducing the idea of male activity and female passivity and victimization. This is partly due to the fact that consent is mostly discussed in the contexts of rape and of 'protection from prostitution' historically (Weait 2004). Accordingly, Humphreys finds in his empirical research that most heterosexuals tend to think that sex is supposed to function naturally, to be spontaneous and unplanned, without any communication, and the partners should be consumed by passion. Heterosexual men actually interpreted communication during sex as a sign of failure (Humphreys 2004: 210). Research reveals that consent is mostly equated with a lack of resistance (Hickman & Muehlenhard 1999: 266; Cowling 2004: 24; Humphreys 2004). But, as Cowling points out, doing nothing may be caused by paralysis or fear (2004: 24) or by not wanting to be impolite (27). Hickman and Muehlenhard, therefore, conclude that showing no response is a dangerous consent strategy (1999: 271). Feminist bloggers also rightly point out that the 'no means no' model of preventing rape is not sufficient, and call for an extended 'yes means yes' approach (Friedman & Valenti 2008a: 6).

Cowling and others object to communicative sexuality as being too far removed from common practices (2004: 27). Yet I have demonstrated how dyke + queer BDSMers successfully practice communicative sexuality through their culture of negotiating consent. Therefore, communicative sexuality is not too far removed from sexual practices per se; rather, it is incompatible with certain heteronormative and harmonicist ideals of how sexual encounters should occur. Interestingly, the norm about sexual communication is reversed in the dyke + queer BDSM community, which values direct and transparent communication: 'I'm attracted to the BDSM community because things are largely as they seem and people say what they mean and are free to say what they feel and that's what they want.' Dyke switch Michaela found it hard in mainstream social etiquette to understand what people say and to figure out what they actually think or mean. In dyke + queer BDSM culture, she did not have to guess, but could trust that there would be direct communication. Communicating sexual desires enhances the quality of the sexual interaction, demystifies it by rejecting the idea of mutual mind-reading and helps to establish valid consent.

Distinguishing working consent from pseudo-consent

'I think that in any given situation it's possible that people can call what they're doing negotiating and yet be in a situation where it's not possible to really negotiate.' As Terry pointed out, there are situations when it seems as if consent is being established when it really is not. Therefore, it is important to be able to distinguish between pseudo-consent and valid consent, or *working consent*. I use the term 'working consent' to refer to experiences of successfully negotiated consent in concrete situations, because consent needs work (specifically, work on the self to know one's desires and limits, and interpersonal skills like communication and negotiation), it is always a work in progress and it 'works' for the practitioners in a given situation or relationship. They have acted according to their own sense of self, their needs and desires, their priorities and values, as opposed to a liberal notion of consent as unproblematically given. Working consent is about a sense of personal integrity and respecting boundaries rather than being based on the myth of equality between partners. Working consent in this sense is often a consequence of personal evaluation in retrospect, and therefore may be messy and not absolute.

In my interviews, dyke + queer BDSMers tried to distinguish pseudo-consent from working consent, discussed the quality of their consent decisions and positioned consent within complex power relations, suggesting ways that critical consent may work in practice. For instance, queer femme switch Katharina saw reflecting one's practices and degree of agency in communicating and negotiating to be significant in the process of establishing working consent:

> How can I generally communicate what I want? How can other people communicate what they want? Because that is not necessarily always the same: how I can do that and how I want to do that. And therefore the point is to always continue learning how, and to expand the repertoire: how can I get answers? How can I find out if someone just simply kind of says yes, because s/he does not dare to say no?

An awareness of the limits of consent and of individual agency in negotiating is necessary in order to assess the validity of the agreements between partners and can be considered a practice of critical consent. For instance, Terry's partner felt too submissive when in his presence to be able to negotiate appropriately; therefore, they negotiated via email instead of face-to-face. The spatial distance between them helped her to keep her boundaries intact. This was a practical solution for a problem of undesirable power dynamics in their negotiations.

One often overlooked criterion for working consent is the ability to fully understand the emotional consequences of BDSM:

> I think new players are totally like that too, they're so into it, like 'let's go', and they dive in and they don't realize just how deep they've gone. I've had people who were in their first month of playing [with] SM, who wanted me to permanently mark them on their face. And I'm just like: 'No.' [laughs out loud] 'But, but, but, it would be adorable.' – 'No. We won't be doing that this week, my precious darling.'

According to Zoe, who had about 20 years of involvement with BDSM at the time of the interview, many people underestimate the depth of the experience and the quality of the bonding that may take place through the intensity of BDSM, especially novices, who may be overwhelmed by the discovery of this new sexual world. As an experienced top, Zoe regarded it as her duty to put a lid on novice bottoms' overenthusiasm in order to prevent regrettable decisions, embodying heightened responsibility. Self-awareness is, thus, another social skill relevant to consent, since inaccurate self-assessments undermine the reliability of negotiations. For bisexual top Franka, checking the self-awareness of potential partners was part of trying to validate their consent: 'So I also test her, [to see] if she is clear. So what she says has to be comprehensible to both of us.' She thus tried to double-check their mutual understanding and the clarity of their agreements. Finally, self-awareness could be increased through the constant practice of negotiating, since it forced one to become clear about what one actually wanted.

Interpersonal power dynamics

The starting ground for negotiated consent was interdependency rather than the autonomy or self-reliance of top and bottom: being a bottom is obviously pointless without someone willing to do things to you, and being a top is pointless if there is nobody willing to place enough trust in you to bottom to you. This insight emphasizes a general view of human subjects as relational (Reindal 1999: 354) and the human condition as one of interdependence and vulnerability, which is common from a disability studies perspective (Galler 1992: 166; Reindal 1999: 353). Acknowledging this basic interdependence of humans has various theoretical, political and practical consequences that are beyond the scope of this work. But, if we understand humans as interdependent rather than autonomous, then all the choices we make are relational in nature. When looking at consent, this means that general statements of the type 'I don't like bondage' are abstract and follow a notion of independence; it seems that I can determine my sexual interests by myself without taking into account how others touch me. If I then meet someone I trust enough to let them put me into bondage, I suddenly may be willing to try it, and I may find that I enjoy it. This would be a concrete example of a realization of interdependence and of how proximity to others can change my boundaries and sense of self. It is for this reason that many interview partners endorsed an approach of 'never say never' or stated that their likes and dislikes in terms of BDSM practices always depended on the situational dynamics with a particular partner.

Yet, interdependence does not mean that all parties involved in any social interaction are of equal status in their dependence on others or in their negotiating power. Rather, interpersonal power dynamics influence the process of negotiating consent, as Teresa reflected:

> We all have power over each other in different ways. I have certain privileges as a femme. Certain people give me some good treatment. And other people who identify themselves as masculine get certain kinds of privileges in the world, because some people take them more seriously. And we all experience privilege in different ways in our lives and we all have different bodies of knowledge. [...] And you can't really measure: 'I have this much privilege from my [type of] privilege and you have that much privilege from being conventionally abled.'

As Teresa pointed out, the power relations between people are complex and cannot be dealt with by adding them up or comparing them on a scale of privilege. Instead, she suggested being 'as conscious of the power dynamics that are going on as possible and actively working to question the privilege that you have and actively working against the privilege that you have'. Thus, one way to address these difficulties is to acknowledge, reflect and act on power differences and one's own situatedness within them. But one needs a certain political awareness of social power structures and the willingness to counter them.

My interview partners displayed an awareness of the power issues around consent and described different techniques to address various kinds of power dynamics. For instance, real-life structural social hierarchies, such as racism, that have an impact on consent might be addressed by the underlying mutual respect of play partners, as dyke/queer butch switch Lola suggested: 'You need both people to have equal amounts of respect in order to have consent. And I think that's regardless of age and other factors. If one person has less, then it's less consensual.' Approaching someone with respect can be a means to acceptance across difference. As opposed to the concept of tolerance, respect is not a paternalizing gesture granting partial acceptance from a position of cultural superiority or hegemony. Rather, respect is about valuing someone in their difference (from oneself), valuing them in their otherness, and thus leaving their otherness intact. Respect can, therefore, be one way of addressing social power hierarchies in situational, personal interactions. While oppressive social structures like racism or ageism are, of course, not overcome through individual respect, their impact may be reduced in a situation of negotiation, because respecting someone's particular choices and ways of being and becoming can enhance their agency in that specific situational encounter. It is, thus, a performative political strategy, because it creates a temporary, situational balance through acting as if all parties hold sufficient amounts of negotiating power.

While all structural hierarchies translate to personal hierarchies between two or more people in any given social interaction, such as who holds more material or cultural capital, there are also additional personal hierarchies that are not related to major social stratifications in any straightforward way, such as communication skills or self-esteem. While the development of these in individual biographies is, of course, also influenced by class, race, gender and so on, it is not determined by these. For instance, a *white* man might grow up with parents who always make him feel inadequate and therefore not develop any sense of self-worth despite his social privilege. So the question is also how individuals are capable of accessing their social capital. Personal hierarchies intersect with structural ones and also need to be addressed when it comes to the validity of consent.

I will restrict myself to discussing the challenges specific to the dyke + queer BDSM context as discussed in the interviews. One personal hierarchy involved performance pressures. Enduring something beyond one's limits might serve as a proof of submission, of love or of toughness. It was, therefore, important that insecurities were acknowledged and accepted as part of play. Shame about having to stop a session might otherwise interfere with the need for self-care. The need for recognition or appreciation also might prevent someone from stating and asserting their actual needs or limits:

> I believe what makes a difference to me is whether I am free enough of wanting to impress her actually. In order to keep my limits. And if I am not interesting [to a top] because I don't like a particular thing or because something is not possible, then that's the way it is.

Culturally lesbian[3] bottom Helene pointed out how tempting it was to disregard one's own comfort zones in order to find more play partners or more acceptance by others. One had to learn, therefore, not to attach one's personal value or self-image as a bottom (or top) to getting recognition from partners. Firesong also saw the danger of wanting to please her top beyond the session. For some, this was a consequence of the way they bottomed, for example wanting to be a 'good boy/girl'. So role personality and everyday personality were not always clearly distinct, which presented challenges to the negotiating process. Thus, dominant/submissive dynamics may start before consent is actually established, as lesbian femme top Frl. R. stated: 'What can of course happen is that the top manager in question is submitting to me somehow non-consensually in this pre-negotiation so to speak. Emotionally. That happens.' Submissiveness might, therefore, become problematic, if someone already entered bottom space while still negotiating. And, as Frl. R.'s usage of the example of a top manager submitting to her demonstrates, submissiveness is not a trait that is per se attached to a certain social position. Therefore, for bottom Leslie, the consent in BDSM worked because the bottom has more decisive power during negotiations: 'In negotiations I often notice that with the things I did, it's often the bottom who makes most of the decisions about what's gonna happen, not the top. So I think the hierarchy is more that in the pre-negotiations [...] the bottom has the most decisive power.' Leslie's strategy of counterbalancing agency works by enabling the one who will be giving up control later to be in charge earlier in order to set clear boundaries. Emotional dependence is subjectively felt, though, and tops also encountered situations where they felt more needy and at the mercy of the bottom in negotiations.

The degree of BDSM experience could also create power imbalances. If someone slipped too easily into a subordinate role during pre-negotiations, many interview partners addressed this by expressly negotiating out of role. This could be facilitated by negotiating away from the BDSM context, as Mistress Mean Mommy explained: 'You don't go meet at the play space and negotiate for ten minutes. You meet over coffee.' If the real-life hierarchical dynamics proved to be too strong, it might lead to the decision not to engage in BDSM with that particular person.

Beyond free choice vs. social determination: Critical consent

Self-awareness (such as of one's own preferences and limits) is a prerequisite to negotiation or is developed through the process of negotiating, but it is not sufficient in itself. It needs to be materialized through accepting and being able to exercise self-responsibility for one's desires and well-being, and this requires some kind of agency. But it is not always easy to judge whether a particular person is capable of understanding and accepting the consequences of BDSM play, for example, due to intoxication or mental health issues. The ability to consent thus seems to be a question of degree and situational circumstances, along with the social context that enables or disables an individual's capacity to enforce their choices. There is also the question of what consent actually means; consenting to something does not automatically mean that this particular action is what is 'best' for the person consenting. In retrospect, people often regret making 'poor decisions'. This is partly because one cannot know all possible future outcomes of a certain decision; uncertainties always remain. Thus, one can never fully foresee and therefore understand all the possible ramifications of a certain act of consent. Furthermore, material dependencies or some emotional spaces that submissives may enter during play may compromise their agency in that situation. Bottom Mik explained: 'So there is a certain danger involved, simply that I encounter the wrong person or that somebody is then leading me somewhere where it's not good anymore. Because I am only capable of acting in a limited way in such a state, which is something like a trance as well.' This speaks to the significance of the integrity of the top, as Terry stressed: 'I think that there's a heightened level of responsibility that is not something that I can ignore or discount that needs to be fully present in the way that I think about how I do play.' This approach stresses the significance of responsibility in regard to risk management in BDSM.

An ethics of heightened responsibility

Responsibility can be understood as a practice of being accountable, and thus having to answer to a third party regarding one's actions, be it legally, materially, psychologically, symbolically, spiritually or otherwise. Focusing on responsibility, therefore, stresses choice and agency. One can only take (full) responsibility for one's actions in a situation of alternative choices. An ethics of responsibility includes the actual consequences of actions on the world rather than just judging the good or bad intentions of an actor. It is, therefore, about practical ethics. My interview partners seemed to endorse an ethics of responsibility, especially in the prospective sense of formulating the duty to take care of their play partners, and to a much lesser degree in a retrospective sense of holding someone accountable for an undesirable outcome of a session. Terry compared the kind of responsibility a top has for a bottom to that of a parent: 'It's that kind of fiduciary relationship where you are responsible for someone else's well-being.' Being responsible for someone's well-being – taking care of someone – means that it is not sufficient during a session to rely on the agreements from pre-negotiations; one must continuously assess the bottom's needs and limits, for they may be subject to change. Hitzler also concluded in his ethnographic research that the top role is characterized by responsibility, risk awareness, technical knowledge and self-control (1995: 141). But interview partners stressed that it is also important that tops acknowledge their own limits and do not burden themselves with a kind of responsibility they cannot carry: 'In terms of rape games, which also belong to a preferred play mode of mine, if the other then absolutely insists on playing without a safeword, it becomes very difficult. I mean, I feel actually somehow overburdened at a certain point with the responsibility.' The issue of being overwhelmed or overburdened with certain kinds of responsibilities, as lesbian top Nico brought up, was not yet part of community discourses. It might conflict with an unrealistic image of the top as always in control and confident. Therefore, the top also has to learn to say no to certain requests, especially since the responsibilities of the top are manifold:

> Likewise, there is the responsibility to bring someone safely back into everyday reality [laughs]. Because you've taken them out of ordinary reality and into another place, and then you need to land them back on their feet. And then maybe check in a couple of times, saying: 'How's your reality going?' in sort of a closure thing.

As Zoe pointed out, the top's task is to transport her charge into another reality and safely back again. Therefore, her responsibilities include protecting a session from unwanted interruptions in a semi-public space and bringing bottoms back to ordinary reality after a session.

The heightened responsibility of a top found its expression in the community practice of aftercare, which extended the obligation beyond the duration of the session itself. But a top's heightened responsibility to take care of a bottom also faced limits, as gay transmasculine switch Craig explained:

> That's the realization that the responsibility is both, the top's and bottom's. Because some people are a bit like: 'I'm a bottom, I don't have any responsibilities, I don't have responsibility for anything.' And up to a certain point, it's correct. You have a bit more responsibility as a top of course, that's a part of the game. But still, everybody has the responsibility to take care of themselves, because even though you can read people very well, sometimes there's just things you can't see.

Since tops are not mind-readers, my interview partners also stressed the need for the bottom to embrace their own agency and take self-responsibility.

Sexual agency

Since agency in this sense was valued and deemed necessary by interview partners in order to practice dyke + queer BDSM in whatever role was chosen, butch-loving femme bottom Lisa rejected an excess of play party rules and unsolicited interventions by third parties to enforce them:

> I experienced that at a party, how a woman thought that a straight wanker – you cannot put it any other way – was too close to a couple that was playing there. And then she went there and put him into his place. And I don't think that is her job. I think that is an incapacitation of both of those playing there.

Lisa rejected this kind of belittling treatment of women as children: 'So why do women need this extra soft, extra safe, extra "we are such an extremely secured space here"? I think that's stupid. [laughs] I find it stupid. We are grown-ups as well, so we don't have to be treated like children.' Some interview partners deemed some community standards to be incapacitating and therefore counterproductive to fostering agency. Mandy and others thought that overprotective rules kept women from learning to accept self-responsibility and from being empowered:

> They're saying: 'Oh, women are weak and fragile, and men have all the strength and the power, so we need to protect the poor, weak, fragile women.' And I'm saying: 'No, the poor, weak, fragile women need to wake up and find their strength and stop being so goddamn weak and fragile!'

Different branches of feminism collide when it comes to the question of how to ensure sexual consent for women. Many interview partners, such as Lisa and Mandy, favored empowering over victimizing approaches:

> I'm not going to choose answers that are outside my power. So the answer that those other people should do something different is like: No, if I play with somebody, then it is my job to learn to voice my needs, it's my job to object to anything I don't like, it's my job to say no to what I wanna say no to. I can't expect the whole society to somehow say no for me. That does not make sense. And to my mind, it does not further feminism.

Mandy's point was that, since it was not within her power to change social power relations or other individuals on her own, she was thrown back to herself and the choices she did have. One option to change her relationship to others was to change herself by claiming self-responsibility.

Various feminist authors have pointed out that women are neither solely the products of their circumstances (victims), nor the producers or in control of their social contexts (powerful agents), but, rather, both (Dunn 1998: 479). Terry and others accordingly characterized agency as actively choosing one option over another (as opposed to a liberal notion of freely choosing). Thus, my interview partners seemed to construct themselves as free in the Foucauldian sense; they saw themselves as having options, albeit limited ones, to act in a field of power (Foucault 1982; 1996: 386). Since all of them were assigned female at birth and/or were raised and/or lived as women, the emphasis on active choosing and initiating is an important rupture with the prescribed passivity for women when it comes to consent. What follows from the fact that free choice is an illusion is that consent is always relative, or, as Sullivan puts it, 'To say that sexual consent will always be constructed within power relations is not to suggest the impossibility of "real consent" but it is to call into question liberal consent (that is a consent negotiated in the absence of power)' (2004: 137). Thus, one's capacity to practice one's freedom or to consent is constructed as an effect of power relations. According to Sullivan, we have to strive to construct our identities, for example as sex workers, women or trans* people, in a way that strengthens our ability to consent, which includes our material conditions. For instance, constructing sex work as *work* will increase agency because new possibilities for workers' rights will emerge in this process (2004: 137). This approach – stressing agency within limited choices and constructing one's sexual practices in a way that allows increased agency as a kind of performative political strategy – was pursued by my interview partners, as I have already shown in their agentic feminism (see Chapter 2). Some interview partners applied an 'as-if' strategy; they acted as if they were in control of certain situations, even though they were aware of the constraints on their choices through social structures such as sexism and racism. This assumption of being powerful and acting accordingly was a performative strategy that seemed to work to a certain degree, effectively bringing about changes in the way they led their lives. Similarly, Dunn (1998: 507) found in her research that women who see themselves as having and making choices are in a better position to negotiate their sexual acts. Klesse (2010: 111, 114) and Woltersdorff (2011a: 13) also described this phenomenon in their empirical research, but saw it as unintentional, whereas in my sample it was not an unintended side effect of ignorance about real-life social hierarchies, but an active strategy to work against them.

Therefore, according to the interviews, agency is not necessarily dependent upon the concept of an autonomous, self-sufficient or sovereign subject or upon a liberal philosophy of equality. It is not a binary matter of possessing either agency or no agency, but how to act within a field of limited choices. Sassen helpfully distinguishes between powerlessness and presence: despite a lack of social power, an individual can still be an actor (Sassen 2007: 165). Social power does not fully determine individual agency; if that were so, resistance and social change could not be explained. McClintock thus calls for opening up notions of power and resistance to a more diverse politics of agency, involving the dense web of relations between coercion, negotiation, complicity, refusal, dissembling, mimicry, compromise, affiliation and revolt (McClintock 1995: 15). She criticizes victim-based feminism for equating agency with context, body with situation, which effectively diminishes the possibilities for strategic refusal (McClintock 1995: 140). Williams also criticizes victim-based feminism because of its effects on sexual harassment policies. In creating the dichotomy of guilty harassers and innocent victims, such policies ignore ambivalences and complicities and tend to reinscribe the powerlessness of the victims of sexual assault instead of empowering them (2002: 112). Williams suggests moving away from re-victimizing practices in the legal system by guaranteeing the right to sexual autonomy (113). Thus, by implication, what is needed is a paradigm shift to a sexual culture of active consent rather than focusing only on instances of lack of consent, for instance, adding the 'yes means yes' perspective to the 'no means no' approach (Friedman & Valenti 2008). This is exactly what the negotiating practices of the dyke + queer BDSM communities were establishing. The kind of empowerment that interview partners experienced can be understood as increasing one's options to make choices and decisions within a social situation of power inequalities, which will continue to structure the playing field.

Agency is not dependent upon the concept of an autonomous, coherent subject. In her queer phenomenological approach, Ahmed (2004) relocates agency from residing in the individual to the interface between individuals and worlds. Agency then becomes a matter of what actions are possible given how we are shaped by our contact with others. Individuals are agents insofar as that which affects them does not determine their actions, but leaves room for a decision. Therefore, to react is not always to be reactionary (Ahmed 2004: 190), or, in Dunn's words, people act rather than simply responding to an environment, and they play a part in shaping it (1998: 481). If we return to Barad's concept of intra-action (instead of inter-action), then agency can be reconceptualized as constantly evolving in the intra-actions of bodies and their surroundings. So not only are individuals agents because they are left with leeway for making choices, as Ahmed rightly points out, but also their acting as an agent in these intra-actions becomes part of the ongoing reconstruction of subjectivities as boundary projects. Thus, making limited choices may also impact my embodied and embedded sense of self, enhancing my sense of agency for future situations. This was evident in the dyke + queer BDSM culture of negotiating consent; the negotiation was constructed as a situation where power dynamics could be engaged with and shifted somewhat. Agency could be accessed and even forced upon someone[4] in a situation that was constructed in such a way as to empower the participants in a semi-contained space, as when Terry was asked the first time to actually own his desires. It is, therefore, not surprising that my interview partners reported a heightened sense of agency in dyke + queer BDSM.

Lorenz attributes the increased agency within BDSM to its function of restaging the apparatus of interpellation of the subject, enabling individuals to rework emotional investments and recast the actors in a type of disidentificatory practice (Lorenz 2009: 136). But she also warns that this re-engagement in the BDSM context does not mean that the scene of interpellation can ultimately be controlled. Social hierarchy reappears unbidden, as my interviews have also shown. Yet BDSM sessions may function as a postponement of social values (141). Barad's intra-active perspective also stresses how bodies resist the closure of boundaries. This became very concrete for Michaela in her bottom space:

> The thing that increases my confidence the most is to be told by a dominant that they find me attractive. Because when I'm in my submissive head space, I will believe anything that I'm told, which can cause problems. [laughs] I have to tell people that, so that they don't implant things I don't want implanted. But to be told that I'm a desirable woman, that I'm attractive, that I'm wanted in that situation, has done me a lot of good.

Michaela's vulnerability and openness was double-edged: it enabled intervention into her processes of subjectification in various ways, such as a reworking of the habitus (Woltersdorff 2011c: 23). In dyke + queer BDSM, this intra-active resistance to closure can be used to enhance the participants' agency and bodily integrity, but, as issues such as abuse or limits to establishing consent show, it can also turn against practitioners if the engagement with BDSM is not power-sensitive and done with care. What all these various poststructuralist theoretical approaches to agency have in common is that they situate agency in the processes of subjectification and they resist closure. This agency is limited, but can be accessed performatively and in inter- and intra-actions that shape bodies and subjectivities, as is evident in the case of dyke + queer BDSM negotiating practices.

From liberal to critical sexual consent

In modern capitalist nation-states, social hierarchy is partly maintained by presenting it as contractual or as self-determined in terms of the equal opportunity ideology. The open acknowledgement of power dynamics within BDSM may serve to expose the myth of social equality and thus present a starting point to look at what consent might actually mean beyond the liberal idea of contractual or egalitarian relations. But it might also reinforce liberal notions of an uncomplicated contractual agreement between self-determined individuals in a social vacuum. Some authors, therefore, call for being 'critically consensual' (Carrette 2005: 26) or have started to focus on the quality or validity of sexual consent, frameworks within which I have discussed consent-making practices in this chapter.

I propose an understanding of the foundation of dyke + queer BDSM practices as *negotiated consent* or *working consent* to stress that consent is not to be taken for granted, but has to be actively and critically established, and even then will always remain relative in a culture of social hierarchies and given its affective character. Explicitly negotiating critical consent and understanding it as ongoing does present a significant improvement in how sexual consent is handled. Therefore, dyke + queer BDSMers can be said to practice a form of critical consent. I understand the concept of consent as critical in two regards. First, it is negotiated in a power-sensitive way. Second, because of the inherent limits to rational control over social interactions, consent is always critical in the sense that it remains precarious and provisional. Understanding consent-making processes as ongoing is, therefore, crucial.

Some authors argue that consenting to BDSM is impossible. These claims tend to be based on questionable a priori assumptions about BDSM or on methodologically problematic generalizations from clinical case studies or fictional accounts to all real-life, negotiated BDSM activities. I will briefly address these theoretical objections from an empirical perspective to conclude my discussion of negotiated consent.

First of all, the common understanding of BDSM as pathological and therefore irrational behavior bars the possibility of consent, because giving consent is socially constructed as rational behavior. For instance, some courts, as in the Spanner case, have denied the very possibility of consenting to BDSM: 'A normal person in full possession of his mental faculties does not freely consent to the use, upon himself, of force likely to produce great bodily injury' (cited in Pa 2001: 75f). Thus, if you do consent to this activity, you are not mentally capable and your consent is irrelevant. Treating BDSM practices as mentally ill behavior in this way is circular reasoning. Hopkins responds that it might indeed be true that one cannot consent to genuine powerlessness and domination, but this is irrelevant, because in BDSM generally one only has to be able to consent to simulated powerlessness and domination (1994: 129). Despite some potential difficulties with this theoretical stance (understanding BDSM as simulation), Hopkins' argument would certainly apply to a lot of the dyke + queer BDSM practices in my sample. Bottoms did not consent to giving up control, but instead they consented to what they experienced on the whole as an *empowering* practice. The social context of BDSM changes the meaning of acts that resemble violence from an outside perspective.

In a related argument, lesbian feminist Sheila Jeffreys holds that women, gays and lesbians are not able to consent to BDSM, because due to self-hatred they do not have any will to protect their own bodies from injury or death (Jeffreys 2003: 119). BDSMers are constructed as irrationally acting against their own best interests, and thus BDSM discursively functions as rationality's other. But this rational self is an illusion, since all people display irrational behavior to some degree; for instance, romantic discourse emphasizes that people act 'crazy' when it comes to 'love'. Decision-making in general is not a purely rational endeavor, since emotions play a role as well. For instance, my interview partners partly based their consent on emotional reasoning or 'gut feelings', such as if they trusted the other person or if there was the right energy or chemistry between them, which could only in part be assessed through 'rational' criteria such as the history of a top with other players, which might provide clues about her integrity. Yet this was not a problem, since working consent was often established through following their intuition on top of the communicative techniques used by interview partners. On the flip side, boundary violations tended to occur if interview partners acted against their intuition, following reasonable arguments or formal rules instead. Understanding consent as ongoing and keeping up communication during any sexual encounter seemed the best ways to deal with ambivalences, rather than ignoring one's intuition or emotional skills. My study shows that dyke + queer BDSMers actually take great care in protecting themselves from injury and harm, contradicting Jeffrey's theory.

Plant points out, based on his analysis of a fictional short story by Kundera, that consent is problematic due to two aspects: the conditions of consent may change over the course of a session, and the trust or goodwill of the participants cannot be established through a contractual agreement, because any such contract or agreement itself relies upon trust or goodwill (Plant 2007: 542). As explained above, my interview partners addressed the first problem by conceiving of consent as ongoing, including the right to veto. Second, they used screening processes and slowly increasing the scope and intensity of play to establish safer play partners. Thus, the trust was not circular, but based on each person's reputation and pre-negotiations and secured through peer control.

But, even if there is consent, this does not necessarily ensure that a situation or relationship is mutually satisfying. Brewis and Linstead argue that a bottom could feel a 'sting' after having been exposed to pain and humiliation without an emotional pay back, or after unresolved misunderstandings during a session, thus stressing the fragility of the BDSM contract (Brewis & Linstead 2003: 142). While this may be the case in some sessions gone wrong, this statement does not take into account that BDSM practitioners usually gain pleasure from what looks painful and humiliating from the outside. Furthermore, one of the motivations to take part in BDSM for my interview partners was self-exploration, which was not reduced to the pleasant sides of soul-searching only. This attitude was complemented by a practice of stressing self-responsibility on the part of the bottom, making it unlikely that a bottom would blame the top for an unpleasant experience as long as it was consensual. The authors are right about the general emotional risk in making oneself vulnerable in intimate interactions, but, again, this is not unique to BDSM. In general, the quality of a sexual interaction is not determined by the presence of consent alone, and simply unpleasant experiences ('bad sex') should not be confused with the absence of consent. And the same holds true for the reverse: just because a sexual interaction arouses someone or makes them feel loved, for example, does not make it automatically consensual, especially not in a cultural context that still encourages women to trade sex for love and so on.

In conclusion, there is no reason why consenting to dyke + queer BDSM should be less possible or more problematic a priori than consenting to other sexual and social activities. What is most important is to have a critical discussion on how to further a culture of sexual consent in general, for instance by supporting communicative sexuality. Dyke + queer BDSM, with its culture of negotiating and practice of working consent, offers a promising starting point.

Dyke + queer BDSM in a society of abuse

My interview partners distinguished between the different kinds of abuse they had experienced, including verbal, emotional and sexual. They also acknowledged 'grey areas' concerning consent and abuse: 'I mean, I wouldn't say I was assaulted a lot, I would say I was coerced a lot. I was in that grey area where I wasn't consenting, and it was coercive, but I wouldn't term it assault.'[5] There were situations and relationship dynamics in which one partner did not actively choose or consent, but also did not know how to or was incapable of asserting his or her boundaries effectively. Thus, the other partner did not actively violate an expressed limit, but did use his or her position of power in a coercive or repressive way sexually, often through psychologically manipulative behavior or through creating a threatening atmosphere. Abuse dynamics might be specific to a certain relationship, in which violent behavior was uniquely perpetrated against one particular partner, as opposed to a general pattern of displaying non-consensual behavior in all one's sexual or BDSM interactions. Some forms of coercive behavior took place in a BDSM context, for example, when a top dominated a bottom without prior negotiations, assuming it was her/his right due to status, effectively misusing protocol. Novice bottoms who did not yet understand what their rights as bottoms were, and what consent in a BDSM framework meant, were vulnerable to being told by someone that certain kinds of non-consensual domination were authentic BDSM.

Certain feminist and psychological theories that seek to pathologize BDSM behavior have linked it repeatedly to experiences of sexual abuse (Richards 1992). A Finnish study (Nordling et al. 2000) showed that the prevalence of self-reported sexual abuse was higher among BDSM practitioners than in the general population, but the sample consisted of only 22 women and was collected via the Internet and not according to socio-demographic features, which hardly makes it representative. A survey among BDSM practitioners in Germany, which reached many more participants from various backgrounds, showed no higher incidence of abuse than average, which makes it likely that the Finnish study suffered from sample bias (Datenschlag 2000). An Australian nationwide representative study also showed that BDSM practitioners were no more likely than control groups to have experience of sexual coercion (Richters et al. 2008).[6] Moreover, the fact that the dyke + queer BDSM community has a high level of open sexual communication and reflection in terms of consent may lead to a higher awareness, an ability to name and thus to report experiences of abuse. Even if future research should show that the prevalence of abuse survivors is above average in dyke + queer BDSM communities, this still does not prove that dyke + queer BDSM is caused by experiences of abuse. An alternative explanation could be that dyke + queer BDSM provides a suitable space to deal with experiences of abuse, for instance through the explicit negotiation of consent, which may be empowering and may enable abuse survivors to have sexual inter- actions in a controlled setting. This is exactly what some interview partners reported.

A personal history of abuse may have an impact on the way some people approach BDSM, though. In the Finnish study, the abuse survivors reported significantly higher incidences of injury during BDSM encounters (Nordling et al. 2000: 58), possibly suggesting challenges with setting appropriate limits and/or seeking out responsible play partners. Abuse survivors were more likely to assume the masochist role (59). The authors propose that this corresponds with the theory that female abuse survivors seek out puni- tive relationships (61), but the argument is flawed, since bottoms do not necessarily regard their position as degrading or punitive. The researchers' conclusion needs further investigation as to the meaning these women actu- ally assign to their submissive roles and their BDSM experiences. The women and trans* people in my sample and in all other recent qualitative studies described bottoming as empowering, not punitive. Thus, instead of inter- preting the choice of the bottom role by abuse survivors as re-victimization, it may, on the contrary, prove to be a self-empowering coping strategy, as evident in the following statement: 'I've used [BDSM] as a tool instead of therapy to work through an incest [memory] that I've had since childhood, a rape issue, because [through BDSM] I was able to take my power back.' Moreover, in my sample, abuse survivors were equally likely to top, bottom and switch.

Due to these widespread pathologizing theoretical concepts, there was a lack of counseling services for abuse survivors who wanted to practice BDSM or for people who had experiences of abuse in a dyke + queer BDSM context. Violence in same-sex relationships is often not acknowledged as a possibility, since abuse has largely been theorized within feminism as a gender issue in heterosexual relationships (Elliott 1996: 3; Merrill 1996), which leads to a lack of services for lesbian victims (Elliott 1996: 6; Renzetti 1996) and perpetrators. When it comes to dyke + queer BDSM, the situation gets worse, because domestic violence shelter personnel and many therapists may confuse BDSM and abuse. My interview partners who experienced abuse in a dyke + queer BDSM context were, therefore, not able to receive professional support.

Certain situations or contexts may make people more vulnerable to becoming the victims of abuse. My interview partners did identify some circumstances or conditions that made them vulnerable to encountering or enduring abuse and that were potentially (if not causally or solely) related to BDSM dynamics. Various personal needs, especially for recognition, might cause a lack of self-protection or a lack of regard for one's partner. Being a novice without an educational and supportive community might pave the way for abusive partners, especially if those partners used misleading images of BDSM to pressure their victims into compliance: 'If I wanna get what I want, I have to accept X, Y and Z.' One person's abusive encounter at a private play party was partly caused by his lack of knowledge and, therefore, insecurity about community ethics and protocol:

> During the whole encounter I had the feeling that I was in a situation where I didn't know the rules. Because I was a novice in the community, I didn't know if he was entitled to do this because he is dominant and I am passive, or is he not allowed to do that? I didn't know for certain. And he acted as if he was allowed to act like this.

The top who violated the boundaries used the novice's lack of knowledge about his rights as a bottom to the top's advantage. And the (heterosexual) community where this occurred did not address these problems adequately or support the bottom afterwards. This stresses the necessity of placing consent not within individuals, but within a community context that actively fosters a culture of consent (see also Barker 2013),[7] because, even for advanced players, a lack of trust might prevent one from safewording. Another novice described a former relationship: 'All of that [the abuse] was done within the context of calling it SM. I think that it was a situation where consent clearly wasn't there. But it was pretended to be there. And where abuse was clearly present, but was called something else.' Considering that abuse taking place in a BDSM context might be disguised as BDSM, and that consent may be an illusion, it is vital to find means to distinguish between pseudo-consent and valid consent, as discussed above.

Looking at theories about sexual abuse and domestic violence, there are some ways in which a BDSM context might present some specific challenges. While the dyke + queer BDSM community has developed ethical standards for behavior, sometimes individuals with a hunger for power come to BDSM to satisfy it without consideration for their partners, or sometimes individuals act out real-life anger in a session. Because abusers are typically driven by a desire for power and control (Elliott 1996: 3–4), and these can also be desirable personal traits for a top in the right ethical context, it may become difficult to judge who is a responsible top to play with and who is not. Merrill identifies three steps that lead to battery or sexual assault (Merrill 1996: 14): the potential perpetrator has to learn to abuse (through role models in the family of origin or through reinforcement that violence is effective and 'rewarding'); s/he has to have an opportunity, a situation where s/he thinks s/he can 'get away with it' (15); and s/he has to decide to abuse (which means that, even though it might not feel like it, perpetrators have a choice). Unfortunately, BDSM may seem to some potential perpetrators to be the right opportunity to abuse someone for various reasons. First of all, it is unlikely that a victim of abuse in a BDSM context will report to the authorities, due to fear of outing themselves as engaging in a socially stigmatized or even illegal activity (for example, in the post-Spanner UK, even bottoms have to fear being jailed for their BDSM activities). Second, as mentioned above, BDSM may present an opportunity due to the fact that unscrupulous tops may convince inexperienced bottoms that BDSM necessarily involves transgressions of limits. Finally, the perception of a potential victim's (social and personal) power plays a significant role in identifying opportunities: people who are perceived as weaker or as incapable of taking care of themselves may seem to be suitable targets for a perpetrator (Merrill 1996: 16). Thus, some individuals may perceive bottoms as suitable victims due to the incorrect notion that equates the bottom role with weakness. Unethical and abusive behavior of varying degrees is expected to exist in the dyke + queer BDSM community, as in any social sphere, yet the nature of the community brings specific challenges when it comes to preventive measures.

Abusive incidents described in my interviews included unsolicited intervention in a session by a third party, toppish behavior without any prior negotiations, being raped within a negotiated session, an expressed limit being consciously violated and safewords being ignored. Contrary to the popular imagination, though, these occurrences were the exception to the rule. Overall, interview partners reported positive experiences with establishing consent in the dyke + queer BDSM context, and the vast majority of dyke + queer BDSM interactions were not abusive. Yet, that a potential for abuse remained despite the ethics of consent in the community has to be acknowledged as well.

Pat (now Patrick) Califia was probably the first to publicly address the issue of violence and abuse in the lesbian BDSM community. In 1996, Califia cited various incidents of different kinds of violence among BDSM dykes in the Bay Area and called for recognition of the issue and the development of strategies to end it, concluding with a checklist for potential victims of domestic violence and a proposed code of honor for leatherdykes (Califia 1996). Since Califia's intervention, the problem of abuse disguised as BDSM has been addressed by some BDSM organizations, starting with the LLC's 'SM vs Abuse Policy Statement' (n.d.), which provided questions about the status of relationships that may help to identify abusive elements. More recently, the discussion about abuse in the heterosexual BDSM community in the US has become more public and somewhat heated (Clark-Flory 2012; Barker 2013).

It is important to understand that the ability to establish consent and enforce one's boundaries has to be learned. Having experienced abuse may turn this into an even more challenging task. One abuse survivor who had also been in an abusive lesbian BDSM relationship had a lifelong struggle with consent: 'The first time I actually had sex with someone where they wanted me to choose scared the shit out of me. [laughs] As if: "What [do] you mean I actually have to own that I want something? What the fuck are you talking about?" [laughs]' This is not surprising, since studies have shown that sexually abused girls are vulnerable to experiencing abuse in adulthood as well, which might be attributed to the fact that they have come to know abuse as part of sexuality (Messman & Long 1996), which is exactly what interview partners described for their sexual development. They had to learn how to actively make choices in their sexual interactions and to claim self-responsibility for their sexual needs and desires, which was unfamiliar and scary at first. But in the long run they were able to increase their sexual self-awareness, and they learned to distinguish between active consent and pressure to comply in sexual interactions. The fact that consent is explicitly negotiated in dyke + queer BDSM enabled some interview partners to develop a sex life as abuse survivors. They therefore saw dyke + queer BDSM as a role model for achieving consent and communicating about power, and thus as a role model for anti-violence work in general.

Likewise, Tanya pointed out how the sometimes dangerous 'games' that are played in non-BDSM flirtation, such as token resistance (see Hickman & Muehlenhard 1999: 259), may be reappropriated as a consensual, explicitly negotiated BDSM practice known as resistance play. Thus, to her, BDSM offered not only options to prevent boundary violations through negotiations but also techniques to integrate sexual responses that might otherwise be harmful, generating sexual tension in a mutually beneficial way. Dyke + queer BDSM can, therefore, function as a way to rebalance the relationship of pleasure and danger in women's lives (Vance 1992a) without sacrificing personal erotic response patterns. It therefore presents a creative path toward a new female sexual agency.

Chapter conclusion

My interview partners were aware that they lived in a society of abuse, in a rape culture. Therefore, they placed great significance on the issue of sexual consent in their dyke + queer BDSM practices, which some also considered to be a role model for other areas of life. While there was no intrinsic connection between being an abuse survivor and practicing BDSM, specific challenges in distinguishing BDSM, with its dramatization of hierarchy and violence, from abuse were identified and discussed in the interviews. Dyke + queer BDSM culture can be read as an approach to sexuality for women and trans* people to find a working balance between aspects of pleasure and danger; it is sex-positive while it also addresses the risks of sexuality through a culture of negotiated consent.

Dyke + queer BDSM stresses communicative sexuality and respecting everyone's limits through installing veto rights. Consent can be defined as an active, ongoing collaboration for the mutual benefit of all involved, helping to establish and maintain each participant's own sense of integrity. Rather than reducing sexual consent to a lack of a 'no', it is about actively choosing. This leads to an ethics of heightened responsibility and accountability for the consequences of one's actions as well as to a sense of increased sexual agency through dyke + queer BDSM practices. Thus, in dyke + queer BDSM space, women and trans* people do not embody the cultural stereotype of women as passive or lacking in desire, but, instead, possess an active sexual subjectivity. Their sense of sexual agency is not based on an ignorance of social hierarchies or norms. Rather, dyke + queer BDSM can be seen as part of a struggle to shatter the myth of equality, working at creating practices to actively establish critical consent, for instance through the insight that, for consent to be valid, actors do not need to be equal (which is practically impossible), but do need to be able to access negotiating power in that particular situation. This is a move away from liberal and rational choice notions of consent and toward consent as negotiated, affective and critical. In practice, this work enables my interview partners to engage in sexual interactions that do not violate, but resonate with their own sense of self. Moreover, it can be seen as one step in acknowledging the human condition as a state of interdependency, rather than acceptance of the liberal illusion of personal autonomy.

5
Exploring Exuberant Intimacies

The concept of exuberance is introduced in this chapter as a queer philosophy of excess and abundance. I take a look at dyke + queer BDSM practices and relationships as exuberant intimacies from a perspective that is critical of mono-normativity. The chapter begins by defining intimacy as access that entails boundary transgressions. It goes on to discuss my interview partners' engagement with BDSM in public as one example of creating intimacy through transgressing the private/public boundary. I then analyze why non-monogamous relationship practices are the (reversed) norm in the dyke + queer BDSM communities. Special attention is given to BDSM-specific kinds of relationship and intimacy, such as the fulltime ownership relationship and sharing intimacy in play party spaces, which leads to synergetic effects.

Containment, accessibility and touch: Intimacy as the crossing of boundaries

Within the organization of social life into public and private realms, BDSM as an explicitly or implicitly sexual or erotic practice is considered to be private. Yet feminist and queer theorists have criticized the very distinction between public and private for a long time. For instance, Valentine (1996) proposes the use of 'street' instead of 'public': the term 'public' is misleading, since many public spaces are not public in the sense of being accessible for everyone, while so-called private spaces are also of socio-political, in other words 'public', relevance. But the street is also not equally accessible to all, and probably there is no space that is equally accessible to everyone across social distinctions. As opposed to heteronormative acts, non-normative sexual and gender expressions are severely restricted and policed in the public and in the private realm, belying the liberal notion of a right to privacy (Duggan & Hunter 1995; Dangerous Bedfellows 1996; Woods & Binson 2003).

Queer sexuality also collapses the public/private distinction in another sense. Gay male sexual culture in particular has pushed the boundary of the private by establishing physically segregated spaces designed specifically for sex. In bathhouses, back rooms of bars and sex clubs, sexual acts are performed in the presence of others; door policies create a semi-contained space distinct from the general public, but shared with others with the same intent (looking for sex with other men). Therefore, I call these *shared contained spaces*, or community spaces. Shared contained spaces are also popular in dyke + queer BDSM culture, as in the form of play parties. Gay men have also challenged the definition of what constitutes a public act. Gay male cruising culture takes place in the public sphere, such as in parks, woods, highway rest areas or public restrooms, yet it is often facilitated in a way that hides the actual practices from the public, creating a contained space within a generally accessible social space.

My interview partners also described their scenes in public as contained, 'private' spaces within public space. Gay transboy and drag king Björn explained: 'That is principally again playing outdoors privately. That is less of a public thing; you just play in a public space. But you hope not to be seen in that public space by any strollers or the like. In that regard it is not public.' Being unnoticed outdoors may be achieved through hiding from sight or, as queer non-defining switch Petra described, through acting as if what happens is 'normal' or through the active ignorance of by-passers, who 'explain' what they observe 'away'. Thus, I call such practices *contained accessible* sex/BDSM. If we define public as accessible and private as being protected from unwanted access, then the terms become relative (Leap 1999: 9) and contested (12). From a critical perspective, they also become prescriptive rather than descriptive, because they do not describe the status quo. Some groups of people are granted access to almost any space they choose to visit and are protected from unwanted access in their own home, but others do not share these privileges.[1] And some groups of people cannot count on wanted access to their homes as a means of protection; for example, in cases of domestic violence some people do not get the support of state authorities.[2] Therefore, I have chosen this alternative terminology around containment and accessibility to critically distance myself from the seemingly uncomplicated public/private dichotomy and to be more specific about how these social spaces are renegotiated and constructed.

Containment can be taken to describe what is commonly referred to as private space, such as the home, but also to describe spaces with intentionally restricted access, such as a club that wants to attract certain clients. Moreover, it can also be used to describe a crucial element of mono-normativity: the dyadic containment of isolated coupledom as the gold standard. There is a spatial and ideological conflation of the private sphere in terms of a household and the romantic couple (or nuclear family) cohabiting in that home. Both are characterized through containment rather than reaching out toward the world, with some so-called 'infidelity experts' even advocating a philosophy of marital isolation as a means of avoiding all risk of contaminating the monogamous couple with extra-dyadic desires (Frank & DeLamater 2010: 14–5). The level of containment does not stop at the material level; even fantasizing about other sexual partners, enjoying time with others, masturbating and having memories of ex-lovers were all rated as 'cheating' by Frank and DeLamater's heterosexual sample (2010: 13). Dyadic containment or, in its extreme, dyadic insulation is associated with images of home, haven, secure base and so on, cushioning those inside against perceived threats from the outside (Finn & Malson 2008: 521). Monogamy as a space of intimacy has to be guarded against intruders (525). This construction of relationships as fortified spaces is a main element of mono-normativity, highlighting the socially isolating nature of monogamy. In this view, the boundaries of relationships are not imagined as semi-permeable and fluid; rather, dyadic insulation upholds illusions of security and stability for those entering couple status. Dyadic containment rhetorically aligns relationships with nation-states, whose borders have to be policed in similar ways and which are also imagined as 'home' to the people. Both seem to function to disable connection and touch across boundaries, isolating people under the pretense of creating emotional bonds via marital or romantic love and patriotism, the love for one's country.

In contrast to the mono-normative ideal of dyadic insulation, the gay male culture of shared contained sex and contained accessible sex historically developed out of necessity due to the lack of options to practice male-on-male encounters within the traditionally private realm (Bérubé 1996), but it has gained sexual value in its own right. Those interview partners who practiced dyke + queer BDSM in what would be considered public spaces did not lack the opportunity to practice it at home or in shared contained spaces. Rather, they enjoyed specific qualities that only accessible spaces offered. For instance, non-defining top MCL used a medieval fair to act out some of hir fantasies:

> We were walking around there and let this whole ambience impress on us. And it was about witches and witch burning and [laughing] such things, about exorcism and who knows what. Yes, and there we simply continued that. I mean, we found a corner for us, but the corner wasn't such a corner that people could not have looked into it, and then we were just engaging with medieval torture methods [laughing]. Which simply matched this ambience quite nicely.

For similar reasons, military play was often conducted outdoors. The context enhanced the atmosphere and the credibility of the scene. While Björn expressed the intent not to be noticed by others sharing the same space, MCL played with the intention of being acknowledged. This kind of play was still contained to a certain degree, since there were boundaries between the players and the audience (which is usual in theater as well: the audience is not supposed to go onstage and participate). But it is better described as *accessible*, since anyone who happens to be there might witness it. All of my interview partners had taken part in play parties, and a minority also played in accessible spaces or extended their scenes into everyday life.

The terminology frequently used in the field of human relating is loaded. For instance, the term 'love' carries the baggage of the discursive history of romanticism; has been used to justify unpaid women's work as labors of love; was historically reserved for *white* heterosexuals (Carter 2007); features prominently in various religious, spiritual and new age discourses and remains heavily invested with emotional attachments, to name just a few issues. Discourses of love were rarely referenced in my interviews, and when they were it was often critically. Therefore, I have decided to work with the term 'intimacy', which remains a compromise because this term is not without its complications either. For one, it has become fashionable in sociology and self-help books, pushing the family off center stage and replacing it with normative discourses about intimate relationships, where intimacy is often understood as being based on a culture of mutual disclosure between equals (Jamieson 1998: 1). That such concepts about the modern form of intimacy as Gidden's pure relationship (1992) are power-evasive and therefore problematic has already been discussed in the previous chapter. Yet intimacy seems to be a much broader term than love and is associated with issues of boundaries and transgressions, which is useful for understanding dyke + queer BDSM ways of interacting and connecting. The term derives from the Latin *intimus*, meaning close, familiar, innermost. In the context of this study, I use intimacy to describe an affective situation or series of situations in an ongoing relationship between two or more people, which touches those involved somehow. They may experience feelings of closeness, intensity, transgression of boundaries, partial connection or complete fusion. In the context of dyke + queer BDSM, intimacy may be understood as situations of shared intense experiences, often incited through boundary transgressions. These situations may be fleeting, leave traces or stay with the participants permanently as emotional attachments.

Intimacy is a highly subjective quality of emotion and can vary in intensity; it is not an either/or question. Feelings of intimacy can be attributed to interactions between people or to relationships. Relationships in the broadest sense can be understood as recurring interactions between people, so that some kind of bond is produced and experienced, possibly an emotional one. Intimate relationships in the context of this study are all those self-defined relationships that were experienced as intimate by the participants. Since this study is about dyke + queer BDSM, the types of relationships discussed usually involve some kind of BDSM, sexual and/or erotic activities, but this does not have to be the case. It would be possible to experience an asexual relationship as intimate, since intimacy is not limited to touch in a literal sense (such as genital interaction), but is defined in a broader sense of crossing boundaries of the self that one does not allow to be crossed mundanely, be they bodily or emotional. My definition, therefore, resonates with Berlant's definition of intimacy as all kinds of connections that have an impact on people and on which they depend for life (Berlant 1997: 284), which once more brings into focus the interdependent nature of human relating in general. Intimacy is a condition one cannot experience in separation or solitude, but only in social interaction. Rambukkana, therefore, rightly points out that the space of intimacy is not actually 'private', but acts as a layer of mediation between our selves and the worlds around us (2010: 239). It is, therefore, not a refuge from the 'public' sphere of economics, politics and social inequalities, but, just like sexuality, love and all those experiences that are constructed as private, it is infused with social power dynamics. This becomes especially evident in BDSM practices that use social hierarchies for generating desires. They demonstrate that the private/public divide is not a strict border, but a porous boundary at best, across which meanings and material effects travel back and forth, cross-pollinating.

Yet popular concepts of intimacy remain invested in the notion of privacy as a privileged space or as containment, and they depend on the prior establishment of a private realm. Simmel (1950: 126–7) points out that the affective structure of intimacy is about showing something to a particular person that nobody else gets to see. Thus, the economy of intimacy in this sense is deeply entwined with a mono-normative ideology of exclusivity and competitiveness, since one only reveals these personal depths or secrets to one particular person. It also seems that intimacy is a limited resource in this logic; if one has already shared a certain special something about oneself with one person, it is used up and cannot generate the same intimacy effect with someone else. Yet intimacy as access can also be understood in a slightly different sense that is more interesting for the dyke + queer BDSM context, namely, as being about crossing boundaries. Even if we question the usefulness and the political effects of the private/public distinction, we can still assume that each individual develops certain boundaries, even needs some boundaries, to achieve a sense of bodily integrity or at least to be able to move purposefully through the world, which otherwise would not be distinct from oneself. These boundaries are individual, but they develop in constant engagement with one's surroundings and are, therefore, social. An intimate situation or experience, then, is created whenever these personal boundaries are touched or crossed in some way. Thus, intimacy has to do with vulnerability, which has several consequences. Intimacy is created by different kinds of boundary-crossings for different groups of people because vulnerability is differently raced, gendered and so on; a situation can, therefore, be experienced as intimate by one person and not the other(s) in an encounter; and intimacy is not a positive experience per se. Since everybody has their own sense of boundaries around the body and the self, what counts as touching, crossing or violating this boundary, and therefore what counts as intimate, is not universal but depends on the individuals in question, their biographies and the social contexts they move in. For example, in Euro-North-American cultures, female breasts are usually concealed, while in some other cultures they are not habitually covered by clothing. Exposing breasts is, therefore, experienced as crossing a boundary by many Euro-North-American women and constitutes an intimate experience, while it probably does not hold the same meaning for a woman whose breasts are not concealed and not constructed as private or shameful body parts.

If intimacy is about access and boundary transgression, feelings of shame and unwanted violations are also experienced as intimate (see also Newmahr 2010: 175ff), but because of the non-consensual context this kind of intimacy is not a welcome, positive experience. In regard to structural violence, such as racism and sexism, we can see that access to bodies is unevenly distributed, such as *white* people touching Black people's hair without permission or men groping women on the street without having to fear any consequences of these violations of bodily integrity. The fact that violations of this kind are experienced as intimate can be used within BDSM: people may choose to explore intimacy in a different context where access is renegotiated. Since sexuality and intimacy are both associated with access and boundary transgressions culturally, this link allows the eroticization of all kinds of social structures and dynamics that are about boundaries and access. Seeking out the kinds of pleasures generated from these boundary transgressions is necessarily ambivalent and ruptures the notion of intimacy as something unambiguously positive and harmonious. It remains significant to distinguish between intimacy as violation and intimacy as a granting of access and as appreciated, welcomed boundary transgression. As I argued in the previous chapter, context matters, and actions change their meanings depending on the presence or absence of negotiated consent. But consent is only a precondition for appreciation of a boundary-crossing. For instance, one may consent to a medical vaginal examination, but not welcome the kind of intimacy this exposure generates. In the context of this study, I will use the concept of touch to refer to a situation of intimacy that is appreciated by someone, whether it is experienced as positive or ambivalent, and the concept of violation to refer to a situation of intimate boundary-crossing that is non-consensual or unwanted and experienced as negative. Being touched is what many interview partners seek out in dyke + queer BDSM. This involves vulnerability, trust, ambivalence and intensity.

As Newmahr points out, much research (and, I would add, much popular discourse) has discussed intimacy solely as a positive, healthy, good feeling (2011: 168). This perspective is also apparent in alternative notions of intimacy; for instance, Klesse observes that, in gay men's discourse, intimacy is reconceptualized as the gentleness of touch or an orientation toward the creation of mutual sexual pleasure (Klesse 2007: 138). While this does away with the reduction of intimacy to (long-term) relationships and enables a perspective of intimacy as a situation, it remains invested in a pseudo-harmonic and socially abstract (and therefore power-evasive) notion of intimacy. Likewise, in the lesbian community, intimacy is often associated with gentleness and closeness only. Queer non-defining polyamorous Petra even spoke of the 'lesbian dogma of closeness':

> I get really annoyed if a woman tells me: 'I need much more closeness.' I go: 'I don't know what you mean by that. I am there, you can rely on me. I am on time, I won't abandon you at a party if I am there with you – how much more closeness do you actually need?' Yes, I've got the feeling that many women actually mean symbiosis, rather than closeness. To me, closeness is a commitment, and about not pretending about some shit to someone that is not true.

What becomes clear in this quote is that there are various understandings of what closeness and intimacy entail. Petra defined it as reliability and honesty, rather than a condition of no boundaries and the fusion of selves culminating in a symbiotic union.

The understanding of intimacy as closeness served as a criterion not only for the quality of relationships but also for lesbian sex as well. Non-monogamous butch-loving femme bottom Lisa described the effect on her sex life once she started participating in dyke + queer BDSM:

> I never was into this kind of sex, like 'Oh, we love each other so much and we are so deep, like completely, sigh, we connect so deeply now, and we are so close now and we give each other so much', and so on. Instead, [BDSM] was really simply something that made sex actually really fun again. Exactly how I wanted it to be, really simply just sex and really just simply fucking. Because of this, I was thinking for a while that maybe I am not a real lesbian, because I don't really like this [laughs] lesbian sex.

For Lisa, the notion of sex as being about intimacy in the sense of closeness, deep connection and love was problematic. The normative power of this ideal in the lesbian community even made her question her identity as a lesbian, because she was looking for sex as an end in itself. Within the dyke + queer BDSM context, therefore, intimacy was not limited to positive feelings of warmth and closeness; rather, it was about sharing intense affects, emotions and physical responses. Physical and emotional/energetic proximity is not necessarily about comfort and harmonious closeness. Dyke + queer BDSM opens up a space to acknowledge and engage with ongoing and pervasive emotional ambiguities and social contradictions. And intimacy may even be created through the employment of pain, humiliation, shame and hierarchy. Therefore, I conceptualize dyke + queer BDSM-specific intimacy as *exuberant intimacy*, since it seeks out the hyperbole of the core themes of intimate access, boundary transgression and touch.

As discussed above, boundary violations are part of hegemonic power relations, which work to police borders, for example, what groups of people are allowed to enter public space without harassment, what kinds of appearances and behaviors they can exhibit without risking losing their bodily integrity and so on. Boundary violations are supposed to be experienced as negative kinds of intimacy, to incite shame, fear and withdrawal. But they also produce unintended excesses of erotic desires, which are exploited in dyke + queer BDSM intimate transgressions. These negative kinds of intimacies are converted into ambivalent and therefore highly intense desires and pleasures, for example in role play based on sexism and homophobia (see Chapter 8). Therefore, the meanings of boundary violations spin out of control, they cannot be contained, they become excessive. In this way, the intimacies generated in dyke + queer BDSM become exuberant as they dramatically engage with everyday technologies of power, or even exaggerate them to gain more erotic intensities.

Transgressing the private/public boundary: Playing in accessible spaces

Those interview partners playing in accessible contexts reported varying reactions of by-passers: surprise and irritation, ignorance or fleeing, voyeurism and wanting to be included, commenting and offering the 'victim' help or calling the police. Negative reactions were partly due to the problem of the intelligibility of certain practices as consensual BDSM or play. Accessible BDSM sometimes was mistaken for violence. Gay transman bottom Mik's top spontaneously started dominating him in an alley one night:

> And then some guy on a bike drove past us, and I waved at him and tried to grin visibly, and I think he did not see the grinning, but only my waving. At any rate, he turned around and came back and wanted to see what was going on there. Which is really laudable about him. And then we both turned around and laughed and said: 'No, we are just joking here', and so on.

Mik did not want BDSMers to involuntarily undermine such sensitivity to street violence and the willingness of passers-by to intervene. To avoid a conflict of interests, he therefore tried to make his consent transparent in accessible BDSM situations by sending out clearly readable signals.

Not only the players' boundaries were at stake in accessible play, but also the boundaries of those with whom they shared accessible spaces: 'If any games in the public are taking place where non-BDSMers don't have any option of avoiding to see the whole thing, then it is simply non-consensual.'

As queer transgender butch Jacky stated clearly, many interview partners considered exposing outsiders to BDSM in shared accessible spaces to be unethical, and as not living up to dyke + queer BDSM's own standards of negotiated consent. In contrast, queer femme Ellen was critical of the heteronormative hierarchy of what is considered acceptable behavior in accessible spaces: 'I think it's fun to freak people out in that way and to challenge people. And to show people that there are so many forms of sexuality and that it can be OK. To show them more aspects than are being shown outside of just sex parties.' Accessible non-normative sexual acts, therefore, became a politically motivated form of sex education to her. This kind of action can be understood as part of a queer in-your-face politics of invading public space and thereby questioning to whom it belongs and who or what kind of practices are excluded (Gamson 1989; Ingram et al. 1997; Mattilda 2004). This was evident in Ellen's anecdote about a group of heterosexuals who played strip poker during the gay night in a local bar, which prompted her and a friend to start a queer BDSM session to highlight the struggle over the accessibility of spaces for queer self-expressions. For MCL, the main motivation of hir public play was the provocation and the taboo-breaking nature of accessible play: 'Yes and sure, [sighs] I of course sometimes intend to provoke people with that and from that provocation I think I also get a kick, which is a fact.' Ze in part gained hir pleasure from other people's discomfort, something other dyke + queer BDSMers might judge as unethical behavior.

Genuine accessible play in this way is distinct from shared contained or contained accessible play. One motive of accessible play is to confront others with non-conforming sexuality and to gain pleasure and/or make political statements through this transgression of social norms. Thus, accessible BDSM sex can be understood as exuberant intimacy, since it flouts the limits of what is acceptable in a public sphere that employs heteronormative double standards and hypocrisies. 'Public' negotiated BDSM performances are condemned as theatrically staging violence, while domestic violence is taking place under the cover of the 'private' home. Accessible dyke + queer BDSM confronts by-passers with these social norms and contradictions. It infiltrates hegemonic spaces with the unintelligible and with 'exaggerated' expressions of sexual difference.

Intimate relationships in the dyke + queer BDSM communities

In the hegemonic cultural context in which my interview partners live, monogamy appears almost unchallenged as the only legitimate way to structure sexual and intimate relationships. Their dyke + queer BDSM practices, encounters and relationships partially reinscribed, but also ruptured these mono-normative ideals in various ways. Based on my interviews, I will discuss the extent to which dyke + queer BDSM presents an alternative approach not only to sexuality but also to ways of relating and sharing intimacy. I again suggest that dyke + queer BDSM is, therefore, best understood as alternative or, more precisely, as exuberant intimacy.

Mono-normative ideologies and lived non-monogamous realities

From an anthropological and historical perspective, monogamy is anything but natural or universal. It was only in 1563 that the Christian Church established the heterosexual marriage as monogamous in Europe. Moreover, the institution of marriage was reserved for a social minority; the rest were excluded from this privilege due to a lack of material resources or to racist constructions of love and marriage (Pieper & Bauer 2005; Willey 2006; Carter 2007; see Bauer 2013b for an overview). At the end of the 18th century, liberal values reconstructed marriage as a contractual relation and infused it with the ideas of the free choice of spouse, egalitarian partnership and romantic love. On the one hand, these are still powerful concepts and emotional codings today, which can also be shown to have influenced social movements. Some strands of feminism, for instance, keep insisting that polygyny proves the cultural inferiority and patriarchal backwardness of Muslim and Mormon cultures without inquiring into the actual advantages and disadvantages of polygyny (and other forms of polygamy) for women. On the other hand, monogamy has been under attack ever since its introduction into Christian Euro-American cultures. Various social movements and subcultures, from the hippies to lesbian feminists (Munson & Stelboum 1999; Jackson & Scott 2004) to anarchists (Goldman 1914; Shannon & Willis 2010: 436), have turned against marriage and monogamy as institutions, propagating such concepts as free love. Since the 1960s we have witnessed rising rates of divorce/separation and rising numbers of single households (Barker & Langdridge 2010b: 752) as well as a pluralization of forms of intimate relationships (Pieper & Bauer 2005). Yet a revival of the ideal of sexual fidelity has also been observed (Burkart 1997: 201; Schmidt et al. 2006). Most people seem to experience sexual attraction to multiple people despite a monogamous commitment, and many act on it secretly, with estimated adultery or 'cheating' rates as high as 50 per cent in the US (Gardner 2005: 5) and up to 60 per cent in Germany (Schmidt et al. 2006: 135). Thus, there are disparities between monogamy as an ideal and people's actual practices, which means that emotional work is necessary to negotiate the contradictions in individuals' lives.

Marianne Pieper and I (2005) coined the term *mono-normativity* to refer to the mechanism that privileges monogamous relationships in both social worlds and scientific discourses alike (Barker & Langdridge 2010a; 2010b). Mono-normativity tends to universalize and naturalize the exclusive, dyadic structure of the loving (usually heterosexual) couple. This complex power relation (re)produces hierarchically arranged patterns of intimate relationships, and devalues, marginalizes, excludes and 'others' any patterns of intimacy that do not correspond to the normative apparatus of the monogamous model. Mono-normativity is based on the taken-for-granted allegation that monogamy and dyadic relationships are the principle of social relations per se, an essential foundation of human existence and the regulation of kinship and intimacy (Schenk 1987; Tyrell 1987; Burkart 1997). From the mono-normative perspective, every encounter or relationship that does not represent this pattern is assigned the status of the other, of deviation, of pathology; it is a sign of being uncivilized, racially inferior, morally inferior, in need of explanation, or it is ignored, hidden, avoided and marginalized. Sometimes monogamy is presented as natural (Mayer 2006), other times as a cultural or moral fact, and often it sets the *white* race apart as morally superior or further developed (Riggs 2006; Willey 2006; Carter 2007). Mono-normativity is also linked with heteronormativity and pseudo-harmonic sex in complex ways.[3]

A minority of people in mono-normative cultures choose a third option besides living monogamously or 'cheating' to solve the dilemma of multiple desires; they practice transparent and negotiated non-monogamies of various kinds. No reliable data about the prevalence of these negotiated non-monogamists exist, but one may tentatively say that this form of non-monogamy is more common among certain communities, such as bisexuals, gay men (Klesse 2007) and BDSMers (Bauer 2010), where negotiating non-monogamies has become a regular part of the subculture. Additionally, with the emergence of the polyamory community beginning in the 1990s, groups have formed solely around the issues of alternative relationship practices for the first time. The term 'polyamory' was popularized by Morning Glory Zell Ravenheart (1990) when a movement formed in the US that demanded the social recognition of alternative relationship forms. The term refers mostly to self-chosen (rather than culturally prescribed) non-monogamous constellations that include multiple relationships or multiple loves, and distances itself discursively from other non-monogamies, such as institutionalized polygamy or promiscuity (see Klesse 2006 for its potentially exclusionary dynamics). Polyamory is also referred to as consensual, responsible, open or negotiated non-monogamy. It may take various forms (Labriola 1999), and there are non-monogamous relationship forms specific to the BDSM community, for instance, the tradition of leather families. These are kinship-of-choice structures involving BDSM power dynamics, which often culminate in shared households with various relationships and interactions among the members (Kaldera 2010: 198–203; 234–63). Leather families may be comprised of gay men and lesbians, because the BDSM aspect is more important than the genital sex and binds the family together (Kaldera 2010: 201–3). Usually, all those involved in these various non-monogamous relationships negotiate individual agreements about their commitments and what can be expected from each other (see also Pieper & Bauer 2005).

While polyamory presents an alternative to mono-normative ways of doing relationships, it is hardly free from mono-normative (and other normative) elements. Jamieson (2004), for instance, shows in her empirical study how, contrary to their own political convictions, in most non-monogamous constellations the role of the couple as the elementary unit remains unquestioned. The most common form of non-monogamous practice, therefore, remains the open marriage or open relationship (see also Wolfe 2003; Cook 2005). If emotional bonding is reserved for one (primary) partner, one may, therefore, also speak of emotional monogamy with sexual non-exclusivity. Finn and Malson (2008: 530) argue that the separation of sex and love helps to construct non-monogamous relationships as fortified spaces via the concept of emotional monogamy, and that the mono-normative concept of dyadic containment is, therefore, perpetuated in many non-monogamous constellations as well, for instance in the practice of 'swinging' (McDonald 2010). Therefore, the distinction between monogamous and non-monogamous relating is complex rather than clear-cut. In the context of this study, I refer to the common definition of monogamy or serial monogamy as sexually and emotionally exclusive, long-term (but not necessarily life-long) couplehood. I label as non-monogamous all those relationship practices that deviate from this commonly understood concept, even though some interview partners may have defined their relationships as monogamous despite sexual or BDSM extra-dyadic activities, for instance because they do not define non-genital BDSM as sex. This is not to disrespect their self-definitions, which I will make clear when discussing their relationships, but in order to focus analytically on the effects and repudiations of mono-normativity. Moreover, there were those who self-identified as monogamous or non-monogamous independent of their current relationship circumstance. Others did not view relationship choices as part of their identity, but were responding to the needs of their current partner(s) and may have chosen phases of monogamy and non-monogamy in their lives without any inner contradictions. Finally, there were gray areas, such as group play. If group play is arranged in a way to preserve the couple structure throughout the encounter, is it a monogamous or a non-monogamous situation?

Non-monogamy as a dyke + queer BDSM community norm

Despite the fact that monogamous practice is much less stable than the norm implies, mono-normativity remains socially effective; for instance, it presents a powerful way of coding emotions even for people who openly embrace non-monogamy. Polyamorous transmasculine switch Craig reports:

> I think for me it's a realization that I have a lot of needs, and my needs are very different. And I think it would be very naïve to believe anybody would have exactly the same match of ideas that I have, even though

I kind of once in a while think: 'Wouldn't that be romantic?' You really do get programmed by society, but I realized this is not the way I actually work.

Craig had intellectually deconstructed the rationale of monogamy as unrealistic and also had discovered that his personality and valuing of difference did not work within a monogamous framework, but he still caught himself being emotionally invested in the romantic discourses to find 'the one and only'. Non-monogamous femme Katharina came up with strategies to counter the interpellations of romantic discourse by using non-exclusive declarations of commitment. She refrained from using clichés like 'You are the best butch in the whole world':

> Rather really saying something like 'You are the best butch I know!' or 'I met so far'. Well this is something I can really be serious about and I don't have to take back if I meet another butch who I also think is great, you know? Or to keep love declarations also open and honest and not to take just any set phrases, just because they are there and I couldn't think of anything better that moment. And also to simply reflect there on: what do I promise people? With Jacky I have more of a thing like: 'I think you're really pretty good, I think I'll keep you for a while!' [laughs]

She renegotiated love declarations to make them more reliable, honest and appropriate to the situation. She disentangled affirmations of commitment to her relationship from the mono-normative ideals of exclusivity and life-long duration. As Samuels points out, part of mono-normativity is the valorization of relational longevity at the expense of relational quality (2010: 220). Katharina's alternatives contained implicit references to the backdrop of the romantic discourse she ironically distanced herself from. Yet her declarations were not emotionally distant; rather, they facilitated bonding through their individuality and their demythologization of love relationships. Therefore, it seems that both secretly practiced non-monogamy and negotiated non-monogamy require emotional and logistic labor, but of different kinds.

In the dyke + queer BDSM communities, negotiated non-monogamies of various kinds were so common that the monogamy norm seemed reversed, not only in terms of prevalence but also as expressed in codes of conduct (see also Bauer 2010). In most dyke + queer BDSM play party spaces, there was an unspoken assumption that it was appropriate to ask any person present for a session, even if they were obviously part of a relationship. As polyamorous lesbian femme Frl. R. observed:

> I also think that it is an extreme standard within the SM community that one should for god's sake not be monogamous at any rate. Well [that is

the case] in the SM scene that I encounter around myself. And it would probably be a major faux pas to say: 'Actually I am looking for a partner for life', you know.

Even though my qualitative study was not designed to be representative, my data confirm this tendency: 80 per cent of my interview partners lived in a self-defined non-monogamous situation, 10 per cent were part of a currently self-defined monogamous couple but planned to open it once it was stable enough or the occasion presented itself, and the remaining 10 per cent self-defined as monogamous, but participated in group settings or extra-dyadic BDSM. They did not consider playing outside of their relationship as non-monogamy, either because they did not define BDSM as sexual or because they were emotionally monogamous despite having sexually open relationships. So not a single person in my sample was monogamous in the commonly used sense of the term (sexual and emotional exclusivity). Instead, various types of non-monogamy and redefined sexual or emotional monogamy were standard. Klesse also found a strong overlap between polyamorous and BDSM communities in his empirical research in the UK (2007:100).

Yet occurrences of jealousy and struggles over status in relationship networks pointed to the fact that mono-normative views and emotional codings remained virulent. But, simultaneously, the normalcy of non-monogamy in the dyke + queer BDSM community depathologized it, enabled its members to experience polyamory not simply as an ideology but as a reality, and provided them with inspiring role models. Non-monogamous genderqueer Femmeboy said:

> So a lot of times, yes, ideally it would be nice to be non-monogamous, but in practice it doesn't work. But when you're in the leather community, you see people living together and people who've been in relationships with each other for ten years, and they have a daddy, and they have a primary partner who's not their daddy, and they have a little girl, and it's working. They're living together, and I think that as a community we need examples of that working.

As opposed to society at large, the presence of role models of successful non-monogamy in the dyke + queer BDSM community made it easier to practice and initiated an upward spiral of ever more people living it. As a result, my interview partners provided rich accounts of how they lived their non-monogamous relationships, but within the scope of this book I will focus on those aspects that are dyke + queer BDSM-specific ways of intimate relating.

Dyke + queer BDSM culture as a medium for inventing ways of relating

Non-monogamous polysexual transwoman Anna stated: 'I consider SM rather as a type of relationship or as a part of a relationship type, where you deal with relationship in a much more reflective way or much, much more thoughtful.' As opposed to viewing BDSM simply as a sexual practice, Anna stressed the relational aspect of BDSM interactions as an alternative intimacy that is characterized by a high degree of reflective relationship dynamics. This is partly due to the fact that dyke + queer BDSM provided my interview partners with a space to explore and deal with social power relations and boundary transgressions differently than in other contexts (see also Chapters 6 and 7). The special communicative sexuality of dyke + queer BDSM opens up spaces for renegotiating relationship forms and doing them differently.

Some interview partners explained the high prevalence of non-monogamy among BDSM dykes + queers with what I have labeled the 'domino effect of perversion', as Frl. R. explained: 'I don't know, maybe it's because you are playing with so many borderline issues anyways already. Well, first you became lesbian, then you are into such kinky stuff on top of it, and yes, I mean then it is not really a necessity anymore to marry, is it?' Frl. R. and other interview partners described a series of coming outs or becoming different in their biographies as initiating this domino effect. That is, once you have crossed a certain line and start to question the culturally available scripts around sexuality and gender, you may proceed to question the validity of other norms. Thus, seemingly private violations of sexual norms may initiate an interrogation of social norms and a subsequent practice of making life choices beyond or outside expected social behaviors and scripts. So the domino theory of perversion represents a positive appropriation of the domino theory of sexual peril (Rubin 1992a: 282), which is the slippery-slope logic that, once a certain (heteronormative) line is crossed, sexual order will inevitably be replaced by sexual chaos or anarchy. Furthermore, feminist and queer traditions of critiquing marriage and (compulsory) monogamy (Munson & Stelboum 1999; Jackson & Scott 2004; Ritchie & Barker 2007) are part of the dyke + queer BDSM community cultural context. This makes the step toward experimenting with non-monogamy even easier, since it will likely be met with approval and support in one's own social contexts.

In Lisa's experience, dyke + queer BDSM culture provided a space for women to disconnect sex from love:

> This SM game [makes it possible] to have this fun, or to live out something without it having to be connected to love necessarily or similar issues. So that works in the SM scene of course much more easily than in the

other lesbian scenes or lesbian worlds, where [sex] mixes so much and so quickly with being in love, and so on.

Even alternative communities tend to perpetuate mono-normative ideologies, such as the normative discourse in the polyamory community that love and sex belong together (Wilkinson 2010: 246). Sex for pleasure outside the context of a loving relationship, and promiscuous behavior, therefore remain stigmatized in various social contexts, especially for women, perpetuating a sexual double standard (Klesse 2005). Women still are confronted with the old Madonna/virgin vs. whore/slut double bind (Dunn 1998: 495–9; Filipovic 2008), which has only become more complicated to navigate, since current norms also demand that women be sexually active. Meanwhile, Black female sexuality is stereotyped as excessive, promiscuous and unrestrained in racist discourse (Hooks 1981; McClintock 1995; Springer 2008), which pressures Black women into proving their respectability through sexual moderation and self-discipline. Dyke + queer BDSM culture provided my interview partners with an environment where they could explore new types of erotic and sexual interactions and intimacy outside romantic scripts and gender-stereotypical limitations.[4] Dyke + queer BDSM women encountered multiple means to experience themselves as active sexual agents in the community: an environment free from cismale intervention, which enabled women to claim the now-vacant space of the (culturally assumed male) sexual initiator; an active part in pre-negotiations; a sex-positive attitude, including spaces like play parties that are specifically designed to allow sexual activity outside a (love) relationship context and an already established culture of non-monogamy.

While dyke + queer BDSM was a context that facilitated a separation of sex from love and relationships, many interview partners experienced a unique BDSM intimacy that created intense emotions, feelings of closeness and deep bonding between play partners, blurring the lines between romantic and purely BDSM relationships. As non-monogamous gay transman bottom Mik experienced it: '[I can] get into a much stronger closeness as well through these intense feelings, be it the level of power or be it the level of pain.' Many others similarly concluded that dyke + queer BDSM generated a heightened level of intimacy through the way one is exposed and made vulnerable, the trust involved and the general intensity of playing with sensations, power, social taboos and boundaries. This is another example of exuberant intimacy. My interview partners saw dyke + queer BDSM as a new way of connecting intimately, and Femmeboy described one experience:

I had my nipples flogged and it was a very intense experience for me, and afterwards I wanted that person to hold me, and I feel there was a part of me that needed just that release: that I can cry and just shake and let go. Like after sex. So it was a new way of connecting with a person that's really intense emotionally. But not necessarily sexual in a way that I would've used to define sex, like having an orgasm, a genital orgasm or something. It's a new way of being connected.

So dyke + queer BDSM contributed to a unique kind of intimacy through shared experiences of intensity beyond genital sex.

Often, deep bonding was facilitated rather quickly between strangers, which became evident in long-term long-distance friendships that originally resulted from a one-time BDSM encounter at a dyke + queer gathering. Because of the intense intimacy that dyke + queer BDSM may generate, non-monogamous lesbian top Nico pointed out: 'Therefore, on the downside, I could also say the potential danger that I fall in love outside of an already existing relationship has increased, maybe because there is so much closeness and trust and a shared emotional world with someone.' Thus, dyke + queer BDSM might also complicate open relationship dynamics if its unique, intimate qualities blur the primary relationship's boundaries rather than containing extra-dyadic activities through the non-genital character of BDSM. This also illustrates how the dyadic containment of mono-normativity is ultimately an illusion and cannot be controlled.

Given these instabilities of dyadic containment, some of my interview partners have redefined faithfulness or fidelity (*Treue*), as Mik explained:

> So faithfulness means that a person has a really high status in my life or even the highest, depending. And that I am there for this person in difficult and good life circumstances, that I am interested in this person, that I relate to this person, also negotiate with this person, if it is also a sexual and couple relationship, that I also negotiate sexuality with this person.

For Mik, fidelity was not about sexual or emotional exclusiveness, but about granting someone a special status, a high priority in life decisions, about being reliable and remaining loyal. The loyalty to a partner or even to a master or mistress was, therefore, not necessarily compromised by extra-dyadic sex or play. Moreover, BDSM etiquette might provide a prearranged structure for non-monogamous or group situations. For instance, if a mistress had to be addressed to ask for permission for any sexual interaction with her slave or property, this introduced an element of respect toward existing relationships as well as communication and negotiation about the potentials and limits of extra-dyadic activities. In this way, BDSM protocol provided a social structure that promoted negotiating individual relationship choices.

Dominance/submission, therefore, structured interactions in ways that facilitated exploring non-monogamy. For instance, a top who felt uncomfortable or potentially threatened by her partner's attention toward someone else might order her partner to serve another top, as queer switch Firesong, who was in a relationship with a non-monogamous partner, stated: 'Picturing her fucking someone is not erotic for me. On the other hand, in play space, if I'm topping her and I ask her to fuck someone and that's negotiated, that's very hot.' Since some of my interview partners reported that jealousy is connected to losing control, being in control of the situation may ease fears and provide positive, mutually pleasing non-monogamous encounters. Generally, DS provided some people with tools to process potential emotional challenges in poly situations. For instance, some submissives can be sexually aroused and emotionally fulfilled by not getting things their way, since it proves to them they are really not in control of the situation. Having to accept their top's sexual interest in others may turn into a positively sexually charged situation, rather than just being an emotionally negative experience of jealousy (Kaldera 2010: 71). So dyke + queer BDSM space produced its own BDSM-specific kinds of intimacy and relationships. Some examples are discussed in the following.

Specific DS (Dominance/Submission) ways of intimate relating

One seemingly paradoxical form of intimacy was objectification or strangeness. Non-monogamous straight-queer femme bottom Teresa enjoyed being objectified. She explained how the degree of intimacy had an impact on her sexual arousal in an encounter:

> The way that I relate to this is sort of strangeness in sexuality sometimes. And sometimes the more intimacy there is, if there isn't also a strong power dynamic with that intimacy, it's too close to home and it turns me off. I've talked to a lot of femmes – who are abuse survivors or not – who the longer they are into the relationship the less turned on they can be, because there's this intimacy then, and I'm less able to feel objectified in sex. […] Yeah, I wanna feel objectified. And if someone's being objectified that means a lack of intimacy.

In this quote, Teresa was referring to intimacy in the sense of familiarity and closeness, and as precluding a great sexual experience. She utilized role play to generate feelings of distance with familiar play partners. Role play can reintroduce elements of unfamiliarity; by acting as strangers and assuming new roles again and again, intimacy is re-enabled in the sense of boundary transgression and touch. Such practices of objectification run counter to the ideals of harmonic sex and romantic relationships. The pleasure lies exactly in the lack of conventional notions of closeness, emphasizing differences between the participants instead. Yet such practices may produce intense sensations and affects. They may even, paradoxically, facilitate bonding or emotional attachments around these common passions or prevent long-term relationships from becoming asexual. Therefore, these objectifying techniques are best understood as a form of intimacy focusing on boundary transgression and access to a body through power dynamics (rather than pathologizing them as fear of intimacy or lack of ability to bond).

DS dynamics also have an impact on how non-monogamy is negotiated. Mik discussed how he would be willing to give up specific sexual liberties for a master: 'What I can imagine rather well is to be under someone else's control, or to be non-monogamous in a controlled way. That my Sir determines for me with whom I have sex and with whom not. That I can imagine rather well. But pure monogamy, I can hardly imagine.' Thus, relationship rules may be part of a protocol for a bottom. Some interview partners who were property had to get permission for sexual interactions with third parties (see also stein & Schachter 2009; Kaldera 2010: 107). In the negotiations for their contract, non-monogamous lifestyle submissive Tanya had granted her daddi[5] control over whom she got to play with outside the relationship. So different rules applied for owner and property in regard to their non-monogamous practices as an expression of their DS relationship. While this seems to limit the options for the bottom, many bottom interview partners in particular fostered a slut identity as a sexually active female subjectivity. The figure of the slut seemed to be especially compatible with the bottom position, reappropriating the sexist stereotypes around women's sexual availability for dyke + queer BDSM pleasures. Even Tanya's rule of having to call her daddi to get permission to play seemed to emphasize her sluttiness and sexual subjectivity, since it forced her to confess to her sexual needs and to become active to get them met, literally 'asking for it'. Thus, all dyke + queer BDSM roles seemed to possess potentials for claiming a non-monogamous practice and an empowered female sexual subjectivity. Another way in which ownership generated a specific form of non-monogamy was the top's right to lend their bottoms to other tops. This non-monogamous practice powerfully demonstrated the extent of the control a top holds. Additionally, it fostered specific intimate connections with other tops through the sharing of bottoms.

Fulltime ownership (24/7)

One DS-specific form of intimacy is erotic ownership. In BDSM fantasy worlds, examples of the fulltime ownership of a slave or a fulltime DS relationship – also referred to as 24/7, lifestyle BDSM or total power exchange (TPE) in community discourse – abound and were referred to by some interview partners (critically) as the 'gold standard'. While this fantasy to live one's whole life as BDSM is obviously alluring and fascinating to many, it is equally disturbing to others and remains one of the practices most criticized and scorned in BDSM communities themselves (see Kaldera 2010: 33–40). Some interview partners simply dismissed it as unrealistic or too much work. Yet the fact that a quarter of my sample were currently or had been previously in a fulltime or ownership relationship proved that it was at least manageable for a certain period of time and was a serious option for a strong minority of dyke + queer BDSM community members.

My interview partners made it work because they adjusted the ideal to their everyday realities. The fulltime relationships of interview partners were configured as master/mistress–slave or daddy–boy/girl, and generally the bottom or submissive was considered to be the property of the top. Gay transman switch BJ described the dynamic:

> I was in a relationship for a number of years where I was owned by this woman where even though I had my daily life to live, for instance school, work, I was owned by her. So at any moment within that 24 hours, she could call me and we would be in the middle of a scene or I'd be in the middle of doing her bidding or whatever.

So 24/7 did not necessarily imply a constant interaction in the roles or identities, much less a total (for instance, economic) dependency on the top, but consisted of a fulltime optional access for the top to her bottom. The power dynamic might intrude into ordinary life at any time (or within negotiated limits, such as no intervention in work life), which demonstrated the arbitrary control the top had. Some interview partners were also cohabiting with their fulltime DS partners. Being owned was the ultimate expression of handing control over one's life to someone else. Yet most interview partners had negotiated clear boundaries even in 24/7 relationships.

If ownership relationships were also non-monogamous, the degree of negotiation increased. For instance, other partners needed to be considered when it came to such questions as prescribed chastity for the property (Kaldera 2010: 61, 88), or if other partners did not want to see their partner in slave modus (87). The blurring of lines in DS poly relationships is also an inherent danger. For instance, the partner of non-monogamous queer trans/genderqueer/butch dyke Scout's Sir expected Scout to serve her as well, even though this was never negotiated (see also Kaldera 2010: 92). Since properties may be non-confrontational or want to please, the heightened responsibility of the top/owner is stressed once more. As Kaldera rightly points out, with privilege comes responsibility (2010: 70), and, if the owner has more than one submissive, s/he is responsible for facilitating the poly situation (47, 122).

For some interview partners, giving up control 24/7 provided them with a sense of security; it structured their life:

> And also just the safety, that I know that there's a place that I can go, where I walk in the door and I'll do the same exact things every single time. There's a place where I know that my body's not gonna be attacked, where I know how my body's gonna be touched, where I know how I can

speak about my body. It just created a safety and a structure in which I could begin to feel in my body at least a little bit.

For Scout, the safety that the 24/7 relationship provided enabled him to connect to his body. The reliable structure of DS protocol may function to help the bottom let go of worries and fears and focus on the moment and the self. Furthermore, Scout's Sir also provided him with material support and a safer space while he was homeless. For Tanya, the security she sought was achieved through a contract that specified the duties of both parties. Tanya was in protocol 24/7: 'So that doesn't really change from moment to moment. I go to work, and I'm in protocol. It's not the same protocol on the high level that I have with my Daddi. But it's still my protocol. And it's who I am.' She described protocol as a set of rules to live by daily, and it defined her sense of self. She was under the permanent control of her daddi, mediated through the protocol. This supported their dynamic and intimacy even in his absence. In everyday life this became manageable through varying degrees of protocol, adjusting to the situation. Therefore, the protocol can be considered a technology of the self, since it requires work and produces a specific kind of subjectivity. Part of her protocol was to ask her daddi for permission to interact with others when he was present. But this was not something that restricted or humiliated her, quite the opposite: 'People shouldn't feel like they have the liberty to come up and touch me without permission. Because I'm special and I know that.' Being a valued property, therefore, can also translate to being unique or special, someone's treasured possession. This may feel validating, bolster self-esteem and enable one to assert one's boundaries more clearly. As is evident in Tanya's quote, being owned by her daddi enabled her, paradoxically, to claim ownership of her own body in relation to others. It was her job to enforce the rule that nobody else was allowed to touch her without permission, effectively changing her embodied subjectivity into one with clearer boundaries.

Besides the practice of collaring (putting a symbol of ownership on the body of the bottom), protocol was another technique to extend the DS relationship into ordinary life and to enrich it subtly. To polyamorous queer femme Emma, living 24/7 was a means to eroticize everyday life, even seemingly mundane tasks: 'My boi at the time actually wrote a poem about how sexy it was to take out the garbage. She just wrote this gorgeous poem about the sweat trickling between her breasts, as she carries the trash. I mean, it was totally eroticized and that was gorgeous.' It can be extremely rewarding to find ways to infuse ordinary life with the erotic, intimate and intense energy of DS. The new meanings assigned to otherwise mundane or looked-down-upon tasks may bring about a different quality of life. If even taking out the trash becomes something special when done for the master/mistress, life becomes elevated. Scout also described his 24/7 experience as all-consuming and his driving force: 'When I got dressed it was like: "Right or left pocket hanky?[6] Right pocket." Everything on my body was designed to his specifications every single day.' Designing his body as an expression of the will of his Sir literally meant constructing his body and identity as a boy in the DS sense and embodying their relationship. Such technologies of the self extended the control of the top beyond face-to-face situations and solidified the power dynamic by inscribing it in the bottom's body and mind, leaving impressions and traces of power and affect.

Finally, DS ownership is interestingly close to romantic discourse, which often utilizes metaphors of possessing someone. It can be seen to make explicit this underlying ideology of love, which is an inheritance of patriarchal marriage as possession. Kaldera even points out that the joy of possessiveness that can be found in ownership may turn a previously polyamorous top into a monogamous owner (2010: 53). In this sense it is a disidentificatory BDSM practice (Muñoz 1999), dealing with affective codings such as jealousy in a caricatured way by making literal the implicit notion of possession in romantic love. Ownership is also a good example of exuberant intimacy, since it performatively exaggerates partners' difference in social status to the extreme. It therefore creates an intensity of experience that may lead to a strong affective bond.

Dyke + queer BDSM culture as fostering non-monogamy

The dyke + queer BDSM communities have developed a specific sexual culture. The high priority of sexual needs and wishes as well as the celebration of sex have fostered an explicit and open way of communicating about sexual fantasies, desires, preferences and practices:

> I think kinky people are at least trying to get over their hang-ups around owning all the things that they want and all the things that turn them on. And once you realize that you can actually access all the things that turn you on, well you also realize that they can't all be matching up with the one person you're in love with. They just don't match up.

Polyamorous transgender stone butch Terry and others described dyke + queer BDSM as a way to experience a multiplicity of desires and to actualize fantasies. But, in practice, the broader the range of specific sexual interests, the more unlikely it was that one partner alone could provide a perfect match. A dyke + queer BDSM coming out thus often functioned as the entrance point into non-monogamy, especially if an existing partner was not interested in BDSM. On the other hand, some interview partners stressed that the great variety of sexual interests and roles they embodied made sexual exclusivity in a relationship work better for them, since their sexual interactions did not become repetitive or boring even within a long-term monogamous relationship. This, of course, depended on finding a partner who shared enough common interests and flexibility in roles.

Dyke + queer BDSM practitioners tended to demythologize sexuality; sexual acts were generally treated like other social activities. Sexuality lost its special status in this sense, getting less burdened with the discursive baggage of love and romance. Therefore, non-monogamy was considered to be a valid way to pursue one's sexual desires, analogous to enjoying one's hobbies with various friends with similar tastes. As a consequence, playing with friends had become so common in this community that the mononormative boundary between friends and lovers became rather fluid. The transgression of this boundary was possibly enhanced through the non-genital focus of many dyke + queer BDSM practices and the fact that some dyke + queer BDSMers separated BDSM and genital sex. Most interview partners played with friends off and on or regularly. Even though the lines between asexual friends and sexual partners, therefore, had become permeable, my interview partners could clearly indicate who counted as a friend and who as a lover or partner. Therefore, the social distinctions that clarified how to interact with certain categories of people were renegotiated but not abolished; the friends who were engaged with in BDSM were still treated as friends socially and not given the specific privileges reserved for partners. This was enabled by the function of BDSM sessions as semi-contained space, as Kelvin, who before entering a monogamous relationship played a lot with a group of friends, described:

> Before I played in a group for the first time – I had never had one-night stands or the like – I thought: 'Are you able to do that? Can you get that close to someone now?' And afterwards, well, the play was now over, and that worked. So there was a somehow special frame. We played and we touched each other's breasts, or body everywhere, and then we exited, and with that the play was over, and with that we were 'zap!' back again in another dimension. And we were completely friends again, with a certain distance again, which is only natural between friends. Maybe you can put it like that, that one actually has a different frame in that moment.

The ritualized beginning and ending of a session may function as a gateway, facilitating the entering into another reality and exiting it again afterwards. This enabled interview partners to share moments of sexual intimacy with friends without falling in love or entering a romantic relationship. At the same time, sharing BDSM experiences was described as enriching and deepening friendship bonds.

Playing with friends, therefore, presented another way in which alternative intimacies were created in the dyke + queer BDSM context. The renegotiation of what kinds of interactions are acceptable among friends, then, may lead to what Ramey has called 'intimate friendships' (Ramey

1976), friendships that include erotic and sexual elements that are usually reserved for primary relationships only. Klesse also finds that polyamory often involves particular philosophies of friendship (2007: 114), which stress the non-exclusive character of friendships as opposed to romantic relationships. Friendships may, therefore, function as models to reconceptualize sexual and love relationships as non-exclusive, since friendships are positive cultural models for being close to more than one person at the same time.

The dyke + queer BDSM communities have developed specific ethics and skills to ensure that BDSM practices and relationships may be carried out in critically negotiated and risk-aware ways. As I showed in the previous chapter, to establish working consent, communication and negotiation skills are crucial. When asked whether he had any explanation for why non-monogamy was so widespread in the dyke + queer BDSM communities, Mik suggested a link between negotiated consent in BDSM and in polyamory:

> This negotiation then offers a lot of chances. That the partners decide together what they wanna do with each other, and each for themselves has to reflect a lot more through these negotiations. What do I actually want? And then non-monogamy or polyamory or however you wanna call it, is negotiated alongside. And consent is established. Since the SM people are used to negotiating sexuality, they negotiate about this aspect in a similar fashion.

So the ethics and skills the BDSM sexual culture had to develop to practice their sexual preferences are not only suitable for approaching BDSM but also work well when dealing with non-monogamy also. Negotiated sexuality may lead to negotiated relationship choices. The possibilities of and limits to establishing consent, as discussed in the previous chapter, can, therefore, roughly be applied to non-monogamy as well.

The self-help discourses that dominate the polyamory communities tend to psychologize and individualize the processes of negotiation, because they follow a liberal ideology of agency and personal autonomy (Petrella 2007). They tend, therefore, to neglect the social construction of emotions and desires (Haritaworn et al. 2006) as well as power dynamics in relationships and their effects on the validity of consent (Klesse 2007). Therefore, I speak of negotiated rather than consensual relationship practices and develop notions of critical rather than liberal consent in the context of openly lived non-monogamies as well. The negotiation culture of dyke + queer BDSM helped to facilitate negotiating non-monogamy for my interview partners and helped to explain the high prevalence of non-monogamies in this community.

Shared intimacy

Dyke + queer BDSM culture provides ample opportunities to play in shared community spaces and in groups. My interview partners reported a great variety of play that involved more than two participants, among which were kinship play, spiritual play like energy pulls,[7] abduction scenes, interrogation scenes and gang rape enactments. The number of participants ranged from 3 to as many as 20 in scenes like outdoor military drills. Larger group events required some preparation, like finding enough compatible co-players, and logistical organization. Therefore, most group play took place as encounters of three to five dykes + queers in private homes, in community spaces and sometimes outdoors. Some group play remained strictly couple-focused, creating an erotic atmosphere among friends, a setting inspired specifically by dyke + queer BDSM fantasy worlds. For instance, for Vito and her wife, Cara, it was important that they had a monogamous relationship despite playing with friends and creating a dyke + queer BDSM and erotic synergy. Therefore, dyke + queer BDSM enabled them to create a new way of intimate and erotic connection beyond the couple while simultaneously preserving their boundaries. Such intimate friendships as a new way of relating were highly valued by them 'because they are really friends with whom you share something else that goes a bit further and goes a bit deeper still'. The sharing of erotic spaces enriched these friendships.

Playing in groups broadened the options for role play and for consensual power exchange dynamics. Some interview partners, like Petra, even had a preference for group play:

> I also extremely like to play in groups, even preferably, because I find that the energy flows even much, much better then. I don't have to work as hard as in a twosome as a top. I can hand her over, off and on, can take a look at what is she doing now, if I hand her over to someone else?

So Petra added further advantages of playing in structures beyond the couple: tops can co-operate and ensure a smoother flow of the action. She also got to see her play partners in other situations, since the dynamic with another top may be different. Thus, one may discover new aspects of the personalities of play partners.

While some interview partners seemed to prefer one-on-one action, others were part of circles of friends who often played together, enjoying the synergy and sharing of intimacy beyond dyadic structures: 'I have an intimate relationship with the whole group, otherwise I would not play with them. I do not play with people with whom I don't have any relationship whatsoever. But the term relationship is defined much narrower by most people.'

As Petra stated clearly here, such group sessions were experienced as intimate and connected, and not as casual or dispersed. She enjoyed a variety of intimate group friendships in this way. The development of such circles of intimate friends and of another phenomenon, polyamory networks, which emerged when individuals formed relationships with more than one partner, was an important part of community-building. Non-monogamous queer/dyke butch Lola and her dyke, trans* and genderqueer BDSM friends came up with their own sexual friendship culture. The inspiration for forming a sexual friendship circle originally came from gay male sexual culture. Yet Lola and her friends did not simply copy it, but, rather, invented their own version of an intimate friendship group:

> One of the complaints that I had about the gay male group and some of the people I know [who] were in that group, was that one thing that was lacking was sort of a sense of political awareness. And sort of what seemed to be kind of a hedonistic indulgence and [emphasizing] just the physical senses with not very much awareness of what's going on outside in the world and sort of a little bit of escapism. And what I really enjoy about the group of people that I've been playing with is that they all are for the most part very political people that also have all sorts of external things going on. So that when we do come together, yeah, we have fun, we have sex, blah blah blah, but we also do talk about politics, too. We also sort of bring our outside life experiences to each other when we're together and when we meet and stuff. So it also becomes this opportunity for political information and skill sharing.

Lola and her friends made radical queer political networking part of creating intimacy among themselves. They did not separate their sexual lives and their ways of relating from their politics. Instead, they discussed how sexuality and relationships were political and how their politics informed their sexual and relationship practices:

> For me, there's a strong connection between non-monogamy and anti-capitalist politics. Because I think part of sort of the consumer's culture that promotes monogamy has to do with seeing individuals as commodities. And that once you fall in love with somebody you own that person and have certain exclusive rights to that person. And if that person is with somebody else, then that's somehow something that's taking away some of your stuff. And it took me many, many, many years of being a really jealous person to realize that maybe I was kinda following what had been fed to me through marketing, through mainstream media, through living in a sort of puritanical Judeo-Christian culture, where sex is seen as bad. So, to me, non-monogamy is sort of a more collective sexual experience, and it sort of opens stuff up.

Lola was not the only interview partner who understood deprivatizing sex and creating collective, non-possessive forms of intimacy in this way as radical political acts. Others discussed this simply in terms of personal preference, fantasy fulfillment and life quality, but many stressed how sharing intimacy with more than one person at a time was part of questioning mono-normative structures, such as emotional imprints:

> I am not really jealous, but rather envious at times. Of good times others have and I do not [laughs], where I always think like: 'Oh man, shit, I want that, too! Why can't I as well? More time, more great people, more sex, more fun, more everything!' But in this case I really find it meaningful to then say: 'OK, how do I get that?' And to focus on that and not on taking away something from other people, since that does not really further universal happiness. Most notably, it does not provide me with anything. Through someone else having even less, I do not have more of anything.

Katharina described how envy as part of mono-normative culture resulted in competitive rather than generous, solidary or collective behaviors. She contrasted this destructive dynamic, based on a logic of scarcity of resources or lack, with a constructive and communal approach of multiplying and sharing sexual pleasures.

Exuberance: A queer philosophy of abundance

In her research on mono-normative discourses, Mayer (2006; 2013) finds that a central feature of mono-normativity is that it operates within an economy of lack. The occurrence of non-monogamous behavior is conceptualized as lack in three different but related discursive strategies: as an effect of a pre-existing deficiency in a relationship (that the 'cheating' partner attempts to counter elsewhere); as a producer of scarcity by reducing limited resources (taking away love, energy, care and so on from an existing relationship by giving attention to someone else); and as a result of a deficiency in the subject (someone is unable to bond, cannot love, is insecure in their gender role, is addicted to sex and so on, and therefore cannot commit properly to a single person). Mayer analyzes self-help literature that gives advice on how to re-establish monogamy in relationships where extra-dyadic sexual activities have occurred. Some authors construct people who act non-monogamously as gender deviant; they posit that non-monogamous behavior serves as a strategy to avoid being a real complement to a real man or woman (Mayer 2013). So, in this perspective, a return to monogamy does not only save relationships but also restores heteronormative gender relations. If one does not share this goal, though, it is possible to look into negotiated non-monogamy as a potential strategy for genderqueerness. Non-monogamy could enable individuals to live out different aspects of their gender with various differently gendered partners. My data suggest that not every partner can interact with each gender aspect of genderqueers, so non-monogamy might actually support those with multiple gender identities in living the full spectrum of their gendered selves. Richards argues similarly that non-monogamy may help trans* people during transition to more fully explore their changing senses of self, body and sexuality, and that multi-gendered trans* persons can express different parts of their gendered identity with different partners (2010: 126ff). Using non-monogamy as a way to express different parts of the self with different partners is not restricted to trans* people, genderqueers and their partners, though; it is a generalized possibility to live one's identities in an exuberant way. Identities are always limited concepts that do not pay justice to the lived complexities of individuals, and therefore necessarily produce excesses. Finn (2010) argues that one function of mono-normativity is to uphold a concept of a subject-in-containment, and that open non-monogamy can potentially allow a subject-in-progress instead. Or, as I would put it, it can open up a space for exuberant selves whose excesses cannot be contained, but that spill over and seek to connect across boundaries such as gender and couplehood. These are dynamics of exuberant desire and intimacy, celebrating multiple selves and multiplying touch across boundaries, replacing mono-normative containment with reaching out. The mono-normative logic, in contrast, relies on an economy of scarcity: intimacy, love, desire, pleasures and attention are all considered to be limited resources. Mayer (2013) identifies some counter-discourses and strategies with which her polyamorous interview partners challenge this logic, such as replacing the image of one pot of affection that multiple partners would have to share (limited resource) with the image of each partner having their own pot (growing resources or renewable energies). Mayer finds those metaphors to be performative insofar as they support individuals in their transitions from mono-normative affective codings to living polyamorously. Likewise, some of my interview partners considered love to be an unlimited resource, available in abundance (see also Halpern 1999).[8]

I would like to contrast the logic of scarcity with a concept of dyke + queer BDSM relationship practices as exuberant intimacy (cf. Pieper & Bauer 2014 for a related theorizing of polyamory as transformative desire drawing on Spinoza, Deleuze and Guattari). Exuberance is a term that denotes excess, a 'too muchness' that has been vital to queer history, culture and politics as part of drag and other flamboyance. Exuberance is derived from the Latin verb *uberare*, meaning to be fruitful (Merriam-Webster 2012). Exuberance denotes an unrestrained and exaggerated enthusiasm, abundance and superabundance, plenitude, lushness, lavishness, effervescence, joyousness, great happiness, excitement, ebullience, animation, liveliness, energy, zest, eagerness, jazziness, exhilaration, lustiness, sprightliness, vibrancy, vigorousness, fierceness and even madness. The adjective 'exuberant' describes something as abounding in high spirits, lavish, effusive, excessively elaborate, growing luxuriantly or in profusion (Farlex 2012; Merriam-Webster 2012). To me, this extensive list sounds wonderfully rich, a set of terms for discussing the excesses that desire produces and that cannot be contained.[9] The myriad meanings of exuberance resonate with a lot of the elements of dyke + queer BDSM practices as detailed by my interview partners.

First of all, polyamory, as the experience of multiple relationships or commitments, and sex-positivism, as a practice of multiple pleasures, can both be seen as based on a notion of an abundance of intimacy, emotional bonds and desires (an antithesis to the notion that a pre-existing lack is constitutive of non-monogamous behavior), as well as multiplying intimacies in the process (an antithesis to the notion that non-monogamy results in a lack in a relationship). A typical dyke + queer BDSM version of the abundance of pleasures is the concept of the (ethical) slut (see also Easton & Liszt 1997). The slut as a self-chosen identity is not burdened with a lack of character or with psychological deficiencies in her subjectivity; quite the opposite. S/he is exuberant in the sense of vibrant, fierce and lavish.[10] The reasons interview partners gave for choosing non-monogamy were also exuberant: the domino effect of perversion can be seen as another antithesis to the ideology of scarcity and lack. Breaking a social norm does not only cost energy but also stimulates further transgressions and may culminate in an identity as a sexual adventurer. This is a dynamic that can be described as exuberant, since it seems to provide my interview partners with more joy, more excitement and a greater abundance of possibilities to live their lives and to connect to others.

My interview partners also stated they had lots of different sexual needs or interests, and therefore not all of them could be met by a single person. This testifies to difference as a basic human principle, and, in this context, implies a sense of constantly multiplying and reinventing pleasures, desires and ways of intimate relating. Dyke + queer BDSM generated its own unique forms of relationship, such as mistress/master–slave, daddi–girl/boi or owner/puppy. The dyke + queer BDSM cultural context also produced intimate or sexual friendships and collective synergies. Sexual or intimate friendships were experienced by interview partners as enriched and animated, because the erotic, BDSM or sexual component added another dimension of vibrancy to a friendship; therefore, they too can be understood as forms of exuberant intimacy. Furthermore, there were synergetic effects described by my interview partners from non-monogamous dyke + queer BDSM practices, such as lending a bottom to another top, group sessions and play parties.

Polyamorous and self-defined slut femme bottom Mandy argued that generally many hands make really good work, and having more than four hands available for any kind of interaction is, I think, nothing but positive in a sort of 'more is better' [laughs loudly]. I used to have fantasies in which I would try to imagine – this is before I was quite into SM, although there was sort of holding down involved, there was certainly helplessness and paralyzing – but I tried to imagine how many people I could actually keep busy in my fantasy, doing things to me at the same time [laughs]. And where would the rest of their bodies go? [laughs loudly]

Mandy clearly described group sessions as a form of exuberant intimacy with her 'more is better' philosophy. Group sessions heightened the intensity for many interview partners; for instance, the experience of being overpowered or in charge was increased if several tops dominated one bottom.

Shared contained community spaces

At play parties, dyke + queer BDSM sexuality was taken out of the closet and celebrated in a sex-positive environment, which made it a good venue for finding play partners and, moreover, inspired many to take advantage of the option to play with more than one partner. My interview partners characterized this kind of play as *shared intimacy*. For many, the degree of intimacy established with their play partners was independent of whether the acts took place behind closed doors, between two people or with others present. Rather, intimacy was dependent on other parameters, such as the level of connection, congruence and focus between partners and the level of emotional involvement, but also on the atmosphere of the play party. Petra held that, while the session might be interrupted by distractions in a shared location, this did not disturb her connection to her play partners. Others found that violations of their play space boundaries might spoil a session, and some, therefore, reserved certain types of play for home. Generally, interrupting, commenting on or otherwise disturbing a scene was not allowed in play spaces. Dykes + queers were selective about whom to share their intimate experiences with. Many sought out women's and queer spaces specifically, as Anna indicated: 'I have personally never played publicly at a heterosexual party or let someone play with me, because I simply found that too intimate. Or where I was too afraid to show that to other people or too shameful.' As a transwoman, she felt too vulnerable to expose herself to heteronormative gazes.

To deal with potential distractions or violations of their space and situation, interview partners came up with ways to construct their own contained space within a shared play space. For many, this happened automatically through engulfment in their session, which made the surroundings disappear. In non-monogamous transwoman switch Daphne's words: 'So especially on the passive side, a bomb could blow up next to me during such play. I don't register it. There is only one person who I see, hear or feel, even if there are 100 000 other people.' To her, it was about a complete focus on her top. If a bottom had trouble in achieving this focus, there were various techniques that helped them, such as sensory deprivation or shielding the bottom from the audience with the top's own body. If partners were still not able to focus on each other, some play spaces provided half-secluded areas. Therefore, intimate erotic and sexual acts were shared in a contained community space in varying degrees.

My interview partners cited various motivations to play in collective spaces. One was the transgression of the social taboos associated with 'public sex': the pleasures of the risk of getting caught, exhibitionism and voyeurism could be acted out consensually and with minimized risk. Non-monogamous transguy top Matt explained:

> It adds to it. To do piss play at home in your shower with someone is one thing, but to be doing it in front of all these other people adds to it, makes it more hot on some levels. It adds a little dynamic of playing with that power of it, of it being socially unacceptable in sort of having people watch you.

So the transgression of certain socially unacceptable practices might be enhanced through exposure in front of others. The fact that sexuality was constructed as private in their cultural contexts enabled my interview partners to play with the feelings of exposure, shyness and shame that might arise when one is being watched during sexual acts. The witnesses function as symbolic embodiments of the culture that judges these practices negatively, and their presence intensifies the players' perception of the situation. So, if situations of intimacy are about crossing boundaries, about being exposed to others, then carrying out such practices in front of an audience increases the experience of intimacy. Therefore, this kind of play can be usefully understood as another way that intimacy can become exuberant. Moreover, the audience members may also experience watching as intimate, creating another layer of shared intimacies in collective spaces.

An intimate audience for an intimate theater

Playing in front of others generated an experience of being exposed, on display or on stage. My interview partners liked to watch others play. Some indulged in voyeurism in the sense that they got aroused, got erotic pleasure out of watching sessions or got into the right mood for their own play. Some enjoyed watching their partners play with others, admiring their session and sharing pleasure rather than reacting with competitive jealousy. This affective alternative could be termed polyvoyeurism and could be considered an erotic version of 'compersion'. Compersion is a term coined by the San Francisco Kerista commune in the 1970s, which means 'the positive warm feeling you experience when you see two of your partners having fun with each other; it is the antonym of jealousy' (Pines & Aronson 1981: 379; Wolfe 2003). The previous lack of a term for the opposite of jealousy is a powerful sign of the mono-normativity of our culture, since it literally makes alternative emotional experiences unspeakable. The polyamory community, just like the queer and trans* communities, is therefore trying to increase the intelligibility of their experiences by inventing new words (see also Ritchie & Barker 2006).

But, besides polyvoyeurism, sometimes my interview partners just liked to watch out of interest, to learn a new technique or get new ideas, for amusement or out of aesthetic appreciation without experiencing personal sexual excitement. My interview partners stated that they had learned a lot from watching others play, and that seeing others play had broadened their erotic horizons. Therefore, Mandy, who at the time of the interview had more than three decades of BDSM experience, concluded: 'It is amazing to me that most people in the world have never seen anyone have sex that they weren't a part of. Probably 99 per cent of the people in the world have never ever observed somebody else having sex. And that is ignorance to me.' This is an instance of reversing the hegemonic norm. To Mandy, it is not watching others have sex that is 'perverse' or in need of explanation; rather, not taking an interest in the different ways people have sex is a kind of (culturally induced) ignorance. This kind of ignorance is one of the ways in which heteronormativity and mono-normativity work to obscure the reality of sexual difference.

Likewise, not all interview partners who enjoyed playing in shared spaces were exhibitionists. There were other motives as well, such as presenting oneself to potential new play partners, demonstrating one's skills and style of play, and teaching and educating. But those who did consider themselves exhibitionistic described various ways in which being watched was gratifying or arousing: 'I am very, very much an exhibitionist. I will get so much more out of a scene if I'm being watched doing it. And it's an odd combination of feeling proud and feeling naughty and dirty [giggles]. But it does greatly increase my enjoyment to be in public.' So, to polyamorous dyke switch Michaela, the pleasures of exhibitionism came from a combination of different and potentially contradictory emotions, such as the shame or joy of breaking taboos ('feeling naughty and dirty') and pride in how she fulfilled her role. Therefore, exhibitionism is another instance of exuberant intimacy through the intensification of affective experiences. This was also evident in non-monogamous gay transman Jonas' case. He distinguished between exhibitionism as the desire to share one's pleasure with the audience, which is an affirmative and positive function, and exhibitionism as humiliation by using the audience as witnesses of shameful actions, thus enhancing negative emotions. For others, exhibitionism was mainly about receiving special attention, as non-monogamous transwoman femme Bell explained: 'I like to be center stage or on stage at least, if not center stage' [laughs]. She enjoyed the spotlight and fed off the energy of being watched. Anna also defined her exhibitionism in this vein, as being 'zeigefreudig' (gaining pleasure from showing off); she, femme Neila and Cara enjoyed the presentation of fetishes and unusual outfits and the admiration of the audience: exuberance in the sense of extravagance and camp.

In addition to erotic voyeurism and exhibitionism, how interview partners described the dynamics between players and audience may better be characterized as the *engaged presence* of others. Sharing their dyke + queer BDSM and sex with others was considered an extension of intimate space and a gift of trust. Furthermore, those watching usually described how they did so unobtrusively, with respect for the players' boundaries. Sometimes they were aware of the significance of being witnesses to certain rituals, and, in Femmeboy's words, were therefore 'engaged through observation'. Sometimes people were even negotiated into a scene as active witnesses: 'It was really nice to do that in front of my entire community, because these are the people that I've played with, that have gotten to cut me, that have shared this with me. So for me to share my final [cutting] with them really was meaningful.' Tanya had to give up being cut by others as part of her contract (which detailed the conditions for being fluid-bonded to her daddi). Therefore, it was important for her to share her final cutting in a kind of closure ritual with significant others who were witnesses, as in other social rituals.

Since a lot of dyke + queer BDSM can be understood as intimate theater (see Chapter 3), having an audience makes a lot of sense, as MCL mused: 'I was thinking about it once that a staging always needs an audience. Yes [laughs] so a role play, what is also a kind of theater, is nothing without an audience.' Likewise, polyamorous high femme Zoe considered the play parties in which she participated in the 1980s to be 'performance art, and we were there to astound each other with what we were gonna come up with today. And we used to do hilarious things on stage, too'. So the creative, artistic and humorous elements of dyke + queer BDSM also possessed an entertaining and inspiring quality for others. This is another way intimacy becomes exuberant – in the sense of flamboyant – in dyke + queer BDSM. Furthermore, the performance aspect is part of queer history and its culture of camp in general, with such institutions as drag shows and the cultural style of the high femme. Therefore, it may not come as a surprise that there seemed to be a strong overlap between some (then nascent) local drag king scenes and the dyke + queer BDSM communities in Germany. But the stage aspect may also have a downside, as Daphne remarked: 'Most of the plays that take place there are unaesthetic. People there play mostly just for an audience, that is somehow like: "Off topic, F, sit down!" [laughs] I don't like that.' So, if the participants are focusing too much on providing the audience with a show, it may be the wrong motivation for play and negatively impact the quality. Some interview partners also felt performance pressure and reported that high expectations might spoil sessions.

Synergies in creating spaces of shared intimacy

One feature of play party culture that interview partners valued could be characterized as synergetic effects, as non-monogamous lesbian butch top Luise concluded: 'And together with the others you create a "Gesamtkunstwerk" [cumulative work of art] in a way.' My interview partners felt they were producing something collectively beyond the individual sessions in shared play spaces. Their experiences were amplified through hearing, seeing and sensing others playing around them, and they enjoyed the visual quality and the sounds of others in proximity. BJ described his experience in play spaces if the energy around him felt right:

> I've been to some parties where it seems that collectively everybody was putting in their really intense energy. It was all very sexual and very hot, and the night really felt powerful and just everybody left charged and up and high. That's what I look for. I look for that kind of larger group of energy, larger group of giving this completeness to my scenes that you can only get playing in groups or in public.

To BJ, the collective experience of sharing BDSM energy in a group setting enhanced the quality and intensity of his BDSM in a way that he could not achieve in more isolated settings. This is some of the excess that is produced by collective BDSM spaces. The usage of the word 'energy' here is typical in that it is a term often used to try to describe something that cannot be captured with language, that represents the limits of discourse. The collectivity created that exceeds the individual is, therefore, another way that dyke + queer BDSM is a form of excessive exuberant experience.

But BJ also acknowledged that this is a fragile balance; just one session that is 'off' could spoil the whole collective experience energetically. Others also pointed out how some people only fed off the energy that was created collectively, but did not give anything back; this was a kind of selfish voyeurism they rejected. One instance of such egocentric behavior was referred to as the 'straight wanker problem': heterosexual cismen who visited mixed play parties to appropriate women and trans* people in particular as involuntary objects for masturbation. Zoe said: 'There were guys jerking off while watching us play. And I was just like: "I'm not your porn star!"' Others described how some heterosexual males objectified and commodified anyone they constructed as female and often displayed disrespectful and violating behaviors. Therefore, most interview partners preferred women's and trans* spaces in which they felt safer to express their dyke + queer BDSM selves and practices. Furthermore, they felt obligated to contribute something to play spaces and not simply act as consumers. If everyone present contributed and shared their experiences, then pansexual femme Neila concluded that a whole play party could effectively establish a situation of group intimacy (see also Newmahr 2010: 181). This is what I consider exuberant intimacy, creating an experience beyond the mono-normative ideas of dyadic containment, of intimacy as necessarily restricted to dyads in an insulated ('private') setting.

This kind of collective experience disrupts the public/private binary as well as concepts connected to it, such as the clear distinction between sexual and non-sexual relationships. What are the potentials of these moments of collective intimacy to disrupt hegemonic ways of imagining identity and community? If BJ rated collective experiences higher than the isolated interactions of couplehood, does this lead to a desire for and practices of communal forms of living beyond heteronormative models? Could it replace a model of sexual competitiveness, scarcity of resources and mono-normative possessiveness with a model of generous and solidary sharing of sexual and other resources?

While these questions might not be answered easily, it was evident that play parties presented a significant part of community-building. My interview partners were able to experience mutual validation, which served to depathologize dyke + queer BDSM and ultimately empowered them. But to be naked or sexual in front of others presented a challenge to some interview partners because of various kinds of body issues:

> Once we were at a play party in another state, and everybody there was just in street clothes and it was a very different scene. She made me put on white baby doll lingerie, white heels, white stockings, and a little pink bow in my hair, and walk all the way across this dungeon. She was at the farthest place. And I wouldn't say I was humiliated, but it was really hard, because there was no one else in lingerie, and I'm totally exposed and it was really hard to do, but I did it. And I got really rewarded. She was really sweet to me and very nurturing to me for doing that, because she knew it was hard.

Dyke femme Mistress Mean Mommy explained how, as a big woman, she always had difficulties feeling sexy and presenting her body in front of others self-confidently. Her top challenged and rewarded her in this instance for mastering such exposure in a kind of ordeal. Dyke + queer BDSMers thus paid each other respect for having the courage to expose themselves and to share intimacy.

Making themselves vulnerable in these ways was only possible within validating environments. It was common in the community to tell someone afterwards that their session was beautiful, fun to watch or made an impression. To Mistress Mean Mommy it made a big difference on the road to self-acceptance to be part of the dyke + queer BDSM community. Community reassurance was a way to fight shame around being different sexually or being openly sexual as women, as Mandy observed: 'But the deprivatization just takes a lot of that certain fear and loathing out of it. And this notion that everything is kind of sick and disgusting. It just takes the disgusting completely out of it.' It is not only the depathologization and the dissolution of shame around dyke + queer BDSM that took place, but, to Lola, Mandy and Emma, it was, furthermore, an appreciation of the beauty of the human body and sexuality per se. Mandy explained: 'You get to see and you learn. I mean, to my mind, everyone looks beautiful at the moment of orgasm. Old, young, fat, thin, whatever. They all look just amazing when they are coming. You see people get turned on and they become radiant. And it's so gorgeous.' So the dyke + queer BDSM shared intimacy culture fostered an acceptance of sexuality as a beautiful expression and generated a general sex-positive attitude. It also worked to foster a positive sense of self through a reality check: 'And so many of my own fears, including those body image fears, go away when I'm in an environment with other people. Because I can look around me, and I see that these people look beautiful to me, so I guess my fears are just fears.' Seeing others' beauty, even if their bodies did not meet mainstream beauty ideals, made Mandy simultaneously realize her own beauty. Interview partners of size in particular endorsed this effect. They all reported that the dyke + queer BDSM community had improved their body image (see Chapter 2 on beauty standards). And Mandy's approach to beauty as a universal condition of human pleasure presented a solidary, win-win alternative to logics of a sexual market of competitiveness, which relies on a hierarchical ranking of body types.[11]

Chapter conclusion

Why were alternative intimacies so common in dyke + queer BDSM communities? They developed a sexual culture that generated excessive desires. Dyke + queer BDSM practices were so multi-faceted and specific that the search for a perfect match in one partner seemed futile. My interview partners possessed highly developed sexual communication and negotiation skills to establish critical consent, and those skills were transferred to relationship practices. At the same time, their demythologization of sex made non-romantic intimacies acceptable, including the sexual friendship model. My interview partners also left behind heteronormative expectations about female sexuality, such as that women (and lesbians in particular in some discourses) are not highly sexual, that they enjoy sex only as an expression of love, and that they prefer to be monogamous. This enabled them to experiment with new forms of intimacies and sexual subjectivities, such as the figure of the slut. Certain properties intrinsic to BDSM dynamics have generated new, dyke + queer BDSM-specific ways of relating, for example using DS as a tool to deal with or overcome jealousy and other emotional inheritances from mono-normative culture. Finally, the domino effect of perversion makes it easier to engage in socially marginalized behaviors.

At this point the dyke + queer BDSM community provides novices with a variety of role models for alternative ways of intimate relating. My interview partners participated in shared intimacy practices, including group interactions and playing in shared contained spaces, such as play parties. Play parties served to deprivatize sex by performing it in front of an intimate audience. Sex could thus turn into a collective intimate experience, creating synergetic effects. These can be understood as a production of excesses beyond dyadic containment and mono-normativity. It is a plus that can be created, but cannot easily be appropriated as a commodity. As the experiences of interview partners have shown, once shared play spaces become more commercial, the group dynamic usually suffers and the creating of something communal is sabotaged, for instance because people who pay a (high) entrance fee might feel entitled to 'get their money's worth' without contributing to the collective situation. Only in contexts where the motives of participants go beyond consumption can these synergetic effects occur and collective experiences be created.

Based on my interviews, I have suggested redefining intimacy as being not simply about positive feelings of closeness, but about boundaries and their transgression, about access and exposure, about violations and touch. I have replaced the problematic public/private dichotomy with a more nuanced and empirical model of social spaces that are accessible, shared contained, contained or insulated spaces, and I have looked at the practices that are contained in accessible spaces. These distinctions are better suited to describing dyke + queer BDSM practices and their significance in terms of the various kinds of intimacies that certain spaces may generate, such as intimate friendships, group play, synergies, objectification, polyvoyeurism and so on. Dominance/submission generates specific kinds of intimacies and relationships, such as objectification and ownership. In general, my interview partners reported that BDSM generates its own unique kind of intimacy through the intensity of the practices and relationships. Therefore, dyke + queer BDSM can be usefully understood as exuberant intimacy, producing excess and abundance in various ways.

6
Exploring and Pushing Boundaries

The semi-contained space of dyke + queer BDSM, with its critically negotiated consent and experiences of alternative and exuberant intimacies, enabled interview partners to explore personal issues as well as social difference. Using this social space for exploration and experimentation was a recurring theme in all interviews. It will, therefore, be given special attention in the following three chapters. This chapter will situate the dyke + queer BDSM experience within the context of dangerous pleasures, of voluntary risk-taking. This sets the stage for exploring boundaries, vulnerabilities and bodies as boundary projects for my interview partners. Side effects included personal growth and healing, which can be transferred to other social realities beyond the semi-contained space of dyke + queer BDSM.

Dangerous pleasures: Dyke + queer BDSM as risk-taking

BDSM was perceived as a risk-taking activity by my interview partners, as lesbian transwoman femme switch Bell made clear: 'I wouldn't have somebody that I didn't trust tie me up, because I'm way too vulnerable.' Bottoms especially put themselves into a position that made them vulnerable to abuse, for instance if they were restrained. But, as Bell pointed out, this is not merely a technical matter of managing risk. Rather, she talked about the presence or absence of trust in the partner as a crucial element of addressing risk. This is significant because the risk-taking concerned not only physical, but also emotional harm, as pansexual femme top Anya stated in a matter-of-fact way: 'It will happen. I've fallen off. It happens. And then you fall back again.' For many interview partners, it was inevitable that some unintended dynamic would develop at some point along the path. Practicing BDSM thus entailed putting oneself in a vulnerable position, but not only as a bottom. Tops might also reveal parts of their psychic life that were usually condemned as ugly, pathological or unethical, and, in addition, in many countries tops especially might get into trouble with the law if anything went wrong. Therefore, all participants needed to be able to trust one another.

If Vance holds that any approach to women's sexuality is in need of a double perspective, that of dangers as well as pleasures (1992a), then dyke + queer BDSM was a field in which both were constantly highly visible, renegotiated and connected rather than posited as opposites or contradictions. Dyke + queer BDSMers used pleasures to work through dangers, both personal and social ones. And they created a space that allowed women to experiment with voluntary risk-taking. The various kinds of vulnerability – physical, emotional, legal – as the point of departure for dyke + queer BDSM encounters made it necessary to create a risk-reducing structure in which those activities could take place.

Safer play: Community guidelines

The dyke + queer and the overall BDSM communities have developed standards to provide their members with safety frames, enabling them to venture into their risk-taking activities in a semi-contained space. Today the most prominent BDSM community guideline is what is commonly referred to as SSC – *Safe, Sane and Consensual*. SSC was originally formulated in 1983 by david stein, and quickly became the most common ethical criteria of BDSM within the community.[1] Most interview partners referred to SSC as their standard, while others questioned the applicability of the concept or admitted to a certain amount of hypocrisy in publicly advocating SSC while not always acting accordingly. Some BDSM safety guidelines were considered suitable for teaching novices and presenting BDSM to the broader public, but too paternalistic for experienced players.

Queer transgender stone butch top Terry criticized the criterion of safety in SSC, because the illusion of absolute safety could provide people with a false sense of security. He drew an analogy to HIV and STD (*Sexually Transmitted Diseases*) prevention: one may choose safer options and practice safer sex, but there is no absolute safety.[2] Some interview partners questioned the concept of sanity as well: 'What sane means is hard to say actually in the light of the day. What is that supposed to be, mentally healthy, according to some psychological-psychiatric manuals, according to the ICD-10 or whatever? Who wants to be the judge?' Gay transman bottom Mik also rejected this criterion because it reminded him of psychiatric discourse and because there was no neutral definition. Others, like queer transwoman bottom Leslie, considered their own practices or inclination toward BDSM as *not* sane: 'And if it's sane – well, if I would be sane, I wouldn't be into S&M, I sometimes think. [laughs] That's also a point that's discussable from my point of view.' Her perspective seconded Mik's question about who gets to define what counts as sane behavior. Leslie's embracing of insanity may represent a powerful rejection of normalizing and sanitizing dyke + queer BDSM and of modern enlightenment discourses of reason in general. Rejecting the ideal of sanity can be considered a queer strategy to question the hegemonic regulations of difference and otherness through the concept of reason and rationality. In one sense, negotiated BDSM culture can be said to show that the alternative to rationality need not be irrational, irresponsible behavior (Ahrens 2006: 292). But, in another sense, the rejection of sanity can go further to radically celebrate the non-rational through exuberant, excessive, perverse and irrational intensity in dyke + queer BDSM practices. This self-positioning as 'crazy' in opposition to 'normal', heteronormative society can be considered another form of exuberance.

My interview partners displayed ambivalences about the dogmatic nature of SSC, but pointed out that sharing spaces required a common under-standing. Therefore, everyone agreed on some community guidelines, such as mutual respect and consideration. Balancing the necessity of guidelines with the restrictive, pleasure-negating and normative dimensions of rules remained a dilemma in dyke + queer BDSM. But the institutionalization and regulation of BDSM that Weiss described for the pansexual Bay Area commu-nity (2011: 74–5) was much less present in dyke + queer BDSM, especially in European contexts. My interview partners did not become BDSM practition-ers through negotiating the boundaries between safe and dangerous play (Weiss 2011: 62), but through engaging critically with power and negotiated consent.

The community was experienced by many interview partners as self-regulating in that it enforced its own standards through social control, such as providing references for responsible players and boycotting unsafe ones. Many interview partners considered playing at play parties to be safer than playing at home due to the public surveillance factor. On the other hand, interrupting a session was also a breach of general etiquette, and therefore people were reluctant to intervene unless it was deemed absolutely necessary. Moreover, most play happened outside the organized (dyke + queer) BDSM communities, and, thus, the social control had limits as well. BDSM culture has undergone significant changes in regard to how to learn to play safe(r)ly since the 1950s, when secretive circles of mostly gay men mentored each novice personally. In the 2010s, practically anyone can find information and like-minded individuals on the Internet.

Risk management strategies

Rather than assuming that BDSM practices can ever be completely safe phys-ically or psychologically, many interview partners identified with the notion of risk awareness, or safer play. Risk denotes the possibility that damage may occur. While in the larger society you are simply exposed to danger, in BDSM you are taking risks by your own decision. Thus, risk awareness stresses individual agency. One may distinguish between risk, as a statistically cal-culable or predictive model that considers the unknown future outcome of events, and uncertainty, as the non-calculable model that is relevant to the creative activity of the entrepreneur in neoliberalism (O'Malley 2000: 462). One might posit the more technical aspects of medical safety in BDSM as risk in this sense, such as acting responsibly on the knowledge that blows to the lower back may cause kidney damage. Then, in contrast, the emotional consequences of BDSM activities might be considered as uncertainty, since they are much less calculable. But one may also group the whole of BDSM under uncertainty in the sense that it is a creative activity with an open-ended outcome. I will follow the community discourse and use risk as a broad umbrella term for both concepts, risk and uncertainty, since these are no clear-cut categories in the context of BDSM.

It seems to me that the decision to take a risk is never based on calculable facts alone, but necessarily involves a leap of faith, since uncertainties always remain. In this, risk-taking is akin to trust; a risk-taker commonly trusts that s/he will not be harmed severely. There are also meta-risks; for instance, risk/danger is not distributed evenly across the population, but members of certain groups are exposed to more potential harms than others are; for instance, studies have shown that lower-class women are more at risk for unintended pregnancies and STDs (Higgins & Brown 2008). Risk, such as loss of health or work, is also (re)privatized in neoliberalism (Pieper 2003; Weiss 2011: 63). Yet this is also not true across the board, as the latest financial crises have shown: bankers are not held responsible for their own risk-taking practices. Thus, risk seems to be privatized for the underprivileged and those most at social risk to begin with. Risk is relative to who you are and how you are positioned socially. Certain areas of a city are perceived as dangerous for some people and as safe(r) for others, and this relative safety also depends on the time of day, whether one walks alone, as a couple or in a group and so on (Corteen 2002). Risk is gendered: in the US, men are 150 per cent more likely to be the victims of violent crimes than are women, but men are more likely to be attacked by a stranger, women by someone they know (Filipovic 2008: 23). Thus, contrary to hegemonic discourses on risk, women are most at risk in 'private' settings and safer in 'public' spheres. But the discourse on risk is gendered in a way that restricts the movement of women and gives (certain) men permission to claim public space fearlessly (Stanko 1987).

The kinds of social risks and dangers people are exposed to need to be taken into consideration when trying to understand the social phenomenon of voluntary risk-taking. In sociology, contemporary Western life has repeatedly been described using the concept of a risk society, positing that we live in a time when potentially catastrophic events are merely foreseeable, but not governable (Beck 1992; Giddens 1999). But these theories of modernization are often based on a romanticizing of 'premodern' times and places. They seem to assume that change, uncertainty, danger and risk are recent social phenomena, while I would suggest they are inherently part of human life. These theories also display an illusionary (masculinist) yearning to be in control of one's surroundings and the future. As one element in these discourses on safety and risk, dyke + queer BDSM can be understood as a phenomenon of voluntary risk-taking (Lyng 1990). Voluntary risk-taking is an interesting social phenomenon, because the subjects of neoliberalism are expected to make use of (rational) strategies to minimize their exposure to harm. Their liberty lies in the capacity to choose rationally among available options of risk management and to assemble a responsible lifestyle. At the same time, enterprising subjects are supposed to be risk-takers as well (O'Malley 2000: 465). These contradictory appellations of the neoliberal subject can be worked at in voluntary risk-taking activities such as BDSM, where one is supposed to be taking risks in a responsible manner.

Risk management in BDSM is one way of practicing care of the self in the Foucauldian sense (Woltersdorff 2010: 10). At the same time, taking voluntary risks in work and leisure is still largely considered a male quality (Nägele 1998). BDSM dyke and trans* interview partners ruptured this discourse. They were taking risks, and, moreover, their risks were purely for the self-serving purpose of erotic gratification, not for activities that women might socially get credit for, such as taking risks to protect their families or feed their children, or for financial gain as in the case of the entrepreneur. They also did not follow a stereotypically male pattern of voluntary risk-taking, which usually involves notions of conquering nature, being in control over the uncontrollable and, therefore, creating (illusory) feelings of omnipotence, and demonstrating special survival skills in a competitive environment (Lyng 1990). Largely, the edgeworkers Lyng describes operate as if in a social and ethical vacuum. In contrast, dyke + queer BDSMers included considerations of the ramifications of their risk-taking, turning it into a practice of taking care of themselves and their relationships to others, rather than creating a spectacle of demonstrating survival skills in a competitive context. They were also not deluding themselves by thinking that they were in control of the situations they entered into when practicing BDSM. Rather, risk awareness for my interview partners meant being informed about the potential risks of their practices and accepting the consequences, including the inevitability of the 'falling off' that Anya referred to. While edgework is certainly gendered, classed, raced and so on, this does not lead to any straightforward conclusions as to who might be interested in participating in voluntary risk-taking. It can make sense to both those who are usually hardly exposed to any risk, to seek a thrill or feel more alive, and those who are most at risk socially, to gain some temporary control over risk or simply face risk in a semi-contained setting.

The basic risk management strategy in dyke + queer BDSM was pre-negotiating to uncover personal limits, as discussed in Chapter 4. It was complemented by more technical guidelines, like avoiding intoxication. Other points were less obvious, such as one's mindset when approaching a scene, including the degree of focus. It was also important to assess the trustworthiness and skills of potential play partners beforehand to minimize risks. One might screen others by watching them play or by getting references from third parties. Certain personal traits set off alarm bells for dyke femme lifestyle submissive Tanya: 'I'm naturally just aware of certain formulas that make somebody not safe to play with. I mean a top or a dom[inant] that has severe control issues, an anger problem and low self-esteem [laughs] is not somebody I wanna play with.' The quality and level of trust of a play relationship was another factor in risk management. Most people restricted riskier activities to well-known partners and took extra safety measures with new partners, like ruling out bondage or playing in a community space to ensure social control.

Regulating levels of intensity during a session was another technique to manage risk. Most tops slowly increased intensity, and followed the bottom's signals and reactions. In order to fine-tune a session, a top needed attentiveness and, therefore, the ability to stay focused. If one paid close attention to a bottom's body language, one was able to 'read' them, a skill that had to be learned with experience, as gay transman switch BJ explained:

> Or you're kinda scared of knives, but you wanna do a knife scene where somebody uses a knife to threaten you and threatens to fuck you with it, but you're scared, yet turned on. I don't need you telling me that, I can read that in the way your body responds to me and the knife. I know.

In general, reading someone reliably improved over time. Medical and psychological knowledge might help to read strangers to a certain extent, but subtle signs like a tone of voice or what silence meant were more accurately interpreted with long-term play partners.

Facing vulnerabilities through trust

Voluntary risk-taking in dyke + queer BDSM meant opening up a space to face one's vulnerabilities. Exploring vulnerability was a significant part of practicing dyke + queer BDSM for my interview partners. Queer femme switch Emma stated: 'So to give up control, to choose to give up control is a very scary thing to do. And women especially have not been given permission to say no.' Overcoming the fear of giving up control, especially for women in a world where their limits are often not respected, was a challenge. Therefore, establishing a framework of emotional safety was important for interview partners: 'I like to clarify beforehand and I am rather someone who prefers a hint too much [pre-negotiation], but then clarified. You can also talk something to death, but I'd rather take that risk then. In that regard my soul is somehow rather important to me, the safety of my soul.' In this quote, pansexual genderqueer femme switch Neila stressed the significance of feeling safe as a precondition for participating in BDSM. Trust in one's play partner was crucial for emotional safety in BDSM (see also Zussman &

Pierce 1998: 23), and, even more broadly, trust is the basis for individual risk-taking behavior and co-operation, performing vital social functions (Möllering 2001: 404).

For my interview partners, trust was a prerequisite for giving up control and taking risks. It was mostly developed over time in an ongoing play relationship, but it was also attributed to a stranger based on references from a trusted third party. Reliability might be understood as specific and limited to a particular thing (such as being reliable in respecting other's limits), while trust might be understood as more encompassing, as in trusting in the overall integrity and ethical behaviors of a person. Yet trust necessarily involves an element of uncertainty, if we follow Möllering's useful definition of trust as a state of favorable expectation regarding other people's actions and intentions (2001: 404), which summarizes the state of mind with which interview partners approached their BDSM encounters. If they did not have these favorable expectations in a particular situation, they usually refrained from playing. Yet they did not base their trust on ruling out certain possibilities or future developments, as some sociologists hold (Luhmann 1979; Lewis & Weigert 1985); rather, they remained aware of the risks they were taking.

Another typical feature of trust highlighted by previous research is that trust takes over where exact knowledge of a situation is not available (Giddens 1990). Exact knowledge is hardly ever available, because the uncertainty of outcomes is a basic persistent feature of social interactions and life in general. Yet people are forced to act even in the absence of trust. What distinguishes social constellations of trust from those without trust is, thus, neither lack of knowledge nor paralysis of action. Rather, trust makes a difference in how the situation is perceived by the individual (expectations of favorable outcome), and, therefore, has an influence on what kinds of risks one is actively choosing or seeking, rather than simply being exposed to them. Furthermore, the perception of heightened risk may increase the experience of trust in BDSM encounters (Newmahr 2011: 150). Following Simmel, Möllering emphasizes that trust necessarily involves an irrational element in addition to rational calculations, which can be best characterized as a leap of faith (Simmel 1990; Möllering 2001). This was most obviously the case when interview partners agreed to play with new partners. What remains problematic about these theories of trust is that they stay attached to a model that privileges the rational 'good reasons' to trust someone over the irrational element, the leap of faith (if they even acknowledge its existence), implying that judgment based on the irrational, the emotional, the intuitive is less reliable than judgment based on the rational. But this was not necessarily the experience of my interview partners, who were very aware of the limitations of predicting risk and safety and often experienced the most favorable outcomes in their BDSM encounters when following their intuition. Therefore, future research on trust needs to pay more attention to the function of the non-rational without the foregone conclusion that this is an element that introduces instability into concepts of trust and safety and into social interactions in general.

Encountering risky and dangerous situations was what gave pleasure to those who enjoyed playing on the edge, yet they were still subject to some degree of risk management. Some enjoyed so-called 'mindfucks', where one partner might really believe the risk is real, when in fact it is not. Bisexual femme lifestyle Mistress Mz Dre described a gun play scene:

> [My slave] said: 'I don't even know if there's bullets in it.' You know what, there was bullets in it, oh shit, that was good. [laughs loudly] There was bullets in it. But I didn't have my hand like this, I had my hand like this [shows how the finger is not on the trigger]. And my hand was stiff, OK? [laughs] But her head was fucked up, saying: 'Is it loaded, or did I take the bullets out?' I was using that as a tease, but at that time of the statement, she'd forgotten herself.

The fact that her slave, who owned the gun that was spontaneously used in the session by Mz Dre, had forgotten herself whether it was loaded or not, made it one of the most intense scenes of her life. Yet her Mistress knew the whole time there was no real danger involved. This intense experience was created by the trust between play partners that enabled them to push the game to the limits and play with the fear of death.

Many interview partners stressed the significance of emotional risks over mere physical risks in dyke + queer BDSM. Most physical risks were largely a matter of technique and could be managed, while the emotional risks could never be completely controlled:

> Because sometimes you're really playing with big things, and sometimes you can't see what's going to happen. Sometimes it's like touchy things and then all of a sudden your mind goes in that direction, and you go into something where you don't wanna be or in a space you don't wanna be.

As gay transmasculine switch Craig discussed here, the psychological dynamics of BDSM functioned according to their own rules and were not completely predictable. For some, a session might always trigger past experiences of traumatization and so on. For queer femme switch Katharina, difficult emotions were part of the motivation to participate in dyke + queer BDSM: 'Why should I practice SM if I don't want to deal with feelings? And those are not always only little, fluffy bunnies that hop around on flower meadows. But it does hurt, and that is one of the reasons why I find SM so intriguing, because it approaches these borderlands.' What was characteristic of many dyke + queer BDSM practitioners was their acceptance of difficult, unpredictable and limit experiences as part of life in general, but

BDSM interactions in particular, since they provided a different setting from everyday reality to deal with difficult emotions. One had to be willing to take the consequences of risk-taking if one pursued this path.

My interview partners accepted challenging or disquieting emotions in dyke + queer BDSM because they assigned great value to the intensity of their experiences. In dyke + queer BDSM, the quest for intense experiences overrode the social imperative to feel comfortable. Affects conventionally considered to be negative and avoidable, such as pain, humiliation, restraint, dependence, deprivation, exposure, helplessness or fear, were infused with different values and different meanings. Intense experiences were created through facing one's own vulnerabilities in a semi-contained setting. Moreover, dyke + queer BDSM served as a space to enable and validate intimate vulnerabilities. Queer-straight femme bottom Teresa described how her little girl persona was treated by her play partners: 'Being valued for my vulnerability, being valued for how much strength it takes in this world to be vulnerable, to not shut down.' In this perspective, opening up to the world bodily and emotionally is an act of strength, requiring agency, rather than a sign of a state of oppression, weakness or passivity. Through this validating context for showing vulnerability and opening oneself to the impressions others leave, dyke + queer BDSM might open up a space for different kinds of embodiments and subjectivities. According to Deleuze, affects (and desires) are what happen to us, across our bodies, as singular events (Deleuze 1996). Therefore, affects are intense experiences, because they force themselves upon us and they cannot be controlled by reason. Intensities, therefore, play an important role in the process of producing what Deleuze and Guattari call a Body without Organs (BwO). To find this BwO, one has to dismantle the self (Deleuze & Guattari 2004: 167), and it is made in such a way that it can be populated only by intensities, which circulate across and throughout it (169). This state of being a BwO was, indeed, described in the interviews, especially in discussions of sensation play and spiritual experiences.

The function of time as linear was one of the partial suspensions of ordinary reality that occurred in dyke + queer BDSM, as described by my interview partners, and this is another way in which it opened up a space for reconstructing bodies and selves or producing a BwO. The semi-contained space of dyke + queer BDSM allowed interview partners to re-enter situations of past violations or other processes of subjectification. Furthermore, an important aspect of BDSM is restraint, the suspension of release. Bottoms especially may spend a lot of time holding out, prolonging the intensity of a situation, resisting early closure and, therefore, opening up intimate spaces for reworking processes of subjectification (see also Freeman 2008: 49). One could, therefore, understand certain dyke + queer BDSM scenarios as providing the space for tarrying. Stephenson and Papadopoulos theorize tarrying as an intervention in time that expands the present (Stephenson &

Papadopoulos 2006: 168).[3] Tarrying entails the dissolution of the reflexive subject, and immanent experience may unfold in space and time without constituting a coherent subject. Tarrying involves a mode of being in the situation, a move beyond the self, enabling the permeation of experience into the world (169). This is exactly the potential dyke + queer BDSM situations hold because of their intensity and depth of experience. Thus, dyke + queer BDSM provides a space to seek out experiences of tarrying to work on subjectivities rather than being dependent upon encountering a space of tarrying by chance. That is why interview partners experienced dyke + queer BDSM as a space of exploration of the self. Stephenson and Papadopoulos understand tarrying as a precondition for micropolitics, because political action involves working with potentials (2006: 169). What they envision as the space of tarrying is not unlike what Deleuze and Guattari describe as the plane of consistency, or immanence. This is the space in which form is constantly dissolved, freeing time and speed; it is the space of deterritorialization, desubjectification, but also of proliferation (2004: 294–7), the space that enables becomings and the construction of the BwO.

Experimentation is a significant mode of the plane of immanence (313). Again, dyke + queer BDSM holds the potential to provide such a space, especially since it keeps the minimum of structure, which Deleuze and Guattari find necessary, through its construction of a semi-contained, safer space in which to experiment. Deleuze and Guattari do indeed discuss masochism as a possible path to the BwO, but they err when they conclude that the masochist has produced a BwO in a way that can only be populated by pain waves (168), perhaps because their understanding of masochism is limited to clinical and literary cases. For my interview partners, the BwO also opened up pathways of becomings and transformations (see Chapter 8). Moreover, in sensation play, pain waves are interwoven with pleasures. But these pleasures are not necessarily reterritorializing either, because they do not always enable a person to find themselves, to return to the state of a subject, as Deleuze and Guattari insist (2004: 173). Rather, these pleasures also turn into waves of intensities, especially the kind of excessive, ambivalent pain-pleasures, powerlessness-pleasures, humiliation-pleasures and so on that are common to the dyke + queer BDSM experience, and these intensities produce BwOs.

This intensity, this depth of experience, was one of the typical characteristics of dyke + queer BDSM and a main reason for many to engage in it. Intensity was generated through the administering of intense sensation/pain, the immobilization of the body, sensory deprivation, surrender and loss of control, the transgression of cultural taboos (for instance, in incest play), the delving into other personalities in role play and generally through the (physical and emotional) risk-taking nature of BDSM. All these intensified sexual and relationship practices can also be characterized as exuberant intimacy, as intimate relating that flaunts social difference and boundary transgressions of various kinds; it is all 'too much'. Indeed, various interview partners reported that they had faced the accusation throughout their lives that they were 'too' something (too dirty, too sexual, too feminine, too butch, too wild), or simply 'too much' without further specification. They were embodiments of exuberance.

Exploring boundaries

One of the risks that interview partners took when engaging in dyke + queer BDSM concerned exploring, experimenting with and transgressing boundaries. Encountering and learning about personal boundaries played a significant role, and for some interview partners it was even the purpose of practicing BDSM, as butch lesbian top Luise put it: 'I think that SM serves to encounter one's limits. I think that is exactly what makes it appealing. And I enjoy playing with that very much.' This entailed stepping outside one's 'comfort zone', making oneself vulnerable and conducting open-ended experiments of the self, but all within a social context, rather than as a supposedly solitary endeavor. The semi-contained space of dyke + queer BDSM provided interview partners with the opportunity to explore their own boundaries, power dynamics and social difference in what could be described as boundary experiences or edgework (Lyng 1990).

Dyke + queer BDSM as a space for exploring

My interview partners experienced dyke + queer BDSM as a valuable tool for exploring social norms and the constitutions of the situated self:

> I think it's because we try to get in touch with a deeper self than the kind of superficial persona that we put out to people. I think that BDSM is about exploration in a very different way. It's about crossing borders, it's about pushing buttons, looking behind things, why is it that way. It's about no longer accepting the party line that good little girls do this and good little boys do that. It's about being a woman and saying: 'I feel like a boy, I feel like a nine-year-old boy, and I want my mommy to spank me for cutting down a tree.' Whatever. It's being able to go outside of your limited world view that you have been taught.

As dyke femme switch Mistress Mean Mommy elaborated, dyke + queer BDSM served as a space to look beyond the social constructions of what it means to be a woman or a man, crossing boundaries of gender and age in particular in order to change one's position in the social landscape and gain a differently embodied and situated perspective. This was possible through the structure dyke + queer BDSM provided; it enabled her to choose her own role or identity in play.

Interview partners again and again stressed that dyke + queer BDSM provided them with a space to explore and experiment through taking on different roles and subjecting themselves to different social situations. Mistress Mean Mommy went on to explain:

> We get to explore. For me it's no different than reading a book. I always use as an example James Joyce's 'Portrait of the Artist as a Young Man'. I can't understand what it's like to be a 15-year-old Irish boy in an all boys' boarding school. But I can read the book and have a sense of what it's like. So if you wanna go out and buy a schoolboy's uniform and wear it and have somebody be the school master and I get to play it, now I have a sense of what it's like, even as me in my body as a woman. I'll never be a 15-year-old boy. I get to experience what I think a 15-year-old boy would be like. And that might be freeing in some way. Maybe it will give me a different perspective, maybe I'll suddenly understand something I never understood about young boys.

While she used the analogy of reading a book, she also pointed out the difference: BDSM not only facilitates understanding different perspectives intellectually, but is also an *embodied* experience. Dyke + queer BDSM provided gay transman Jonas with opportunities for embodied reflexivity:

> What is, I think, really important to me is that I get things clearer in my head if I do them instead of talking about them. Intellectually, I can talk about all kinds of things really wonderfully and babble on for years, and still nothing happens in the heart. But my possibility to really engage with something is to experience it.

Jonas was not the only one who found that experiencing specific situations in BDSM gave him the ability to deal with personal issues with much more depth of engagement and understanding, because it is embodied and affective and not restricted to intellectual investigation of the self. Mistress Mean Mommy's quote also highlights the simultaneity of differing realities, like the experience of being a 15-year-old boy in a grown woman's body. She was aware that whatever understanding she might gain was not identical to the experience of the original boy, but was *her* perspective on *his* position. Yet she also knew that it might facilitate connections across social boundaries: 'maybe I'll suddenly understand something I never understood about young boys'. Thus, dyke + queer BDSM as practiced by my interview partners may function to produce those partial connections that Haraway has envisioned as the basis of an alternative way of knowing through situated knowledges:

> The knowing self is partial in all its guises, never finished, whole, simply there and original; it is always constructed and stitched together and

therefore able to join with another, to see together without claiming to be another. Here is the promise of objectivity: a scientific knower seeks the subject position not of identity, but of objectivity; that is, partial connection.

(1991: 193)

Although my interview partners might not necessarily think of themselves as scientific knowers, they, nonetheless, were invested in the project of investigating and understanding themselves in a network of social power relations. They were highly aware of the partialness and embodied situatedness of their perspectives and were, therefore, able to explore realities different from their own, to potentially see together without claiming to be another. In this sense, dyke + queer BDSM might become a tool for building solidarity as critical, power-sensitive connection across differences.

Another way to understand the processes in dyke + queer BDSM explorations is the framework of becoming developed by Deleuze and Guattari (2004). As explained above, dyke + queer BDSM can be conceptualized in various ways, such as intimate theater, a game, playing and so on, depending on the specific acts and personalities involved. But it also represented its own kind of reality to interview partners, its own particular kind of social space, its own type of energies, intensities and embodied experiences, which were distinct from anything else they encountered in their lives. This is why the concept of becoming by Deleuze and Guattari captures the potentials of the dyke + queer BDSM experience more accurately than merely understanding it as play-acting, for instance. According to these theorists, becoming is a process that goes beyond playing, imitating and identifying, beyond dreams and fantasies (2004: 262). Rather, it produces nothing but itself and its own kind of reality (263). Coming back to Mistress Mean Mommy's example, we can see that embodying a schoolboy as a grown woman is not about imitation or playing in the sense of deluding herself that she actually is that particular boy from the novel or an ordinary boy from down the street. Rather, what happens in this kind of dyke + queer BDSM practice is that the individual enters into a composition with other elements (schoolboy uniform, headmaster, punishment with a paddle) to produce a situation of becoming (289). This becoming is a process of desire (300); starting from the position of a grown-up woman, she transforms herself and enters a zone of proximity with a molecular other (303), in this case a young boy, but it might also be an animal, a vampire and so on. Deleuze and Guattari contrast the molar with the molecular; the molar is the overcoded category, like 'the human', 'the woman', whereas the molecular entity is the effect of deterritorialization, of becoming, of multiplicities. All becomings are molecular (303). A becoming is the in-between, the border or line of flight; as in Mistress Mean Mommy's quote, it is not about actually being a boy or 'the boy', but about becoming boy in the body of woman, experimenting with what that body can do as a boy. It, therefore, creates something else entirely, neither boy nor woman; it is its own reality.

Age play practices in general represented a way to enter a block of becoming-child. As Katharina explained:

I believe [my girl persona] communicates, it is her voice which speaks then. But it is not necessarily her body things are being done to. That to me is always a bit diffuse, that I experience such strange parallel realities then like: I am talking with a five-year-old voice, the body feels simultaneously somehow teeny-like, somehow puberty-like, but simultaneously also really grown-up, female at the same time or femme respectively.

Katharina remained aware that she was enacting a girl persona with the actual background, experiences and body of a 34-year-old; she experienced simultaneous realities in age play and engaged in adult versions of certain child ages. Deleuze and Guattari insist that there is a reality specific to becoming (2004: 263), and that becoming is an anti-memory (324); in other words, becoming-girl in age play is not about re-enacting scenes from one's actual childhood, but a molecular child is produced that co-exists with Katharina in a childhood becoming (324). This was evident in the self-dynamics these personas often developed. Sometimes they even got their own names. Often they resembled in part a child one could have been in a kind of alternative time-line or reality, for instance, becoming another gender. This molecular child changed both the state of being adult and the meaning of childhood (Deleuze & Guattari 2004: 324) for interview partners; it expanded the repertoire of their 'adult' behaviors. My interview partners traded on social constructions of children to enrich their emotional lives by freeing them from the constant social pressure to act 'grown-up' and rational, entering processes of becoming-child.

This kind of becoming-child also questioned the logic of the molar child whose future is the adult in terms of gender; a child does not necessarily grow up to be an adult in the gender they were assigned. For many interview partners from the FTM spectrum, the lack of a boy childhood was a significant one, which they could compensate for through the boy/i role. While these practices were related to the actual childhoods of interview partners, they were still becomings rather than simply reterritorializing engagements with memory, because they invented new ways of being-child in the present (see also Bauer n.d.).

Becoming can also be seen as another element of exuberance, since it is about the expansion of desires and intensities beyond the containment of the subject. It opens up the body to connect across boundaries with other heterogeneous elements to produce individuals that are infinite multiplicities (Deleuze & Guattari 2004: 280).

One of the preconditions for using dyke + queer BDSM as a space for sexual exploration was the crossing of the line of what was socially accepted sexuality and embracing an outsider status: 'Once we got outside the box, we were outside the box. We were just: "All right, let's go!" So yeah, we did piercing, we did branding, mummification, suturing, suspension, what else? Flogging, caning, scarification, cuttings, we were just like: "Yeehaw, let's go!"' In queer high femme switch Zoe's perspective, once she was not tying herself to society's expectations anymore, the doors opened to vast experimentation. This resonated with Foucault's description of gay BDSM spaces in San Francisco and New York City as laboratories of sexual experimentation (1996: 330). Related to this was an attitude of staying open to new experiences as a community value, as queer femme bottom Ellen pinpointed: 'I also think it's good to not put limits on this and say: "I'm never gonna do something."' This 'never say never' attitude stemmed from a common experience in the community that boundaries were constantly changing, and practitioners usually expanded their repertoire of practices significantly over time. Thus, if one did not stay open to experimentation, s/he risked missing out on great new experiences.

Playing taboo: Cultural boundaries

Terry and others considered dyke + queer BDSM to be a role model for how to deal with personal as well as cultural boundaries. Cultural boundaries were often discussed as taboos: specific cultural prohibitions that are not to be touched, that are not to be spoken out loud. Bataille points out that transgressing a prohibition or taboo suspends it temporarily without abolishing it (Bataille 1994: 38), and often the transgression is as regulated as the law itself (65). This was also the case for dyke + queer BDSM with its community standards. Bataille holds that the taboo is eroticized because it is waiting to be violated; without violation, it would not exist. And he sees this transgression as the main element of the erotic (327). The erotic is about intensity (13) and the dissolution of constituted forms (21). The erotic to Bataille is sexuality as self-experience (315). Thus, to Bataille, taboos are erotically charged, and transgressing them may provide one with an especially intense erotic experience.

Dyke + queer BDSM made use of this mechanism. There were various ways in which interview partners explored taboos from their social contexts through role play: gender privilege play (play that draws on cultural sexism), homophobia play, transphobia play, incest or intergenerational play (see Chapter 8). Hornsby holds that lesbian BDSM incorporates roles that play on the taboos that Bataille deems particularly transgressive, such as incest and rape (1999: 67–8). Cultural taboos were one way dyke + queer BDSMers referred to the real social world to generate pleasures. But engagement with certain cultural taboos, such as racism, in BDSM still remained too loaded for most interview partners. Thus, it is necessary to differentiate between the various kinds of social differences and cultural taboos.

Pushing boundaries

My interview partners engaged with cultural taboos as well as with personal boundaries. Partly, personal boundaries coincided with cultural taboos, such as incest or piss play, but not all personal boundaries resonated with society's value judgments. A lot of personal limits had to do with individual histories and individual personalities. My interview partners used dyke + queer BDSM practices as a way to deal with these boundaries and limits. Because complete self-transparency is impossible, crossing limits was a regular part of exploring through BDSM, since one could not possibly know all one's personal boundaries before encountering them. Yosh, who defined as a bottom and was biologically female but felt in-between genders, even planned a session to detect her personal limits:

> I am incredibly curious in regard to that. On the one hand I am a bit nervous, anxious, because I don't know where we will end up finally. But on the other hand rather curious as well, because I want to know where the hard core is, where this point is inside myself where I say of my own volition: 'No step further.' Where such a self-defense thing applies then as well. Because I have never felt that until now, and I don't know where it is, if it exists at all. And I am simply really curious about it, so there is rather a huge, huge amount of self-awareness involved.

Pushing against personal limits served to gain self-knowledge in the eyes of interview partners, because it was the only way to find out where the personal boundaries were and what they meant to the individual. This resonates well with phenomenology-inspired approaches to understanding the body as the basis of interacting with the surrounding world.

It is only through pushing oneself to the limit that a self is actually experienced as distinct from its surroundings. In Yosh's description, the lack of what she calls a basic mechanism of self-defense or self-preservation suggests a state of the self as not ultimately distinguishable from its surroundings. What Yosh seems to have sought in the planned session is a process of reterritorialization in a situation that resembles the plane of immanence in the sense that her body is almost imperceptible (Deleuze & Guattari 2004). Jonas thought that people with boundary issues might be drawn to dyke + queer BDSM for this very reason, which was double-edged:

> That's an important problematic issue I believe, because in my experience a relatively high share of SM practitioners have issues with their own boundaries. That is a reason for many to practice SM in the first place in

order to encounter their own limits, to locate their own boundaries in the first place.

On the one hand, dyke + queer BDSM provided a frame in which to learn about one's boundaries; on the other hand, not being aware of one's own limits complicated negotiating consent.

It was significant that many interview partners de-dramatized boundary violations if they happened within a consensual and respectful BDSM framework. Lesbian/bisexual butch switch Erika believed that 'finding limits and definitions should play a conscious role in the life of a human and that you can approach these boundaries playfully and should do so to rob them of their severity and heaviness'. So dyke + queer BDSM often provided a space to learn about personal limits. Moreover, the trust that boundaries would be respected enabled interview partners to renegotiate and push them, as Emma explained: 'Once we have a "no" that we absolutely believe will be heard and respected, it allows us to go a little bit further with our "yes".' Because you can push that boundary knowing that at any point you get to say "no".' So, respecting boundaries did not necessarily consolidate them, but, rather, made them more porous, permeable and fluid.

A lot of dyke + queer BDSM was about pushing boundaries within a secured setting. It, therefore, presented a space suitable to work on becoming a Deleuzian/Guattarian BwO, because it provided situations of deterritorialization coupled with processes of reterritorialization, avoiding the danger of annihilation (Deleuze & Guattari 2004: 167–83). For instance, queer/gay transguy top Matt pointed out that it was important to distinguish between the boundaries to push and those to keep:

> I don't like it when people touch my chest. And I am having chest surgery in a couple of weeks actually, but that's not something that I would be interested in changing. That's just how it is. It doesn't bother me. There are certain boundaries I have for other reasons, because of socialization or fear or whatever, and those are things that I'm interested in changing, for example penetration.

To Matt, it did not make any sense to try to change limits that were part of his transmale identity. But other boundaries were limiting his options in play and life in general, and, therefore, he was interested in overcoming them eventually.

Many interview partners shared the value of pushing boundaries in this way. To some, transgression represented a progressive micropolitics, as queer genderqueer switch Femmeboy stated: 'Anything that limits me feels repressive and is against my political stance.' Deleuze and Guattari (2004) also call for a focus on how we might become, how we might extend life to its fullest potential, expand life as a whole beyond limited and limiting perspectives. Femmeboy's stance of pushing all boundaries through dyke + queer BDSM practices can, therefore, be considered an example of leaving behind morality, with its distinction between good and evil, and developing an ethics of potentialities instead, maximizing the power of producing new and previously unimagined styles of thinking and being. To others, like Teresa, transgression might also become a reactionary goal: 'I think that trying to be transgressive is kind of reactionary, because it stops being about what feels best to you and following your pleasure. And it becomes about reacting to the Victorian morals.' Thus, if transgression is reduced to a counter-reaction to hegemonic values, it may block the process of following one's own path and restrict choices once again (to counteridentifications instead of disidentifications or deconstructions). The logic of transgression may also unwittingly promote one-dimensional perspectives on social hierarchies, since it furthers images of clear-cut binaries, which are separated by a line one may cross (Haritaworn 2005; Klesse 2007: 16).

What counts as transgressive depends on the social context. For instance, the Victorian morals Teresa referred to are race, gender and class-specific. Thus, sexual behavioral limits are not identical for women from different class and racial backgrounds. This complicates any notion of what makes a transgression subversive or reactionary. Moreover, a politics of transgression faces clear limits when it comes to the material aspects of oppression (Raymond 1997). Woltersdorff asks: if the erotic is theorized as the desire to transgress, from which positions of stability does this desire depart in the first place, such as economic privilege (2011b: 167)? This is also a problem with Deleuze and Guattari's concept of becoming, which, for them, is necessarily about becoming minoritarian (2004: 320–3). This makes the minoritarian the matrix of becoming for majoritarian subjects without a critical discussion of the costs of such processes of appropriation. For instance, if middle-class interview partners fetishize working-class bodies as sexier (see Chapter 7), transgressing the class line may be liberating for them, but not necessarily for working-class people, since it reinscribes sexual stereotypes about them. Therefore, it is important to understand transgression as a concept of limited political value and to distinguish transgressions that purely generate pleasures or other benefits for majoritarian subject positions from those that also effectively bring about social transformations. For example, if role-playing across class lines provoked further interrogations of class privilege and informed future political actions, it might become transformative. On the other hand, Teresa also held that it was necessary to transgress limits that were based on social norms and related fears. To her, extending boundaries could then become a tool to counter social domination.

Ahmed states that fear involves reading the openness of the body to the world as dangerous, and therefore the body shrinks in fear (Ahmed

2004: 69). Consequently, a politics of fear is often narrated as border anxiety (76). The semi-contained space of dyke + queer BDSM may serve as a tool to approach such fears and to establish a different relationship with them, as Teresa proposed, especially since dyke + queer BDSM as a disidentificatory practice enables the simultaneous welcoming and shrinking away of the body when playing with fear. My interview partners reported feeling liberated after pushing a boundary because the fear associated with that particular limit or taboo vanished. This, in effect, broadened the choices of actions available to them in life. Through testing limits, my interview partners learned not only about the nature of their boundaries, but also about the significance of possessing boundaries and how to assert them. Dyke + queer BDSM became a practice field for setting and keeping boundaries.

There were also limits to explorations and transgressions, such as the political beliefs of interview partners. The great majority avoided playing with racist[4] or Nazi scenarios. This was one difference from the pansexual BDSM community Weiss studied (2011: 187–231), and shows that the politics of BDSM are negotiated differently in different community contexts. These kinds of community ethics and regulations might be one of the reasons why some interview partners sought to find ways to preserve the transgressive nature of dyke + queer BDSM through what they called *edge play* or *nonconsensual consensual play*. There seemed to be two different definitions of edge play. One approach was to call any play that confronted an individual with a personal boundary edge play. Thus, to one person eating from a bowl on the floor may be humiliating edge play, while for another it was just a fun part of becoming-dog. The other definition was more specific and mostly referred to practices that challenged the notion of SSC. Edge play in this sense included practices that were considered to be of high risk, such as asphyxiation; practices that confused the boundaries between fantasy and reality, such as certain mindfucks; practices that played on the theme of transgressing the notion of consent, such as rape or abduction scenarios or playing without safewords; and, finally, practices that violated social or community ethics, such as racially degrading play or incest play.

Some interview partners felt restricted by community norms and kept their edge play private to avoid judgments, while to others challenging community members with their edgy practices was another sexually stimulating boundary transgression. Those who identified their own practices as edge play in this latter sense, therefore, positioned themselves discursively as the rebels within the community. This self-positioning documented arguments about the ethical boundaries of what counts as responsible BDSM. It cannot be taken as proof that the rest of the BDSM dykes + queers did not play with and push their own edges, but, rather, that those activities experienced as edgy by them were not considered unethical, dangerous or politically suspicious by community standards. While edge play in the second sense was restricted to a subset of my sample, edge play in the first sense of confronting and pushing personal boundaries in dyke + queer BDSM practices was a common theme in all interviews.

My study, therefore, confirmed Newmahr's characterization of BDSM as edgework (2011: 144–86). While Weiss only considers edge play in the second sense as edgework (2011: 87), my findings suggest that exploring and pushing boundaries applies to the dyke + queer BDSM experience in general, and that BDSM is, therefore, usefully understood as intimate edgework. Newmahr draws on Lyng's concept of edgework (1990), but reassesses it from a feminist and BDSM perspective as collaborative, contextual and including the realm of emotional risk-taking (160). Lyng defines edgework as voluntary high-risk behavior involving negotiating the boundaries between chaos and order, life and death, consciousness and unconsciousness, sanity and insanity (1990: 855f). Edgework activities involve a threat to one's physical or mental well-being or one's sense of an ordered existence (857), testing limits of body and mind (858). Edgeworkers experience an alteration in perception and consciousness and a heightened sense of self (860–1). Many of these elements are describing an out-of-the-ordinary experience that is typical for BDSM, but Lyng's edgework differs from dyke + queer BDSM in the feelings of omnipotence (861) and the illusory conviction of the edgeworkers that they are controlling the uncontrollable (859, 872), while a lot of dyke + queer BDSM situations are precisely about giving up control and acknowledging that being in control over life is a delusion. This illusion of control is stereotypically part of the construction of male subjectivities. In contrast, Newmahr points out that collaborative edgework, as opposed to solitary male adventuring, creates the surplus thrill of being dependent on each other (2011: 181).

Generally, the concept of edgework has to be expanded to include a consideration of social power relations. Moreover, my data suggest that dyke + queer BDSM is not simply about playing with edges as a serious leisure activity (which is the framework Newmahr suggests), but about pushing one's limits and changing one's relationship to the boundaries one engages with, ultimately leading to a transformation of the self, to processes of resubjectification. I therefore understand dyke + queer BDSM not simply as playing with edges, but as going further to desire vulnerability and to renegotiate bodies as boundary projects through exploring and pushing limits.

Encountering the limits of bodies: Desiring vulnerability

As a result of the exploring and pushing of boundaries, dyke + queer BDSM may also point out the limits and vulnerabilities of bodies. Lesbian butch transwoman top Kay's activities were constrained by her disability. But she was the owner in a 24/7 relationship, and BDSM provided Kay with a structure to get her needs met from a position of power rather than from a position of dependence. Her situation confirms Smith's speculation that a DS relationship in which an able-bodied person submits to a disabled top might transform 'the concept of caregiving into erotic servitude' (Smith 2005: 186). This might also be a powerful way to counter the social construction of the disabled (woman) as asexual (Galler 1992; Tremain 1996: 15; Reynolds 2007; Iantaffi 2010). As Galler points out, the discourse about the lack of perfection of disabled bodies translates into their not being entitled to a sex life (Galler 1992: 168). The disabled are constructed as child-like and, therefore, asexual (Iantaffi 2010: 161).

Being non-disabled means being capable of the 'normal' physical actions required in specific systems of labor (McRuer 2006: 8). But this capability is not sufficient; the myth of bodily perfection holds that all humans can and should strive to achieve perfect bodies (Stone 1995: 413). In Christian belief systems, disease and dysfunction are not considered part of human diversity, but evidence of moral failure, which causes shame in those who are sick (414). Yet everyone has experiences of disability, no matter how fleeting (415), and all humans have limits to their abilities (416). Bodily suffering and discomfort are part of the human experience (422). Therefore, disability studies have come up with the concept of the vulnerable body, stressing the fact that each body, not just the already disabled one, is prone to violations and disability through accidents, diseases and aging, which are all part of life in general. For instance, Mandy, who was 60 at the time of the interview, felt that her aging body was betraying her and feared that her ability to play would cease someday in the future.

Bodily differences are real, and the binary of abled/disabled produces real and material distinctions, which regulate access to participation in life. Since there are moments when we all experience disability, McRuer poses the question: what would it mean to welcome the disability to come, to desire it (McRuer 2006: 207)? Some BDSM practices may be seen as re-enacting, eroticizing and therefore desiring this vulnerability and these disabled moments through their manipulations of the body, such as playing with pain and immobilization. Disabled performance artist and 'super-masochist' Bob Flanagan used BDSM as a way to simultaneously submit to the sick body and gain control over the effects of his illness (Reynolds 2007:11). Reynolds criticizes the fact that disability studies, with its focus on the social conditions of disabilities, tends to neglect corporeal pain as part of the disabled experience (2007: 7). Flanagan managed to discuss in his performances both the limits of his body and the social construction of the disabled. Even when he performed as a superhuman, he was not fooling himself or the audience into embodying this new counter-stereotype of disabled people heroically overcoming the limitations of the disabled body, which Clare calls the 'supercrip story' (1999: 2). Rather, the toll of his flying in the air through suspension bondage as 'bizarre Superman' with an erection showed clearly in his stressed body afterwards (Reynolds 2007: 21). Moreover, the ways he used his body were productive (of pleasures, of social connections with his partner and audience), but did not turn him into a productive member of a capitalist workforce or into a respectable, heteronormative citizen.

MacKendrick stresses that practices of restraint as well as the useless invoking of pain generally disrupt the productive efficiency that is demanded of good subjects in capitalist societies (MacKendrick 1999: 106; 110). Restraint and pain provide the individual with an experience of intensity that disrupts the organization of subjectivity (107). So some BDSM practices could be considered to be the desire for disability practices, resisting the interpellation to capitalistic productivity and forging alliances across difference. On the other hand, they are problematic in that they also rely on ableist notions of what is considered normal, which privileges regular bodies. The erotic value of immobilization for the non-disabled lies exactly in the fact that it presents an out-of-the-ordinary experience of helplessness, dependency and denial of privilege; thus, it is potentially an experience of humiliation, rather than being considered a legitimate way of inhabiting the world. Therefore, BDSM practices seem to simultaneously embrace and reject the desire to become disabled. But BDSM may still heighten awareness of the vulnerability of bodies. As dyke + queer BDSM enables one to experience bodies as boundary projects, it stresses their limits. Desiring and experiencing situations of disability through BDSM practices may become transforming rather than just transgressive, if it leads to a lasting awareness of the general vulnerability of bodies and of interdependency as a human condition, revoking the myth of bodily perfection and imploding the binary of disabled and non-disabled.

Transforming pain into sensation in body boundary projects

In daily life, people are not always aware of their bodies. Mostly, body awareness is initiated through the boundaries, limits and vulnerabilities of the material body, since they become felt when one is in close contact with other people or objects. The more intense the touch, impact or restraint, such as in pain, sickness, violation, immobilization and sexual pleasure, the greater the awareness of the body. As Prosser points out in the context of transsexuality, pain can be used to feel the alienated body's surface and can help to establish bodily boundaries for the self (1998: 74). Playing with intense sensations and pain in BDSM, pushing their bodies to their limits, therefore turned into an experience of the body as a boundary project for interview partners and transformed their embodiments.

The physical impacts of dyke + queer BDSM became evident in sessions including sports, resistance or sensation play in general. Such play equipped lesbian Connie, who bottomed a lot, with the ability to deal with rough handling in everyday life and to stand her ground, changing her bodily subjectivity. In her queer phenomenology, Ahmed suggests that pain creates the very impression of bodily surface (Ahmed 2004: 15). This impression of a surface is an effect of an intensification of feeling (24). The body is often forgotten in ordinary reality, disappearing from awareness, and experiences of pain become lived as a return to the body (26). Ahmed makes the general statement that pain leads to a body turning in on itself, while pleasure tends to open up bodies to other bodies (26). This is complicated by the kinds of pleasure-pain generated in sensation play. Mistress Mean Mommy explained the distinction between pain and sensations as they are administered in BDSM:

> Pain is when it's something unexpected. You stab your toe and it hurts. But when you're watching a needle come toward you or you know you're gonna be hit with something and you're expecting it, it's sensation, because you are welcoming it, you are expecting it. It might still be pain, but it's a different kind of pain, because you're absorbing it, you know it's coming, you prepare your body for however you do it, you breathe deep, you close your eyes, whatever.

So what we culturally define as pain is often unexpected, or at least unwelcome (as in pain from surgery or chronic illness), and, therefore, it is an unpleasant and sometimes even negating experience. It is not pain in this usual sense that BDSM practitioners seek out, but carefully selected sensations in a specific context that prepares them for the stimulation and gives the sensations a different meaning from ordinary pain. There are various techniques one can learn to manage pain, such as visualization, breathing and welcoming the pain. Intense sensation in this context may, therefore, also lead to orienting and opening one's body toward the person inflicting the pain, welcoming the pain as well as the liminal, boundary-shifting state this paradoxical situation entails and transforming it into something pleasurable or experiencing the simultaneities of pleasure and discomfort.

Many interview partners stated that they only practiced sensation play within the context of a certain role and only liked specific kinds of pain. The role transformed the sensations into something meaningful or pleasurable, as queer genderqueer switch Firesong described: 'Maybe there's different parts of my body that can perceive reality differently when I'm in role. My senses probably change. When I'm in role, the way I experience sensation is totally different.' Again, BDSM can be considered a specific state of mind that enables one to experience sensations differently than in other contexts (see also Mains 2002: 65). This context, in turn, enabled my interview partners to utilize sensation play to feel more grounded in their bodies or to let go. They characterized the effect of sensation play as entering a certain space, as Emma described: 'When I have experienced sensation play and really gone into that transported place, it's this kind of trancy, floaty experience, not leaving my body, but sort of out my mind basically and more into my body.' This out-of-mind experience was altering, and Emma compared it to hallucinogenic drugs. My interview partners also referred to it as an 'endorphin high'. This goes back to Mains' physiological explanation that sensation play causes the body to release endorphins and may thus produce a biochemical state of euphoria or bliss (2002: 61–5).

In her ethnographic study, Newmahr identified four different community discourses for framing and making sense of pain in BDSM (2011: 134): transformed pain, when pain is actually turned into pleasure; sacrificial pain, when pain is suffered for a greater good, such as pleasing the top or achieving a certain state of mind (137); investment pain, when enduring pain is traded for something else, such as sexual favors (138); and strength and fitness, as in hypermasculinist discourses of 'no pain, no gain' or 'taking it like a man' (Savran 1998). The first three are actually disavowals of pain. Pain itself remains something adverse. Only the fourth kind, autotelic pain, admits to enjoying actual pain without redefining it (Newmahr 2011: 139–40). Those types of addressing pain were found in my sample as well, but I do not interpret the first three as disavowals of pain so much as examples of how the context of a situation changes meanings and enables the experience of simultaneous realities, for instance if a bottom hates the pain, but loves enduring it for her top. Rather than disavowing pain, these contradictory simultaneities create affective intensities.

Receiving intense sensations in a dyke + queer BDSM setting also enabled some interview partners to refocus through letting go of their mundane worries. The intense stimulation of the body may clear the head and enable one to stay completely focused in the moment. Many spiritual practices, such as meditation, are also aimed at reaching this state of being. It may, therefore, not be surprising that, for many interview partners, BDSM sessions turned into spiritual experiences, and some BDSM sessions were planned with the intent to enter a spiritual space. This is a widespread phenomenon, especially in the queer BDSM communities in the US (Thompson 1997: 19; Zussman & Pierce 1998: 17; 31–6; Mains 2002; Easton & Hardy 2004; Kaldera 2006). For instance, interview partners reached an elevation of the experience or moment, or a state of altered consciousness, through out-of-the-ordinary experiences in dyke + queer BDSM, which are also characteristic of spiritual experiences, for instance in rituals (Turner 2000).[5]

Interview partners experienced bodies as boundary projects, but these boundaries were not prefixed; they were constantly renegotiated in social interactions (Haraway 1991). So, if bodies are boundary projects and dyke + queer BDSM is an intimate, embodied limit-experience, it opens up the space to renegotiate and shift bodily boundaries in their intimate intra-actions. This is why interview partners also experienced transformations or transmogrifications through pushing limits in dyke + queer BDSM, resulting in personal growth. On the other hand, following Haraway and conceiving of the material body as a trickster also points out that there are limits to the remaking of the body. Individuals are not in complete control over their lives and the bodies they inhabit, and the materiality of the body does constitute a limit in itself, even if the boundaries are not sitting still and are not necessarily identical with the material form. Some phenomenological approaches to understanding the body have, therefore, been proven useful in transgender studies (Prosser 1998; Henry Rubin 2003; Salamon 2010), and they might also further illuminate the concept of bodies as boundary projects and how these are reworked in dyke + queer BDSM. Queer theorizing following Butler's focus on the performative aspects of sex, gender and sexuality has privileged discourse over materiality in such a way that material bodies have been reduced to an effect of discourse.[6] Feminist science studies scholars like Haraway and Barad have provided alternative accounts, and phenomenology has also been useful in theoretically refocusing on the body. Butler's concept of performativity focuses heavily on the visual surface of the body and neglects the feeling of being embodied (see also Prosser 1998 for a detailed critique from a transsexual perspective) and how the boundaries of the body are drawn through touch.

Phenomenology, on the other hand, starts with the body as its point of departure, from which one reaches out to the surrounding world. French psychoanalyst Didier Anzieu's concept of the skin ego holds that the body's surface is fundamental in forming the ego through its handling, touching and holding and the individual's experience of its feel (Prosser 1998: 65). The skin functions as the interface between the self and the other. As Salamon elaborates, following psychoanalyst Schilder, one is only able to perceive the body's surface when it comes into contact with other surfaces. Touch is, therefore, constitutive of body (Salamon 2010: 30). And in dyke + queer BDSM, because it is working with intense forms of intimate touch, this effect is amplified. The body schema is, furthermore, relational; it cannot be chosen freely (Salamon 2010: 31). My interview partners were able to make use of this relationality to re-co-construct their bodies in dyke + queer BDSM interactions (see Chapter 8 on *gender reassigning*).

It is interesting that Schilder and Anzieu distinguish between the material body and the body image, a mental representation of the body that is constructed over time. The body image is multiple, flexible and arises from relations with others, and its contours are rarely identical to the outlines of the body as it is perceived from outside (Salamon 2010: 29). Moreover, changes in the body image tend to translate into changes in the material body (32). Therefore, Salamon concludes that the body image allows the resignification of materiality itself (38). While this opens up intriguing possibilities, for instance in reshaping the body via reworking the body image through dyke + queer BDSM boundary-shifting practices, it sounds too much like a reduction of materiality to a blank page to be written upon once again. Rather, while materiality is certainly influenced by social contexts and interactions, it also resists. This is a painful experience for trans* people who are unable to pass in their gender identity because of the way their bodies are shaped (rather than how they present or perform their gender). Therefore,

Haraway's image of the material body as a trickster remains the more convincing and the more dynamic theoretical model. Yet, what is useful about Schilder and Anzieu's work is the emphasis on the significance of the skin as a boundary in the construction of the self and the conclusion that the body image is not necessarily identical with the material body. The latter is of great interest in understanding transgender embodiments. The former reinforces the notion of bodies as boundary projects.

In dyke + queer BDSM interactions, it becomes clear that these boundaries do not sit still and are not absolute. They are fragile and temporary constructions, which are important to the sense of self, which remains a changing self. And the porosity of the boundaries is important for intimate connection. Dyke + queer BDSM is about those boundary-crossing, boundary-shifting moments, moments of resisting the closure of the self, moments of reopening the body image to reworkings. Therefore, it is not surprising that my interview partners experienced personal growth and healing through their BDSM practices. To conclude this chapter, I will briefly summarize the healing effects discussed by interview partners.

Personal growth and healing through limit experiences

To my interview partners, dyke + queer BDSM had a therapeutic function (see also Kaldera 2009: 158; Newmahr 2011: 95), most often as a side effect, but sometimes deliberately pursued. More generally, it promoted and catalyzed personal development and change. This was related to dyke + queer BDSM as an exploration and the pushing of boundaries, because it confronted interview partners with unresolved issues, challenges, past traumatic experiences and personal weaknesses and strengths. For Tanya, eroticizing trauma was a way to work through it. But why was this potentially healing for many interview partners, and not simply re-enacting or retraumatizing?

First of all, and most significantly, queer/dyke high femme bottom switch Mandy explained:

> We can make it come out different. And if I did a scene in which I brought up some old abuse and did not come to a conclusion in that scene, I can go back with my partner and say: I wanna do a different scene with those same characters and go back and pull up that same part of myself, but have it come out different, thank you.

A crucial aspect that is damaging to the self in real-life rape or abuse is the experience of the loss of self-determination. Dyke + queer BDSM can provide a space in which to regain control, either as top or bottom, through its negotiated nature. The bottom gets to choose the ending of the scene, and is, therefore, able to re-emerge with self-chosen, or at least renegotiated, boundaries. Another interview partner also pointed out that the intent of the persons involved matters: 'If I do a rape scene now, I know the intent is not to make me a little child and hurt me and overpower me.' Rather, the intent is mutual pleasure and the empowerment of grown-ups. BDSM was, therefore, experienced as nurturing and validating by interview partners.

The specific context of BDSM functioned to reinscribe past experiences with new emotional meanings and memories, and, therefore, transformed the meaning of the earlier events in retrospect. BDSM was not simply repetitive, but transformative; the repetitions served to shift the meanings of past experiences and, therefore, brought about therapeutic change.

Tanya and Connie also used BDSM to move themselves through unfounded or irrational fears. Mastering a situation of fear or anxiety by living through it in a semi-contained setting may help one to overcome it. Other examples were the process of regaining the ability to trust someone through BDSM, finding a constructive space for formerly destructive behaviors such as self-harm-related cutting, and being able to reconnect to one's own body and gain a sense of physical strength after being socialized into feeling weak and frail as a feature of *white* middle-class femininity.

In summary, BDSM provided interview partners with new behavioral paths, and, as queer genderqueer switch and therapist Femmeboy pointed out, if a transfer to everyday life happens, it does not matter how the new pathway was established. Thus, dyke + queer BDSM with good aftercare had some therapeutic effects.[7]

Integration

BDSM provided interview partners with a space to explore, acknowledge and embrace all parts of their selves, from gendered identities to personality traits that were commonly thought of as negative or unethical:

> I feel more complete since I began to practice SM. Somehow more whole. So it is the case that SM is a place for me where things are simply possible, which are simply not possible otherwise. But they belong to me in whatever kind of way as well, or maybe also things that I don't really like so much about myself and that I actually don't really want to be or don't want to be in everyday life, but which can come out in SM.

Neila used dyke + queer BDSM as a semi-contained space for aspects of the self that were unwelcome in other areas of life. It helped her to make peace with sides of herself that she did not really like, and therefore fostered self-acceptance.

Thus, another significant mechanism that BDSM provided for healing was integration. Many interview partners used dyke + queer BDSM in this sense, not only to embrace their 'monsters', to use Zoe's word, but also to express subjectivities that are simply not welcome in ordinary life because they would impede one's functioning in the world or because they are socially stigmatized, such as childish emotions and behaviors. Mandy used the Jungian concept of the shadow to explain healing through integration within BDSM. It enables practitioners to enter the shadow realm and bring a forbidden and splintered-off part of the self back to consciousness in the presence of a play partner as a validating mirror who finds exactly these 'ugly' parts of the self desirable, for instance 'the pathetic child' or 'the manipulative bitch'. This process also helped BDSMers to deal with parts of the self that were not allowed to come out due to heteronormative society. For instance, queer trans/genderqueer/butch dyke switch Scout found it healing to be able to take care of and nurture his inner boy in the relationship with his Sir until he felt that 'I'm whole and that little boy is happily in his bed sleeping, and he's fine.' Healing through integration was especially significant for gender-variant interview partners and will, therefore, be revisited in Chapter 8.

Chapter conclusion

The semi-contained space of dyke + queer BDSM provided interview partners with the opportunity for intimate exploring through experiencing and pushing boundaries. They valued intensity of experience, such as desiring vulnerability, over what usually counts as pleasant. The voluntary risk-taking and the desiring of moments of vulnerability depended upon the establishment of trust, which could not be reduced to a process of rational calculation and the suspension of risk-awareness. Trust was part of the renegotiation of danger and risk through pleasure in dyke + queer BDSM. Moreover, my data suggest that dyke + queer BDSM was not simply about playing with the edges as a serious leisure activity, but about pushing one's limits and changing one's relationship to the boundaries one engages with, ultimately leading to transformations of the self, to processes of resubjectification. I therefore understand dyke + queer BDSM not simply as playing with the edges, but going further to desiring vulnerability and renegotiating bodies as boundary projects through exploring and pushing limits. As a side effect of these boundary transgressions, my interview partners experienced personal growth and healing dynamics.

The dyke + queer BDSM experience highlights that bodies are boundary projects, and that pushing boundaries in dyke + queer BDSM may open bodies up to transformative subjectification processes and becomings. I understand dyke + queer BDSM encounters to be apparatuses of phenomena that produce situationally determinate boundaries in intimate performative intra-actions of bodies. The meanings, properties and boundaries of the bodies that enter the dyke + queer BDSM encounter have not been settled yet; they are redrawn and renegotiated in the intra-action. Dyke + queer BDSM seems to be a social phenomenon that increases the likelihood of transformations in such intra-actions because of its intimate intensity and performative character. It holds the potential to create situations in which processes of tarrying can be entered and/or a BwO can be produced.

7
Exploring Intimate Power Dynamics

Dyke + queer BDSM opened up a space to explore and experiment in different ways for interview partners. Besides exploring and pushing boundaries, it also enabled them to engage with power dynamics, social hierarchy and difference. If we return to the definition of intimacy as being about access and the transgression of boundaries, it becomes evident that social power dynamics and structural power inequalities involve intimate touch. Who has a right to bodily integrity or 'privacy' in society is dependent upon such differentiating markers as race, gender, class, age and ability. For instance, Black people's hair is touched without permission, genderqueers are interrogated by strangers about the status of their genitals and so on (see also Conradi 2011: 28–9). These are intimate moments of the violating kind, even though they may not be experienced as such by the privileged intruder because they are simultaneously an expression of 'normality'. Because interactions structured by social hierarchy are of an intimate nature in this sense, it is not surprising that power may become eroticized.

BDSM represents one way of engaging with this eroticization of power and social hierarchy. The following two chapters will discuss how my interview partners used the social space of dyke + queer BDSM to explore power dynamics and categories connected to social hierarchy, specifically race, class, age and gender. This chapter interrogates how my interview partners understood power dynamics in their BDSM practices and in everyday life contexts. I apply various power theories to show how social hierarchy is constructed in dyke + queer BDSM sessions and in what ways interview partners were erotically invested in power, domination and subversion. Finally, I ask why dyke + queer BDSM does not engage with all types of social hierarchies but focuses on only a few.

Dyke + queer BDSM perspectives on power

As Newmahr points out, few theorists are concerned with an empirical investigation of power (2006: 37). BDSM offers a field to study power dynamics, especially how they travel through and across bodies, generating pleasures, transgressions and transformations. From a dyke + queer BDSM perspective, it becomes evident that all social relations are infused with power dynamics. The so-called private sphere, including the field of sexuality, is no exception to this: 'I would also say that this is very important to me with vanilla sex – well, certainly, power-free sex is nonsense anyways. But I am also less into vanilla sex, which plays with this idea of power-free sex, or which does not concern itself with [power].' As *white* queer transgender butch switch Tony's remarks illustrated, there is no power-free sex (see also Brickell 2009: 57). My interview partners could, therefore, be said to follow a feminist analysis summarized in the slogan 'the personal is political' as well as a Foucauldian perspective on power as biopower. So, rather than BDSM sex being about power and non-BDSM sex being free of power dynamics, non-BDSM sex plays with the illusion of a sexuality devoid of power, or it simply ignores the issue of power altogether.

Power dynamics in dyke + queer BDSM are negotiated and made explicit, while the trend has been to cover them up or deny their existence or significance in other sexual interactions, for instance in post-feminist discourses and other myths of equality. *White* Jewish queer transgender stone butch top Terry therefore identified a political value in dyke + queer BDSM from his activist perspective, stating:

> There's an open acknowledgment of power hierarchies. But the goal isn't to get rid of power altogether, which is often a feminist and anti-violence goal. I think anti-racist folks are less deluded about the possibility. [laughs] The feminists are not and the anti-violence folks are definitely not. They're still way deluded. They think they can get rid of power. And what SM does, it actually says: Yes, of course there's power dynamics. And they're incredibly important and they are not only a source of oppression and violence, but they're also a source of strength and power like personal empowerment and pleasure and desire. You don't have to throw out power altogether. In fact not only is it impossible, but it's not ideal.

Many interview partners echoed the approach to power captured by Terry here. They valued dyke + queer BDSM for its open acknowledgment of and engagement with power. They shared the assumption that power dynamics were intrinsic to social life per se and could not be abolished. Moreover, they held that power was not only oppressive, but also productive, for instance of pleasures and a sense of agency. They argued that acknowledging the ubiquity of power was the essential first step in dealing with power relations in a less oppressive and more productive and transformative way. Therefore, they tried to engage in power-sensitive practices, which can be considered a form of micropolitics, located in what Deleuze and Guattari call the zone of indiscernibility of central power, which describes the fact that power and social hierarchy are diffused throughout the microphysical fabric of society (2004: 249), including sexuality.

Power and sexuality are inextricably entwined. My interview partners understood power almost as a neutral currency, an energy running through bodies and social relations with various effects, good and bad. In dyke + queer BDSM, power could be put to use in ways that celebrated life and passion, dyke + queer bodies and identities, processes of transmogrification and becoming. This corresponds with certain feminist theories that define power as a capacity to transform and empower oneself and others (Held 1993) and as creative (Hoagland 1988). While some of these theorists tend to locate power in the individual, as 'power-from-within', they simultaneously understand it as a life-affirming force or as energy (Hartsock 1983), much as it was described in the interviews. On the other hand, the flow of power can be blocked, and power can turn into structures of social hierarchy. It seems as if hatred and prejudice can then infuse and contaminate power; oppression and domination seem to stick to power, and this power is often metaphorically or literally sexualized. Sexuality also serves as a trope for other power relations, for example the feminizing of the 'virgin land' in colonialist discourse (McClintock 1995: 14) or making sense of cultural traumas like the Holocaust (Moore 2005). Such legacies of discursively connecting sexuality with technologies of power and domination may be the reason why very different kinds of social power relations seem to be suitable as materials for eroticization in BDSM. It seemed that, for interview partners, dyke + queer BDSM could become an intimate social space where this kind of 'contaminated' power was converted into 'good' power by deflecting it from its original purpose of disconnecting bodies in hatred and prejudice. Instead, power was infused with erotic value and turned into a means to establish intense intimacies, which opened up bodies toward each other.

Because power was negotiated, play was experienced as empowering to bottoms (see also MacKendrick 1999; Newmahr 2011: 54–5). According to my interview partners, this was because all parties started out with a degree of negotiating agency, and through the element of consent the bottoms did not give up their control on an underlying level, but granted the tops their position of power. For the tops, using this position was only attractive if they evoked a positive and erotic response, not in order to non-consensually dominate someone. My interview partners, therefore, described a paradoxical structure of power dynamics in dyke + queer BDSM. Queer femme bottom Ellen explained: 'Very often, the dynamic is the top is doing whatever they can to try to get the bottom off. The bottom is really holding the power in the situation. And it's usually a bottom who you'll see say their safeword more than anyone else in the scene.' While on the level of the game's reality the top was at the apex of the hierarchy, on the simultaneous level of ordinary reality the bottom never gave up her control over the situation. So, rather than competing for power positions in the strategic game of power (Foucault 1996), tops and bottoms used a cooperative mode of distributing power differently on simultaneous levels of reality, potentially following feminist visions of a model of 'power-with' rather than 'power-over', as dyke/queer femme Mandy put it, a distinction that is attributed to Follett (1942).

Dyke + queer BDSM also provided a space to be in a powerful position without some of the ethical downsides or consequences, as *white* Jewish queer femme bottom Ellen described:

> SM is this one place to me where power exists, but you can play with it and it's not about profit. It's about playing with it under the dynamics you wanna play with it. So someone can be a slave and someone can be a master, and in 15 minutes you can switch that. But in the real world, like the work world or something, someone's a boss and someone's serving, and you can't change that in 15 minutes. So it's about playing for power but outside of the capitalist profit structure.

Power was not only taken outside the capitalist structure in this sense, but also denaturalized in that it was disassociated from the social privilege associated with race or gender, for example. Some authors celebrate this 'denaturalization' of positions of power in BDSM and the disconnection from privilege (Califia 2000: 166; Sullivan 2003: 161), and Foucault discussed the strategic situation of power in BDSM as fluid (1996: 387). But my data showed empirical limits to this theoretical fluidity, such as individual capacities to eroticize or convincingly embody a certain role.

Dominance, for instance, was performed through a certain way of inhabiting space and a particular style of claiming significance that not anyone could display at will, since it was also connected to social status such as gender, class, race and able-bodiedness. One might not have learned to move through the world with a sense of entitlement, one might lack the self-confidence for this kind of performance or one's personal way of embodying dominance might not be accepted by others. *White* bisexual woman top Vito reported that in her local heterosexual BDSM group she faced sexist comments by male tops: 'Well it wasn't all of them, but there were like two of this kind sitting in a talking round, who were saying something along the lines of: "Yeah sure, you just don't have a guy, otherwise it would be different with you as well. Then you would also submit nicely." ' Thus, the discourses of 'natural male dominance' were put to use by some heterosexual men to question the credibility of female tops. This attests to a gap between the hypothetical liberty to claim any role in BDSM and the actual opportunity in various social contexts. While male tops were able to claim their position without opposition, Vito had to fight to claim her right to be a dominant woman.

In contrast, my interview partners rejected the practice of simply acting out their social positions in play. BDSM to them precisely offered an opportunity to consciously reflect on their own embedding in power structures. They generally observed that their awareness of power structures and power games in ordinary life had increased through practicing dyke + queer BDSM, as *white* lesbian femme top Frl. R. described:

> I am, for instance, more aware of power imbalance or not and that would not hurt a lot of other people either [laughs shortly]. Yes, also because my experiences with the few vanilla, non-SM lesbians with whom I interact is that they deal with power in a very non-reflective way and find it somehow rather funny to dominate someone or the like. And I then say: 'Yes, but [what you do] is mean after all! You [should] negotiate this beforehand!!' [laughs]

She described a common double standard, in which BDSMers were often accused of immorality and abuse of power, while in her social contexts non-BDSMers were often much less self-aware of how they acted out power in an uncontained and violating way.

So interview partners found that dyke + queer BDSM held the potential to deal with and to deconstruct power. They believed that, if power issues were not dealt with in a constructive way, they would become displaced and might have destructive effects through being acted out non-consensually. They would agree with Cooper's feminist adaptation of Foucault's theorizing of power, which stresses that power has the capacity to shape, facilitate and generate practices, processes and social relations, and that what is necessary, therefore, is the development of an ethics of power rather than eschewing it altogether (1994: 436).

Power theories revisited

The term 'power' is derived from the Latin *potere*, meaning to be able. Most commonly, power is understood as the capacity to exert influence by individuals, groups or institutions on others, or as a capacity for action (Barnes 1988). Some theorists stress that it is a potentiality (Lukes 2005). Of central significance for this study are concepts that understand power as relational; most significantly, Foucault analyzes power not only as repressive, but also as productive. For Foucault, discourses play a central role. A discursive regime determines what can be discussed, and how, in a specific historical moment, and therefore predefines possibilities of agency, subjugating those practices, selves and connections that are not socially intelligible. Discourses produce subjectivities, social realities and truths. Therefore, power is also productive in terms of generating specific forms of subjectivities and practices (Foucault 1978).

The concept of biopower is especially significant in the context of researching dyke + queer BDSM. According to Foucault, this particular kind of power emerged in the 17th century. From the sovereign's power over death, the focus shifted to power as controlling life according to the interests of the nation-state, governing the populace through technologies that regulate reproduction and health (Foucault 1994). Biopower thus simultaneously targeted the individual and the social body. The logical consequence was the emergence of a normalizing society. Since life itself had to be governed and administered, subjects were increasingly measured against norms that they were supposed to fulfill. Sexuality plays a crucial role in this context. It connects the axes of disciplinary technologies and the regulation of the population within biopolitics (Foucault 1978; Pieper 2007: 218). Life in its totality is subjugated to the primacy of productivity (222). State institutions today still use sexuality as a means of intervention to regulate the population, as is evident in political struggles over STD prevention and reproductive rights. Therefore, Foucault speaks of the advent of a new discursive regime, that of sexuality. For the citizen of the modern nation-state, sexuality is access to the truth of the self and the body; 'discovering' one's own true desires equates to speaking one's own inner 'truth'.

Foucault is interested in the type of power that turns individuals into subjects, the processes of subjection (1982: 781). This is the inheritance of a specifically Christian form of power: pastoral power. It targets the individual for the sake of the salvation of the soul. Rather than merely regulating the actions of humans, pastoral power developed new technologies of power, like confession, to gain access to thoughts and emotions. This produced the concept of secret feelings and the privacy of emotions, which are then invaded (by the priest, the psychiatrist, the media and so on) to evoke shame. So this focus on the 'soul', the interior, in pastoral power produced specific kinds of subjectivities. The power technologies of the Enlightenment are based on control through surveillance (Foucault 1996: 232). The rationale behind this is not only to keep people from committing crimes, but also to anchor inside them the wish not to do evil, to be good citizens. Everyone becomes their own overseer, and power is no longer identified with a particular person, but becomes a decentralized machinery that nobody can control (234). The modern state has generated a new form of pastoral power to integrate its citizens, producing compliant, economically capable individuals (783) and this type of power has spread into the whole social body (1982: 784). But Foucault, according to Bartky's criticism, has ignored how these disciplinary practices are gendered and how they make women's bodies more docile, for instance through self-surveillance practices such as dieting or learning not to take up too much space (1990). In any case, power is decentralized, and there is nothing that is outside power relations. Moreover, Foucault's concept of subjection emphasizes how the processes that produce subjects simultaneously subject individuals to power relations, which leads Butler to question the political usefulness of the very category 'woman' (1990). And, I would add, the element of (gendered/sexed) access to the body and interiority is what biopower and intimacy have in common (as well as the prior assumption that there *is* such a thing as an interior of the subject). It is not surprising that even non-reproductive sexuality such as dyke + queer BDSM plays a major role in processes of subjectification.

Foucault defines the exercise of power as a process in which certain actions modify others (1982: 788). A power relation does not act directly upon persons, but upon their actions. Cooper extends this concept of interpersonal power through structural power into a definition of power as the *differential* ability to cause (1995). Thus, power and agency are not distributed evenly across populations. Like Hannah Arendt (1960), Foucault distinguishes power from violence; violence acts upon bodies, it forces and destroys, it forecloses all possibilities. Likewise, domination occurs when an individual or group succeeds in blocking a field of power relations, preventing any reversibility of movement (Foucault 1996: 434). A power relationship may rely on consent or violence or both, but it can only exist if there are possibilities to act, even for the one who is subjected to that power: 'a way of acting upon an acting subject or acting subjects by virtue of their acting or being capable of action' (Foucault 1982: 789). To characterize this kind of power, Foucault uses the term 'government' in its original, broad sense as structuring the possible field of action of others. This includes enabling structures, not only limiting fields of action. Cooper rightly points out that control and dominance may work more successfully by creating certain possibilities rather than by simply denying things (1994: 437). But, again, these possibilities are not accessible in the same manner to all.

Foucault considers power relations to be a strategic situation, which always holds possibilities for change (1996: 386). It follows from Foucault's distinction between violence and power that power can only be exercised over free subjects, in the sense that they are capable of choices for actions, however narrow these might be (Foucault 1982: 790). In this sense, no society or social situation can exist without power relations, since there must always be possibilities for actions upon other actions. This is why Habermas' ideal speech situation (1984) has to remain utopian and is not fit for practical use. It relies on the myth of equality. Rather than ignoring the pervasiveness of power relations in social spaces, one has to acknowledge them and act accordingly, situating oneself, taking responsibility for one's actions and developing strategies to shift and rebalance them. Acknowledging that there will always be power relations, of course, does not mean that existing power relations cannot or should not be challenged or changed (Foucault 1982: 791). According to Foucault, we have to look for ways that allow us to play these games of power with as little domination as possible (1996: 446). It is clear that the picture is much more complex and power more elusive than the simple idea of clearly identifiable entities possessing it. Rather, as Young (1990) describes, following Foucault, power is relational, situational and omnipresent. It is a dynamic that structures social interactions. Newmahr argues that this becomes especially evident when looking at BDSM: because power is played with in BDSM, its externality to the individuals becomes obvious (2006: 57); it is not a thing possessed, but a condition we live in, a context in which we interact (56). Yet, in her conviction that power is external, Newmahr fails to consider how power is also part of embodiment and subjectification processes, and therefore is internalized by individuals and inscribed on their bodies. If power were simply external to persons, one could not explain why not every member of the BDSM community is a switch. Obviously, the eroticization of power is differently inscribed on bodies. In the BDSM community studied by Newmahr, this is clearly observable, for instance in the fact that it was predominantly men who took on the role of the top. Thus, while power dynamics are a social context, this context is prestructured in certain ways, which has an impact on how power is played out in BDSM, because BDSM is part of the social fabric as well.

Constructing social hierarchy through technologies of power

In dyke + queer BDSM, power was obviously performative. Being rather tall and physically strong, Tony had to remind hirself when bottoming in resistance play to keep up the illusion that s/he was weaker than the top. This example shows that hierarchy in a dyke + queer BDSM session was actively co-constructed, for example through performing a certain kind of habitus, by the participants. The roles chosen clearly indicated a power differential, such as master/slave, vampire/human or daddy/girl. Hierarchy was often further cemented through a set of rules for bottoms' actions (referred to as protocol). The discussion that follows relates to the level of role play reality and how power relations are constructed for play, not the power relations among the everyday personalities of the parties involved.

In the descriptions of their BDSM practices, it became evident that my interview partners utilized different modes and technologies of power to co-construct their power-based erotic interactions. Despite their creative adaptations, all these technologies of power that served to create hierarchy and inequality can be found in society at large as well, even though they differ in significance in certain historical and social contexts. While there is a tendency to theorize BDSM as romanticizing past modes of oppression and power, I believe this rests on a false theoretical assumption about technologies of power. While it may be possible to identify new modes of power that emerged in specific historical circumstances, such as biopower or governmentality, this does not mean that other, older technologies of power suddenly ceased to exist or were replaced completely. Rather, they have tended to co-exist, such as the monopoly on violence (by the state) or the objectification of humans (see Young 1992 on various faces of oppression). The neoliberal mechanisms used to make citizens govern themselves clearly have limits, and the state, co-operative businesses and individuals resort to other modes of power, including physical violence if necessary (see, for instance, Snorton & Haritaworn 2013 for a discussion of necropolitics in regard to trans* people of color). In the following, I briefly present the technologies of power that were used by interview partners to co-construct power differentials in their dyke + queer BDSM encounters and relationships.

Power as contract. A basic distinction on the play level was voluntariness versus force. Voluntary submission to an authority or higher power, for whatever reason, could be considered to be a contractual power situation. For gay transman switch Wolf, voluntariness and pride in service were indispensable when submitting to someone. His image of bottoming was characterized by loyalty: 'Such an officer, who goes down with his emperor or general or is bound to him in whatever way that he executes all kinds of orders, is able to leave, right? There is an element of voluntariness there.' His fantasies centered on being sworn to a superior, for instance being the second man behind a warlord who was willing to give everything for that lord out of his own free will or personal convictions. For some interview partners, there were obviously affective rewards connected with voluntarily agreeing to subordination, including moral validation ('being good', 'acting reasonably' and so on).

Power as setting parameters. Power was often established through superiority or through an advantage in resources on the top's part. Power as superiority was not dependent on loyalty or co-operation to succeed. For instance, the superhuman superiority of the vampire made resistance futile. In this power dynamic, interview partners in the top role enjoyed exerting their authority to the fullest, including being ruthless and narcissistic. Many invented their own rules and therefore structured the field of possible action for the bottom in a Foucauldian sense.

Power as control. As a consequence of being able to set parameters, people in power gain control over others and their actions. This was crucial for my interview partners. To many, power play was mainly about consciously exercising or giving up control. Being dominated put gay transman bottom Mik into a space of vulnerability and complete focus on his top: '[I am] very strongly focused on the other. I am reacting almost automatically then or immediately if he says anything to me. And I react very strongly then in what I do and how I do it; I execute it very intensely.' What Mik described here was a trance-like state of being completely controlled by the top through being enthralled. He ceased to feel a will of his own and became the instrument of the will of the top. Situations of power exchange were, therefore, experiences of great intensity and of exuberant intimacy. Control was present in dyke + queer BDSM in various ways. Some practices of control were closely linked with surveillance as a technology of power; others seemed to resemble hypnosis, if the control was aimed at the mind of the bottom, as in Mik's description.

Objectification and dehumanization. Some bottoms wanted to be considered an object. This was achieved through being owned, being used, being put on display, being lent to someone else, being humiliated or being robbed of privacy. In summary, they were treated like a possession and not a human being. Being treated as less than human is a strong expression of the exertion of power. It is a part of racist, sexist and transphobic technologies of domination, and the desire to be objectified could be related to these very real histories and ongoing realities. But being an object in a context of negotiated power exchange may also become an opportunity to completely abandon everyday responsibilities, in a similar move to entering the role of a small child or animal. The desire of some to move to a stage beyond or below humanity in the semi-contained space of dyke + queer BDSM could, therefore, be seen as a desire for a different kind of existence than that of the subject. Gay transmasculine switch Craig stated: 'It's really fun to be a puppy. It's really nice. No worries at all. Have to play and eat and pee and whatever they do [laughs].' This state of being was one of blissful abandonment, rather than humiliation.

Service. Service can be considered both a benefit of possessing the power to make others work for oneself and simultaneously part of constituting power relationships. Historically, service played a role in constructing a middle-class identity (McClintock 1995). Therefore, service can be considered as playing with class status. Some interview partners enjoyed the culture of service, as queer femme switch Emma explained: 'I find it sexy when somebody knows how I like my beverage and goes and gets it and kneels in front of me with it and will stay there holding it until I take it.' Thus, service entailed taking care of details, of making everything perfect for the top. This also points to the intimate nature of service. Servants have access to spaces and sometimes zones of the body considered to be private, for instance when bathing their mistress. Service represents complex embodied crossings of class boundaries in hierarchical intimate interactions. Therefore, it offers a rich resource for dyke + queer BDSM to exploit erotically.

Power as denial. One way of demonstrating power and exercising control was the denial of rights or privileges, such as using the toilet, touching oneself, having an orgasm or touching the top. Bottoms might be released 'hungry'. Denial and the delay of gratification were technologies that increased the intensity of the situation. The various technologies of power utilized by my interview partners showed that no bodily or psychological practice was per se indicative of status, but each was dependent upon the assigned meanings. For instance, top status might find expression through being untouchable (the bottom is constructed as unworthy of touching the top), or through being touched constantly and very intimately in certain kinds of service situations, like being bathed, massaged or serviced sexually (the body of the bottom is denied attention).

Power as benevolence. Being in charge provided tops with the power to be magnanimous, as Vito explained:

> Out of that situation I can then be very, very generous. So occasionally I provide physical fulfillment after a long tantalizing [session], even if others then maybe say: 'Man, you could have stretched that out another half an hour!' I then say: 'No, I know my wife, and I want her to realize in that moment exactly that it is my generosity which allows for this to happen.'

Tops were often nurturing, protective and compassionate. Certain gestures might be rewards for good behavior or a means to facilitate bonding through making the bottom feel loved or creating the impression that they owed their tops something in return. Being generous might also have proved that the top was so secure in her position that she was not dependent upon cruelty to reign. Benevolence also plays a role in fiduciary relationships, such as parent and child, where the caretaker's power comes with responsibility. In any case, benevolence is an integral structure of hierarchical relationships, because it depends on someone having greater resources and who then deigns to be generous.

Power as irrevocable responsibility. My interview partners described the ways power operated in age play as complex. The point of departure was a clear hierarchy, because the responsible adult was superior and had the power to make decisions on behalf of the child/youth, who was totally dependent on the caretaker. This is because, as Millett points out, the authority of parents is the greatest in society (besides the state): since children have no status and no resources of their own (1992: 217), they are in a state of dependency (221) and are property (222). The extent of this real-life power, therefore, made the caretaker–child dynamic an interesting one for erotic power exchanges. But, in my interview partners' age play, power flowed both ways, as pansexual genderqueer femme Neila explained:

> Playing on top in age play is in principle a lot about having more power to start with. But therefore also having more responsibility and therefore having a very special kind of affection, that kind of weakens one somehow again. So in that moment where one is not so clear and

structured and rational anymore, but in the moment where a specific kind of affection develops, a weakness emerges somehow as well.

Thus, power was connected to irrevocable responsibility and a specific emotional bond with the youngster. These parental emotions and duties weakened the top's power position. Elias (1998), therefore, developed the notion of power chances. He observed that a child has power over its parents, not intrinsically but because of the social context, which makes the parents receptive to their children's needs because of the value they see in them. The child can draw on power through demanding care and attention and can use the irrevocable responsibility of the parent to her/his own advantage through manipulation. It was the complexity of these power dynamics that made age play so interesting. For example, boy and girl roles possessed more liberties and power than other bottom roles had; these bottoms had the privilege to demand things of their caretakers. Most of the girl or grrrl personas of interview partners, for instance, were neither submissive nor obedient, but were often bratty or princesses.

Betrayal of responsibilities. Misusing one's social or institutional position of power presented another dynamic to play with. This was the opposite of ruling through benevolence or paternalism. My interview partners described this type of power as betraying responsibility and trust and manipulating their bottoms, as in incest play.

Ordeal. Power was also manifested as pushing boundaries through presenting the bottom with challenges or leading her through ordeals, from playful daring adventures to rites of passage. This offered the bottom the opportunity to experience her own strength and to be proud of her successes. This type of play was one of the ways in which bottoming could result in an increase of self-worth. Here, the power was about the authority of the top, which needed to be tied to a position that had been earned, such as that of a master of ceremonies or an elder who had mastered similar challenges before.

Resistance play. Resistance and force were ways to test (and ultimately solidify) power relations. Some interview partners liked to play on the theme of rebellion. Overcoming resistance and forcing someone to do something against their will was an intense form of power play. Mandy stated: 'My fantasies are largely of non-consent. So the submission is always kind of dragged out of me, and it's not something that I really want to offer.' Some bottoms drew their sense of self-worth and pride from the fact that they were submitting of their own free will and therefore were really in control of the situation, while others drew their own sense of strength from their resistance and not giving in to power easily. Resistance play is interesting in that some theorists argue that one can only gain knowledge about power and domination through resistance (Cooper 1994), because pushing against hierarchy can expose it.

Power as monopoly on violence. Power may also be backed up through possessing the monopoly on violence. Some tops threatened or disciplined their bottoms into obedience, including the administration of punishment. Punishment might be used 'fairly' for actual misconduct, bringing about redemption for those bottoms invested in 'being good', or arbitrarily, which stressed the state of being at the complete mercy of the top.

Erotic investments in power, domination and subversion

Even though dyke + queer BDSM was a semi-contained space, it was not a completely separate set of realities, but was embedded in the larger social worlds surrounding it. A lot of the power exchange was based on real-life social power relations as a resource for erotic fantasies, but they were engaged with according to the different rules of the dyke + queer BDSM framework. My interview partners acknowledged how being situated within specific socio-political contexts shaped their sexuality and provided the framework for their BDSM:

> Power is something that we're constantly facing and that exists in our society. Sex is all about power, power play I think for me. And I think that we're so fucked up by living in a capitalist society, I mean in America living in an oppressive police state. I just think that's part of just being honest about what we find hot.

So *white* gay transguy top Matt positioned dyke + queer BDSM within the context of an oppressive society that is damaging to marginalized groups.

Being subjected to oppressive power structures on a daily basis shapes one's sexuality and creates a connection between desire and power. From lesbian feminist anti-BDSM discourse to recent queer theorists, the libidinous dimension of compliance with one's own domination (Linden et al. 1982; Chancer 1992; Woltersdorff 2011c) has been pointed out again and again. BDSM is just one expression of this phenomenon. Non-BDSM sexuality that is based on the illusion of equality and synchronicity in desires also helps to eroticize one's own oppressions by romanticizing and glossing over the actual ongoing inequalities in intimate relationships. Dyke + queer BDSM offers a different way of engaging with these erotic investments in structures of social power, since it exploits them knowingly and manipulatively, and thereby creates potentials to rework embodied emotional attachments through replaying them in the semi-contained space of dyke + queer BDSM. Furthermore, the vulnerability that is created by erotic investments in structures of power and domination may also work to reshuffle situations of agency in intimate intra-actions. For instance, Arthur Munby's desires gave Hannah Cullwick a degree of control over him despite her lower social status as a working-class woman (McClintock 1995: 146–7). Moreover, what is missing in the theoretical debates about BDSM is the acknowledgment of erotic investments in subversion and resistance, which clearly showed up in my interviews as well. Dyke + queer BDSMers did not simply eroticize their own oppressions in their BDSM interactions, even though that was part of it. They also used the space of dyke + queer BDSM to work on their emotional attachments to social power, and to live out their erotic investments in subverting and resisting structures of domination and social norms. Thus, it seems that not only power, but also emotions and affects, circulate, travel across and through bodies, happen to bodies, excite them momentarily, leave impressions and uproot subjectivities through their unbidden appearances.

McClintock (2004) understands BDSM as an economy of conversion of specific social values. This was also evident in my interviews. My interview partners gained pleasure from the bottom role, for instance when providing service for a top, which proved that even socially devalued labors and positions provided affective rewards and that hegemonic values were not all-encompassing. Many bottoms possessed pride in their skills in that role, which might have helped them to integrate and value this part of their personality, providing a sense of dignity in a capitalist and hierarchical culture that only values those on top. McClintock's theory, therefore, has to take into consideration that these conversions would not work if there were no emotional attachments to the devalued activities in the first place, for instance an ability to erotically enjoy shame or humiliation in a disidentificatory way. So it is precisely those emotional attachments to subjugation that, paradoxically, may initiate setting an upward resignifying spiral into motion; debased positions and practices are infused with erotic value, and the potentials for questioning hegemonic meanings arise, such as an acknowledgment of the human condition as a state of interdependency rather than autonomy. This is an instance of how systems of domination and subjugation may produce excesses that lead to unintended subversions or perversions of hegemonic values. As the case of dyke + queer BDSM shows, desires are powerful, and power is mediated, perpetuated and challenged through intimate investments and attachments. Because of the intimate and erotic quality of social power, anti-oppression politics cannot ignore the workings of desires.

Not all social hierarchies are equal game

Though, theoretically, all areas of discrimination could provide themes to play with, none were as popular among my interview partners as gender, sexuality and age, and some were not addressed at all:

> Gender, sexuality, and age are the main societal structural hierarchies I have played with. I am less comfortable engaging with race and class in BDSM play, perhaps because I have privilege in those areas, and been very

politicized around that. Anti-racist is one of my core activist identities. Those things feel very loaded for me.

As a *white* Jewish middle-class anti-racist feminist disabled queer transgender butch and fat activist, Terry's BDSM games exploited gender, sexuality and age, but not race, class, anti-Semitism, fatness or disability. It was, there-fore, certainly not the loadedness alone that kept him from engaging with these, since due to his social positioning he was surely emotionally invested in sexism, homophobia and transphobia as well. More likely, it was exactly the loadedness and taboo character that made those boundary transgres-sions sexually interesting. It was also not only the fact that he possessed privilege around race and class. Although this obviously made him uncom-fortable because of his political convictions, being exposed to discrimination himself seemed to give him emotional and political permission to play only with gender, age and sexuality, but not with anti-Semitism, fatphobia and ableism.

Obviously, not all social hierarchies provided interview partners with equal opportunities to produce bodily pleasures and desires (see also Bauer 2008b). Therefore, I find it helpful to distinguish between acts in which *transgressing* individual and/or socio-cultural boundaries generates (or pre-vents) a pleasure experience in terms of violating a taboo and *transformative* acts, which additionally create new meanings that might hold promising utopian and/or political potentials beyond the semi-contained BDSM set-ting. In the case of the dyke + queer BDSM communities, gender-based play created new subcultural skills around sex/gender (sometimes as they inter-related with age, sexuality and class), which were partially transferable to the everyday lives of my interview partners and intervened in processes of embodiment and subjectification. These types of play may thus be viewed as transformative, while no such skills had been developed in regard to race. Transgressive acts were those in which players found pleasure in the violation of boundaries without changing the status quo. Transformative experiences, on the other hand, resulted in shiftings or changes within the individuals which enabled them to relate differently to their social contexts. Some practices might also be considered transgressive by society in terms of violating social norms, but experienced as transformative by interview partners, such as cross-dressing.

Colorblindness as *white* privilege

Commonly, *white* interview partners did not perform race consciously in role play. To some, this was because they generally felt that they remained themselves and they did not invent a fictional character. In that case, they stayed *white*, they remained in their everyday gender and so on. For instance, if they expressed their partial identity as a slave, the question of skin color did not come up for them when entering the slave head space: they were embodying themselves *as* slaves. Yet, it remained a *white* privilege not to concern oneself with one's racial status and history when taking on the role of a slave or slave-owner. While interview partners were aware of the performativity of gender in their roles even if they did not cross gender lines, they did not acknowledge the performative character of their race as *white* in this regard; there was no racial equivalent to gender-variation play (see Chapter 8). They did not explore or discuss how different roles might shift the meaning of *whiteness*, for instance. Even play that was highly racialized historically and culturally, like master–slave, was deracialized by *white* players in monochromatic constellations, as *white* transman Jonas observed:

> There is play with colonial history and slavery, what was indeed a clearly ethnically specific matter in reality, but in the transfer to the SM game, this is not evident. Or very, very, very rarely evident. It probably only comes to the fore if those who play have an African-American or [African-] European background.

In the dyke + queer BDSM context, a curious disconnection from the historical reference to slavery took place, which only resurfaced if Blacks, as obviously racialized, were part of the play.

This kind of 'colorblindness' is part of a post-racist myth of equality that helps to deny institutionalized racism and enables *whites* to imagine their play as not racialized and therefore not politically relevant (see also Weiss 2011: 197). Weiss argues that BDSM performances in this way may appropriate racist histories and realities, trivializing them (198). To me, this danger seems to be inherent in the extensive use of the term 'slave', which is circulated widely in the BDSM communities as a BDSM-specific technical term, so that its meaning is shifted in a way that seems to disassociate it from its racist history politically, while at the same time exploiting the emotional attachments to this history for sexual pleasures. This phenomenon is not unique to BDSM, since the term 'slave' has been used as a metaphor for eternal devotion in discourses of romantic love as well, for instance in popular music. The effects of these kinds of circulations of metaphors in affective discourses warrant further investigation.

Impact of race on BDSM, sex and gender

Cultural racism has limited the options for play for dykes + queers of color in various ways. First of all, dykes + queers of color might not feel comfortable with certain practices in an interracial context, as *white* genderqueer Femmeboy reported: 'a friend of mine, an African-American woman, said she wouldn't be comfortable bottoming to six *white* tops, for instance. She would have a problem with it. Historically.' *White* middle-class bisexual Franka also reflected upon the historical and current impact of racism on her BDSM, stating that negotiations with a person of color should include what kind of comments or actions would be reproducing real-life experiences of racism.

Part of racist discourse depicts people of color as possessing a non-normative sexuality, for instance as hypersexual, dangerous, depraved or carnal (Stokes 2001; Khan 2009: 94–5), while *whiteness* functions as the 'unmarked signifier of sexual purity' (Khan 2009: 95). There is a *white* standard against which Blacks are constructed as masculine and hypersexual (Davis 1983), Asians in general as hyperfeminine and Asian men as desexualized (Schiebinger 1993). In this sense, people of color have never had the privilege of being sexually 'normal', a point that *white* queer theories about heteronormativity and heterosexual privilege often overlook (Cohen 2005; Haritaworn 2007). Springer, therefore, suggests that the Black woman was always already queer, as the *white* norm's other (2008: 86).

The history and contemporary reality of continuing racism impact the affective meanings of certain racial positions in play for dykes + queers of color themselves, but also for potential *white* partners, who may be prejudiced or struggling with *white* guilt (Winant 1997: 41), which is especially problematic given that the majority of potential play partners are *white* due to the racial composition of the community. *White* dykes + queers might feel uncomfortable topping a Black person or even seeing a Black bottom. *White* gay transman Wolf recounted an instance in the German dyke + BDSM community:

> This Black woman had made SM a big thing in [this town] with her lover in the first place back then. And she was running around there, and the other one was leading her on a leash. And at the time I had made an attempt of a fling with a femme, completely odd story [laughs shortly], and then she says to me: 'And the Black woman was even wearing the collar.'

The *white* woman assumed she was in a position to judge the Black woman's decision to bottom and insinuated that she did not deal appropriately with her own history or social position as a Black woman. This assumption attests to *white* arrogance and unearned moral authority (Bérubé 2001) and, possibly, discomfort with being confronted with historical racism as a *white* person. Sometimes Black bottoms could not find *whites* willing to top them, and Michaela described her own *white* discomfort: 'I'm not sure how comfortable I'd feel with bringing race into play, for example, if I was dominating a Black woman. I'm not sure if I could tell if I was dominating her because she was Black. Consensual or not, I would feel uncomfortable with that.' Thus, race can be seen to introduce an unwelcome social inequality to the presumably egalitarian (women's) community. The possibility of negotiating consent was not questioned among monochromatic *white* women and trans* people, but between women of different skin colors, destroying the illusion of a community devoid of predefined power relations and posing the threat of naturalized and imposed, as opposed to performed and self-chosen, power hierarchies. This *white* discomfort also created a double standard, since dykes + queers of color were not credited with the same kind of agency. Therefore, it had an impact on both their possibilities of finding play partners and the kind of play that was available to them.

While interview partners were able to see sex/gender, age and class as performative and transformable, the same did not seem to hold true for race (see also Weiss's description of a Black bottom in a 'slave auction' community event; 2011: 3–4). While I am far from suggesting that transgressing 'racial taboos' in a community dominated by *white* dykes + queers would in itself be a politically progressive act, the problematic dynamic remained that gender, sexuality, age (and to a lesser extent class) received a lot of attention and were consciously negotiated in dyke + queer BDSM spaces, while the racialization of the *white* majority went largely unnoticed, remained unexplored and functioned as a non-transgressable and probably also non-transformable cultural taboo when it came to the interracial imaginary. Thus, *white*ness remained invisible as a racial norm (see also Weiss 2011: 193ff) and the space of dyke + queer BDSM was not used to critically engage with it.

Race-based play

Play that made explicit use of racist stereotypes was a hard limit for most (*white*) interview partners. Only a few mentioned fantasies in that direction, but most of them had not enacted them yet. Even though it was usually not public in the overall dyke + queer BDSM community, race play does take place. At this point it seems that predominantly BDSM people of color or those with a Jewish background consciously engage with it and openly and critically discuss it, for instance in the context of the concept of cultural trauma (Hernández 2004; Berlinger 2006; Koone 2008; Plaid 2009; Weiss 2011). Various Black BDSMers have discussed race play as a productive and healing way for them to engage with racism (see Dark Connections n.d; Julien 1994: 126; Reid-Pharr 2001: 137; Freeman 2008: 43; Plaid 2009). Historical slavery play can, therefore, be seen as a way to renegotiate racist histories that stick to the present through disidentification. In a public BDSM performance called 'The Black Confederacy', African American Mistress Mz Dre inflicted everything on her *white* bottom that historically *white* people had done to Blacks in the US, including tarring and feathering her. This was obviously too much to handle for the predominantly *white* audience members. They did not seem to be able to experience the reversal that Mz Dre offered as a form of critique, reconciliation or catharsis. Instead, their discomfort in being confronted with racist history prevailed. This experience shows that there are still limits to the parodying potential of BDSM when it comes to race, even though Mz Dre did not let herself be limited by this in her way of playing.

Class: Between being unissued and fetishized

Most interview partners claimed that class was not an issue in their BDSM practices. But Scout, a *white* working-class queer, analyzed how experiences of violence were class-related and how that informed BDSM practices. *White* genderqueer Firesong, who was of a middle-class background growing up, also acknowledged that class-related experiences of physicality impacted approaches to BDSM:

> I was a very protected kind of child. I was a musician. I grew up not being allowed to ride a bike, because I might hurt my hands. This is such a different experience than someone who grew up beating up their brother, in terms of how I'm gonna bottom. To me, my whole experience bottoming, or topping for that matter, inflicting pain or receiving pain, is completely different from someone who played in the streets, totally different.

Thus, class differences were inscribed on embodied subjectivities in various ways. As Firesong showed, members of different classes might develop different kinds of relationships to their body due to the kind of work and leisure activities they performed. Dyke + queer BDSM could be used as a way to work through these kinds of embodied subjectivities and potentially change one's embodiment.

Stereotypical constructions of class are evident in the fetishization of working-class people and culture in the gay, lesbian and queer BDSM communities. Lisa found her middle-class real-life persona unsexy and preferred to play a lower-class slutty girl in her BDSM sessions. This is a heritage of discourses that posit working-class women as biologically driven to excess, while upper-class women are constructed as naturally indifferent to the flesh (McClintock 1995: 86). Gay transman Wolf, who came from a white-collar background but was of precarious socio-economic status at the time of our interview, rejected the contemporary working-class fetishes of middle and upper-class gay men:

> [Craftsman pants] are not a fashion accessory, boys, but work clothing. I think they are very sexy and I would like to have a pair myself, but there is the matter of 'I am not buying it, because there are people who simply have to wear them as work clothing and those are damn hard jobs.'

Wolf criticized the consumption and fetishization of working-class clothing from a position of socio-economic privilege because it exploited working-class people erotically without doing anything to redistribute economic power or to improve working conditions.

McClintock interprets fetishization as the displacement of social contradictions that the individual cannot resolve at a personal level onto an object (or person) (1995: 186). The individual gains symbolic control over what might otherwise be terrifying ambiguities (184). In the example Wolf discussed, the fetishization of working-class clothing and men could be seen to embody the contradictory social values of class position and what is considered to be authentic masculinity. Middle and upper-class gay men desire masculine embodiments that display traces of hard physical labor, but not the social status and the material consequences associated with that labor. Therefore, class remains paradoxically unissued. It is considered not relevant (not an issue), and at the same time it is effective enough to produce fetishes, reducing it to a question of cultural form rather than of material significance.[1]

Class-based play

Some of the role play of interview partners was consciously designed to draw on class dynamics. As Tony, who was a student with a precarious socio-economic status at the time of the interview, explained, the theme of economic exploitation can provide a lot of material for BDSM role play, for instance in scenarios involving sex workers. As Björn, who also had a precarious socio-economic status, pointed out, one might use role play to embody class positions one would never inhabit in real life. For Lola, who was downwardly mobile, playing with class helped her to work through feelings of disenfranchisement. Therefore, real-life class issues did inform my interview partners' BDSM practices.

Chapter conclusion

My interview partners considered power to be intrinsic to the whole of the social fabric, including sexuality. They valued the transparency of negotiated power dynamics in dyke + queer BDSM. Negotiating power into one's relationships might present a challenge to non-consensual oppression in the regular world through the experience of new kinds of agency.

Emotional investments in power were partially transfigured in dyke + queer BDSM, with its erotic and emotional attachments to practices and positions of little or no social value or recognition. These re-evaluations of negative emotions and devalued objects, bodies and practices may offer hope for micropolitical interventions. They show that there is always an excess of emotions and desires that can intervene in unpredictable ways in hegemonic processes of subjectification.

Yet, not all social hierarchies were addressed in a similar fashion in dyke + queer BDSM communities. Transformative acts occurred mainly in terms of gender, sexuality and age, while class-based play seemed to be purely transgressive for the most part, and consciously race-based play seemed to present too strong a taboo within the mostly *white* community to be employed for either transgressive or transformative practices. Most *white* interview partners only acknowledged race when people of color entered the scene, which racialized the context that otherwise seemed free of racial dynamics. This was due to *white* privilege, which enabled interview partners to ignore their own racial position. Moreover, the unacknowledgment of *whiteness* seemed to enable transgressions in other realms, because it reduced complex, simultaneous social systems to polarities (such as man–woman instead of raced genders). This move established a clear line between the polar opposites that one could transgress, rather than just repositioning oneself with ambiguous and contradictory results. For instance, claiming a slut identity was a transgression of sexual norms for *white* women of a certain class background, but not necessarily for Black women, who have historically been constructed via their deviant sexuality. This also highlights the need to move beyond an understanding of transgression as subversive per se to a politics of transformation, which is less unidirectional in its perspective.

8
Exploring Intimate Difference Through Gender

One of the crucial practices in the dyke + queer BDSM communities was gender-based play. For some interview partners, like bisexual woman Vito, this was at the core of their practices: 'We have also thought about it before if we could refrain from playing with that role and that gender, but to me it is completely essential. So for me it is a very, very strong lust motivation on top of it.' Because of this major significance of gender-based play for generating desires and pleasures as well as for transformations of the self, this chapter investigates dyke + queer BDSM as a space for exploring and experimenting with gender as an example of intimate difference. I consider relations of social difference to be intimate, because they involve touch and boundary transgressions. Intimacy in the sense of access to bodies and its flip side, rights to bodily integrity, are distributed unevenly in society. Power circulates through bodies and produces erotic investments in social structures of domination and in subversive practices. Dyke + queer BDSM as an erotic practice highlights this intimate character of social difference and exploits it in play.

Duncan discusses dyke BDSM as a site of cultural conflict (1996: 87). As such, BDSM holds the potential for reconceptualizing notions of social difference. This renegotiation of identity is enabled by the fact that both identities and power are constructed, imaginary, negotiated and constantly shifting and by the fact that BDSM is based on difference and the eroticization of that difference (88). For the women in Duncan's interviews, within the structure of BDSM scenes, identity became malleable (101) and a site of transformation (103), a finding that was confirmed by my data.

Dyke + queer BDSM community context as a space for exploring gender

The dyke + queer BDSM community seems to provide a special space for exploring gender, since no other subset of the BDSM community is composed of such a diversity of genders and such a culture of exploring and playing with gender. In the gay male BDSM community there is practically no gender play except for playing on variations of the theme of polarized masculinity. In the mixed, heterosexually dominated BDSM communities, playing with gender basically is reduced to the forced feminization of biological males.[1] Anti-trans* sentiments also remain a part of the non-BDSM lesbian communities, which are partly justified through a discursive construction of transwomen as dangerous to women (Salamon 2010: 107). This leads Salamon to demand that feminism accept and respond to the fact that there are more than two lived genders (2010, especially Chapter 4). Even non-BDSM queer or trans* communities can be rather normative in what kinds of gender expressions are allowed. My interview partners agreed that the dyke + queer BDSM communities were extraordinarily accepting of gender difference. I was interested to look for possible explanations of what set this community apart from others in regard to this queer gender potential.

Culturally lesbian woman Helene suggested that in women's spaces the position of men became vacant through their absence and was available to be filled through play in creative ways, while in the straight community this position was already occupied and therefore was harder to claim by women. Likewise, pansexual genderqueer femme Neila argued that the lack of culturally predefined gender hierarchies in women's communities opened up a space to express genders in ways that were not possible elsewhere. And lesbian Connie and gay transman Wolf pointed out the high motivation for dykes and trans* people (who possess low status in the heteronormative social hierarchy) to embody masculine roles that could open up new worlds, while for gay and straight men embodying a different gender role would suggest a loss of status and, therefore, of possibilities.[2] This also explains the tendency to privilege expressions of female masculinity (Rick 2007), since this means embodying the space that has been structurally denied to women. So the separatist space was one factor in allowing gender experimentation.

Additionally, interview partners understood gender exploration to be an extension of the more general exploration enabled by dyke + queer BDSM. Choosing a gender different from one's own might be interesting because it offered an insight into another perspective on the social world. For instance, dyke woman Michaela enjoyed the insight she gained when she adopted the role of a straight male character in role play. Neila added that a cross-gender expression as a simple reversal of one's assigned gender role was the first obvious step in exploring gender within a binary construction. Then, over time, the community became more sophisticated in playing with and inventing new genders beyond the binary. Dyke femme Mistress Mean Mommy observed:

> You wanna come up with something new, and you just go around to people and say: 'Hey, guess what my new thing is, I'm gonna be a princess

daddy. That to me is somebody who's really stern and parental, but wants you to carry them around in a little litter or something. That's my princess daddy version.' – 'And what the hell is a princess daddy?' I was just like: 'Who knows? I'll just invent it. I'll be me, and that will be what a princess daddy is.' Ten years from now, there'll be dyke princess daddy contests.

This humorously illustrated the inventiveness and the general climate of acceptance of new gender variations and identities in the community. Once a certain multiplicity of gender expressions in the community was established, it became a supportive environment for experimenting further. Queer genderqueer/transgender Firesong discussed how exploring gender affected the community: 'As I recognize different roles in myself, that's an experience of diversity. So if that's something that people are exploring individually, then in the community that would probably be reflected as a common acceptance of valuing diverse expression.' Firesong implied that experiences of difference within the self could lead to an acceptance of interpersonal difference; the valuing of difference on the community level, then, was a result of reflecting on one's own gender and sexuality and experiencing it as difference-within through partial selves.

The US transgender activist and performer Kate Bornstein sees a connection between BDSM and gender in terms of performativity:

Sadomasochism intersects with gender at the point of *performance*. We perform our identities, which include gender, and we perform our relationships, which include sex. Transgender is simply identity more consciously performed on the infrequently used playing field of gender. S/M is simply a relationship more consciously performed within the forbidden arena of power.

(1994: 124; Bornstein's emphasis)

She points out one main element of the binary gender system: 'The current gender system relies heavily on everyone's agreement that it's inflexible. Key to doing away with gender is the ability to freely move into and out of existing genders and gender roles' (121). This is exactly what my interview partners used the semi-contained space of dyke + queer BDSM for, as queer transgender butch Tony described:

Nobody comes along and says: 'but you are actually ... '. You interact on a completely safe level with people who perceive you as exactly what you want to be perceived as, no matter how out of this world it may be. It is simply completely all right, and it matters to nobody how it is acted out or how it is performed, but it is simply as it is.

My interview partners felt that dyke + queer BDSM was a safe space in which to choose any gender they wanted to embody, as opposed to everyday life, where gender was not self-determined and subjective, but assigned according to sex, which is seen as an underlying objective truth: 'but you are actually...'. In the dyke + queer BDSM communities, in contrast, 'gender is not based on biology at all', as queer/gay transguy Matt stated. The dyke + queer BDSM communities have developed subcultural techniques for recognizing and reading all kinds of queer genders. This recognition of queer genders within the community stood in stark contrast to society's pressures for gender conformity. The potentials of expressing partial identities were also related to gender hierarchies, as queer genderqueer Femmeboy explained: 'I'm more comfortable as a boy actually. I feel very vulnerable when I'm dressed in femme drag. I don't know what to call it, but it doesn't feel safe to me. I can feel sexy that way, but I also feel very vulnerable that way.' The erotic value of a feminine presentation was double-edged, as it made her feel like a sexual object for men and a potential subject of harassment. Thus, everyday sexism restricted her options to freely express all of her partial gender identities and skewed her presentation toward the masculine range, while feminine expressions were kept more to contained spaces.

Gender agency through dyke + queer BDSM

My interview partners reported that dyke + queer BDSM functioned to support them in developing gender agency. It might even 'force' them to develop that agency, as queer transgender butch Tony explained: 'So I believe if I couldn't say with a certain self-confidence of myself as well: "In this moment I have a male body", then the session wouldn't function either. Then I would feel uncomfortable and then it would not work out.' Thus, the credibility needed for BDSM roles provided an incentive to learn how to perform certain genders convincingly and to develop a certain gender habitus as well as an inner feeling of embodied congruence with that performance and habitus. At the same time, gender self-confidence was fostered because gender was differently and much less policed within dyke + queer BDSM. Rather, interview partners described gender as a conscious and active co-construction, as Femmeboy emphasized in regard to her FTM lover: 'That's very important to me that I'm fucking my lover, his body, in a way that is constructing that body, perceiving that body in a way that the person wants to be perceived.' This statement points at the performative embodiment of gender: the sexed body only becomes meaningful within a social interaction, not in a vacuum.

Co-constructing genders, therefore, involves work for the actors. Lorenz understands sexual labor as doubly productive: it produces value and subjectivity (Lorenz 2009: 15). Answering interpellations means work for the (aspiring) subject, who in turn calls on others to perform sexual labor on his/her behalf (17), but the efforts of the processes of subjectification vary for different individuals (18). For instance, my interviews showed that marginalized subjects like trans* persons had to do more gender and sexual labor than did majoritarian subjects. On the other hand, Salamon points out how the request by trans* individuals to be seen as something specific, for example for transmen to be seen as men, is a temporal reversal of Althusser's interpellation (2010: 123–4). But demanding or expecting things of others is also part of male privilege. Thus, from the perspective of femmes, who are supposed to co-construct transmen as men by being their female counterparts, Ward defines gender labor as the affective and bodily efforts to give gender to someone (Ward 2010: 237).[3] In her study on the gender labor that femmes perform in relationships with FTM partners, Ward finds that it serves to solidify a binary between transgender and fixed-gender subjectivities (2010: 248), positioning femmes as women who are naturally comfortable with their female embodiment, rather than disidentifying with it in a sexist culture (250). While Ward's analysis is significant, the partners of trans* people in my sample painted a somewhat different picture of gender labor. They enjoyed co-constructing bodies to make gender consensual, and they described these acts not only as work, but also as emotionally rewarding and sexually gratifying, and therefore productive of gender identities *and* queer desires and pleasures.

In a heteronormative culture, gender norms are an imperative that one has to resist actively, as trans/genderqueer/butch dyke Scout observed:

> I also participate in separatist community space once a year, and this space is very important to me, because even though I try not to, I find myself modeling my masculinity or adjusting it to not-trans-male masculinity throughout the year in ways. Then I get in women's space and realize it is not inherent or natural in the way I understand my masculinity to be, but rather is a shield I put on to pass through the world, to make myself more comfortable or more stereotypically 'desirable' to others.

In heteronormative environments Scout participated in a self-dynamic of adjusting his masculinity in a way that enabled him to move through the world free of harassment and with a sense of desirability. Only in women's space was he able to construct his own masculinity without the constant reference to cis-masculinity and was able to refocus on his own queer feminist standards. Thus, a non-normative gender performance may require conscious gender labor and specific social spaces in order to actively resist normalization. Hale suggests that leatherdyke boys are less constrained by hegemonic notions of masculinity because their gender performances are embedded in a subcultural or scene context, which he calls 'a culture of two'[4] (2003: 65) and which I refer to as semi-contained space, yet these gender performances are regulated nonetheless in order to stay intelligible as queer masculinities (62). A culture of two still remains imprinted by the social contexts around it, but different kinds of social contexts provide different kinds of gendered interactions and different options for co-constructions.

My interview partners had developed strategies to deal with heteronormativity through dyke + queer BDSM. For instance, some trans* people chose to top as a way to stay in control of their bodies, which was otherwise denied to them. Kaldera also stresses that BDSM negotiations in general enable control over what happens to one's body, and that this is helpful for trans* individuals (2009: 51). Queer femme Katharina used a session where she embodied a pirate queen with a captive boy to reassign power to feminine artifacts and acts:

> And after the young man was not quite so reluctant anymore and started to find the woman pirate rather fascinating, I took this clothespin and first made the connection: this is women's work, it is devalued work this stands for. But I use this clothespin now as an instrument with which I can exercise power. And at the same time a power over this young man. And through the fact that this exercise of power also provides him with lust, it is also something that increases its value on various levels, so to speak.

She used BDSM to infuse feminine artifacts with power through transforming them into a tool of domination and pleasure. She also used her long fingernails in a similar way. This empowering of femininity in play served as a balance for other social contexts she had to move through, which constantly addressed feminine women as inferior.

Exploring gender in dyke + queer BDSM

Gender is a social power relation and was therefore complexly interwoven with power and with other social categories in dyke + queer BDSM interactions. For instance, the term 'boy/boi' connoted a certain gender expression and a BDSM position. It was a specific bottom role that was characterized through a boyish masculinity that was not related to real-life age or sexed body type. There was the lesbian boi, who was distanced from hegemonic understandings of boy through the spelling, and a gay male version of boy, both of which existed in the dyke + queer BDSM communities. What was not discussed by interview partners was that using the term 'boy' for grown-ups also has a racist and classist history, since slaves, men of color and men from the lower classes working in the service industry were and are still addressed as 'boys' to belittle them. This was one way in which racial references were unacknowledged in the community.

In contrast, the association of gender with power was apparent to my interview partners. They cited the social construction of how gender is infused with power relations and used it for their own play, such as under-standing aggression and dominance as masculine traits. To queer-straight femme Teresa, masculinity was inherently dominant, and being the object of that desire was part of her femme identity. The general cultural deval-uation of women and femininity was exploited in play, but also restricted play options. For instance, interview partners struggled to find powerful feminine roles without having to rely on importing masculine stereotypes. Butch-loving femme Lisa considered her own submissiveness to be an effect of gender socialization. She therefore admired women who were dominant and was at first resistant to bottoming due to her feminist convictions. Gen-der hierarchy also affected safety, especially for bottoms. Teresa explained why she did not play with cismen:

> Living in a sexist society, and having a relationship to masculinity where it's about it dominating me, it doesn't appeal to me to be a lot with bioboys. Because it's just like: 'You were born with that power!' So I feel that bioboys have to totally unlearn their dominance before they can come full circle to topping me.

What was essential to Teresa was to bottom to someone who was aware of the performative character of her gender identity and power within dyke + queer BDSM; cismen who were born with gender privilege often inhabited a naturalized position of power and were not aware of their own sense of entitlement. Therefore, the gender, sexuality and BDSM practices of my interview partners were impacted by sexism and heteronormativity.

Generally, gender functioned as a lens through which interview partners looked at their BDSM interactions. They consciously drew on gender as a rich cultural resource for play. Especially for trans* individuals, gender was always an undercurrent in play, even though it might become less so with familiar partners. There was great variety in how interview partners played with gender in their BDSM. I identified seven different dynamics or types: gender privilege play, gender identity exploration play, gender sliding play, gender variation play, gender polarization play, gender nonconformity play and gender validation play. These categories were not part of community discourse; instead, all of these were commonly grouped together under the umbrella of gender play. My potentially artificial splitting of the commu-nity term into various subcategories serves to demonstrate the myriad ways in which gender was employed, co-constructed, reinvented and multiplied in dyke + queer BDSM practices. It is meant to illustrate the richness of the dyke + queer BDSM culture in this regard. In practice, many of these categories overlapped and intersected and were not neatly distinguishable. Furthermore, I have certainly not captured all the dynamics and motives involved in gender play in the community, especially as these are always in the process of evolving.

Gender privilege play

The social gender binary and the gendered and sexualized hierarchies among men, women and trans* people presented one point of departure for gender play, employing gender privilege and gender policing to evoke dynamics of power and humiliation. These are two different but related elements in heterosexist societies. Sexism connects the male sex/gender with privilege. In regard to sexuality, it constructs women as passive, but tempting, or within a 'virgin/whore' dichotomy (Filipovic 2008). Men, as the supposed polar opposite to women, are constructed as active and libido-driven, which presents them with a (sexy) 'asshole'/(asexual) 'nice guy' double bind corresponding to the 'virgin/whore' double bind for women (Serano 2008: 232ff). These constructions of gender and sexuality also intersect with race, class and ability to create various stereotypes and differentiated, sometimes contradictory, moral interpellations. Gender privilege tends to only privilege cismen and certain FTMs who pass as male.

Gender policing is a technology of power and domination that serves to uphold the gender binary, since it punishes those who do not fit in with gender norms. A lot of anti-queer violence, targeted at both gays and trans* people, is actually about policing gender presentations, and those outside gender normative presentations are most at risk (Namaste 2000: 136). Gender policing, therefore, is not identical with sexism, since it may target members of all sexes/genders, but it helps to sustain sexist social structures by patrolling the borders between the sexes to make sure every individual stays 'in their place' within the gender hierarchy. Gender policing is also connected to cultural anxieties about difference. As Salamon points out, difference that masquerades as sameness is perceived as dangerous, and therefore passing transsexuals cause discomfort (2010: 112). According to her, the primary anxiety today is not that trans* people may not pass, but that they may pass too well, that one cannot tell them apart from cispeople. These are fears that mirror anxieties about sleeper spies and porous national borders in a post-9/11 world (192). Therefore, trans* individuals find themselves in a 'lose–lose situation' whether they are visibly different or whether they pass; in each case, they cause anxiety and often experience violent reactions to being different and to exposing the unreliability and constructedness of sex/gender.

My interview partners drew on these realities and discourses for their dyke + queer BDSM scenarios. For polysexual transwoman Anna, being turned into a 'stereotypical woman' and used sexually as a doll was a major fetish fantasy, which exploited the fact that women are considered sexual objects. Transgender stone butch Terry played scenes that were based on discovering someone's 'hidden gender'. Given the fact that many trans* people face the need to hide their genital status in order to feel safe, this drew on actual trans* realities. In public and legal discourses, such non-disclosure of a trans* status is considered to be deceit and fraud (Beauchamp 2013), and is regularly used as a justification for violence against trans* people (Genschel 2000; Bettcher 2013). Thus, dyke + queer BDSM provided a space for trans* individuals to work through these dangerous scenarios.

Gay transman Jonas used humiliation in BDSM as a way to deal with his trans-related body issues:

> The quite most humiliating thing for me is to be seen as a woman, play as a woman and to be forced to disclose my female genital parts. And that has to do a lot with my being trans. And I think that I chose SM for myself consciously or unconsciously as a possibility to get something positive out of this humiliation. Namely to become aroused by it.

The exposure of body parts coded as female was humiliating for Jonas as a transman. Putting this into a dyke + queer BDSM context converted shame into something positive through infusing it with erotic value (see also Kaldera 2009: 95–6). On the other hand, Jonas was not sure whether this way of dealing with body dysphoria was a successful coping strategy or also, in part, self-destructive. Either way, dyke + queer BDSM provided him with a space for gender identity exploration.

Clearly, even 'negative' affects such as shame and humiliation can be productive, if not painless, in dyke + queer BDSM. Ahmed attributes the power of shame to the feeling of exposure, which is intensified by being seen by others who witness the failure to live up to an ideal and whose moral judgment matters (2004: 103–6). In shame, the subject may have nowhere to turn (104). Therefore, shame can be intensified in a BDSM situation of restraint, which literally makes it impossible to turn elsewhere. Lorenz frames shame more in terms of being exposed in one's social status before witnesses (2009: 66). Shame triggers intensive affective work on the self (69). Ahmed also points out that shame can be the affective cost of not following the scripts of normative existence (2004: 107). The element of exposure and the invasion of personal space that these theorists attribute to shame also make it an experience of intimacy. In dyke + queer BDSM practices, staying with shame rather than trying to avoid it can function to intensify this negative emotion. Or, alternatively, the semi-contained space of dyke + queer BDSM may serve as a refuge from shame, infusing shameful activities with erotic value and postponing the engagement with or changing the relationship to this bad feeling. In Jonas' case, his play led not only to affective, but also to material work on the self: he transitioned to male in (at least partial) response.

Gender identity exploration and transformation play

Dyke + queer BDSM provided a space for interview partners to explore their gender identities, as genderqueer Femmeboy put it: 'For instance, if I'm role playing I could be a girl one day and a boy the other day in the leather community. Because people are into role-playing and taking on different personas, it opens up the possibilities for exploring gender.' This exploration helped them to discover aspects of their identities, and their overall gender identity might coalesce through dyke + queer BDSM. This prompted Terry to ask: 'Is that gender play? I don't know. It probably started out being gender play and now is part of their identity.' Therefore, this exploration was not limited to the BDSM space, but led some interview partners to change their gender in everyday life. Thus, gender play did not stop at being a transgressive practice for sexual pleasures, but also became transformative, changing the embodied self. For instance, it fostered Anya's coming out as femme, and that of many FTMs in my sample. Kaldera's (2009) findings confirm that BDSM involvement facilitates transitioning for trans* people.

BDSM also helped genderqueer interview partners to specify their gender position and facilitated working out and consolidating a boy identity for transgender butch Tony: 'So by now I would say that in my everyday life specific reactions on my part to my partner or other people have something very boyish about them, but which I only can name like this since I have worked out this identity in play.' Play partners became mirrors or gender mentors in this process, co-constructing each other's gender. Exploring gender was a practice that produced pleasures not only for those who were playing with their own gender, but also for their counterparts in a session. The multiplication and specification of genders was, therefore, a community value and had generated subcultural skills that I have called *renaming/reassigning*, *recognition* and *integration* (see also Bauer 2007b). In the following two sections, I will develop the first two categories from my interviews, while integration is discussed later.

Reassigning bodies: Cybercocks and holodicks

Gender play enabled my interview partners to recode bodies. Through dyke + queer BDSM practices, the social significance of the gendered body could be changed without modifying the body. This was a solution to a certain extent for some, but others moved on to alter their bodies through hormones and surgery. Transwoman Daphne referred to her (by then removed) biological penis as her 'second appendix'. It is an interesting analogy, since the appendix is a part of the body that may have to be removed if it gets sick. So, for some individuals, removing the penis is part of a healing process (instead of a mutilation of the body). This resonates with Hayward's concept of the cut as a possibility of transsexual becoming (2008: 72). Hayward complicates the concept of bodily integrity, since bodies are never pure; embodiment is still coherent, however, because 'I am always of my tissue even in its ongoing transformation' (73).

In Anglo-American law, the bodies of the citizens belong to the state, which is evident, for instance, historically and currently in the laws against the self-mutilation of slaves, prison inmates, soldiers and the poor, acts which could all be considered to be resistance against forced labor (Loeb 2008: 49–50). One's sex is also not the private property of the individual, but belongs to the state as well, as the legal administration of transsexuals highlights (Salamon 2010: 183). The entitlement of *white* men to the integrity of their bodies started in the mid-19th century, but that standard still does not apply to non-normative bodies, such as intersex people or Black women (Loeb 2008: 50ff). But the right to bodily integrity is not simply about keeping one's body in its 'original' state; there are people who wish to transform or regenerate their bodies, including transsexuals. I therefore propose a reimagination of the concept of bodily integrity as a state of being that makes the individual feel most in synchronicity with their sense of self. Bodily integrity could be understood as a state in which the body matches the body image, and others respect this. In this case, bodily integrity would mean different things to different people; it might include changing the material body to conform to one's body image, as in the case of transsexual body modifications. Moreover, with Hayward, bodily integrity would simultaneously mean coherence and constant transformation.

Not all trans* interview partners desired hormonal or surgical transformations. For some, a succession of play sessions led to *reassigning* body parts with different gendered meanings, which found its expression in the creative use of language to rename body parts. Anna reassigned her non-operative MTF body by distinguishing between medical definitions and lived identities or individual self-definitions: 'I define my own body rather in a way that I am saying: each woman somehow has her own personal body, one has large breasts, the other has a small clitoris or however.' First, she distinguished between sex as a prototype and individual sexed bodies, which were always different from the prototype. Then, she considered her body of birth to be her individual version of a woman's body, similar to ciswomen, whose individual bodies might not fit into gender norms in every aspect either. This was a different strategy from modifying one's body to synchronize it with one's body image, further extending difference within one category of sex. This is not as unusual as it may sound at first, since there are individual cismen whose breasts are larger than those of some individual ciswomen, for example. And the science of biology in general is unable to find unambiguous criteria to determine someone's sex, since it depends on many different markers that may be in conflict with each other, such as genetic, hormonal, gonadal and phenotypical sex (Fausto-Sterling 2000).

Once gender identity and body image are added to the picture, the situation gets even more complex. While Anna was shifting the hegemonic meaning of well-established terms, trans/genderqueer/butch dyke Scout and his Sir were developing their own language to talk about their bodies: 'So being a boy, he was trying to teach me how to have a boy cunt and reassign my body in a way that I could survive in it.' By combining two apparent contradictions, 'boy' and 'cunt', they carved out a space for genderqueer realities and bodies and created new meanings. Deleuze (1994) also stresses the power of language to transform itself through sense, for instance through combining two words to create a new meaning. Therefore, these choices are not about representation or naming, but about creating worlds of sense that interact with other material worlds, such as bodies. Scout and his Sir can be seen to have enacted this kind of creative function of language, inventing a new sense by combining the seemingly contradictory terms 'boy' and 'cunt'.

In the case of strap-on dildos, reassignment was taken a step further to (re)incorporate what is commonly considered to be a technical artifact (a sex toy) as a body part, as a penis. To interview partners on the FTM spectrum and to those who played as men in dyke + queer BDSM and their significant others, dildos were not dildos, but genuine parts of their bodies, and they referred to them as their dicks or cocks (while, if more femme or woman-identified individuals strapped one on, they more often remained dildos). Scout discussed his relationship to his cock:

> Fucking with a dildo is like, when I'm feeling it, I'm connected to it. And playing in bed in the morning when waking up and fucking, we call it a dick [even] when I don't have anything on. It's in my brain and she still comes; it's also really intense. So there's this kind of tricky thing. We call it a dick for a lack of a better word, but it's not like I desire a dick, a flesh penis dick. I don't have a desire for that.

So strapping on a dildo gave a material form to his cock or infused it with life; he felt it like any other part of his body. In Scout's case, though, it was not a substitute for a penis made of flesh, because his butch transmasculinity did not cause him any desire for a cismale body.

Other interview partners also stressed that their dildos were part of their bodies in this way. Therefore, I refer to them as *cybercocks*. As for cyborgs, for trans* people and genderqueers these artificial extensions of their body are incorporated and become part of the self, expanding bodily integrity to a hybrid of flesh and artifact, a cyborg embodiment. Grosz also holds that anything that stays in contact long enough with the body surface can be integrated into the body image (1994: 80), and, I would add, this integrated part became receptive to sensations for interview partners. Trans* bodies have been described as unnatural and monstrous (see Stryker 1994: 245 for a subversive narrative of the transsexual as Frankenstein's monster) in a move that appropriates the function of monsters as heralds of the extraordinary, eluding gender definition (247) and becoming something other and more than their makers intended (248). Haraway utilizes the metaphor of the cyborg, a postmodern monster, to conceptualize the subject more generally. The cyborg embodies partiality, irony, intimacy, perversity, opposition, utopia and a lack of innocence. Through its position at the interface between organism and machine, the cyborg necessitates a redefinition of 'nature' and 'culture'. Cyborgs are children of militarism and patriarchal capitalism, but as illegitimate offspring they are not necessarily loyal toward their culture of origin (Haraway 1991: 151).

Cyborgs are an especially productive metaphor for dyke + queer and trans* BDSM subjectivities. They generate perverse kinds of kinship, embodiment and desires, crossing boundaries like those between human and machine/artifact, nature and culture, man and woman, blood and chosen kin, reproductive and recreational sex. And, as children of a heteronormative system, they are betraying their origins. According to Haraway, cyborgs have more to do with regeneration than with rebirth, and a limb regrown after injury can be monstrous (1991: 181). Regeneration as a dyke + queer embodied practice is a (re)iterative enactment not only of growing new boundaries (rebodying), but also of imperiling static boundaries (Hayward 2008: 75–6), as in the changeling body ('a body who's changing sex from one day to another') Eric inhabited. Monster, alien, changeling and cyborg are forms of subjectivities that exceed regulation, creating uncontained excesses of signification and potentials to create something beyond the human.

The cyborg element in dyke + queer BDSM was not necessarily restricted to dildos that were incorporated into the body (image) as dicks, but could also be found in the usage of other implements, such as whips, which extended the body. Weiss suggests that BDSM tools in general become a part of the body when used, and that this use transforms the body (2011: 133–4). Yet my interview partners did not tend to view these implements as parts of their body or body image in the same way as they saw their (and others') cybercocks. This suggests that, as opposed to what Grosz posits, not all artifacts that are in contact with the body or used by humans as tools are integrated into the body, at least not in the same way. Rather, some remain tools and others become extensions of the body with their own sensations, such as dildos and prostheses. Weiss theorizes BDSM toys as stand-ins for missing social relations, following a Freudian pathologizing concept (2011: 128; 130), yet later she shows with her own data how toys produce connection and intimacy (132; 135). The social relations deprivation theory seems to stem from nostalgia for an age that never existed, where humans are imagined to have lived in a natural state without any use of technological artifacts. Sexuality seems to be the one area left that is supposed to still be 'natural' and free from the use of technology in this mythical sense. In contrast, I would rather follow Haraway in accepting the human condition as that of a cyborg. Positing that tools deprive humans of social relations per se also risks supporting an ableist and transphobic discourse, pathologizing those bodies more in need of extensions of the flesh than others. The cyborg metaphor, on the other hand, emphasizes the fact that all humans are dependent upon some kind of artifacts and technologies for survival, thus stressing interdependence as the human condition.

But the dildo as part of the body was not the only alternative concept of understanding bodies in the excerpt above from Scout's interview. He also described possessing a non-material dick that could be interpersonally experienced as a penis, as proved by the fact that his partner was able to orgasm from being penetrated with this non-material entity. One may compare this to the phantom limbs of people who have lost body parts, but continue to feel them as part of their body. This would fit into transsexual narratives of dissonance between material and perceived or felt bodies. FTM scholars Jay Prosser (1998) and Henry Rubin (2003) developed theories about transsexuality utilizing the writings of French existentialist Merleau-Ponty and psychoanalysts Anzieu and Sack about phantom limbs and the opposite phenomenon, agnosia. Merleau-Ponty defined agnosia as the failure to recognize a part of one's own body as one's own. Therefore, he defined body image as the mental representation of the body as it is for the subject, which need not correspond directly with the physical body (Henry Rubin 2003: 28). Prosser observes that for transsexuals the body image clearly already has a material force (1998: 69). And both phenomena are relevant for transsexuals: the feeling of phantom 'limbs' such as cocks for FTMs or breasts and vaginas for MTFs, as well as agnosia, the felt absence of women's breasts for FTMs or penises and scrotums for MTFs. Scout's quote shows that this is not restricted to transsexual identities, but includes genderqueers who do not wish to alter their body. Precisely the fact that the body image already has such a material existence may be the reason why altering the body surgically may *not* be necessary for some individuals. Therefore, the materiality of the body image does not determine whether a trans* person decides for or against bodily interventions. Psychoanalyst Sack's research has shown that phantom limbs are not necessarily a negative side effect of amputation, but may enable the amputee to use a prosthesis more efficiently (Prosser 1998: 85). Scout's phantom penis enabled him to feel the strap-on dildo like a fleshly penis, rather than a disconnected piece of silicone.[5]

One may also interpret this phenomenon within an immaterial framework. Trans* people, then, would possess an energetic body that matches their gender identity. Sticking to the science fiction metaphors, I propose the term *holodick*, a reference to the 'holodecks' in the US science fiction TV series *Star Trek*. Holodecks are spaces of simulated reality, which also transgress the boundaries between what is generally thought of as material reality and what is seen as simulation or immaterial imagination. Humans and those aliens that are also embodied life forms enter the holodeck with their real bodies, move in this simulated reality as in a role play scenario, and experience real bodily affects while some aspects of ordinary reality are suspended; for instance, weapons are not lethal. Therefore, the holodeck reality has much in common with the reality of the semi-contained space of dyke + queer BDSM. The holodick could thus be considered an artifact from this other reality that has been brought back into ordinary life. When switching from one type of reality to another, structures of relevance are left behind (Schütz & Luckmann 2003: 182). When it comes to the reality of dyke + queer BDSM, interview partners were able to leave the relevance of the binary gender system behind. Schütz and Luckmann define a symbol as a theme that covers two spheres of reality, for instance interpreting a dream while being awake (183). Those themes may leave behind enclaves in ordinary life, like the holodick. This underscores the fact that these different realities are not completely separate; there is cross-pollination. Both the cybercock and the holodick are ways of reassigning and reinventing sexed bodies that transgress the boundaries and transform the meanings of the body and bodily integrity.

Recognition

Related to the subcultural skill of renaming/reassigning was *recognition*. Transgender butch Tony recalled a situation:

> I played as bottom as boy, and my partner undressed me and put me in front of a mirror. And for the first time really I actually consciously saw in that naked body an absolutely boyish or masculine body. And then afterwards I had this experience of 'what biology tells us is simply complete bullshit'. [laughs] I see what I want to see, and my partners can also see what they want to see.

Here, the act of recognition referred to an insight that occurred during a scene and reassigned a heteronormatively female-coded body as boyish or masculine. It was not planned or actively sought; it happened rather spontaneously (of course, also due to the history and context of the situation). Tony suddenly *saw* himself as differently gendered than before.

'Seeing' is a term that was commonly used by interview partners in both a literal and a metaphorical sense, referring to seeing themselves, but even more so to seeing others: recognizing somebody else's partial, play or all-encompassing gender identity from the outside, which stressed the importance of being recognized as how you define yourself. Interpersonal recognition in general is an important feature of social life. Henry Rubin thus understands FTM body modification as a situated, contextual project of authenticity based on the principles and demands of recognition in modern society (2003: 15), but this also extends to non-body-modifying trans* subjectivities. Smith points at the 'ultimate irony of identity': the development of identity is dependent upon the recognition by another, and therefore subjectification always implies objectification to a certain degree (2005: 181). Her conclusion that the gaze, therefore, plays a major role in BDSM culture (182–3) was echoed by my interview partners, who also stressed the significance of recognition when it came to (partial) gender identities. This is part of the interpellation of the subject. Where I depart from Smith (2005: 184) is her insistence that the self/other binary is psychologically inevitable for subject formation. She does not explain why one necessarily needs to become a subject – which is a specific socio-historical invention – or why no other subject positions or developments are imaginable. My model of *integration* (explained below) demonstrates an option to develop an identity that does not rely on rejecting or expelling an imagined or real 'other' in order to become a 'self'.

Since Tony, interestingly, stood in front of a mirror, s/he was able to recognize hirself, so to speak, from the outside perspective. Prosser holds that the mirror sets the transsexual plot in motion, since it shows that 'I am not my body' (1998: 100), yet obviously the mirror can also show a self beyond the visual surface of the body or can readjust the vision to reinterpret the meaning of that visual surface. While, in the Lacanian mirror state situation, the mirror serves to foster an illusion of wholeness of the self and, therefore, ultimately represents a misrecognition (Lacan 1977), in the trans* experience the mirror may, rather, show the ruptures in the self and the limitations of attaining a self from the projection of a surface, since their body image is not derived from the projection of the bodily surface the mirror reflects. Therefore, the mirror can also function as a means to illustrate the fragmented and incoherent character of a self that consists of multiple partial selves or of a self in transition.

Other interview partners described one function of a play partner as being a mirror to reflect parts of one's personality that had not been acknowledged previously:

> A couple of people that I have been playing with the longest started out kind of like 'I'm a dyke, and I'm in the middle'. But when I looked at them, I was like 'I see a boy. How do you feel about me calling you boy?' And by this point they're boy identified in a big way, and it's a huge factor in how they see themselves.

Terry's description showed how far the subcultural skill of recognition had been developed. It was not only about being able to read someone as the identity they consciously and purposefully expressed or performed, but it was also a way to recognize, for example through mirroring back one's own gender expression, an identity or partial self that had not yet surfaced. This adds a temporal dimension to the concept of identity-at-a-distance. Salamon, drawing on this concept by Silverman, points out how there is always distance in identity, because identifying with an idealized image necessarily involves an image that is outside the self (2010: 23). This is what an encounter with a mirror illustrates literally. I would add that, in trans* trajectories, this includes a temporal distance, since one may identify with a post-transition, future self (see also Carter 2013 on the folding of time). And the goal of transitioning may be precisely to become recognizable (Henry Rubin 2003: 143). Rubin holds that intersubjective recognition first requires recognition of the self (15). Yet Terry's narrative suggests that being recognized as one's gender by another can precede self-recognition. This partly invokes notions of authenticity in terms of a 'true' self. Queer high femme Zoe put it slightly differently:

> I see beauty in people that have never seen the beauty in themselves, and it's really nice to see people bloom into being recognized for being a boy, say. Just being able to mmmmmhh [enjoyably] shine under being recognized for their beauty. And be sort of stunned like 'I've always been told I'm a sport of nature, a freak, and I'm ugly and undesirable', and to have them come into this community that recognizes them: 'You're not an ugly duckling, no, you're a swan, baby' [laughs]. 'No, you're not unattractive, you're a really handsome butch' [laughs].

This quote shows that recognition does not rely on a notion of authenticity, but can also be understood as a subcultural technique that acknowledges that concepts such as beauty are dependent upon context and that the butch–femme and dyke + queer BDSM communities have constructed different kinds of gender expressions that generate other ways of seeing and different kinds of beauty standards.

The kind of recognition described here is unique to certain subcultural contexts, since mainstream heteronormative society is not able to see or read gender expressions in this way, because it neither mirrors nor desires dyke + queer genders. All the elements of processes of recognition – the literal mirror, the metaphorical mirror and recognizing and validating others – resemble the active co-construction of gender expressions and identities that are in a stage of becoming. Therefore, gender identity exploration play does not stop at exploring, but goes further to enter processes of becoming and transformations. Recognizing, as a dyke + queer subcultural skill, is no logic of discovery, but an ever-emergent, context-related process of subjectification that includes gender labor for all participants. But, in dyke + queer BDSM, it involves not only gender labor, but also gratifications and benefits in the form of the erotic and sexual pleasures to be gained from recognition and from gender identity exploration play in general.

Gender sliding play

There were various motivations for adopting in play a different gender position from one's everyday gender identity. For bisexual woman Vito, the experience of taking on and exploring a different personality in role play became more intense through switching gender. Embodying another gender also presented a greater challenge in regard to the credibility of a role to her. For Vito, embodying another gender was akin to embodying a vampire, which also gave her the thrill of becoming-other. Therefore, the basic attraction of switching gender was the allure of otherness and experiencing difference, as well as intensity. But it might also be a representation of a partial self.

Some interview partners slid in and out of different genders, sometimes even within a session, as gay intersex transman BJ described:

> I've actually fluctuated. I've seen myself do it in scenes as a bottom, fluctuate in and out of being a boy or a girl in the scene. Depends on what was happening. Once you stick your fist in my cunt, I don't care what I was doing beforehand. I'm a little girl. If you're fucking me in the ass, I'm a boy.

BJ fluctuated between genders depending on the context or the activity; for instance, sexual acts involving certain body parts invoked a gendered response. This shows how sexed embodiment and cultural stereotypical associations continued to matter; the vagina was still associated with femaleness, anal sex with gay men. Often, gender was also influenced by the partner's gender expression. For instance, when Connie's genderqueer lover radiated a straight male energy, she responded by turning into a slutty femme.

Gender sliding was not restricted to movements from female to male. Rather, the multiplicity and specificity of gender identities in the dyke + queer BDSM communities built a multi-dimensional landscape in which to move. For instance, gay transman Wolf's FTM lover once cross-dressed for him in a session:

> Such a real drag queen queeny dress, such blue sequins. Don't ask me, I was so gasping for breath. My eyes were blindfolded, and then opened and then he stood there in the room. He also had a wig on and a bit of lipstick. And I said: 'take off the wig', and the wig came off and it was his real, short hair and it was incredibly beautiful.

The cross-dressing or criss-cross-dressing of FTMs in feminine or androgynous attire pushed the edges in the community, as queer femme Emma pointed out. This seemed to follow a logic of being allowed to cross gender lines only once (if at all), which is evident in the treatment and legislation of transsexuals (Lindemann 1997). But this was a rule that many interview partners did not adhere to, and they slid in and out of genders. Wolf's lover did not restrict his gender expression after transitioning to stereotypically masculine. Rather, he drew on gay male drag culture to expand his options genderwise, and Wolf adored the campy genderfucking presentation of his short-haired lover in a dress. As opposed to the norm in gay male BDSM culture, Tony also found erotic value in gay camp: 'I especially like the fact about being queeny [tuntig] that the role opens up space for intelligent play-fulness. I like queens [Tunten]. And I definitively think they are sexy.' This implies that interview partners did not simply copy gay male culture. Rather, they treated it as a rich resource for their own becomings. Here, they rein-scribed the *Tunte*/effeminate fag with erotic value, cross-pollinating it with the butch–femme tradition of eroticizing queer femininities.

For Deleuze (1994), freedom requires moving beyond the concept of the human to affirm the flow of life itself; we no longer know what or who we are, but experience the differences, intensities and singularities that move through us. Impersonal joy, then, is about affirming what increases our power to become. Singular experiences can be understood as moving through individuals rather than belonging to them, a process Stephenson and Papadopolous call individuation (2006: 163). They use the example of aging, but within the context of this study I would suggest that the movements of experiences of power, as well as masculinity, femininity and genderqueerness, are also examples of singular experiences without a mate-rial attachment to bodies or individuals per se, but, rather, moving through and across them in particular situations, as evident in the gender sliding practices. Some may stick and leave an impression on bodies and identi-ties, becoming part of subjectification processes or transformations of the self; others may move on. But all these singular experiences may serve to connect individuals across difference and may spark forms of collectivity that are not dependent upon the subject, but are based on those partially shared experiences of singularities (Stephenson & Papadopoulos 2006: 132). These kinds of collectivities composed of singularities open up social and erotic spaces that enable the emergence of new desires and pleasures, and increasing differentiation. This was evident in the dyke + queer BDSM com-munities with their constant invention of new erotic practices, pleasures and identities, which demonstrates their exuberant character. Their desires cre-ated excesses that escaped discourse and produced, in the words of Deleuze and Guattari, a thousand tiny sexes, which were uncontrollable becomings (2004: 307).

Becoming-fag

A specific form of gender sliding play that was very popular in the dyke + queer BDSM community was *fag play*. Many interview partners enjoyed gay male fantasies and erotica. Queer femme Katharina had a gay leatherdaddy fetish, which she attributed to having been socialized into gay male BDSM and having gay men as her first role models. While some interview partners transitioned to gay men and entered the actual gay male BDSM community, most enacted their partial identities as fags within the dyke + queer BDSM community. My interview partners redefined fag/gay male sexuality as an interaction of masculine energy with masculine energy instead of the interaction of two cismale bodies. For queer transgender butch Jacky, this gay male desire developed in response to his femme partner's inner fag boy. And fag play illustrated how singular experiences move through bodies, sticking to some and sliding across others, but creating unexpected connections, such as between a femme and a gay leatherman. The practice of fag play, therefore, can serve as another example of becoming in the Deleuzian sense, and can be characterized as becoming-fag, not imitating gay men, but entering the zone of proximity of a micro-fagness that produces a molecular fag in a female or trans* body (Deleuze & Guattari 2004: 304).

Gender variation play

Not all playing with gender involved a movement across the binary gender line, as queer high femme Zoe summarized her play with FTM partners: 'I think my point of origin with them is that they're male, and then I play with variations on that theme.' So playing with gender could also be about exploring various kinds of masculinity or femininity. Thus, gender variation play brought into focus the variety within the categories of male and female. For example, age play provided a space to explore alternative masculinities and femininities, since gender expressions and stereotypes are age-specific: different behaviors and styles are expected from a girl aged four than from a teenage girl, a young woman or a grandmother. Therefore, playing in a different age opened up possibilities for inhabiting different gender positions as well.

Dyke femme Tanya's seven-, nine- and 12-year-old girl personas were tomboys: 'They're all little tomboys, they wanna wrestle, they wanna play cars and trucks, they wanna wrestle some more' [laughs]. Tanya had girl personas of different ages, which allowed her to draw on very different kinds of femininities through the varying ages, from good girl to tomboy to slut. In general, femme interview partners used age play to explore alternative, non-mainstream ways to become-girl. Emma connected her grrrl persona to riot grrrl and queer culture. On the flip side, many FTMs seemed to feel uncomfortable with the associations of the label 'man' (see also Noble 2013), and so 'boy/boi' offered a different kind of masculinity to identify with, one less associated with patriarchal power. For some FTMs this also seemed to be a process of going through a masculine boyhood, which had been denied to them during their actual childhood/adolescence, and eventually growing into an adult and becoming male (see also Bauer n.d.).

While daddy was a very popular role and received a lot of attention, mommy was much less prevalent and less visible (see also Bauer 2007a). My interview partners attributed this to the fact that mothers are not seen as powerful or sexual and are perceived as much less abusive in a sexist culture. Mothers were held to be more sacred than fathers and were not sexy as a stereotype. Many interview partners did not identify with those mother clichés, but few players in dyke + queer BDSM broke the taboo of sexualizing the asexual figure of the mother.

Gender polarization play

One type of gender variation play was the polarization of genders within the binary. My interview partners enjoyed amplifying their masculinity or femininity in dyke + queer BDSM. This included playing with stereotypes and clichés and was clearly visible in the butch–femme community (see Chapter 3). This polarization enhanced the construction of difference, which was alluring for many dyke + queer BDSMers, as Emma explained:

> I find that the way that my desires are structured is tension-based. That I am not attracted for the most part – there's always exceptions – but for the most part I am not attracted to people who reflect back to me my gender presentation. What is interesting to me in the dynamic is the polarity.

Her desire was based on the tension that arose from difference, be it gendered or power difference. She enjoyed the intensity of experience that was an effect of the tension created by polarity. Furthermore, gender stereotypes provided a rich cultural resource for role play. For instance, high femininity clichés bore potential for being bitchy as a top, according to Tony.

Gender nonconformity play: Situated becomings

My interview partners also experienced dyke + queer BDSM as a safe space in which to construct and express subversive genders. This encompassed a whole range of possibilities, from a girl role who did not adhere to conventional sexual morals to incongruent embodiments, as queer femme Anastasia stated: 'I have a lover, he's a transguy, who's totally passing, big bear and everything. And he has a cunt and he says so, and I think that's really cool. I think that's power outside the lines.' She experienced her FTM lover's embracing of a male body with a vagina as undermining hegemonic gender notions.

Female masculinities (Halberstam 2002) – masculine gender expressions starting from a female body – in various forms were a major way in which gender nonconformity was explored within the community. For many, the ruptures, the frictions, the inconsistencies from a binary perspective of gender were enticing, as bisexual woman Franka described: 'I tell feminine women: "So today, you are my butler; today, you are really the butler. And then I want as well that you keep in style and that you dress accordingly, with a tie, and simply realize how that feels, this male clothing, these ruptures."' Performing and embodying female masculinities highlighted that masculinity is not restricted to male bodies, but can travel across various bodies. As the example of the butler shows, these masculinities were not necessarily a rise in social status, but were mediated by class, age and other markers of social distinction. Therefore, the practices of female masculinities were not necessarily associated with the top role; many interview partners played as boys or other male characters on the bottom.

The deliberate practice of combining various elements of stereotypically gendered items and behaviors to create an incongruent and potentially confusing gender presentation was referred to as 'genderfucking' in the dyke + queer BDSM community. In my sample it was predominantly femmes and genderqueers who participated in genderfucking in this way, especially through strapping on a dildo while wearing a skirt or other (high) femme attire. Queer high femme Zoe said:

> I used to pack a dick in my toys, and I'd be wearing a dick under my skirt and stuff, right? I guess I did that in my thirties too; it was pretty fun. And I can remember these two guys seeing me on the street, grabbing each other and screaming. And this guy saying: 'I like it, I like it. I don't know what it is, but I like it' [laughs].

While those in the dyke + queer BDSM community put a great emphasis on understanding and recognizing different gender expressions, Zoe's encounter with the men on the street highlights the role that desire plays as a catalyst for exploring sexual and gender otherness, even if you are not able to comprehend that otherness (yet), or maybe precisely because it forces you to question your usual categories. This desire that is not fixed, that is not understood and that confuses one's categories may be called a queer desire.

Salamon draws on Deleuze and Guattari and considers the transitioning process of trans* individuals as a continuous becoming rather than a one-time event or crossing (2010: 116). This is also true for genderfucking, which is open-ended rather than oriented toward a *telos*. Deleuze and Guattari ask us to reveal and intensify the production of images, becoming-other, multiplying intensities and affects to produce further possibilities for experience. This is exactly what happened in the semi-contained space of dyke + queer BDSM, which served to push the boundaries of all kinds of experiences of difference and otherness. Singer also considers the trans* proliferation of bodies and identities as bordering on the sublime, confronting us with a vision of potentially infinite specific possibilities for being human (2006: 616). To Deleuze (1994), all beings are just contractions of flows of becoming, or relatively stable moments in a flow of becoming. The chaos or flows of difference that are life are located within the plane of immanence (Deleuze & Guattari 2004) that precedes a distinction between inside and outside. Deleuze (1994) calls for becoming-imperceptible in this flow of difference and asks us to abandon the point of view from which we judge and order life. This sense of becoming-imperceptible, though, is in danger of falling prey to the illusion of the possibility of a neutral position, reinscribing the god-trick (Haraway 1991) and a power-evasive perspective. The differentiations that the plane of immanence produces are ordered hierarchically in social worlds; it matters how beings become and how they are differently situated in structures of power. Therefore, a power-sensitive approach like Haraway's situated perspectives is needed in order to reimagine how becoming can actually serve to restructure social hierarchies. Multiplying genders, sexualities and ways of being and becoming does not automatically do away with oppression. (It may even follow the logic of an ever-expanding capitalist market, looking for new products to sell and to consume.) But acknowledging one's social situatedness is about vulnerability and, therefore, resists closure and finality (Haraway 1991: 196). This is a different kind of becoming, one that remains accountable for its positioning in social structures of power and therefore open to ongoing reconfiguration and regeneration, as in the practice of genderfucking, which acknowledges its own social contexts while generating differences and singularities. I therefore call it *situated becoming*.

Gender validation play

My interview partners used the space provided by dyke + queer BDSM to respect, validate and celebrate queer genders. This validation of his masculinity opened new doors for gay intersex transman BJ:

> It was getting the focus on: 'Oh, I like my vagina. And actually the sensation feels really good. Maybe it's not so foreign, if I learned how to play with it in this context.' And doing SM and being able to be a boy and being able to identify as male, which was easier to do in the SM community than in the dyke community, I was able to get a lot more comfortable with it. And now I love it. Now I can't even imagine having surgery to change it.

The validation he got for his queer masculinity in the community enabled BJ to reconnect to his vagina, eroticize it and increase his overall acceptance of his body. It therefore enabled him to live in a space beyond the gender binary. Play partners of trans* people often actively worked to validate their genders. They even organized gender celebration play parties. Again, as opposed to the scholarship that describes gender as labor, with the accompanying issues of exploitation, burnout and so on, this work of co-constructing genders was described by my interview partners as mutually pleasurable and rewarding. The concept of the gender celebration party illustrated this rather well.

But, even within the dyke + queer BDSM community, gender intelligibility and validation had limits; for instance, some butch interview partners described that with the vanishing of the butch model they were increasingly read and addressed as transmen, which ultimately reinforced the hegemonic assumption that certain expressions of female masculinity implied a wish to be a man. But many butches did identify as women, as lesbian butch Luise stressed: 'I believe I don't have to feel like a man to look like a man. It's still me, and I am still a woman.' Therefore, the community faced the challenge of equally validating a range of different gender choices rather than reinstalling new norms.

Gender integration through play

All the various kinds of gender play discussed above could be seen as part of exploring and transforming gender. Gender-based play presented a possibility to explore multiple and partial identities and personas: 'I've been able to kind of get to terms with parts of me that I may have rejected or that have been splintered off. I feel role play's been one of the most integrating things I've done.' As Firesong pointed out, this practice went beyond mere role play; it provided an access to lost parts of the self that could be permanently reintegrated through BDSM. If new parts of the self emerged in play, this could lead to a renegotiating of one's gender identity.

When queer femme Katharina encountered her inner fag boy unexpectedly, she had

> a kind of transgender identity consolidation in a minor dimension throughout an evening, maybe for two hours. Then the gathered girls, so to speak, which in this case includes grown-up femininities and female-nesses, somehow had to negotiate like: 'Now what about the nail polish and the long fingernails and the long hair?' The boy said he definitely does not want to wear a skirt [laughs].

This quote demonstrates the internal dynamic of partial selves, as Katharina's inner fag boy appeared spontaneously, out of her control, and made demands of her. And it shows that a whole inner team of partial girl identities had coalesced over time, assembling her femme identity. The potential incongruence of catering to a boy, therefore, needed negotiation and was only partially dissolved, but the boy was successfully integrated.

Integration in this way can be seen as an alternative mode of subjectification. As Derrida (1991) and Kristeva (1982) have shown, part of identification processes in Western cultures is the expelling of the other, the *abject*, in order to establish the self. Therefore, Derrida (1991) criticizes all identifying as excluding and binary thinking, since it is based on various kinds of hierarchical dichotomies. An example is the expelling of same-sex desires to form a heterosexual subject, which produces homophobia as a result of the inner constitutive boundary of the self. Subjectification in this sense, therefore, serves to construct and maintain difference as the foundation of social hierarchies and violence against the other. An integrative process of subjectification, on the other hand, as my interview partners described it, continuously expands the self by including difference rather than expelling it in processes of abjection. The multiplicity of the self that emerges is not dependent on expelling and downgrading the other in order to become a subject, but also does not dissolve the contradictions of these partial selves on a higher level; rather, they co-exist. Integration can, therefore, be understood as an example of practiced *différance*, according to Derrida, since it exceeds a dialectical understanding. It is about inhabiting a position of ongoing contradictions between the lines. This form of subjectification can also be understood within Haraway's (1991) concept of articulation, as a process in which different elements are brought together in order to create something more encompassing, but not a fully integrated whole, since these genderqueer subjectivities are never absolute, finished or free of contradictions. They are not about romantic illusions of wholeness, but ongoing difference within the self.

(Not) Identifying and becoming: Situational positionings and fixed points on gendered landscapes

Identifying sexually and genderwise or refusing to identify within these categories was a matter of great importance in the dyke + queer BDSM communities in general, and this was reflected in the interviews. Asked for their identification, most interview partners gave elaborate and sophisticated answers, sometimes delighting in their senses of self, sometimes struggling to get them across even to me as a member of the same queer subcultural contexts. They were aware of the fact that they constantly related to the world as gendered and sexual selves, whether voluntarily or involuntarily, and of the positive, negative and ambivalent emotional investments this entailed. This was especially evident for those whose own identity was incongruent with the hegemonic assignment of their gender and for those born intersex, such as BJ:

> I got diagnosed at eleven with GID [gender identity disorder], but it wasn't until I was three years into my transition that my mom told me that I was born with Klinefelter syndrome. So she kept it from me forever. Now if she would have told me sooner, I probably would have had a much different life.

By deciding to have him surgically altered, by raising him as a girl and by not telling him about his intersex history, the medical establishment and his parents took away BJ's self-determination over his gender and his body (Fausto-Sterling 1993; 2000; Chase 1998; Reiter 1998). Through transitioning to male, he reclaimed self-definition of his gender, without realizing the extent to which it had been denied to him in the first place until his mother finally informed him. This was one of the narratives that attested not only to the non-consensual and violent nature of gender policing inherent in the very formation of subjectivity, but also to the resistant excesses that cannot be disciplined or contained. BJ did not end up leading a heteronormative life as a woman, but inhabited a very queer location. He was even planning to design his own intersex genitals surgically.

My interview partners felt social pressure to identify in general, and as either man or woman and as gay or heterosexual in particular. This was manifested in interpellations, in Althusser's sense of the term, to function as their biological sex dictated. According to Foucault, the main interpellation for individuals in neoliberalism is to become subjects, which prompted him to suggest that the point is not to know who we are, but to refuse what we are, to liberate the individual not only from the state, but also from the processes of subjection that are imposed on us (1982: 785). Lorenz distinguishes between the interpellation to become a subject and the call to become a specific kind of subject (2009: 93). She reimagines Althusser's model as a sexual scene of interpellation (23). Likewise, Muñoz considers queers to be people who have failed to respond to the 'Hey, you there!' interpellating call of heteronormativity (1999: 33), and Lorenz understands interpellation as a theatrical sequence of scenes that are open to new casts and reworkings (2009: 69). Therefore, interventions into normative processes of subjectification are possible. My interview partners could be said to have employed Lorenz's model literally: they used the intimate theater of dyke + queer BDSM to restage social interpellations and invent their own scripts, characters and endings, resulting in different kinds of subjectivities.

My interview partners experienced hegemonic sexual and gender interpellations as emotional burdens; this was especially true for those who failed or refused to comply with these categories. Some rejected these categorizations and carved out spaces to live outside conventional definitions. When transwoman Daphne was prompted for her identity, she replied: 'I don't like all those boxes. And I decline them more and more as well.' MCL completely refused to identify in terms of gender and positioned hirself and others on a hard–soft spectrum (which was not simply equating hardness with masculinity and softness with femininity) instead. Therefore, ze chose an acronym of three differently gendered names to express hir positioning. This shows that Henry Rubin is right when he points out that dislocation still provides the individual with subject positions, since dislocatedness is not the absolute absence of location (2003: 336). Rather, MCL and others built new locations, new social spaces to inhabit.

Eric gave his obsession for football priority over his gender and even moved beyond the human when positioning himself as 'born female, but I feel more comfortable in alien SM body than like woman or male body'. Pansexual FTM alien/unisexual Eric defined his gender as alien, which illustrated his complete separation from the binary gender system and how others perceived him as 'out of this world', dislocated from Planet Earth.

On the other hand, the figure of the alien provided him with a strong positive image that described an experience of difference so basic that it excluded him from what was considered human, as opposed to the derogatory, dehumanizing discursive strategies used by transphobes, such as calling trans* people 'it'. The self-positionings put forth by MCL and Eric can be considered strategies of decentering gender and sexuality as identity categories, while still acknowledging the impact on their lives, and becoming-other.

Due to a lack of suitable identity categories or because of possessing fluid identities, some interview partners could not put any label to their identity. Some employed relatively vague, undefining terms such as 'queer' or 'transman', which stood for a range of identities and opened up a space to move in rather than restricting their genders and sexualities, extending the boundaries of these categories. Only a few interview partners favored a utopian future of no identities, though. For the majority, identities remained important and part of the richness of their lives. They could, therefore, be characterized as 'genderphiles': 'A genderphile is someone who loves gender. Someone who is attracted to the what and the how and the when and the joy of how people create and remix and imagine' (Blank 2006: 1). Yet utilizing gender stereotypes for erotic enhancement in dyke + queer BDSM contexts, such as in the gender polarization play described above, could at times turn into a burden, for instance when gender norms pressured butches and femmes to conform their gender expressions to conventional or subcultural beauty standards:

> I know a lot of femmes who struggle with to what extent we accept conventional beauty standards as things that give us pleasure. Do we accept, do we wanna reject them? And to what extent do we feel pressured to shave our legs, pressured to wear high heels? Fit into that traditional pretty – well I think – as opposed to that fierce queer femininity.

This quote from queer-straight femme Teresa demonstrates a moment of disidentification: stereotypical femininity gave her pleasure, but also put her under pressure to conform to beauty norms she rejected. The fact that dyke + queer communities politically valued fierce femmeness over other forms of femininity provided the individual femme with a counter-pressure. She had to navigate through the complex webs of her own desire and mainstream, subcultural and personal norms. A partial solution to dilemmas like this was to distinguish between stereotypes in play and in real life; some butches and femmes used the erotic potential of gendered stereotypes without restricting themselves to them outside the bedroom or play space.

Gender, desire and sexuality as context-dependent

My interview partners acknowledged that their desires and identities were context-dependent in a variety of ways, and different or shifting contexts might produce shifting identities. For some interview partners, shifts in their gender identity caused changes in their sexual preference, most notably with FTMs who went from lesbian to gay male identified (see also Kaldera 2009). Identities could also be dependent on the kind of partner one was with, as queer-straight femme Teresa described: 'And it used to be with non-trans boys I felt kind of like a fag, with girls I felt kind of like a dyke.' She concluded that different partners could bring out different sides of her. Identities could also be dependent on cultural contexts, for instance on the availability of identity choices. Femmeboy had to wait for the emergence of the concept of a femmeboy to find a suitable definition of self, and lesbian/queer transgender Kelvin had to move to a larger city to encounter queerness.

Sometimes, identities could also be strategic (Minh-ha 1986/7), which is how queer transgender butch Tony employed the label 'lesbian': 'I would, for instance, now as well position myself as lesbian in my relationship in a purely heterosexual context if it seems important to me to express this kind of lifestyle or make it visible.' Even though s/he had never identified as lesbian, s/he found political value in self-positioning that way in heteronormative contexts. Others had stopped using the term 'bisexual' because it reinforced the notion of binary gender, instead using 'pansexual' or 'queer' to point out that there are more than two genders. Zoe, a queer high femme, followed another strategy of resistance, refusing to be judged by the dominant paradigm:

> Some small-minded literalists were applying the dominant paradigm to my community, but my community is above and beyond the dominant paradigm. We're doing our own thing, and I'm sorry that you're so locked into the dominant paradigm that that's all that you can see when you see me – somebody who's selling out to patriarchy. Because my thing is so much more fabulous and exotic than that. [laughs loudly] You need to get your glasses checked. [laughs loudly]

To her, context mattered, and therefore an interpretation of butch–femme culture within the dominant gender paradigms – interpreting femininity per se as a sign of female oppression – was doomed to fail. She connected her high femmeness to a queer culture of fabulousness and camp instead; thus, high femme can be seen as an exuberant gender expression.

Simultaneous processes of subjectification

One way in which context mattered was through simultaneous processes of subjectification. I am following Erel et al.'s suggestion to conceptualize interlocking systems of differentiation and hierarchization as simultaneous processes rather than as the intersections of categories such as race and gender, as if these were originally 'pure' and distinguishable until they encounter another category (Erel et al. 2007). Rather, any given process of subjectification is always already multiple and simultaneously positioned within complex webs of social power.

For instance, it seems to be necessary to possess a specific gender identification in order to connect with potential partners, since sexual dynamics are always already gendered, and, as Salamon points out, desire is experienced through one's gender (2010: 127). Thus, it proved hard for interview partners with indeterminate or nonconventional gender positionings to locate themselves sexually in heteronormative contexts where desire was based on the construct of a gender binary, and to attract the right partners. Likewise, one's sexual and BDSM practices could also impact one's gender and other identities. Before applying for surgery, Anna had thoroughly examined her wish for female breasts to determine whether the desire was motivated by sexual fetishism or whether breasts were necessary for her everyday life as woman. She concluded that her fetishizing of female breasts was a small part of it, but not the main reason, pointing at the simultaneity of sexual and other aspects of gender identity. Making a clear distinction between transvestitism as an erotic practice and transsexualism as a gender identity issue, as in the diagnostic manuals (DSM and ICD), is a theoretical issue, not based in the complex lived realities of trans* individuals.

Therefore, the now common distinction between gender and sexual identity/practices in theorizing has to be re-examined. Erotic desires can conflate, confuse and contradict this neat analytical distinction, as my interviews and Valentine's research on communities of poor queers of color in New York City show (2006: 409). Yet, the analytical distinction between gender identity and sexual identity has proven to be an important tool for transgender activism and to highlight the specific needs of trans* people. Many trans* activists and theorists have pointed out the negative effects of being subsumed under the gay/queer umbrella and the discrimination that trans* individuals face in gay communities and in queer theory (Stryker 1994; Namaste 1996; Prosser 1998; Namaste 2000; Haritaworn 2005). The distinction between gender and sexuality also faces limits, however, and whether it is a useful political strategy will continue to depend on the context (see also Bauer 2009).

For Scout, who grew up poor in a rural area, his class background was also tied into his struggle to find an appropriate gender identity:

> Do I go on testosterone and identify as genderqueer and use male pronouns while I'm on testosterone and kind of be like 'fuck the world and their designed binary genders'? But by doing that, I felt like I was erasing my class background of where I came from. It had a lot to do with my brothers and my father and how like: Did I want to be like them? No. Did I feel like it was a curse that I wasn't born with the body of my little brother? No. But did I think it was fucked up that I got my ass kicked

because I dressed like my little brother? Yes. So it's the struggle of just being real with myself and how I identify myself in the cultural context of all of my life.

While Scout had been presented with the possibility of living as genderqueer in the metropolitan area he moved to, he ultimately rejected that option as too disconnected from his class and rural background. So part of finding a suitable gender identity was how to negotiate its various aspects and integrate it into one's socio-geopolitical–biographical contexts. Since certain queer identities were firmly situated within *white* middle-class culture and values, to most *white* interview partners finding queer identities seemed to simply be a question of renegotiating sex and gender in heteronormative society, when, more accurately, this necessarily entailed a renegotiation with their racialized and classed family and community backgrounds as well. But these processes went unnoticed through the assumed normality of *whiteness* (Carter 2007: 2).

Crossing and becoming: Gendered landscapes under construction

From a gender binary perspective, anyone who does not fit into the categories of man and woman is deviant, but there are many possibilities for *how* genders may depart from hegemonic norms. My interview partners brought up various axes on which their genders could be positioned. One was whether gender was fluid or stable, as Firesong explained: 'To me, genderqueer doesn't necessarily mean that it shifts, because I mean I could have a genderqueer identity always with the same balance of gender expression. The fact that it's fluid is more like it's a different scale. That's the scale of how stable the identity is.' Firesong made an important distinction between the degree of stability of a gender identity and the degree of unambiguousness or quantity of the identity. One may have multiple gender identities that are absolutely stable, one may have a stable gender identity that combines masculine and feminine aspects in a genderfucking way, one may have a gender-fluid identity that means switching back and forth between traditional notions of man and woman, one may move fluidly through all kinds of unconventional gender expressions and so on. The possible combinations seem unlimited.

For many interview partners, gender was a fluid spectrum or a three-dimensional landscape that they either positioned themselves in permanently or navigated through, depending on the situation and context. Identifying was understood as becoming: a continual, open-ended process with the constant possibility of change. Sometimes, becoming was channeled into a kind of reterritorialization, resulting in queer identities like transman, femme, genderqueer and so on, or it even had an expressed goal, like becoming a man or a woman for some trans* individuals. But, sometimes, becoming was just the process of constant experimentation, change and transformation. I call this dynamic becoming-other, in a double sense. In the first sense, becoming-other is simply about becoming something (anything) different from the current self, the basic process of life as change. In the second sense, becoming-other is about becoming something that cannot be articulated yet, because it does not exist in the current social and cultural contexts, like genderqueerness. In this sense, interview partners could not strive to become something specific, like becoming-animal or becoming-woman, but had to push the experimenting even further and be completely open-ended in becoming.

To some, finding an identity in heteronormative culture presented an ongoing struggle. Scout was dealing with unanswered questions about the extent of his intersex history. His 24/7 DS relationship provided a framework within which he could explore these complex identity issues, although he acknowledged that some might remain unresolvable: 'It's still very complicated, because I can't tell where the line is between my body dysphoria because I'm trans, and my body dysphoria because I was mutilated. So I still don't know the answers to these questions. Maybe I never will.' Scout pointed at a general problem in regard to trans* identities: how to evaluate one's discomfort with certain body parts in the context of a range of possible causes, like intersex-related body mutilation, sexual abuse or sexist discrimination. Some of these questions could not be answered, which pushed my interview partners to invent their own gendered embodiments, or to accept living in the in-betweens. One transgender butch, for instance, refrained from pursuing trans*-related body modification until he could be certain it was not a reaction to a recent experience of sexual abuse.

Many interview partners described multiple, not necessarily linear, coming-out processes, especially those arriving at queer, genderqueer, femme and trans* rather than lesbian and ciswoman identities. Femmeboy felt lost not fitting into any of the communities she encountered because her desire and gender expression were outside the norms:

> If I went to a butch–femme club, I would be attracted to the butches, but the femmes would be attracted to me. So that's what would happen, and I don't usually date femmes. And I'm usually not as attracted to femmes, but the butches are more attracted to the femmes than to me. I feel sort of lost. And I don't identify as androgynous either, so where do I fit in?

Not fitting in is not simply an emotional burden, but, as this quote demonstrates, may also lead to isolation and a lack of potential partners. Femmeboy finally found a suitable self-description with the emergence of the new concepts of genderqueer and femmeboy, the latter denoting a boy with a feminine expression.

While Femmeboy and others had to search for new terms or invent them to position themselves, for MCL the struggle was about arriving at a place of non-definition of self:

> I was on the search for myself for decades. That is especially difficult in the realm of non-definition that finally came out of it. Simply because society forces definitions on us that I have also tried to orient myself with just to discover again and again: somehow they all do not fit.

Thus, inventing new gender identities and refusing all categorization were two different strategies to deal with the limitations of the gender binary. My interview partners could be categorized into genderphiles and gender-refusers in this way.

Coming out did not necessarily mean the discovery of an inner essence, core or truth, but was described by many interview partners as a repositioning on an ever-evolving gender landscape. Both the landscape and its inhabitants were subject to change, becoming travelers at times or constantly. Therefore, gender and sexual identity appeared to be constantly changing, in flux, in motion, as Teresa summarized:

> Since I've come out to [this area] I realized that I'm not really attracted to feminine people significantly enough for me to wanna pursue it very often at all. And I'm also usually not attracted to non-trans boys. I've sort of gone from feeling lesbian/fag to queer-straight femme. So that's the gender identity of the day [laughs].

Often, gender presentation was only temporarily and situationally fixed, as Teresa's 'of the day' implied. For genderqueer Femmeboy, it was a conscious decision each day whether to express her girl or boy side, while transgender butch Tony used a combination of names and pronouns that left it up to the people interacting with hir in a given situation which way to address hir genderwise. Many interview partners were open to further changes in the future, fostering a sense of identity as provisional and becoming.

Cross-gender identifications: The (transgender) butch

Many interview partners defined not as woman, man or middle ground, but as cross-gender, for instance as transwoman or transmasculine. One common cross-gender practice or identity in dyke + queer BDSM communities was the butch or transgender butch. Butches are recognizable as gender non-conforming in public. Anti-butch sentiments are common in mainstream society and in the lesbian community, and sometimes in the FTM community as well due to the policing of boundaries. Butch women and transmen renegotiate the boundaries of the definitions of woman and of man (Rubin

1992b; Halberstam 1998; Hale 1998; Henry Rubin 2003). Butches also face the problem of intelligibility in regard to their gender. The dyke + queer BDSM community provided them with a space where they were mostly read correctly and erotically valued.

To some butch interview partners, their masculine gender expression was no contradiction to their identity as female or woman. They defined butch as female, but not feminine. To them, it was a subcategory of lesbian/dyke. Mostly, it is implied that a butch is born female and theorized as female masculinity (Halberstam 2002), but Kay was a butch transwoman, which entailed a double gender transgression, first from being born male to living as a woman, and then from (feminine) woman to butch. Her biography thus complicated the notion of butch as someone born female who transgresses her socially assigned gender role. Rather, Kay's identity stressed the fact that butch is not necessarily best understood on a scale moving away from one's assigned gender, but as relating to varying degrees and kinds of masculinity (and femininity) in specific contexts, repositioning oneself over time.

While some butches identified as women, transgender butches did not identify as women, but as in between genders or as primarily masculine. Some still identified as lesbian, while others rejected that label; that is why Tony used the prefix transgender to qualify which kind of butch s/he was. Since s/he positions hirself between man and woman, s/he used both pronouns and different names to express hir various gender identities. Transgender butches claimed a predominantly masculine body image despite, or independently of, their female anatomy. This put them technically in close proximity to non-transitioning transmen, but they were not simply the missing link between butches and transmen. Rather, they presented their own distinct gender with varying degrees of masculinity. Thus, butch, transgender butch and transman can be best understood on their own terms, with each containing a range of gender expressions (Rubin 1992b; Hale 1998: 321). These terms are self-definitions, expressing a complex process of negotiating one's own sense of the gendered and erotic self in various cultural and erotic contexts. Therefore, there are no other criteria to neatly distinguish the concepts of butch and transman from each other (Nataf 1996: 47), and sometimes an individual actually defines as both (Hale 1998: 322). Salamon, therefore, argues that, rather than idealizing the straight cis-male as the reference and understanding masculinity as a continuum with him at one end, relations among transmen, butches and genderqueers can be understood as circuits of sameness, resulting (potentially) in a solidarity in masculinity, rather than reproducing the hegemonic competitiveness between men over masculinity (2010: 120). This corresponds with how my interview partners handled masculinity, which was not attached to certain bodies or identities, but could even be embodied situationally by femmes as well.

But, even within dyke + queer contexts, there were certain norms that one had to fulfill to be fully recognized as a butch, including a certain style and certain acts and behaviors. Thus, not just anything could count as queer masculinity. Tony emphasized that being penetrated did not compromise hir butchness in hir view, despite the expected sexual profile of butches. Because being expressive and talkative was associated with femininity, transgender butch Jacky had to renegotiate how this personal trait could be integrated into his identity. He solved this apparent contradiction by attributing it to his inner fag, thus drawing on a gay, camp version of masculinity and employing a strategy of queering traditional notions of butchness. Furthermore, as with any gender, butchness is always already racialized, and butch and femme remain discussed and measured against *white* standards of masculinity (Goldman 1996; Lee 1996).

Gendered multiplicity of the self

Overall, the interviews painted a picture of a gendered and sexual multiplicity of the self rather than a unified, single entity. Many interview partners used the label 'queer' to describe their sexual preference as opposed to the more binary-gender-based concepts of lesbian/gay, straight or bisexual, and even those who used the latter terms often did not use them in the conventional sense, but specified redefinitions that stressed a sense of fluidity and becoming. Many subjectivities were composed of various partial selves, and experienced difference within. Rather than resolving those differences into a synthesis in a dialectical movement, in the dyke + queer BDSM model of self or identity these partial selves were not assimilated into a unified whole, but remained a collection of singularities that were expressed situationally in different contexts.

One particular feature of the term 'queer' for some interview partners was connected to the fact that they multiplied genders by *specifying* them. This was one reason why they created a multiplicity of genders, rather than simply a bi-gendered self, for instance. They described their identities as complex and complicated. For instance, Lola used the term 'dyke fag' to express an identity as a butch dyke attracted to other butch or boyish dykes. She did not simply describe her desires in terms of belonging to a certain sex and desiring another certain sex, but specified her own way of being a woman as well as her lovers' ways of being women and transgender. Thus, while from the perspective of heteronormative culture her acts would be categorized as lesbian (two biological women interacting sexually), the dynamics had a different meaning to her that was not adequately captured by the term 'lesbian'. Therefore, interview partners displayed rich ways of specifying their gender and sexual dynamics.

Many interview partners also had multiple partial gender and sexual identities. Since, in the dyke + queer BDSM communities, genders were multiplied, there were more than two genders for people with multiple, partial selves to use as identities. Examples of such partial identities of interview partners were teenage boys, fag boys, daddies, high femmes, girls of varying ages, in-between genders, aliens and so on. These were often distinct partial selves, as genderqueer Femmeboy explained: 'I don't feel much in between. I don't feel androgynous. Definitely everyday I feel I'm gonna be a boy or I'm gonna be a girl. It's a conscious decision.' This was how interview partners used the term 'genderqueer': to describe an identity that consists of multiple, partial selves that are distinct. The genderqueer couple Firesong and Femmeboy also invented the term 'genderslider' to express how their genders shifted between various positions, and Eric invented the term 'unisexual' for

> a body who's changing sex from one day to another. So some days you feel like a male and the next day you feel like an alien with a mixed body, like a male chest and woman pussy [laughs]. And the next day, you maybe have a male proper body, then you wear a strap-on as well.

What is interesting in Eric's description is that he was referring to his body, not only his inner sense of self or his presentation, as changing between male and alien/mixed. In this concept of a changeling body, he radically altered heteronormative perceptions of reality and materiality. From his perspective, material reality (his body) and immaterial reality (his body as changeling) merged into one. This is significant, since many trans* people and genderqueers questioned the pre-eminence of a heteronormative, rationalist reality and confronted it with their own realities and perceptions of their bodies and identities, as when Tony stated that s/he and hir partners could see in hir body what they wanted to see. This is a radical act in a post-Enlightenment and positivist culture that relies on discounting various simultaneous realities that cannot be captured in empirical science to establish a single reality that is the same for all, independent of difference. Claiming the validity of other realities is taken as a sign of racial inferiority, gendered hysteria, religious superstition or mental disease. Discourse on cross-gender behavior also relies on the validity of a single reality in which bodies can be assigned as male or female (and sometimes intersex as a medical condition) and trans* subjectivity is understood as a false representation of the underlying truth of the biological sex (Stryker & Whittle 2006: 9). Therefore, Eric's refusal to accept this hierarchy of realities can be seen as a radical queer questioning of the foundations of Western hegemonic thought. Humanity does not share one unified reality, but various co-existing realities, which overlap but are not completely congruent.

Besides shifting from one gendered location to another, some interview partners also inhabited different positions on the three-dimensional map at the same time; thus, multiple identities could be characterized as either temporally distinct or simultaneous. Intersex transman BJ stated: 'It's very interesting, because I feel equally both male and female most of the time and have my whole life.' Mandy identified simultaneously as hyper-femme and androgynous, and Craig both as gay male and as a daddy to a girl. Thus, inhabiting what would be considered incompatible spaces from a heteronormative perspective was not contradictory to them, as Femmeboy described her own label: 'Wow, that makes sense, that I'm a boy to [my mother], but I'm a femme. So when you put it together, it made a lot of sense.' Femmeboy's mom called her 'son', while insisting that on the butch–femme scale she was more femme. In the concept of the feminine boy, those apparent contradictions were merged into a meaningful identity for both of them. Some gender expressions were thus meant to remain contradictory, combining elements of femininity and masculinity in incongruent ways, as in the practice of genderfucking, discussed above. These practices could also be about balancing gender. Lesbian/queer transgender Kelvin used a male name and masculine clothing to balance the outer female appearance since s/he identified as both male and female.

Gender as trickster

The way interview partners described how gender functioned in their lives could be summarized as performative embodiment. While they experienced gender as being constituted and crystallized through performative acts, this did not explain how they arrived at a certain gender identity, especially a non-normative one:

> That is something that I had to deal with recently, because I was labeled as butch and was very indignant at first, because I actually never wanted any such definition for myself ever. But when I look at myself throughout the years, then I have turned into a big, large butch from a baby butch; that is clearly evident. But not because of some role models, but simply because I am that way.

While Luise's butchness can still be seen as performative in terms of being enacted through a series of certain gender performances, it cannot be easily attributed to a recital of gender norms. The theory of gender performativity (Butler 1990) cannot account for *why* Luise turned into a butch instead of responding to society's gender imperative to become a feminine woman, other than interpreting her gender expression as a failed performance or drag, but she was not a drag king parodying masculinity. Rather, she successfully performed a butch gender, and for her it would be a failed performance to try to present as feminine. Thus, one may postulate the existence of a resistant excessive or exuberant self, the trickster element that eludes not only individual, but also social, control.

In this sense, Haraway calls upon us to recognize the world's independent sense of humor. She reimagines the world as a witty agent and uses the figure of the Native American trickster, Coyote, to describe a situation in which we give up mastery but keep searching for fidelity, knowing all the while we will be hoodwinked (Haraway 1991: 199). In Native American mythology, the trickster has created the world and possesses all kinds of magical power, which he (ab)uses to his own advantage, trying to manipulate others into stealing food or to attain sexual favors. But he keeps failing, thus ending up hoodwinked himself (Swann 1996). While Haraway refers to Coyote, trickster-figures are not limited to the Native American context, but are part of folk tales and myths in cultures all over the world, including European ones, for instance in tales of Fox or Rabbit. Moreover, tricksters tend to be gender changelings. Therefore, this metaphor captures quite well the way gender worked in the self-descriptions of my interview partners. Sullivan proposes the concept of transmogrification to describe the strange and grotesque transformations, characterized by distortion, exaggeration, extravagance and unnatural combinations (2006: 553), that are typical of trans* and queer ways of being and becoming in the world. Transmogrification is a concept closely related to the trickster and to intimate exuberance, and it too captures quite accurately the practices of my interview partners. Sullivan understands transmogrification not only as a specifically queer act, but also as an expression of a fundamental human condition, part of the process through which everyone negotiates the boundary between self and other, and through which we perpetually transform ourselves in relation to an other (552). She, therefore, calls for an incorporeal ethics that recognizes and welcomes one's own strangeness as well as the strangeness of others (552), not unlike the process of integration through gender play.

My interview partners encountered not only the limits of hegemonic interpellations, but bodily and habitual limits to the possibilities of choosing self-definitions as well: 'I will never pass as femme. Then I look like a queen' [Tunte]. Luise *could not* convincingly perform a feminine gender expression. Therefore, the performativity of gender has limits; people cannot convincingly, intelligibly perform any gender at will. Likewise, Femmeboy pointed out that she could not be butch, even if she wanted to, due to her dancer's way of moving. This was exactly the demarcation between gender experienced as innate and as performative, since this 'failure' to pass convincingly as butch was in part due to the limits of Femmeboy's bodily and habitual repertoire of behaviors and in part due to community norms about what counted as butch. Thus, interview partners also had a sense of themselves as performing gender in a way that was almost contrary to some elements of Butler's concept of performativity. They were very aware of it and even employed it intentionally rather than unconsciously, not on stage, but in their daily lives (while they were also always citing a copy of a copy of a gender, not an original one; this aspect of Butler's theory of performativity remains applicable). They carefully chose their style of clothing and their general outer appearance, as well as habitus and body modifications, to express their – sometimes differing – sense(s) of self, but were also aware of the limits of performativity. Interestingly, these were not only limits to the self-definitions of queers, but also precisely the limits to gender-conforming processes as well: if Luise failed to answer the gender interpellation to perform hegemonic femininity, this displayed the trickster nature of gendered bodies and beings. This trickster element is the exuberance of life that cannot be contained.

Not only did my interview partners feel they were performing gender when embodying a cross-gender expression; ciswomen also felt they were performing gender when presenting as feminine. To dyke femme Mistress Mean Mommy, femme was a practice, an alter ego, not an identity: 'To me, it's just drag, it's fun. It's probably like a butch putting on a suit and facial hair.' The analogy to drag stressed not only the performativity of femininity, but also a femme's awareness of her gender's performative character and the use of it for her pleasure, which Duggan and McHugh call for in their 'fem(me)inist manifesto', in which they position the femme as 'Girl-by-Choice' (2002:166).

Femme coming-out narratives served as a marker of femme as a gender and a sexual identity. In some cases this seemed to be connected to an understanding of femmeness as essential or natural, as dyke femme Tanya stated: 'I'm naturally very feminine, and it's just part of who I am and what I'm comfortable as.' Yet Tanya and many femme interview partners recalled a tomboy prehistory, and not only in childhood. Sometimes, the coming out as femme had taken place in the woman's thirties, as Anya described: 'It started, I think, ten years ago, that I more wanted to define myself as a woman. And although I was born a woman, to come out as a woman with the typical womanly things.' As this quote demonstrates, Anya had to claim her own femininity although she was born female. Therefore, femmeness is not to be understood as a natural trait caused by a woman's sex, or as 'successful' gender socialization, but, rather, as a *reconstructed femininity* that is attained through negotiating one's own gender positioning within various social contexts. As queer femme Katharina explained,

> That is not always that easy, because something always drops out of the picture that is not perceived or is then prevented through [my femininity]. And that is a bit of a constant rebalancing of outfits and behaviors and interactions and so on. Yes, and thus it is a work in progress.

A femme identity, therefore, entailed constant gender labor, especially since third parties were quick to put women with feminine presentations into boxes they might not feel they belong in. Femme is, therefore, also an exuberant gender identity, always containing more aspects than are apparent on the surface. It can also be understood as an example of becoming

a molecular woman, according to Deleuze and Guattari; femme interview partners, indeed, 'conceive of a molecular women's politics that slips
into molar confrontation, and passes under or through them' (2004: 304)
through their reconstructing of femininities as drag, as girl-by-choice and as
non-conforming female subject positions, such as brat or slut.

So interview partners, from FTM to femme, made conscious gender
choices. Teresa regarded all genders as roles in general and explained:

> I think the main thing that's important is not whether it's real or not;
> it's whether it's consensual. If I feel my gender is a role, that doesn't
> make it not real. And the way I think about gender is coming from my
> genderqueer sort of queer radical perspective, which is that all genders
> are roles and that they all should be respected highly. And just because
> we choose something, it doesn't make it less real.

With her insistence that choosing an identity or role does not have an
impact on the reality of the lived experience, Teresa rejected as victimizing
the 'no choice' or 'born this way' discourse of queers seeking to gain acceptance for their sexualities and genders. She held that asserting one's sexual
and gender choices was empowering. Gay transman Mik also contemplated
the epistemological status of one's inner sense of gender: 'Is it gender play
what I am doing, or am I a transsexual? So that is the question of constructivism and essentialism in principle: Am I a man, or do I play a man?' The
question he raised – whether he was playing/performing as a man or simply
was a man – became confusing from his position and remained unanswered.
Obviously, even if people rejected essentialist notions, as Mik and Teresa did,
this did not lessen the impact of gender and the necessity to be able to live
one's gender of choice. In this sense, gender could be understood as a serious game, just like BDSM itself, but with more material consequences. And, if
we think of hate crimes toward trans* people and women and other forms of
sexist violence, this is a deadly serious game. In the experiences of my interview partners, the question of essentialism versus constructivism became
another false binary opposition; rather, their identities were experienced as
simultaneously essential and performative, strategic and situated.

My interview partners were consciously choosing gender, and, therefore,
not only could gender as an epistemological entity be usefully understood
as a trickster, but dyke + queer BDSMers also claimed the position of gender
tricksters themselves. As genderphiles they manipulated the hegemonic system of gender performativity to their own advantage, such as inventing new
pleasures. Simultaneously, they were aware that gender remained ultimately
beyond their control. Sometimes they 'irrationally', stubbornly, kept struggling against the limitations of the binary gender system; at other times they
accepted the limits with a sense of self-irony or found loopholes.

One gender trickster strategy could be to manipulate the gender system by passing, as in femme Lisa's concept of femmeness as subtle power beneath the surface:

> If I move simply in straight contexts or however, I always realize that it is a rather good rupture, that is also quite interesting. So it then is this completely different kind of provocation because they think: 'Ooh, this lovely, nice, blonde, blue-eyed girl and so cute!' [But] I think, the way that I live from my inner life is absolutely not in accordance with that cliché. And I think that is also important. So that is already such a rupture, so that it does not mean that just because someone is somehow high-heeling around in a miniskirt, she is at the same time absolutely non-feminist or whatever.

To her, the passing femme may unlock subversive power because she is irritating to and interrupting heteronormative assumptions about the meaning of femininity by exposing the dissonance between what is expected of her as a woman with a feminine presentation and how she actually moves through her life, as a feminist and non-conventional woman. Lisa's political stance as femme was 'to show that anything is possible' and that gendered assumptions are often not valid, exposing the queer trickster element. While passing in this way holds potentials and benefits in certain situations, most femme interview partners would decidedly prefer to be recognizable as queer or lesbian. Therefore, femmes actively worked to enhance their recognition, as Emma did through her style: 'Combat boots with skirts and things like that, that kind of style. And that, to me, is a dyke style, it's a grrrl style.' The downside to this strategy was that this could also be read as a straight punk style and was continuously being mainstreamed and robbed of its intended statements; the queer trickster can be hoodwinked herself.

Cross-pollinations between dyke + queer BDSM space and 'straight worlds'

Members of the dyke + queer BDSM community assigned different meanings to their gendered BDSM practices, as the transmasculine gay bear and daddy Craig reported:

> I'm having an ongoing discussion with my girl about role play, if you're playing role play or not. And I don't feel it's role play, because I feel that I'm just a Daddy. So I don't feel like I'm taking on a role: 'I'm in my Daddy role right now.' I'm a Daddy. I just feel like a Daddy most of the time.

For some, their persona was role or gender *play* and for others it was their identity, as in *being* or expressing certain aspects of themselves. However, this differed from ordinary everyday identities in the sense that these identities were more consciously chosen and performed.

My interview partners stressed that BDSM in dyke + queer contexts had the effect of increasing awareness around gender identity issues and social power relations. Teresa and others gained sexual pleasure from using heteronormative and sexist dynamics and stereotypes in dyke + queer BDSM interactions:

> A lot of the super non-consensual power dynamics that exist between straight folks, or just between men and women, like non-trans men and non-trans women, I do eroticize a lot of those dynamics and want to play them out with people who don't actually have those privileges in the rest of the world.

The possibility of actually playing with and experiencing such stereotypes, dynamics or even just the staging of binary genders as pleasurable depended on the fact that in daily life interview partners did not have straight (or male) privileges:

> Though there are SM people who I don't know but I see around, the straight ones supposedly, the straight ones who are really well dressed, who wear lots of leather, go to clubs. I don't know these people, and I should know them better before I talk about them. But I see this sort of yuppie consumption of SM culture as being super apolitical in a lot of ways, and the way they can play with gender and race – I'm amazed that they have no fucking idea what oppression is. I don't know how they can really engage in healthy SM, when they're not understanding how what they do is different than oppression, because they don't know what oppression is. But the SM community that I experience is a community of other folks who understand what it feels like to be non-consensually dominated or oppressed, queers and trannies and sex workers and people of color and working class, poor folks who understand that our gender's a creative response to our oppression. And our sexuality's a creative response and a healthy response.

Teresa and others stressed the importance of reflecting first on their situatedness within social hierarchies in order to be able to consciously play with and perform gender and power in BDSM space. Moreover, queer genders and sexualities were considered to be ways to engage with oppression and normalization critically and productively in processes of disidentification. For Teresa, this set BDSM in dyke + queer contexts apart from straight BDSM.

Many interview partners had stopped attending mixed play parties in the 'pansexual'/straight BDSM communities, because the subcultural skills of reassigning and recognition had not been developed there or had been reduced to a fetishizing, appropriating gesture of domination:

> If a straight person who doesn't really understand the value of a trans person, if a straight person is watching my trans lover being fucked in the cunt, that person may be perceiving my trans lover as a woman, having breasts. They may not be able to construct in his head the body that my trans lover has constructed. And that's very important to me that I'm fucking my lover, his body, in a way that is constructing that body, perceiving that body in a way that the person wants to be perceived. And if there're people watching who perceive it differently, I think it would be unsafe.

These differences in subcultures had the effect that dykes + queers did not see their identities recognized, respected and valued in straight-dominated spaces, and thus those spaces did not provide the kind of semi-contained space or playground that was the prerequisite for exploring, playing with and expressing queer genders, as Femmeboy described above for her trans lover. The audience would unwittingly co-construct a different gender than Femmeboy and her partner constructed, intervening into their gender labor practices. Only gay transman Mik regarded the straight BDSM community in Germany as trans* friendly, whereas transwoman Anna said that this community treated transvestites and transwomen as inferior, placing them on the lowest rank in the internal social status hierarchy.[6]

Given that there were norms and hierarchies in the dyke + queer BDSM community as well, the question became for whom and under what circumstances this social space was actually a space to explore social difference and at which times and places it was also illusionary. A few comments showed that the dyke + queer BDSM space was also not free of conflict surrounding trans* and gender issues, let alone other power dynamics. The dyke butch Luise, for example, was repeatedly asked for her male name, although she identified as female. Some dykes participated in gender play mainly because their partners wanted to, rather than because they found it especially attractive. Some also faced limits when it came to trans* intelligibility. Still, even those members of the dyke + queer BDSM community who did not have the desire to participate in the exploring of gender usually respected and accepted the genderqueer and trans* roles and identities in their midst. But, even though interview partners built a bridge between dyke + queer BDSM space and everyday life, for example through integration, in daily life gender was not safe, sane and consensual, as Bornstein (1994) points out. In any case, transgender butch Tony acknowledged that s/he gained not only gender awareness but also *gender self-confidence* through gender play, which helped hir to defend hir identity in everyday life.

Chapter conclusion

My interview partners generally celebrated difference. In this regard they were part of a broad theoretical and political tradition that considers difference as not simply something to be tolerated or accepted, but as the creative function of life (Derrida 1991; Lorde 1998: 111; Deleuze & Guattari 2004). I have argued that we should conceive of difference as *intimate difference*, since social hierarchies are always infused with erotic investments and are a site of touch and boundary transgressions. Through exploiting the erotic potentials entailed by intimate difference, dyke + queer BDSM acknowledged these emotional investments.

The multiplicities and becomings of queer genders in the dyke + queer BDSM scene have been fostered by a combination of certain BDSM characteristics and the exclusion of privileged genders (specifically, cismen), which created a social space that was perceived as a safer playground in which to explore and experiment with gender, often simultaneously with age. The possibility of playing with, experiencing, transgressing and transforming the stereotypes and dynamics associated with gender, sexuality and age in a pleasurable way seemed to depend on the fact that in daily life the members of the dyke + queer BDSM communities did not have straight (or, for the most part, male) privileges. On the other hand, the fact that most members of this community had racial privileges seemed to prevent them from experimenting with and transforming race and race relations in a similar fashion. Yet it was not the gender segregation of the dyke + queer BDSM space alone that made it such an interesting venue for engaging with and transforming gender, but that BDSM in general encourages a playful and erotically charged, embodied and intimate engagement with power, social roles and cultural stereotypes.

Dyke + queer BDSMers sought out intimate intensity; performing another gender or age and playing with difference held the potential for intense experiences. Furthermore, dyke + queer BDSM combined elements of power exchange and role play that stressed the performative character of gender and sexuality with elements that stressed the material limits of the body (sensation play and bondage), thus providing BDSM dykes + queers with a potential starting point for experiencing and discussing their bodies and sexual acts as material-semiotic entities. As a consequence, within the community the sexed and gendered body was generally perceived as more performative than in mainstream culture; its boundaries were not necessarily restricted by its own skin, as cybercocks and holodicks illustrate, but the limits to its semiotic reinvention were also acknowledged (for instance, through witnessing previously identified non-op FTMs starting to transition). This highlights the need to reassess the usefulness of the concept of bodily integrity as reduced to keeping the body safe from interventions and change, and also emphasizes the need to take into account that life itself is characterized by constant change and that the body is vulnerable.

Gender exploration led to certain insights and awarenesses, especially to an embodied understanding of non-heteronormative gender identities. It created an expansion of gender concepts and identities that, in turn, enabled specific subcultural skills to emerge, which I have called *reassigning*, *recognition* and *integration*. The fact that co-constructing gender held a lot of pleasure for interview partners adds another dimension to theories that consider such practices solely as gender labor or that neglect the erotic and intimate rewards entailed. Furthermore, gender labor is not only performed when giving gender to someone, but is also expected of gender noncon-formists to save others from irritation. My interview partners sometimes disappointed these expectations by going on strike and thus redistributing gender labor.

Integrating split-off parts of the self and other in dyke + queer BDSM play presented an alternative mode of subjectification that was not depen-dent upon excluding an 'other' to become a 'self'. Moreover, the space of dyke + queer BDSM facilitated becoming-other for interview partners in various ways: becoming another gender, a child, an animal, an alien, a vam-pire, an object. My interview partners described dynamics of individuation, singular experiences moving through them. They did not only become a previously defined other, but also created new gendered and sexual subjectiv-ities through processes of transmogrification. Some experienced a constant sliding or shifting of these singular experiences. Therefore, their becoming may best be understood as becoming-changeling and becoming-trickster, not simply becoming a predetermined, fixed other. This becoming is elu-sive and slippery. In order to avoid a power-evasive concept of becoming, we need to understand it as situated, paying attention to the conditions of various becomings.

The presence and performance of partial and situational identities trans-lated into valuing gender difference on a community level and provided interview partners with the potential for partial connections across dif-ference. These practices were sometimes transferred into everyday life, especially in terms of identities. Femmeboy described her fag play with her FTM lover, their mutual becoming-fag:

> Some people would say we were not really [being fags] because 'you're not a fag and he's not a bio boy' or whatever, but I really felt that I was exploring that fag part of myself. So it's not just a fantasy, it's a real part of me. You know, I feel it. So there's a bridge, there's a bridge.

While fag play enabled Femmeboy to become-fag and express a real fag part of herself in everyday life, any transfer to other communities and main-stream society, however, remained limited due to heteronormative social structures, as her comment on how outsiders perceived them reveals. This shows that, while different realities co-exist, they are not considered equally valid in society, which seems to echo McClintock's conclusion that BDSM points to the limits of the concept of individual agency as resolving social dilemmas, since it remains paradoxical (2004: 251). Yet what happened within the space of dyke + queer BDSM had social effects. This was true even for practices that seemed to simply repeat social structures of power and domination, and for those that transgressed them ambiguously or that actually transformed or transmogrified them. Dyke + queer BDSM was effective not only in restaging social conflicts and personal trauma, but also in transforming past experiences and the self while working through past challenges. When interview partners carried these transformations outside their bedrooms and dungeons, they did have an effect on their social contexts.

9
The Sexual Politics of Exuberant Intimacy

As I have shown, dyke + queer BDSM provided a semi-contained space that enabled interview partners to explore boundaries, intimate difference and ways of becoming. I have discussed instances of dyke + queer BDSMers becoming-other in desiring moments of disability, vulnerability, becoming-child, alien, vampire, fag, object and, finally, gender trickster. The emotional and erotic dynamics of dyke + queer BDSM reject the ideal of harmonic sex and relationships, prioritizing experiences of social difference, intensity, non-innocence, disidentification, excess, polyfidelity, insanity and exuberance. In this chapter I will discuss the potentials of dyke + queer BDSM in terms of transformative, rather than just transgressive, micropolitics. I will also expand on my conceptualization of dyke + queer BDSM as a social space of excess, abundance and exuberance.

Historically, excess has been the antidote to reason, and a judgment of excessive sexuality has been assigned to those who were constructed as irrational, especially Black men and women (McClintock 1995: 113). Therefore, excessive erotic practices, like dyke + queer BDSM, with its focus on boundary transgression, intensity and pleasure for its own sake, as well as its eroticization of everyday social worlds, may serve to disrupt the hegemonic notions of reason and sanity (Derrida 1976). Furthermore, these practices also reject enlightened and modernist imaginings of relationships as egalitarian or 'pure' (Giddens 1992), which leads to the creation of various kinds of alternative intimacies. These non-innocent forms of social relations, which do not fall prey to the myth of equality (Klesse 2007) but, rather, acknowledge the ubiquity of power dynamics, may lead to acknowledging one's own social positions and one's emotional investments in them, such as eroticizing power relations. At the same time, they may provide access to excesses of sexualities that may be used productively to infuse socially devalued practices with erotic value and to create desires for subjugated and subversive social positions, not in the sense of eroticizing one's own oppression, but of imagining and experiencing spaces beyond hegemonic values and subject positions. For my interview partners, desire was a strong incentive to disrupt normalizing processes, and they took pleasure in practices that deconstructed and reconstructed the gender binary. If we can come up with ways of desiring to become-other without appropriating this other and rein-scribing social hierarchies, our sexual desires might thus create new political affinities and solidarities.

Power-sensitive transgressions and social transformations

According to Foucault, pastoral power turns individuals into subjects. It is a technology of power that guides subjects through 'truth', and often it is the individual's sexuality that is constructed as that which reveals a person's innermost truth and secrets, and therefore determines who they are. Biopower works through (flexible) normalization rather than exclusion, and makes direct resistance obsolete (Foucault 1976; 1978; 1982). There-fore, one path of resistance is to subvert processes of normalization by cultivating marginal practices and embodying alternative social relations (Stephenson & Papadopoulos 2006: 127). These kinds of micropolitics can take part in processes of social transformation and, therefore, deserve the attention of sociological research. This study has taken an empirical look at a set of social practices, subjectivities and phenomena collected under the umbrella of dyke + queer BDSM, interrogating whether and how they con-tribute to social transformations. More specifically, are these practices and identities simply transgressing social norms and cultural taboos, or are they actually transforming or transmogrifying embodied subjectivities and social relations?

Weiss holds that the circuits of BDSM work when connections are made between realms imagined as being isolated from each other, such as sexuality and politics (2011: 7), and that BDSM can be transformational when it con-nects what happens in a BDSM encounter to social contexts (227). I have demonstrated that dyke + queer BDSM is a social and political space that produces new marginal embodiments and (temporary) identities and prac-tices; it transmogrifies processes of subjectification. Furthermore, it produces alternative intimacies that may serve as a foundation to create alternative social relations, which becomes evident in a sexual culture that values differ-ence and develops out-of-the-ordinary notions of gender, sexuality, consent, beauty, friendship, relationship and intimacy. A lot of dyke + queer BDSM connects the semi-contained space of BDSM with other social realities and with spaces of ongoing social hierarchies and processes of normalization, partly transferring realities from play to everyday life, especially when it comes to gender, but hardly ever when it comes to race.

My interview partners were often simultaneously located in different real-ities, such as the reality of a multiplicity of genders in dyke + queer BDSM spaces and the reality of a binary gender society. On the one hand, they func-tioned as bridges between these worlds, connecting them and facilitating transfers of meaning and embodiment across the porous boundaries of these realities. On the other hand, one has to wonder about the social and political consequences of such parallel realities, which sometimes had little overlap and, therefore, produced in society at large little intelligibility of the alternative subjectivities that my interview partners embodied. It is up to the inhabitants of non-hegemonic spaces to navigate the social contradictions that this entails. Nonetheless, dyke + queer BDSM can be said to hold the potential to be transformative according to Weiss's criterion. While there are certainly situations (like deracialized slave play) that de-emphasize and separate sexuality and BDSM from their social embeddedness, there are also moments and dyke + queer BDSMers who actively connect their sexuality with social histories and contexts, and use dyke + queer BDSM to work through social contradictions and normalizations, with various outcomes. It becomes clear, then, that dyke + queer BDSM is socially effective, and not an isolated phenomenon with only temporary individual transgressions in a presumably 'private' setting. Yet these social effects do not automatically subvert social hierarchies and normalizations; the politics of dyke + queer BDSM can be effective in all kinds of ways, both reproducing hegemonic relations – to the body, to the self, to others, to larger social worlds – and subverting and transforming them. Therefore, the issue of whether dyke + queer BDSM, or even BDSM as a whole, is subversive or conservative per se has to be rejected as a false question, since it minimizes social complexity and thus impoverishes social theorizing. Rather, we have to keep paying attention to the social contexts of sexual practices, identities and relationships and give detailed and differentiated, rather than overgeneralizing and oversimplifying, answers. This is why I prefer to speak of the *potentials* of dyke + queer BDSM rather than positing it as subversive per se. Whether or not its power-sensitive and subversive potentials are put into effect depends on the situational context of the specific actions and individuals in question.

In a lot of queer politics and theorizing, transgression per se has been hyped as subversive. Yet a politics of transgression is severely limited for various reasons, as I have discussed in previous chapters. Some transgressions, such as fetishizations of marginalized subjectivities, even present technologies of domination and social hierarchy themselves. Sexual practices focused on transgression and self-exploration are in danger of promoting individualistic understandings of agency, treating people as if they were acting in a social vacuum and implying the possibility of 'private' solutions for social problems. As Savran points out, sexual dissidence discourse often lacks collective vision (1998: 239). He characterizes gay and lesbian BDSM as providing a kind of psychic alchemy, transforming abjections into gold and offering a genuine, if limited, sense of empowerment without altering the social structures (233).[1] Obviously, the pleasures that interview partners gained from dyke + queer BDSM were genuine, and there are good arguments for leaving it at that and refusing to discuss potential political values as additional justification for these sexual practices – especially in light of the fact that non-BDSM sexuality is not scrutinized in the same manner, establishing a moral double standard. Therefore, it might be politically dangerous to engage once more in a discussion about the political use value of marginalized sexual practices such as dyke + queer BDSM. On the other hand, the opponents of BDSM argue precisely that it is reproducing oppression and should, therefore, not be engaged in. Since my interview partners did not experience it in this way, this assumption needs to be addressed and countered. But, more significantly, and independently of anti-BDSM sentiments, dyke + queer BDSM, like any other human interaction, is entirely social and therefore cannot be discussed in isolation from the social contexts it is embedded in. While following Savran, we can argue that any individualistic benefits that subjugated queer subjects may gain from engaging in BDSM are all the justification it needs, and we can also, at the same time, ask ourselves whether and how dyke + queer BDSM can support social transformations to improve the living conditions of these very subjects beyond the semi-contained space of dyke + queer BDSM. After all, my interview partners fought for the recognition of their non-normative genders, for instance.

We, therefore, have to move beyond the benefits that individuals may reap from their BDSM experiences to the alternative intimacies that are created through partial connections across difference in dyke + queer BDSM and explore the potentials they hold for reimagining collectives that may bring about social change.

Genderqueer Firesong explained that, to her, dyke + queer BDSM was political because

> I'm constructing and deconstructing power for myself in a very intimate way, and what is a political structure but a power structure. And so if you have a power structure that's based on people's need to exert power and control that for whatever reason is less than thoroughly examined, then any work to deconstruct that is actually political work. Politically, I identify as an anarcho-communist, that's my political orientation. And I feel my SM practices enrich that orientation, because it gets me familiar with how I use power and what my power needs are. It gives me a form to play that out, and so maybe I'm more clear about that when I come to a meeting with people. Or knowing myself in that way and knowing my needs, knowing my range and my capacity helps me make better choices of how I am with other people in group situations and in organizational structures. And so that's really political, because I feel in a lot of activism the weak link is always communication and organizational structure. And so to have an organizational structure with people who know themselves in that way, to me, would be really revolutionary.

For Firesong, dyke + queer BDSM offered a space to explore her own invest-ments in power dynamics and to better understand political structures. In many political groups or contexts where the goal is to question hege-monic relations of power, power games and power struggles are still played out in the very same ways they are criticized theoretically. Exploring power in an erotic, intimate, embodied and emotional setting helped interview partners to experience their own embeddedness in power structures in ways that held the potential to transform their daily and political actions more deeply than via intellectual, 'rational' engagement alone. Technologies of negotiating consent in a power-sensitive way in dyke + queer BDSM that increase agency for all parties involved can serve to envision new ways of community-building.

Firesong went on to observe how partial connections across difference could translate into collective action. As a genderqueer, she developed

> a desire to be with biofags who may not be politicized or have a clue about how to play with me. What do I do with that desire? But it's my sexual desire that's leading me to make those [politics]. And I think people are able to commit to their sexual desires almost better than they can commit to any other agenda actually.

Firesong made a strong statement about desire as a catalyst for people's actions in general, and in politics as well. As a consequence, desire and sexuality cannot be neglected in any political analysis or context. Firesong here echoed Deleuze and Guattari's (2004) insistence that desire pervades the political. This also implies that desires could be productively used to generate politics, starting at a small level of organizing to create spaces for those partial connections across difference, such as between female-bodied genderqueers and gay cismen. Terry, for instance, was organizing queer com-munities across such boundaries, producing unexpected connections and solidarities. These kinds of community-building can be seen as generating rhizomes according to Deleuze and Guattari, since heterogeneous elements (different sexual cultures) are brought into close proximity, and the interac-tions between them parallel becomings (becoming-fag for the dykes and vice versa). They, therefore, constitute processes of deterritorialization (Deleuze & Guattari 2004: 11). Desire is the driving force behind these new forms of social collectives, the excess that cannot be contained within the binaries of sex/gender and of homo/hetero, but reaches out to generate new becomings across boundaries.

My interviews have shown that dyke + queer and trans* BDSMers are cre-ating new social relations and collective visions, such as building spaces where gender becomes self-determined. But how can a socially marginalized group like dyke + queer/trans* BDSMers intervene effectively in hegemonic

structures of power and bring about social change beyond their own community spaces? I do not claim to have an answer to this question, but
I do believe that dyke + queer BDSM offers new perspectives on processes
of subjectification, pain, desire, power, critical consent, negotiating agency,
intimate difference, privatization and social relations in general, and that
these are all issues that play a significant role in reinventing collective spaces
and movements across social boundaries. A lot of dyke + queer BDSM may
be about transgression and self-exploration, but it does not stop there. There
is a difference between exploring the self in a purely individualistic fashion,
as evident in most of the self-help literature and the New Age boom, and
exploring the self as a social entity and its embeddedness in social relations.
With its focus on power, social difference and imagining alternative realities
of gender and sexuality, dyke + queer BDSM fosters a socially critical culture
of exploring, thus intervening in processes of normalization rather than simply answering the neoliberal interpellations to be good consumer-subjects
who govern themselves.

A politics of exuberant intimacies

Difference is of great significance in contemporary social theory. What is
important from my perspective is not to try to justify or functionalize difference as something that is worthwhile striving for because it promises certain
benefits, as in many multicultural discourses. While it is certainly the case
that difference enriches life, this is beside the point. The kinds of discourses
that posit difference as a recent social invention (such as the 'detraditionaliz-
ing' discourse) have the problematic effect of implying that there was a time
in history before difference became fashionable (presumably only in the cultural West, at that), which, in turn, implies that the original state of the
world was one of homogeneity, uniformity and 'tradition' in the sense of sta-
sis. Instead, my study has been situated within those theoretical approaches
that hold that difference and variation are the basic principle of life (for
example, Rubin 1992a: 283; Deleuze & Guattari 2004).

Moreover, life generates not only difference, but also an abundance of
practices, bodies, relationships and meanings that exceed discourse. Therefore, life in general is characterized by abundance rather than scarcity, as,
for example, Bataille shows in his theory of economy (2001: 289ff). According to Bataille, the earth produces excesses of energy, which can only be
used for growth of the system or be wasted (290). He contrasts the economy of capitalism (accumulation) with the economy of the festival, which
is about wasting the excess without maximizing the production potential
(299). Bataille considers the latter to be the logical choice and favors a
wasting of the excess energy through living completely in the moment, celebrating life through means like art or games and (non-reproductive) sex,
which wastes resources without a real purpose. Yet he seems to overlook

that these may be wasteful activities in the material sense, but they are, nonetheless, productive of the social.

Art, games and sex generate affects, social relations, identities and cultures. Moreover, the production of excess is not limited to the physical world. Excess comes into play in various forms in social relations, such as the productive ambivalences of communication, which necessarily produce excesses of meaning (Stephenson & Papadopoulos 2006: 85), as in the invisible gender subversion of the queer femme. Even more generally speaking, human intentions rarely produce what is intended (91). As Deleuze and Guattari point out, the segmented lines of macropolitics are always immersed in and prolonged by micropolitics that continually reshuffle and stir up its segments, and something always escapes the molar structures (2004: 240). There are always lines of flight. For instance, the polyphony of criss-crossing interpellations (Pieper 2007: 231) produces excesses in the processes of subjectification: if you cannot answer all interpellations at the same time, you are forced to choose between them, and thereby produce subject positions that cannot be described within a simplistic framework as either 'hegemonic' or 'subversive'; instead, you are engaged in simultaneous but contradictory social dynamics. This is, for instance, evident in contradictory interpellations of heteronormativity and neoliberalism, with heteronormativity asking subjects to form nuclear families that share a home, chronic interaction and continuity (Tyrell 1987), while neoliberalism simultaneously requires us to adjust to the needs of international corporations, which demand mobile and flexible subjects. This, paradoxically, opens up options for agency in the interfaces, with such phenomena as non-monogamous constellations providing alternative lifestyles. Hardt and Negri (2000), for instance, locate resistance potentials in the excesses of the creative powers that are produced by capital but not completely appropriated. One may consider dyke + queer BDSM tools and toys such as whips, handcuffs and dildos as an instance of objects that are a commodity and create niche markets, but have not been completely appropriated, since they still embody the hope for something that is beyond commodification, as Weiss showed in her work on how non-BDSMers perceived the BDSM film *Secretary* (2006a).

In the case of dyke + queer BDSM, certain forms of social collective or community may also not be appropriated, since they do not cater to the logics of commodification, such as non-commercial play parties and the synergetic effects they create. Criss-crossing interpellations of the gender binary and queer subcultures, with one calling for stable genders and the other for deconstructing genders, also produce excesses in subjectification processes. These meet in dyke + queer BDSM, where all kinds of renegotiations of these interpellations can be eroticized: disidentificatory practices that celebrate gender polarity as well as gender fluidity and multiplicity. Yet Lorenz warns that the management of competing interpellations has clear limits (2009: 183). For instance, those interpellations that individuals need to answer in order to make a living may outweigh others. And the solution of compartmentalizing subjectivities that answer to work demands versus other, for instance, sexual demands, may become a burden for the individuals who have to navigate these restrictions. These burdens are logistical as well as emotional if certain aspects of the personality have to remain hidden, as evidenced by Terry's practice of transforming his embodied work self into his 'real', trans* and BDSM embodied self in the subway or public toilets.

In dyke + queer BDSM there are further phenomena of excess. For instance, BDSM toys/tools can be considered to hold an excess of meaning. They are often everyday objects, such as clothespins, kitchen foil or medical equipment, that are used for something they were not intended for. This was especially true for those interview partners who had to resort to creative solutions because they could not afford specialized equipment, such as Mistress Mean Mommy, who referred to herself as 'the budget dom[inant]'. As I have elaborated, the very power of dyke + queer BDSM desires produces its own excesses of unpredictable and unexpected emotional investments that may paradoxically open up new forms of agency, as in disidentificatory practices and identities (Muñoz 1999). With its exaggerated style, BDSM generally reveals that the social order is unnatural, scripted and invented (McClintock 1995: 143; Duncan 1996). Dyke + queer BDSM disassociates sexuality and the erotic from reproduction and other 'usefulness' (such as in medical discourses that hold that sex is good for your health), appropriating parts of the body and everyday life for sexual pleasure, twisting their social significance. It shows, therefore, that the sexual is excessive and cannot be limited to reproduction, the genitals or even the material body, as having an orgasm from getting one's back flogged and the concepts of the cybercock and the holodick illustrate.

The perspective that sees sexuality as a social sphere of excess, abundance and exuberance, therefore, also resists the urge to look for 'explanations' for 'deviant sexuality' or difference in general, or for any functions outside itself. A theory of sexual exuberance refuses what Deleuze and Guattari (2004) refer to as 'interpretosis': the assuming of some meaning or truth behind the appearances that is just waiting for interpretation, revelation and disclosure. In contrast, Deleuze (1994) advocates a transcendental empiricism, which is thinking of an experience, life or becoming as having no ground outside itself. This was also evident in my interview partners' stances. They refused to rationalize or justify their dyke + queer BDSM through discourses that presumably provided them with some respectable social value or function. Rather, they stressed that the motivations to practice BDSM were the inherent, inexplicable pleasures, as queer femme Emma stated:

> asking why my sexuality is the way it is, or anybody's sexuality is the way it is, anybody's sexual orientation or gender identity, is ultimately not a

really useful question. It's like asking: 'Why do you like the kind of music you do? Why do you like the kind of food that you do?' And I think the best answer is just 'because'. Because it's my preference, because this is what I react to, because when I taste Ethiopian food, it tastes good to me.

So Emma clearly rejected the search for a reason behind her sexual preferences. This kind of approach seems to fit better within Bataille's economy of the festival than within capitalism, wasting the body and one's energies for pleasures rather than for material productivity, and producing queer subjectivities, social relations and collectives instead.

The sole aim of exuberant sexuality is self-serving pleasure and desire in the sense of a state of joyful being in the moment, bodies stretching out to touch others, an intensity of experience, an expression of excess. MacKendrick, therefore, holds that pleasure is only subversive as long as it is not turned into something 'useful' beyond itself, even if that is the political goal of subversion (MacKendrick 1999: 12). So, paradoxically, trying to infuse BDSM intently with subversive value might sabotage its subversive potentials. My interview partners sometimes struggled with the imperative to justify their BDSM by giving it a higher purpose, such as spirituality, therapy or subversion, when it came to defending themselves against the negative public or subcultural image of BDSM. Queer femme Ellen discussed the question of BDSM's political aspects as problematic:

> I'm not queer and I don't practice SM just because I view it as political. Because I think, just like people who rationalize the lesbian thing because they see it as political and outside of patriarchy, I think that degrades the sensuality aspect of it. So, for me, SM is political, but it's also incredibly sensual, and I think that that's really important to recognize in it. I wouldn't do it if I didn't get off on it.

To Ellen, the micropolitics of BDSM were unintended side effects, and the reasons she practiced dyke + queer BDSM were self-serving: the sexual pleasures it provided. She rejected a rationalization of her sexual preferences. Therefore, dyke + queer BDSM remained a 'useless', excessive, intense, exuberant intimate practice. Its excess, its hyperbole, its intensity defied reason and (re)productivity. It was a life force in the sense that it did not strive for a goal, sometimes not even for sexual gratification, since the prolonging of tension enhanced its power and the intensity of the experience.

My concept of exuberant intimacy is not uncritically in favor of wasting resources and transgressing all limits without ethical and political considerations, however. The focus of 'no limits' philosophies, as put forward by theorists like Bataille and by some queer theorists and sexologists who celebrate boundary violations without any risk-reducing frameworks and sometimes criticize negotiated BDSM (or communicative sexuality in general) as not transgressive enough (for example, Schmidt 1998; Downing 2007), is a privileged one. These kinds of transgressions are only possible for (or are the taken-for-granted entitlement of) dominant subjects. For instance, it is easy to criticize the 'boredom' of negotiating consent from a *white* male perspective since that subject position hardly ever faces violations of sexual boundaries. Moreover, 'no limits' secures the status quo of sexist sexual violence. Propagating an economy of the festival without further qualification may also ignore the realities of poor people struggling for material survival, who will hardly perceive life as full of abundance in this regard. And, in times of environmental destruction, it has to be made clear what kinds of wastefulness one is talking about. Wasting natural resources in terms of deforestation and increasing consumption, for instance, is hardly anti-capitalist (but, of course, this is not an instance of the economy of the festival as conceived by Bataille). Clearly, a simple philosophy of hedonism without social and environmental responsibilities as integral components would do more harm than good in the 21st century.

The same may be true when it comes to dismantling the subject. Even Deleuze and Guattari, who call for deterritorialization and the construction of a Body without Organs, rightfully warn that wildly destratifying is not an option and would result in death; a bare minimum of the subject has to remain in order to survive (2004: 177–8). Or, differently put, along with the various deterritorializations, reterritorialization has to occur as well.

In contrast to the 'no limits' philosophies, dyke + queer BDSMers could be said to have followed Deleuze and Guattari's advice and Haraway's (1991) demands, since they were trying to create pleasurable yet responsible ways of confusing boundaries in order to open up bodies and connect across differences. While this may seem less exciting to some theorists, I hold that ethical and political considerations, most basically understood as taking into account and being accountable for the consequences of one's actions, such as the effects on others, social contexts and 'natural' environments, are indispensable. And the presumably 'private' realm of sexuality is no exception, since it is part of the social worlds we inhabit.

This also applies to researchers and theorists, of course. Haraway's situated knowledges (1991) are one way of opening oneself to being held accountable for the kind of knowledges one produces. Namaste (2000) also reminds researchers who study marginalized groups of their responsibilities, asking: what do research subjects need in terms of social and political policies? In the case of my interview partners, the answers were manifold, from the decriminalization of BDSM and sex work to legal and medical options to live a life beyond the gender binary, to BDSM-friendly women's spaces (including shelters and therapists), to programs for queer youth to prevent homelessness. As researchers, we should strive to produce another kind of excess regarding our work: one that spills out of our pages beyond the intrinsic relevance for the academic world and back into other social worlds to bring about social transformations.

In summary, dyke + queer BDSM can be conceptualized as holding potentials for and actually creating exuberant intimacies, practices and subject positions through intense experiences that reject reason, moderateness, mediocrity, harmony, the myth of equality, reproduction and usefulness. Instead, these exuberant moments celebrate difference, tension, intensity, risk, excess, ecstasy, wastefulness, perversity, campy extravagance, fluidity and insanity, as well as becoming something beyond the human, becoming-other, becoming-trickster. I consider dyke + queer BDSM practices to be exuberant intimacies, opening up different kinds of queer worlds beyond the illusion of egalitarian relationships and mythical connections across difference (as in heterosexual romance discourses). I see a world of situated embodiments and desires, dykes + queers taking pleasure in the perversion of hegemonic boundaries, becoming tricksters and claiming responsibility for their own non-innocent but productive emotional and political investments in structures of social hierarchy and domination. A politics and ethics of exuberant intimacies would, then, exploit intense sensations and emotions to be in the moment, to prolong that moment, and to stay with the social contradictions that produce these pleasures and their accompanying ambivalences and pains. All of this would create a social space in which structures of social hierarchy, norms and social contradictions, such as between the myth of equality and the social reality of inequalities, can be engaged with in an embodied, intimate and affective, rather than just intellectual or rational, manner. This kind of engagement with the histories and realities of social difference frozen into hierarchy may contribute not only to transgressions, but also to transformations and transmogrifications.

This concept should not be confused with Giddens's notion of the pure relationship (1992), though. The concepts of exuberant intimacy and the pure relationship have in common that sexual activities and the sharing of intimacy are mostly self-serving, and they do not focus much on the more functional aspects of relationships. Or, as lesbian Cara described her criterion for finding a suitable partner: 'There has to be a compatibility of crazinesses.' A compatibility of crazinesses can be considered an expression of an exuberant (or pure) intimate relationship concept, far removed from the imperatives for the usefulness of traditional marriage in terms of reproduction or building an economic unit. But it is of great significance that Giddens's concept of the pure relationship ignores ongoing social power dynamics and structures, while exuberant intimacy actively engages with power and social difference. My interview partners were not deluded into assuming their relationships were pure or innocent or outside power structures. Moreover, the wastefulness and playfulness of exuberance should not be confused with capitalist consumerism, the exploitation of others and environmental destruction, but should be focused on the celebration of the intense and ambivalent pleasures and pains generated by human bodies interacting sexually in a social context. The intensity of the dyke + queer BDSM experience, including its boundary-crossings, extravagant gender play, gendered multiplicities, synergetic effects of group play, shared intimacies and other phenomena, shows that desire is not lack, but a spilling over across the boundaries of individuals. Bodies are not closed, but open and vulnerable boundary projects always in the processes of becoming, experiencing the intensities of the moment and stretching out to touch. Desire is about exuberant intimacies.

Conclusion

This empirical study has focused on dyke + queer BDSM practices, subjectivities and communities. The analysis of the interviews has shown that this small, socially marginalized subculture has interesting perspectives to offer on issues that are of great significance for current theorizing about gender, sexuality, consent, intimacy, power, community, subjectivities, embodiment, agency and social spaces.

While refusing to reduce the broad range of social practices that constitute dyke + queer BDSM to a single explanation, I have proposed an understanding of dyke + queer BDSM within a framework of exuberant intimacy. This seems appropriate because the interviews highlighted the production of various kinds of excesses. First of all, desire itself constitutes a force that cannot be contained; for instance, the erotic appreciation of trans* individuals has served as a catalyst to expand the women's BDSM community into a dyke + (queer) one. I have argued that both desire and pleasure hold potentials for deterritorializations as well as reterritorializations. Desire reaches out, while pleasure encourages touch, prolonging the moment. Desires travel through bodies and are shaped by individual and social histories. Therefore, social power relations also produce excesses of desire in disidentificatory ways, as the eroticization of hierarchy and of socially devalued positions in dyke + queer BDSM proves. Thus, there is always an excess of desires and emotions that can intervene in unpredictable ways in hegemonic processes of subjectification. Furthermore, gender functioned as a trickster in the experiences of my interview partners. They described various processes of becoming, becoming-other and transmogrifications; they possessed identities in transition, in flux or multiplied. Dyke + queer BDSM represented a semi-contained social space for exploring and experimenting. It allowed interview partners to continuously expand the self by including difference rather than expelling it. This kind of integration can be understood as an alternative to hegemonic processes of identifying that work via exclusion of the other. The semi-contained space of dyke + queer BDSM also enabled interview partners to explore and push boundaries in regard to personal limits as well as cultural taboos. In general, I have proposed an understanding of intimacy as access, as boundary transgressions in terms of touch and violation. Intimacy, therefore, has to do with individual and social vulnerabilities. Difference is always already intimate difference, since social hierarchies are sites of such boundary transgressions. Dyke + queer BDSM, with its active renegotiations of power, can be said to unmask and defy the ideal of harmonic sex and the myth of equality.

This kind of edgework generates intense experiences. My interview partners valued intensity over comfort, which is another element of the exuberance of dyke + queer BDSM in the sense of hyperbole. Moreover, pushing against limits produced experiences of bodies as boundary projects. A space was opened up that allowed the production of a Body without Organs and that redrew the boundaries of the body and subject in intimate intra- and interactions. My interview partners used this for healing as well as to co-construct trans* and genderqueer embodiments that expanded their material limits, presenting another kind of excess, as the examples of cybercocks and holodicks illustrated. The latter can be understood as artifacts from another reality that was as valid to my interview partners as the reality of reason and scientific materiality. Bodily integrity could, therefore, be redefined as a state in which the body matches the body image and others respect this personal reality. Thus, dyke + queer BDSM excess can be understood as producing another kind of reality, the intimate theater and out-of-the-ordinary (such as spiritual) space interview partners entered when they left ordinary reality behind.

My interview partners also shared intimacy in community spaces, a practice that holds the potential to create synergetic effects, which represent another kind of excess that is produced. This collective experience resisted commodification and held potentials for the creation of new forms of social relations. These sometimes followed a queer philosophy of exuberance, as exemplified in how interview partners created communities that valued difference and intimate relating beyond dyadic containment. But these practices did not take place in a social vacuum, and, therefore, social position and situatedness continued to matter. The dyke + queer BDSM community developed technologies of negotiating critical and affective (rather than liberal and rational-choice) consent that offered a promising tool to invent new power-sensitive ways of dealing with difference and social hierarchy. Starting from an acknowledgment of interdependence rather than personal autonomy, they replaced the illusion of equality with the criterion of negotiating agency, which enabled individuals to state their desires and set limits in concrete, contained situations. The notion of agentic feminism that prevailed in the community entailed claiming one's own agency both to empower oneself and to interrogate one's own position of power critically.

As the first to extensively document the dyke + queer BDSM community, this study has covered a broad range of topics. While some questions have been tentatively answered, new ones emerged in the process of analyzing these practices, subjectivities and communities in more detail. Thus, future research is needed to further investigate such issues as sexual consent, power and agency. It seems that the dyke + queer BDSM community is a unique social space in some regards (gendered multiplicity, negotiating critical consent). Comparative studies with other subsets of society could bring about further insights: for example, how do participants in different social contexts establish sexual consent? Are there social spaces that hold the potential to also transform and transmogrify other social categories that were ignored or left to transgressive politics within the dyke + queer BDSM sample of this study, such as race and class? How can such promising concepts as becoming and transmogrifying be put into everyday social practices and resistant politics? What does it mean for marginalized subjectivities if they live in realities that are not shared, understood and accepted by society at large? Do an ethics and micropolitics of exuberance suffice to bring about social change?

To start to answer some of these pressing questions, more empirical research and theory-building are needed. Through this study, I hope to have made a contribution by shedding some light on social practices and spaces that have been neglected in research and politics so far, with the goal of bringing about social change in the long run. For that to happen, we must keep interrogating our desires and their reaching out into the social worlds around us from a power-sensitive perspective.

Annex: Alphabetical List of Interview Partners

Situated according to their self-definitions at the time of interview. Gender and sexual identities, relationship status and occupation have changed for quite a few individuals since.

Anastasia was a *white* queer femme from the US in her early 20s, preferring the bottom role. She was in a non-monogamous relationship and identified as polyamorous.

Anna was a *white* (East) German polysexual transwoman of low socio-economic status (SES), a switch preferring the bottom role. She was non-monogamous, sexually active and single, aged 32, and had worked as a sex worker at times.

Anya was a *white* European pansexual femme, top in a non-monogamous relationship. She was middle-class and aged 43.

Bell was a *white* US lesbian transwoman femme switch. She was in her 40s, of low SES and in a non-monogamous relationship.

BJ was a *white* US gay transman who was born intersex. He was a switch and in a polyamorous situation. He was of precarious SES and aged 40.

Björn was a *white* German gay transboy/drag king and switch. He was 31, of precarious SES, non-monogamous, sexually active and single.

Cara was a *white* German lesbian woman, bottoming to her wife, with whom she was in a monogamous relationship. She was 37 and of middle-class SES.

Connie was a *white* German lesbian switch, preferring the bottom role. She was 25, of precarious SES and lived polyamorously.

Craig was a *white* European gay transmasculine switch leaning toward top. He was 33, working-class, chronically ill and in a polyamorous relationship.

Daphne was a *white* German transwoman switch with no sexual preference besides BDSM. She was in her 40s, of low SES, non-monogamous, sexually active and single.

Ellen was a *white* US queer femme bottom of Jewish background who worked in the sex industry. She was in her early 20s, of precarious SES, non-monogamous, sexually active and single.

Emma was an Ashkenazi Jewish/*white* US queer femme switch. She was 50, middle-class, single and polyamorous.

Eric was a *white* European pansexual FTM alien/unisexual top. He was 30, leading polyamorous DS relationships as Master, and chronically ill. Eric died two years after the interview.

Erika was a *white* (East) German lesbian/bisexual butch switch who was mostly topping. She was 28, middle-class and cohabited with her wife in a non-monogamous relationship.

Femmeboy was a *white* US queer genderqueer switch. She was 30, upwardly mobile middle-class, non-monogamous, sexually active and single.

Firesong was a *white* US queer genderqueer/trans switch. She was in her late 20s, of precarious SES and in a non-monogamous relationship.

Franka was a *white* (East) German bisexual woman top. She was 43, middle-class and in a non-monogamous relationship.

Frl.R. was a *white* German lesbian femme top. She was 44, middle-class and polyamorous.

Helene was a *white* German culturally lesbian woman and bottom. She was 34, middle-class, sexually active and single.

Jacky was a *white* German queer transgender butch switch. He was 35, working-class and in a non-monogamous relationship.

Jonas was a *white* German expatriate gay transman switch. He was 32, upper middle-class and in a non-monogamous relationship.

Katharina was a *white* German queer femme switch. She was 34, middle-class and in a non-monogamous relationship.

Kay was a *white* US lesbian transwoman butch top. She was 30, lower middle-class, disabled and in a polyamorous triad.

Kelvin was a *white* German lesbian/queer transgender top. He was 27, of precarious SES and in a monogamous relationship.

Leslie was a queer transwoman bottom. She was 20, grew up as an Asian adoptee in Europe, and was a lower middle-class sex worker in a monogamous relationship.

Lilly was a *white* German lesbian woman top and professional. She was 25, of precarious SES and in a non-monogamous relationship.

Lisa was a *white* German butch-loving femme bottom. She was 32, middle-class and in a non-monogamous relationship.

Lola was a *white* Jewish US dyke/queer butch switch who was mostly topping. She was 40, downwardly mobile lower middle-class, and in a non-monogamous relationship. She had done professional topping.

Luise was a *white* German butch lesbian woman top. She was 37, middle-class and cohabiting with her wife in an open relationship.

Mandy was a *white* US queer/dyke high femme bottom switch. She was 60, middle-class, chronically ill, polyamorous, sexually active and single.

Matt was a *white* US-based queer/gay transguy top. He was 20, middle-class and in a non-monogamous relationship.

MCL did not define in terms of gender and sexuality. She was 37, a *white* German middle-class top who was sexually active and single.

Michaela was a *white* European dyke woman switch. She was in her 30s, middle-class, polyamorous, sexually active and single.

Mik was a *white* German gay transman bottom. He was 35, of precarious SES, non-monogamous, sexually active and single.

Mistress Mean Mommy was a *white* dyke femme switch of Jewish ancestry from the US. She was 43, middle-class and in a non-monogamous relationship.

Mz Dre was an African American bisexual femme lifestyle Mistress and professional. She was in her 50s, of precarious SES and in polyamorous DS relationships.

Neila was a *white* (East) German pansexual genderqueer femme switch. She was 27, unemployed and in a monogamous relationship.

Nico was a *white* German-based lesbian woman top. She was 38, of low SES, disabled and in a non-monogamous relationship.

Petra was a *white* German queer switch who was biologically female but did not identify with any gender category. She was 43, middle-class and polyamorous, and had been a sex worker during her life.

Scout was a *white* US queer trans/genderqueer/butch dyke switch. He was 21, of low SES with experience of homelessness and in a non-monogamous relationship.

Sophie was a *white* German bisexual woman switch who had worked as a professional. She was 28, precarious middle-class, sexually active, non-monogamous and single.

Tanya was a dyke femme lifestyle submissive of *white* and Native American background. She was 26, disabled, of low SES and in a non-monogamous DS relationship.

Teresa was a *white* US queer-straight femme bottom who had worked as a sex worker and BDSM professional. She was 21, precarious middle-class, sexually active, non-monogamous and single.

Terry was a *white*/Jewish US queer transgender stone butch top. He was 30, chronically ill, middle-class and in a polyamorous situation.

Tony was a *white* German queer transgender butch switch. He was 25, with a precarious SES and in a monogamous relationship.

Vito was a *white* German bisexual woman and top. She was 32, middle-class and lived in a monogamous relationship with her wife.

Wolf was a *white* German gay transman switch. He was 46, with a precarious SES and in a non-monogamous relationship.

Yosh was a *white* German expatriate biologically female bottom who felt in between genders and had a sexual preference for butch women. She was 39, upper middle-class and lived with her wife in an emotionally monogamous relationship.

Zoe was a *white*/Jewish US queer high femme switch. She was 44, had serious health issues, was of precarious SES and was in a polyamorous situation.

Notes

1 Introduction

1. In the German contexts, trans* is used increasingly to refer to all individuals who do not live fulltime according to the gender they were assigned at birth. It is, thus, an inclusive umbrella term that sidesteps the necessity to refer to either sex or gender as the transgressed aspect (as in transsexual or transgender).
2. 'Trans' means 'across' and 'cis' means 'on the same side'. The prefix 'cis' is used by the trans* community and others to refer to people who live in the gender category they were assigned at birth (in opposition to trans*). This terminology has the advantage of avoiding the logic of 'normal/other' and of avoiding the privileging of biology/anatomy as a point of reference. It serves to rupture the invisibility or assumed naturalness of this gender location. It has also increasingly replaced the formerly common term 'biological' men/women, since that term seems to suggest that only non-modified bodies are 'biological', and that gender identity is derived from the sexed anatomy of bodies without complications. Using 'cis' may, thus, point at the social constructedness of *all* gender positions.
3. 'Othering' is a commonly used concept in various fields of studies, originating in feminist and post-colonial theoretical contexts. De Beauvoir (1974) analyzed the social construction of man as subject and woman as other. In post-colonial theory, othering describes the process of constructing a specific complex and diverse group of people, such as 'Arabs', as a homogeneous category. Differences rather than commonalities between the self and 'other' are stressed in order to establish this category as a polar opposite to the imagined position of the self, misrepresenting and exploiting this image of the other in order to define one's own position as normal, superior and so on (Said 1978; Hall 1997).
4. The capitalization of racializing terms like 'Black' serves to point out that these are not natural or self-evident categories, but social constructions with political consequences and meanings. Science studies scholars have shown that races do not exist biologically (Livingstone 1993). Therefore, my employment of racializing terms is not meant to perpetuate this false notion, but to make visible social relations of power and hierarchy that continue to mark certain individuals as racial others with very material consequences. Moreover, the capitalization of Black has been a part of Black anti-racist politics. I choose not to capitalize but to italicize *white* because naming this racial category is not part of a liberationist struggle, but a means of critical (self-)positioning and, therefore, a claiming of political responsibility for *white* privileges.
5. Several authors have, therefore, called for the removal of section F65 (Moser & Kleinplatz 2005; Reiersøl & Skeid 2006; Kleinplatz & Moser 2007). Reiersøl and Skeid point out that, if any distress is caused by sexual behaviors, non-sexual diagnosis criteria, such as compulsive behavior, exist to address the issue (2006: 248).
6. I use the term 'colonialist' to indicate that I am not simply referring to a bygone period of history called colonialism, and that the discursive and material effects still structure the societies and cultures of both former colonizers and colonized

peoples. Furthermore, indigenous and aboriginal peoples are still actively col-onized today, such as the violent displacement of Amazon tribes from their ancestral homelands and the deforestation of those lands. We do not live in post-colonial but in colonial times.

7. It is beyond the scope of this work and largely irrelevant to my sample to present the details of this debate. For counter-arguments to Sontag, see, for example, Van Lieshout (1995) and Moore (2005).

8. There is definitely a minority of BDSM practitioners who practice explicit Nazi play, although, due to its taboo nature, it is hard to estimate how many people engage in this kind of role play and why. Further research into this issue is war-ranted. None of my interview partners reported personal experiences of such play, although one German interview partner expressed a conflicted potential inter-est in it, and one US interview partner showed me an SS uniform in her BDSM wardrobe. Weiss observed that the politics around Nazi play in the SM commu-nity she studied were reduced to the question of what can be done in public and what should remain in private (Weiss 2011: 207).

9. For a more detailed discussion of this part, as well as many other chapters and themes, see Bauer (2013a).

10. I am critical of the concept of justice, since it is too often used as a decontextual-ized, abstract yet normative ideology. Therefore, I use the term 'fairness' instead as a localized, situated, contextualizing, power-sensitive and messy attempt to address power imbalances and structures of domination and exploitation. Fair-ness may include renouncing one's own 'rights' and entitlements in order to achieve a settlement in situations of conflict. Fairness is not falling prey to the illusion that true justice can be achieved, but tries to work toward a world with fewer social hierarchies, knowing that this is always only partially possible.

11. I will situate interview partners the first time they are mentioned in each chapter, but not each time, except when I think it is necessary in order to understand the context of their statements. A list of my interview partners and their socio-political positioning is provided as an annex.

12. For an excellent example of reflective power dynamics in research, see Chapter 2 of Klesse (2007).

13. What stood out was the impact of transitioning for both MTFs and FTMs, which resulted in becoming downwardly mobile or staying poor, which confirms the findings of studies on the discrimination that trans* people face (FRA 2009; Franzen & Sauer 2010; Grant et al. 2011).

14. Anna used the term 'polysexual' to state that individuals of all genders were potential sexual partners for her.

2   The Culture of Dyke + Queer BDSM

1. My US interview partners preferred the term 'dyke' over 'lesbian', since it stood for a more confrontational, rebellious, 'in-your-face' attitude, as in the 'dykes on bikes' culture. In Germany, the differentiation between 'dyke' and 'lesbian' does not exist, so that all German interview partners who positioned themselves as 'lesbisch' have been translated to 'lesbian' as the more neutral term.

2. Personal communication with CHC member Ian Gurnhill, 4 June 2012.

3. 'Pansexual' as an identity marker should not be confused with its function as a BDSM community marker. It has become fashionable for the heterosexual BDSM

communities in the US to call themselves 'pansexual', since they are theoretically open to all genders and sexualities. In practice, though, these communities are overwhelmingly straight, with a number of bisexual women in mostly heterosexual relationships among them, as opposed to bisexual communities that actually consist of mostly bisexual, pansexual and queer individuals (see Newmahr 2011; Weiss 2011, who both describe the set-up of the 'pansexual' communities they studied in this way).

4. No such gender-neutral pronouns have been introduced in German to my knowledge as of yet.

5. For Terry, it was the way of negotiating power that drew him to BDSM from his previous engagement with anti-racist communities. So, approaches to BDSM can be very different in their relation to racial politics.

6. To recount the ongoing discussion about how racism is mediated through socio-economic exclusion goes beyond the scope of this work. But I encourage theorizing that looks both at the intersection of various processes of social exclusion and at each category's unique dynamics. That being said, I always assume that the monochromatic nature of a space is caused not only by economic issues around race, but by cultural racism as well.

7. Kate Bornstein is a US lesbian/queer transwoman artist and activist.

8. Critiques of the category 'woman' by feminists of color, such as Minh-ha, have been broader, though, including criticism of the exclusion of women of color from that category. In queer community discourse, this has been largely reduced to an argument about whether biological sex determines gender and thus membership under the signifier 'woman'.

9. Of course there are trans* individuals who themselves endorse the binary gender system. I am concerned here about what being judged according to gender stereotypes means for those individuals who are not able to (or do not want to) pass.

10. See Kaldera (2009: 233–43) for an introduction to the issues surrounding the inclusion of FTMs in gay men's sexual spaces.

11. This 'bad person precedent dynamic' was also described by Kaldera's informants (2009: 217; 224–5).

12. This, in turn, might result in feminists accusing MTFs of 'exaggerating femininity' or of reproducing patriarchal stereotypes without analyzing their own role in (re)producing these normative standards.

13. See Kaldera (2009: 258ff) for a discussion of various disclosure strategies.

14. See also Kaldera (2009: 207) on the fetishization through pornographic stereotypes of MTFs in BDSM communities, resulting in an image of MTFs as 'free hookers'. Moreover, in BDSM contexts, trans* status is often not acknowledged as a gender, but simply considered to be another fetish.

15. Sexologist discourses differentiate between cross-dressing for the sake of sexual arousal, thus reducing certain trans* practices to sexuality alone, and transsexuality as a body dysphoria that prevents the individual from having any sexual interaction at all, turning pre-op transsexuals into asexual beings (World Health Organization 2010: F 64).

16. Fat female bodies can also be seen as exceeding femininity since they take up more space, which is a feature of demonstrating masculinity. Yet, the girls in Rice's study also reported that they were not able to assert an identity as a tomboy either, since the definition of boys as wiry and strong also conflicts with the image of fat bodies as inert and weak (Rice 2007: 168). Therefore, fat girls and women

are assigned a genderless rather than an androgynous or genderqueer kind of not-womanhood through mainstream discourse.

17. Some interview partners refused to name themselves in terms of gender and/or sexual preference. Therefore I situate them as non-defining.
18. Some queer BDSMers appropriate the term 'pervert' as a self-description to affirm the outlaw status of non-conforming sexual tastes.
19. I will discuss some of these theories in the context of the issue of consent in Chapter 4.
20. Since, to lesbian feminists, consent to BDSM activities is invalid, all those practices amount to sadomasochism in the pathological or criminal sense.

3 Renegotiating Dyke + Queer BDSM

1. Stone is a term from butch–femme culture. Those butches and FTMs who do not let their partners touch their chest and genital areas in sexual interactions are referred to as stone.
2. Newmahr also reports that tops in her sample consider themselves 'reaction junkies' (2010: 326).
3. A third one could be about desiring masculinities in all possible bodies and identities, but this remained a marginal preference among femmes in my sample, especially when it came to their actual sexual practices, which usually excluded cismen.
4. A packy is a device that is worn inside underpants to mimic the bulge of a penis and balls.
5. I did not interview any people who felt they were ever in danger of acting out non-consensual sadism. Since my interview partners stated that BDSM gave them more peace of mind, future research should inquire whether this function of BDSM as an outlet for aggression may actually serve to decrease the chance of becoming violent for some individuals.
6. Connie used the word 'lesbian' as a marker for both sexual and gender identity.
7. This German term has no equivalent in English, but it refers to the mind as a movie theater, a movie running in the mind.

4 Negotiating Critical Consent

1. This may be a research bias from studying only specific subsets of the community. For example, in professional settings, it could be expected that sessions are much more scripted due to the service provider–client dynamic.
2. In community discourse, terms such as 'Mistress' referring to the top are often capitalized to emphasize the difference in status between top and bottom.
3. By calling herself culturally lesbian, Helene expressed that she had been socialized in lesbian culture and felt connected to it, even though her desire was not always exclusively directed toward women, but included FTMs.
4. For instance, interview partners reported that, if one were too passive in pre-negotiations, one might be prompted to reveal one's interests or even be shunned as a play partner, since many players refused to risk a session going wrong because of inadequate information.
5. Because the community I'm researching is rather small and because sharing one's experiences of abuse is an extremely personal matter, I will refrain from identifying the quotes in this section.

6. Since I was conducting face-to-face interviews, I did not consider it appropriate to include a mandatory question about experiences of abuse. I felt that the decision to discuss this matter should be left to my interview partners. Therefore, I cannot provide any definitive statistics about the prevalence of abuse in my sample. Sixteen per cent of my interview partners identified themselves as abuse survivors without being prompted while discussing topics like consent or age play.

7. Barker (2013) discusses various mechanisms that have prevented the (heterosexual) BDSM community from developing a culture of consent so far, like the dogma that BDSM is not abuse, victim blaming, reducing consent to the area of genital sex rather than whole relationships, the myth of the mind-reading dominant, social pressures on women to present as desirable and discourses that romanticize men as predators and women as infantile.

5 Exploring Exuberant Intimacies

1. To discuss this in detail would go beyond the scope of this work. Examples of groups of people who are not able to access certain spaces due to social barriers include people of color, people assumed to be Muslims, the disabled, the poor, the homeless, sex workers, drug users, HIV-positive people or those with AIDS, children, women and trans* people. Groups of people who cannot be sure of unwanted access to their private spaces, or who do not even possess privacy in the general sense at all, include the disabled, the homeless, old and sick people in need of care, the incarcerated, children, people taken to be Muslims, queers and sex workers.

2. Think of victims of domestic violence who are not taken seriously or who cannot call for help due to financial dependencies or lack of legal status.

3. Most communes founded in the wake of the 'sexual revolution' of the 1960s rejected monogamy, but did not question the naturalness of heterosexuality at all. On the other hand, the change of gay liberation into a gay rights movement with a priority on lobbying for same-sex marriage entailed a loss of any critique of this mono-normative institution along the way. Today only a marginalized minority in the gay community questions the usefulness of focusing on same-sex marriage, among them radical queers and queer theorists who criticize the underlying hetero- and mono-normative structures of society, which find their expression in the institutions of marriage, the nuclear family and so on.

4. Sheff (2005) and Mayer (2013) have also observed this kind of strengthening of female sexual subjectivity in their empirical studies on polyamorous women in general.

5. The spellings 'boi' and 'daddi' are used in the community to make it clear that these are not real-life boys or fathers, but grown-up, non-blood-related dykes + queers who are embodying these archetypal roles.

6. Colored hankies are used in the community to signal BDSM interests; for example, wearing a hanky in the left back pocket of a pair of pants means top, while the right pocket means bottom.

7. BJ described an energy pull as a group session in which the participants insert hooks in the skin of their chests and connect them to each other using rope or chains. They then lean back, balance their weight against the others and pull and manipulate the chains/ropes and hooks, creating intense sensations for all participants.

8. The two resources they discussed as limited were time and money. While one may be able to love and desire many people, one only has limited time to spend; this usually restricted the number of partnerships people engaged in on a longer-term basis, while limited budgets restricted the possibilities of long-distance relationships.

9. I owe the inspiration for appropriating this term in the context of my study to the inspiring work of queer biologist Bruce Bagemihl and his suggestion for a new biological paradigm (1999).

10. The appropriation of the term 'slut' is not uncontested. Given that certain groups of women are constructed as excessively and pathologically sexual, such as Black women and sex workers, this strategy is more risky for them than for those women constructed as lacking sexual interest, such as *white* middle-class women.

11. Many of these notions, such as enhanced bodily and sexual agency, are echoed in the results of an ethnographic study of a Canadian lesbian/queer bathhouse (Hammers 2008). Some of the downsides Hammer discusses, like the pressure to possess a specific sexual capital, were not discussed or were countered by my interview partners. For instance, because BDSM skills balance the value of age and appearance, this may point to the fact that BDSM dykes + queers have developed a different sexual culture from that of non-BDSM queers.

6   Exploring and Pushing Boundaries

1. Stein himself is now critical of the popularity of that slogan and its effects. He states that it was never intended as a fixed rule to police behavior, but was supposed to initiate dialogue (2002).

2. Gary Switch from the BDSM organization 'The Eulenspiegel Society' has, therefore, proposed an alternative: *RACK – Risk Aware Consensual Kink* (2001). Switch argues that safety is relative, risk is part of the thrill and there are no objective criteria for sanity.

3. Freeman seems to think along similar lines when she theorizes that BDSM as a corporeal way of engaging with the historical past (2008: 40) has the potential of refusing historical moments (such as slavery) the closure of 'pastness' (42), because it uses physical sensation to break apart the present into fragments of time that may not be one's 'own', and one may embody aspects of the historical past (38). Unlike tarrying, this effect does not expand the present, but the past, fragmenting the present. But both concepts share the resistance to closure.

4. My interview partners avoided racist scenarios in a conscious, explicit way. This, of course, does not mean that some of their actions were not unwittingly racist or did not make references to cultural and everyday racism.

5. For more examples of how BDSM was spiritual for my interview partners, such as through worshipping or surrender, see Bauer (2013a).

6. It is beyond the scope of this work to discuss how much this is inherent in Butler's theory or a misconception in the reception and appropriation of her work. What is important here is that her work has inspired a line of theorizing that tends to neglect the significance of the material body by overprivileging the power of discourse.

7. Some authors identify potential downfalls of the healing narratives. These narratives might imply that everyone in BDSM is damaged because they are in

need of healing, or that BDSM is only valid if its goal is the higher cause of healing (Barker et al. 2007; Lindemann 2011). My interview partners, in general, did not perpetuate this sanitizing discourse. Rather, they stressed that erotic pleasure was the reason to practice BDSM, not the healing, spiritual or political aspects, although these were often welcome side effects.

7 Exploring Intimate Power Dynamics

1. Another twist in my concept of class as unissued is that one's class status is, in principle, issued, that is, given to one via birth rights to the resources (or lack thereof) of one's parents and so on, yet in democratic discourse it is constructed not as issued via birth and social contexts, but as self-earned. This aspect was not part of my study, though.

8 Exploring Intimate Difference Through Gender

1. Newmahr argues in favor of the presence of gender subversion on various levels in the pansexual/straight community she researched, but this remains dubious. For instance, she refers to the option of gender role reversal in BDSM, which, according to her own statements, hardly ever takes place in this community (2011: 117–8), a fact that also contradicts her claim that the top/bottom hierarchy has replaced the gender hierarchy in the BDSM community as the most significant social differentiation (106). Newmahr also detects what she calls incidental androgyny in her sample (2011: 29ff), but this concept is dependent on heteronormative polar gender presentations as standard (for Newmahr, a woman is already androgynous if she is not using make-up daily).
2. Yet this ignores the fact that, in the straight BDSM community, gender play is mainly practiced by men who erotically enjoy being 'degraded' to the status of woman. Possibly this is not alluring to gay men, since part of their stigmatizing remains their depiction as feminized, not 'real' men. And straight women might not embody male roles as much because there is a lack of erotic appreciation of masculine women by straight men. More research is needed to confirm these possible explanations.
3. I would expand the concept of gender labor to include the work that trans* people and genderqueers are expected to perform to become intelligible and to make others comfortable by avoiding any blurring of the gender binary (see Chapter 2).
4. I would not restrict this to a culture of two, but would expand it to the dyke + BDSM community culture as a whole.
5. For a discussion of a different kind of 'cockplay' see Bauer (2005).
6. Further research might reveal whether certain heterosexual communities are more accepting of FTMs than MTFs, for example.

9 The Sexual Politics of Exuberant Intimacy

1. Savran also makes a convincing argument that considering male masochism as subversive per se is misguided. Masochism enables men to master that which they imagine to be the feminine and to abnegate masculine privilege temporarily, but

to be able to take it up again at the end of the performance (1998: 252). Savran shows that, rather than being a subversive practice, masochism proves masculinity by demonstrating that one is able to 'take it like a man' (205). I share his critique, but it does not apply to my sample of dyke and trans* BDSMers, since they are not framing their practices in this way.

References

Ahmed, Sara (2004): *The Cultural Politics of Emotion*. Edinburgh: Edinburgh University Press

Ahrens, Sönke (2006): Die paradoxale Grundstruktur des Sadomasochismus. *Zeitschrift für Sexualforschung* 19: 279–308

Alison, L., P. Santtila, N.K. Sandnabba & N. Nordling (2001): Sadomasochistically Oriented Behavior. Diversity in Practice and Meaning. *Archives of Sexual Behavior* 30(1): 1–12

Anderson, Benedict (1983): *Imagined Communities. Reflections on the Origin and Spread of Nationalism*. London: Verso

Anzaldúa, Gloria E. & Analouise Keating, eds. (2002): *This Bridge We Call Home. Radical Visions for Transformations*. New York/London: Routledge

Arendt, Hannah (1960): *Macht und Gewalt*. München: Piper

Athanassoulis, Nafsika (2002): The Role of Consent in Sado-Masochistic Practices. *Res Publica* 8: 141–155

Atkins, Dawn, ed. (1998): *Looking Queer. Body Image and Identity in Lesbian, Bisexual, Gay and Transgender Communities*. New York: Haworth

Bagemihl, Bruce (1999): *Biological Exuberance. Animal Homosexuality and Natural Diversity*. New York: St. Martin's Press

Balzer, Carsten (2009): Every 3rd day the murder of a trans person is reported. Preliminary results of a new Trans Murder Monitoring Project show more than 200 reported cases of murdered trans people from January 2008 to June 2009. Accessed 23 May 2010, http://www.liminalis.de/2009_03/TMM/tmm-englisch/Liminalis-2009-TMM-report2008-2009-en.pdf

Barad, Karen (1996): Meeting the Universe Halfway. Realism and Social Constructivism Without Contradiction. In: Lynn Hankinson Nelson & Jack Nelson, eds. *Feminism, Science and the Philosophy of Science*. Dordrecht: Kluwer, 161–194

Barad, Karen (2003): Posthumanist Performativity. Toward an Understanding of How Matter Comes to Matter. *Signs* 28(3): 801–831

Barker, Meg (2013): Consent is a Grey Area? A Comparison of Understandings of Consent in Fifty Shades of Grey and on the BDSM Blogosphere. *Sexualities* 16(8): 896–914

Barker, Meg & Darren Langdridge (2010a): Introduction. In: Meg Barker & Darren Langdridge, eds. *Understanding Non-Monogamies*. London: Routledge, 3–8

Barker, Meg & Darren Langdridge (2010b): Whatever Happened to Non-Monogamies? Critical Reflections on Recent Research and Theory. *Sexualities* 13(6): 748–772

Barker, Meg, Camelia Gupta & Alessandra Iantaffi (2007): The Power of Play. The Potentials and Pitfalls in Healing Narratives of BDSM. In: Darren Langdridge & Meg Barker, eds. *Safe, Sane and Consensual. Contemporary Perspectives on Sadomasochism*. Houndmills: Palgrave, 197–216

Barnes, Barry (1988): *The Nature of Power*. Urbana: University of Illinois Press

Barrett, Jenny (2007): 'You've Made Mistress Very, Very Angry'. Displeasure and Pleasure in Media Representations of BDSM. *Participations* 4(1)

Bartky, Sandra (1990): *Femininity and Domination. Studies in the Phenomenology of Oppression*. New York: Routledge

Bataille, Georges (1994): *Die Erotik*. München: Matthes & Seitz
Bataille, Georges (2001): *Die Aufhebung der Ökonomie*. 3rd Edition. München: Matthes & Seitz
Bauer, Robin (2005): When Gender Becomes Safe, Sane and Consensual. Gender Play as a Queer BDSM Practice. In: Eleha Haschemi Yekani & Beatrice Michaelis, eds. *Queer durch die Geisteswissenschaften – Perspektiven der Queer Theory*. Berlin: QuerVerlag, 73–86
Bauer, Robin (2007a): 'Daddy liebt seinen Jungen' – Begehrenswerte Männlichkeiten in Daddy/Boy-Rollenspielen queerer BDSM-Kontexte. In: Robin Bauer, Josch Hoenes & Volker Woltersdorff, eds. *Unbeschreiblich männlich. Heteronormativitätskritische Perspektiven*. Hamburg: Männerschwarm, 170–180
Bauer, Robin (2007b): Playgrounds and New Territories. The Potential of BDSM Practices to Queer Genders. In: Darren Langdridge & Meg Barker, eds. *Safe, Sane and Consensual. Contemporary Perspectives on Sadomasochism*. Houndmills: Palgrave, 177–194
Bauer, Robin (2008a): Zwischen Phantasie und Realität – Die Debatte um BDSM in queeren Räumen. In: Elisabeth Tuider, ed. *QuerVerbindungen. Interdisziplinäre Annäherungen an Geschlecht, Sexualität, Ethnizität*. Berlin/Münster: Lit Verlag, 69–88
Bauer, Robin (2008b): Transgressive and Transformative Gendered Sexual Practices and White Privileges. The Case of the Dyke/Trans BDSM Communities. *WSQ* 36(3/4): 233–253
Bauer, Robin (2009): 'Ihre Eltern dachten, dass sie ein Junge wäre.' Transsexualität und Transgender in einer zweigeschlechtlichen Welt. *Queer Lectures* 7, ed. Tatjana Eggeling. Hamburg: Männerschwarm
Bauer, Robin (2010): Non-Monogamy in Queer BDSM Communities. Putting the Sex Back Into Alternative Relationship Practices and Discourse. In: Meg Barker & Darren Langdridge, eds. *Understanding Non-Monogamies*. London: Routledge, 142–153
Bauer, Robin (2013a): *Dyke+Queer BDSM as Exuberant Intimacy. Exploring Intimate Difference and Power*. Dissertation zur Erlangung des Doktors der Philosophie im Fachbereich Sozialwissenschaften der Universität Hamburg. Unpublished Dissertation Thesis, available on request from the author
Bauer, Robin (2013b): MonoPoly. Monogamie-Norm und Polyamory auf dem Spielfeld von Besitzansprüchen, Treue und Bekanntgehen. In: Ilse Nagelschmidt, Britta Borrego & Uta Beyer, eds. *Interdisziplinäre Dispute um Methoden der Geschlechterforschung II*. Frankfurt/Main: Peter Lang, 143–168
Bauer, Robin (n.d.): Bois and Girrrls Meet Their Daddies and Mommies on Gender Playgrounds. Gendered Age Play in the Dyke+Queer BDSM Communities. Unpublished Manuscript
BDSM Berlin (n.d.): Timeline. Eine kurze Geschichte des Sadomasochismus in Berlin. Accessed 17 October 2009, http://www.bdsm-berlin.de/timeline.html
Beauchamp, Toby (2013): Artful Concealment and Strategic Visibility. Transgender Bodies and U.S. State Surveillance After 9/11. In: Susan Stryker & Aren Z. Aizura, eds. *The Transgender Studies Reader 2*. New York/London: Routledge, 46–55
Beauvoir, Simone de (1974): *The Second Sex*. New York: Vintage Books
Beck, Ulrich (1992): *Risk Society. Towards a New Modernity*. New Delhi: Sage
Beckmann, Andrea (2001): Deconstructing Myths. The Social Construction of 'Sadomasochism' Versus 'Subjugated Knowledges' of Practitioners of Consensual 'SM'. *Journal of Criminal Justice and Popular Culture* 8(2): 66–95
Beckmann, Andrea (2007): The 'Bodily Practices' of Consensual 'SM', Spirituality and 'Transcendence'. In: Darren Langdridge & Meg Barker, eds. *Safe, Sane and Consensual. Contemporary Perspectives on Sadomasochism*. Houndmills: Palgrave, 98–118

Beinstein, Krista (n.d.): Kurzbiographie. Accessed 17 October 2009, http://www.kristabeinstein.de/bio.html

Bell, David & Jon Binnie (2000): *The Sexual Citizen. Queer Politics and Beyond.* Cambridge: Polity

Bell, Kirsten & Darlene McNaughton (2007): Feminism and the Invisible Fat Man. *Body & Society* 13(1): 107–131

Berlant, Lauren (1997): *The Queen of America Goes to Washington City: Essays on Sex and Citizenship.* Durham: Duke University Press

Berlinger, Cain (2006): *Black Men in Leather.* Tempe, AZ: Third Millennium Publishing

Bérubé, Allan (1996): The History of Gay Bathhouses. In: Dangerous Bedfellows, eds. *Policing Public Sex.* Boston: South End Press, 187–220

Bérubé, Allan (2001): How Gay Stays White and What Kind of White It Stays. In: Birgit Brander Rasmussen, Eric Klinenberg, Irene J. Nexika & Matt Wray, eds. *The Making and Unmaking of Whiteness.* Durham/London: Duke University Press, 234–265

Bettcher, Talia Mae (2013): Evil Deceivers and Make-Believers. On Transphobic Violence and the Politics of Illusion. In: Susan Stryker & Aren Z. Aizura, eds. *The Transgender Studies Reader 2.* New York/London: Routledge, 278–290

Blank, Hanne (2006): Tits of Clay. Genderphilia and Changing the World, one Lipstick at a Time. Accessed 10 May 2011, http://www.hanneblank.com/pdf/Femme2006_Keynote.pdf

Bornstein, Kate (1994): *Gender Outlaw – On Men, Women and the Rest of Us.* New York: Vintage

Brat Attack, ed. *Fish.* San Francisco: Self-Published

Brewis, Joanna & Stephen Linstead (2003): *Sex, Work and Sex Work. Eroticizing Organization.* London: Routledge

Brickell, Chris (2009): Sexuality and the Dimensions of Power. *Sexuality & Culture* 13(2): 57–74

Bullough, Vern & Bonnie Bullough (1977a): Lesbianism in the 1920s and 1930s. A Newfound Study. *Signs: Journal of Women in Culture and Society* 2(4): 895–904

Bullough, Vern L. & Bonnie Bullough (1977b): *Sin, Sickness and Sanity. A History of Sexual Attitudes.* New York: New American Library

Burkart, Günter (1997): *Lebensphasen – Liebesphasen. Vom Paar zur Ehe, zum Single und zurück?* Opladen: Leske und Budrich

Butler, Judith (1990): *Gender Trouble. Feminism and the Subversion of Identity.* London/New York: Routledge

Califia, Pat (1996): A House Divided. Violence in the Lesbian S/M Community. In: Pat Califia & Robin Sweeney, eds. *The Second Coming. A Leatherdyke Reader.* Los Angeles: Alyson Publications, 264–274

Califia, Pat (1997): *Sex Changes. The Politics of Transgenderism.* San Francisco: Cleis Press

Califia, Pat (2000): *Public Sex. The Culture of Radical Sex.* San Francisco, CA: Cleis Press

Carrette, Jeremy R. (2005): Intense Exchange. Sadomasochism, Theology and the Politics of Late Capitalism. *Theology & Sexuality* 11(2): 11–30

Carter, Julian (2013): Embracing Transition, or Dancing in the Folds of Time. In: Susan Stryker & Aren Z. Aizura, eds. *The Transgender Studies Reader 2.* New York/London: Routledge, 130–143

Carter, Julian B. (2007): *The Heart of Whiteness. Normal Sexuality and Race in America, 1880–1940.* Durham, NC/London: Duke University Press

Chancer, Lynn S. (1992): *Sadomasochism in Everyday Life.* New Brunswick, NJ: Rutgers University Press

Chase, Cheryl (1998): Hermaphrodites with Attitude. Mapping the Emergence of Intersex Political Activism. *GLQ* 4(2): 189–211

Cho, Margaret (2008): Foreword. In: Jaclyn Friedman & Jessica Valenti, eds. *Yes Means Yes! Visions of Female Sexual Power & A World Without Rape*. Berkeley, CA: Seal Press, 1–4

Clare, Eli (1999): *Exile & Pride. Disability, Queerness, and Liberation*. Cambridge: South End Press

Clark-Flory, Tracy (2012): When Safe Words Are Ignored. Accessed 1 March 2012, http://www.salon.com/2012/01/29/real_abuse_in_bdsm/

Cohen, Cathy (2005): Punks, Bulldaggers, and Welfare Queens. The Radical Potential of Queer Politics? In: Patrick E. Johnson & Mae G. Henderson, eds. *Black Queer Studies. A Critical Anthology*. Durham, NC/London: Duke University Press, 21–51

Conerly, Gregory (1996): The Politics of Black Lesbian, Gay, and Bisexual Identity. In: Brett Beemyn & Mickey Eliason, eds. *Queer Studies – A Lesbian, Gay, Bisexual and Transgender Anthology*. New York/London: Routledge, 133–145

Conradi, Elisabeth (2011): *Kosmopolitische Zivilgesellschaft. Inklusion durch gelingendes Handeln*. Frankfurt/Main: Campus

Constantine-Simms, Delroy, ed. (2000): *The Greatest Taboo. Homosexuality in Black Communities*. Los Angeles/New York: Alyson Books

Cook, Elaine (2005): Commitment in Polyamorous Relationships. MA Thesis, Regis University. Accessed 7 November 2007 http://www.aphroweb.net/papers/thesis/thesis.pdf

Cooper, Davina (1994): Productive, Relational and Everywhere? Conceptualizing Power and Resistance Within Foucauldian Feminism. *Sociology* 28(2): 435–454

Cooper, Davina (1995): *Power in Struggle. Feminism, Sexuality and the State*. Buckingham: Open University Press

Corinna, Heather (2008): An Immodest Proposal. In: Jaclyn Friedman & Jessica Valenti, eds. *Yes Means Yes! Visions of Female Sexual Power & A World Without Rape*. Berkeley, CA: Seal Press, 179–192

Corteen, Karen (2002): Lesbian Safety Talk: Problematizing Definitions and Experiences of Violence, Sexuality and Space. *Sexualities* 5(3): 259–280

Cowling, Mark (2004): Rape, Communicative Sexuality and Sex Education. In: Mark Cowling & Paul Reynolds, eds. *Making Sense of Sexual Consent*. Aldershot & Burlington: Ashgate, 17–28

Cowling, Mark & Paul Reynolds, eds. (2004): Introduction. *Making Sense of Sexual Consent*. Aldershot & Burlington: Ashgate, 1–14

Cross, Patricia A. & Kim Matheson (2006): Understanding Sadomasochism. An Empirical Examination of Four Perspectives. In: Peggy J. Kleinplatz & Charles Moser, eds. *Sadomasochism. Powerful Pleasures*. Binghamton: Harrington Park Press, 133–166

D'Emilio, John (1983a): *Sexual Politics, Sexual Communities: The Making of a Homosexual Minority in the United States 1940–1970*. Chicago: University of Chicago Press

D'Emilio, John (1983b): Capitalism and Gay Identity. In: Ann Snitow, Christine Stansell & Sharon Thompson, eds. *Powers of Desire. The Politics of Sexuality*. New York: Monthly Review Press, 100–116

Dangerous Bedfellows, ed. (1996): *Policing Public Sex*. Boston: South End Press

Dark Connections (2004): Viola Johnson. Dark Connections Featured Member April 2004. Accessed 16 October 2009, http://www.darkconnections.com/featuredmember/featuredmember14.htm

Dark Connections (n.d.): History of Black BDSM. Accessed 10 May 2011, http://www.darkconnections.com/history/history01.htm; http://www.darkconnections.com/history/history02.htm

Datenschlag (2000): Datenschlag Peinliche Befragung I. Alte Fragen neu gestellt. Ergebnisse Frage 25. Accessed 5 January 2012, http://www.datenschlag.org/umfrage/dpb1_ergebnisse25.html

Davis, Angela Y. (1983): *Women, Race and Class*. New York: Vintage

DeBlase, Tony (n.d.): Leather History Timeline. *Leather Archives*. Accessed 28 September 2009, http://www.leatherarchives.org/exhibits/deblase/updatetimeline.pdf

Deleuze, Gilles (1994): *Difference and Repetition*. New York: Columbia University Press

Deleuze, Gilles (1996): *Lust und Begehren*. Berlin: Merve Verlag

Deleuze, Gilles & Felix Guattari (2004): *A Thousand Plateaus. Capitalism and Schizophrenia*. London/New York: Continuum

Delgado, Richard & Jean Stefancic, eds. (1997): *Critical Whiteness Studies. Looking Behind the Mirror*. Philadelphia: Temple University Press

Derrida, Jacques (1976): *Die Schrift und die Differenz*. Frankfurt/Main: Suhrkamp

Derrida, Jacques (1991): Die différance. In: Peter Engelman, ed. *Postmoderne und Dekonstruktion*. Stuttgart: Reclam, 76–113

Downing, Lisa (2007): Beyond Safety. Erotic Asphyxiation and the Limits of SM Discourse. In: Darren Langdridge & Meg Barker, eds. *Safe, Sane and Consensual. Contemporary Perspectives on Sadomasochism*. Houndmills: Palgrave, 119–132

Duggan, Lisa & Kathleen McHugh (2002): A Fem(me)inist Manifesto. In: Chloë Brushwood Rose & Anna Camilleri, eds. *Brazen Femme. Queering Femininity*. Vancouver: Arsenal Pulp Press, 165–170

Duggan, Lisa & Nan D. Hunter (1995): *Sex Wars. Sexual Dissent and Political Culture*. New York/London: Routledge

Duncan, Patricia L. (1996): Identity, Power and Difference – Negotiating Conflict in an S/M Dyke Community. In: Brett Beemyn & Mickey Eliason, eds. *Queer Studies – A Lesbian, Gay, Bisexual and Transgender Anthology*. New York/London: Routledge, 87–114

Dunn, Jennifer L. (1998): Defining Women. Notes Toward an Understanding of Structure and Agency in the Negotiation of Sex. *Journal of Contemporary Ethnography* 26(4): 479–510

Dyer, Richard (1997): *White*. London/NewYork: Routledge

Easton, Dossie (2007): Shadowplay. S/M Journeys to Our Selves. In: Darren Langdridge & Meg Barker, eds. *Safe, Sane and Consensual. Contemporary Perspectives on Sadomasochism*. Houndmills: Palgrave, 217–228

Easton, Dossie & Catherine A. Liszt (Janet Hardy) (1997): *The Ethical Slut. A Guide to Infinite Sexual Possibilities*. San Francisco, CA: Greenery Press

Easton, Dossie & Janet Hardy (2004): *Radical Ecstasy. SM Journeys to Transcendence*. Oakland, CA: Greenery Press

Echols, Alice (1992): The Taming of the Id. Feminist Sexual Politics, 1968–83. In: Carole S. Vance, ed. *Pleasure and Danger. Exploring Female Sexuality*. London: Pandora Press, 50–72

Elb, Norbert (2006): *SM-Sexualität. Selbstorganisation einer sexuellen Subkultur*. Gießen: Psychosozial-Verlag

Elias, Norbert (1976): *Über den Prozess der Zivilisation. Soziogenetische und psychogenetische Untersuchungen*. Frankfurt/Main: Suhrkamp

Elias, Norbert (1998): The Civilizing of Parents. In: Johan Goudsblom & Stephen Mennell, eds. *The Norbert Elias Reader*. Oxford: Blackwell Publishers, 189–211

Elliott, Pam (1996): Shattering Illusions. Same-Sex Domestic Violence. *Journal of Gay and Lesbian Social Services* 4(1): 1–8

Ellis, Carolyn & Arthur P. Bochner (2000): Autoethnography, Personal Narrative, Reflexivity. Researcher as Subject. In: Norman K. Denzin & Yvonna S. Lincoln, eds. *Handbook of Qualitative Research*. 2nd Edition. Thousand Oaks: Sage, 733–768

Eng, David L. & Alice Y. Hom, eds. (1998): *Q & A. Queer in Asian America*. Philadelphia: Temple University Press

Erel, Umut, Jinthana Haritaworn, Encarnación Gutiérrez Rodríguez & Christian Klesse (2007): Intersektionalität oder Simultaneität?! – Zur Verschränkung und Gleichzeitigkeit mehrfacher Machtverhältnisse – Eine Einführung. In: Jutta Hartmann, Christian Klesse, Peter Wagenknecht, Bettina Fritzsche & Kristina Hackmann, eds. *Heteronormativität. Empirische Studien zu Geschlecht, Sexualität und Macht*. Wiesbaden: VS Verlag, 239–250

Farlex (2012): The Free Dictionary. Exuberance. Accessed 21 February 2012, http://www.thefreedictionary.com/exuberance

Fausto-Sterling, Anne (1993): The Five Sexes. Why Male and Female Are Not Enough. *The Sciences* (March–April): 20–24

Fausto-Sterling, Anne (2000): *Sexing the Body – Gender Politics and the Construction of Sexuality*. New York: Routledge

Filipovic, Jill (2008): Offensive Feminism. The Conservative Gender Norms That Perpetuate Rape Culture, and How Feminists Can Fight Back. In: Jaclyn Friedman & Jessica Valenti, eds. *Yes Means Yes! Visions of Female Sexual Power & a World Without Rape*. Berkeley, CA: Seal Press, 13–27

Finn, Mark (2010): Conditions of Freedom in Practices of Non-Monogamous Commitment. In: Meg Barker & Darren Langdridge, eds. *Understanding Non-Monogamies*. London: Routledge, 225–236

Finn, Mark & Helen Malson (2008): Speaking of Home Truth: (Re)productions of Dyadic-Containment in Non-Monogamous Relationships. *British Journal of Social Psychology* 47(3): 519–533

Firestein, Beth A., ed. (1996): *Bisexuality. The Psychology and Politics of an Invisible Minority*. Thousand Oaks: Sage

Fish (1993): When Good Gossip Becomes History. Fifteen Years of Dykes Doing SM. *Brat Attack* #4: 4–15

Follett, Mary Parker (1942): *Dynamic Administration. The Collected Papers of Mary Parker Follett*. New York: Harper

Fontana, Andrea & James H. Frey (2000): The Interview. From Structured Questions to Negotiated Text. In: Norman K. Denzin & Yvonna S. Lincoln, eds. *Handbook of Qualitative Research*. 2nd Edition. Thousand Oaks: Sage, 645–672

Foucault, Michel (1976): *Mikrophysik der Macht*. Berlin: Merve Verlag

Foucault, Michel (1978): *The History of Sexuality Vol 1. An Introduction*. New York: Pantheon

Foucault, Michel (1982): The Subject and Power. *Critical Inquiry* 8(4): 777–795

Foucault, Michel (1990): *The History of Sexuality Vol 2. The Use of Pleasure*. New York: Vintage

Foucault, Michel (1994): *Überwachen und Strafen. Die Geburt des Gefängnisses*. Frankfurt/Main: Suhrkamp

Foucault, Michel (1996): *Foucault Live. Collected Interviews, 1961–1984*. Ed. Sylvère Lotringer. New York: Semiotext(e)

FRA (European Union Agency for Fundamental Rights) (2009): Homophobia and Discrimination on Grounds of Sexual Orientation and Gender Identity in the EU Member States. Part II: The Social Situation. Updated Version. Luxemburg. Accessed

30 June 2014, http://fra.europa.eu/sites/default/files/fra_uploads/397-FRA_hdgso_
report_part2_en.pdf

Frank, Katherine & John DeLamater (2010): Deconstructing Monogamy. Boundaries,
Identities and Fluidities Across Relationships. In: Meg Barker & Darren Langdridge,
eds. *Understanding Non-Monogamies*. London: Routledge, 9–20

Frankenberg, Ruth (1993): *White Woman, Race Matters. The Social Construction of
Whiteness*. Minneapolis: University of Minnesota Press

Franzen, Jannik & Arn Sauer (2010): Benachteiligung von Trans*Personen, insbeson-
dere im Arbeitsleben. Eine Expertise. Berlin: Antidiskriminierungsstelle des Bundes.
Accessed 30 June 2014, http://www.transinterqueer.org/download/Publikationen/
benachteiligung_von_trans_personen_insbesondere_im_arbeitsleben.pdf

Freeman, Elizabeth (2008): Turn the Beat Around. Sadomasochism, Temporality,
History. *Differences: A Journal of Feminist Cultural Studies* 19(1): 32–70

Freud, Sigmund (1991): *Drei Abhandlungen zur Sexualtheorie*. Frankfurt: Fischer

Friedman, Jaclyn & Jessica Valenti, eds. (2008): *Yes Means Yes! Visions of Female Sexual
Power & A World Without Rape*. Berkeley, CA: Seal Press

Friedman, Jaclyn & Jessica Valenti (2008a): Introduction. In: Jaclyn Friedman & Jessica
Valenti, eds. *Yes Means Yes! Visions of Female Sexual Power & A World Without Rape*.
Berkeley, CA: Seal Press, 5–11

Galler, Roberta (1992): The Myth of the Perfect Body. In: Carole S. Vance, ed. *Pleasure
and Danger. Exploring Female Sexuality*. London: Pandora Press, 165–172

Gamson, Joshua (1989): Silence, Death, and the Invisible Enemy: AIDS Activism and
Social Movement 'Newness'. *Social Problems* 38(4): 351–367

Gamson, Joshua (1995): Must Identity Movements Self-Destruct? A Queer Dilemma.
Social Problems 42(3): 390–407

Gardner, Timothy Joseph (2005): Queering Polyamory. Configurations, Public
Policy and Lived Experiences. MS Thesis, Minnesota State University. Accessed
30 June 2014, http://www.ibrarian.net/navon/paper/Queering_Polyamory__
Configurations__Public_Policy.pdf?paperid=10978012

Genschel, Corinna (2000): Wann ist ein Körper ein Körper mit (Bürger-)Rechten? In:
Quaestio, ed. *Queering Demokratie. Sexuelle Politiken*. Berlin: Querverlag, 113–129

Giddens, Anthony (1990): *The Consequences of Modernity*. Cambridge: Polity Press

Giddens, Anthony (1992): *The Transformation of Intimacy. Sexuality, Love and Eroticism
in Modern Societies*. Cambridge: Polity Press

Giddens, Anthony (1999): Risk and Responsibility. *Modern Law Review* 62(1): 1–10

Goffman, Erving (1974): *Frame Analysis*. Cambridge: Harvard University Press

Goldman, Emma (1914): *Marriage and Love*. New York: Mother Earth

Goldman, Ruth (1996): Who is that *Queer* Queer? Exploring Norms Around Sexu-
ality, Race, and Class in Queer Theory. In: Brett Beemyn & Mickey Eliason, eds.
Queer Studies – A Lesbian, Gay, Bisexual and Transgender Anthology. New York/London:
Routledge, 169–182

Grant, Jaime M., Lisa A. Mottet & Justin Tanis (2011): Injustice at Every Turn. A Report
of the National Transgender Discrimination Survey. Published by the National Center for Transgender Equality and the National Gay and Lesbian Task Force. Accessed
18 June 2012, http://www.thetaskforce.org/downloads/reports/reports/ntds_full.pdf

Grosz, Elizabeth (1994): Refiguring Lesbian Desire. In: Laura Doan, ed. *The Lesbian
Postmodern*. New York: Columbia University Press, 67–84

Guter, Bob & John R. Killacky, eds. (2004): *Queer Crips. Disabled Gay Men and Their
Stories*. Binghamton: Harrington Park Press

Habermas, Jürgen (1984): *Vorstudien und Ergänzungen zur Theorie kommunikativen Handelns*. Frankfurt/Main: Suhrkamp

Halberstam, Judith (1998): Transgender Butch: Butch/FTM Border Wars and the Masculine Continuum. *GLQ* 4(2): 287–310

Halberstam, Judith (2002): An Introduction to Female Masculinity. In: Rachel Adams & David Savran, eds. *The Masculinity Studies Reader*. Malden: Blackwell, 355–374

Hale, C. Jacob (1998): Consuming the Living, Dis(re)membering the Dead in the Butch/Ftm Borderlands. *GLQ* 4(2): 311–348

Hale, C. Jacob (2003): Leatherdyke Boys and Their Daddies. How to have Sex Without Women or Men. In: Robert J. Corber & Stephen Valocchi, eds. *Queer Studies. An Interdisciplinary Reader*. Malden, Oxford, Melbourne & Berlin: Blackwell, 61–70

Hall, David S. (1998): Consent for Sexual Behavior in a College Student Population. Appendix A: The Antioch College Sexual Offense Policy. *Journal of Human Sexuality* 1. Accessed 12 July 2012, http://www.ejhs.org/volume1/conseapa.htm

Hall, Stuart (1997): The Spectacle of the Other. In: Stuart Hall, ed. *Representation*. London/Thousand Oaks: Sage, 223–290

Halperin, David (1990): *One Hundred Years of Homosexuality and Other Essays on Greek Love*. New York: Routledge

Halpern, Ellen L. (1999): If Love Is So Wonderful, What's So Scary About MORE? In: Marcia Munson & Judith P. Stelboum, eds. *The Lesbian Polyamory Reader. Open Relationships, Non-Monogamy, and Casual Sex*. Binghamton: Harrington Park Press, 157–164

Hammers, Corie J. (2008): Making Space for an Agentic Sexuality? The Examination of a Lesbian/Queer Bathhouse. *Sexualities* 11(5): 547–572

Haraway, Donna J. (1991): *Simians, Cyborgs, and Women. The Reinvention of Nature*. New York: Routledge

Hardt, Michael & Antonio Negri (2000): *Empire*. Cambridge: Harvard University Press

Haritaworn, Jin, Chin-Lu Lin & Christian Klesse (2006): Poly/Logue. A Critical Introduction to Polyamory. *Sexualities* 9(5): 515–529

Haritaworn, Jinthana (2005): Queerer als wir? Rassismus. Transphobie. Queer Theory. In: Elahe Hashemi Yekani & Beatrice Michaelis, eds. *Quer durch die Geisteswissenschaften. Perspektiven der Queer Theory*. Berlin: Querverlag, 216–237

Haritaworn, Jinthana (2007): (No) Fucking Difference? Eine Kritik an 'Heteronormativität' am Beispiel von Thailändischsein. In: Jutta Hartmann, Christian Klesse, Peter Wagenknecht, Bettina Fritzsche & Kristina Hackmann, eds. *Heteronormativität. Empirische Studien zu Geschlecht, Sexualität und Macht*. Wiesbaden: VS Verlag, 269–290

Hart, Lynda (1998): *Between the Body and the Flesh – Performing Sadomasochism*. New York: Routledge

Hartsock, Nancy (1983): *Money, Sex and Power. Toward a Feminist Historical Materialism*. Boston: Northeastern University Press

Hausen, Karin (1976): Die Polarisierung der 'Geschlechtercharaktere'. In: Werner Conze, ed. *Sozialgeschichte der Familie in der Neuzeit Europas*. Vol. 21. Stuttgart: Klett, 363–393

Hayward, Eva (2008): More Lessons from a Starfish. Prefixial Flesh and Transspeciated Selves. *WSQ* 36(3/4): 64–8

Hegel, Georg F.W. (1993): *Phänomenologie des Geistes. Werke 3*. Frankfurt/Main: Suhrkamp

Hein, Hilde (1982): Sadomasochism and the Liberal Tradition. In: Robin Ruth Linden, Darlene R. Pagano, Diana E.H. Russell & Susan Leigh Star, eds. *Against Sadomasochism*. Palo Alto, CA: Frog in the Well, 83–89

Held, Virginia (1993): *Feminist Morality. Transforming Culture, Society and Politics*. Chicago: University of Chicago Press

Hernández, Daisy (2004): Playing with Race. *ColorLines 27*. Accessed 16 January 2011, http://colorlines.com/archives/2004/12/playing_with_race.html

Hickman, Susan E. & Charlene L. Muehlenhard (1999): 'By the semi-mystical appearance of a condom'. How Young Women and Men Communicate Sexual Consent in Heterosexual Situations. *Journal of Sex Research* 36(3): 258–272

Higgins, Jenny A. & Irene Browne (2008): Sexual Needs, Control, and Refusal: How 'Doing' Class and Gender Influences Sexual Risk Taking. *Journal of Sex Research*, 45(3): 233–245

Hirsch, Joachim (1995): *Der nationale Wettbewerbsstaat. Staat, Demokratie und Politik im globalen Kapitalismus*. 2nd Edition. Amsterdam/Berlin: Edition ID-Archiv

Hitzler, Ronald (1995): Sadomasochistische Rollenspiele. Ein Beitrag zur Ethnographie algophiler Milieus. *Soziale Welt* 46(2): 138–153

Hoagland, Sarah Lucia (1988): *Lesbian Ethics. Toward a New Value*. Palo Alto: Institute of Lesbian Studies

Hole, Anne (2003): Performing Identity. Dawn French and the Funny Fat Female Body. *Feminist Media Studies* 3(3): 315–328

hooks, bell (1981): *Ain't I a Woman. Black Women and Feminism*. Boston, MA: South End Press

Hoople, Terry (1996): Conflicting Visions: SM, Feminism and the Law. A Problem of Representation. *Canadian Journal of Law and Society* 11(1): 177–220

Hopkins, Patrick (1994): Rethinking Sadomasochism. Feminism, Interpretation, and Simulation. *Hypatia* 9(1): 116–141

Hornsby, Teresa J. (1999): Gender Role Reversal and the Violated Lesbian Body. *Journal of Lesbian Studies* 3(3): 61–72

Houlihan, Annette (2011): When 'No' Means 'Yes' and 'Yes' Means Harm. HIV Risk, Consent and Sadomasochism Case Law. *Law & Sexuality. Review of Lesbian, Gay, Bisexual and Transgender Legal Issues* 31: 31–59

Humphreys, Terry P. (2004): Understanding Sexual Consent. An Empirical Investigation of the Normative Script for Young Heterosexual Adults. In: Mark Cowling & Paul Reynolds, eds. *Making Sense of Sexual Consent*. Aldershot & Burlington: Ashgate, 209–225

Iantaffi, Alessandra (Alex) (2010): Disability and Polyamory. Exploring the Edges of Inter-Dependence, Gender and Queer Issues in Non-Monogamous Relationships. In: Meg Barker & Darren Langdridge, eds. *Understanding Non-Monogamies*. London: Routledge, 160–165

Ingram, Gordon Brent, Anne-Marie Bouthillette & Yolanda Retter, eds. (1997): *Queers in Space. Communities/Public Spaces/Sites of Resistance*. Seattle: Bay Press

Jackson, Stevi & Sue Scott (2004): The Personal *is* Still Political: Heterosexuality, Feminism and Monogamy. *Feminism & Psychology* 14(1): 151–157

Jamieson, Lynn (1998): *Intimacy. Personal Relationships in Modern Societies*. Cambridge: Polity Press

Jamieson, Lynn (1999): Intimacy Transformed? A Critical Look at the 'Pure Relationship'. *Sociology* 33(3): 477–494

Jamieson, Lynn (2004): Intimacy, Negotiated Non-monogamy and the Limits of the Couple. In: Jean Duncombe, Kaeren Harrison, Graham Allan & Dennis Marsden, eds. *The State of Affairs*. Mahwah, NJ: Lawrence Earlbaum Associates, 35–57

Janus, Samuel S. & Cynthia L. Janus (1993): *The Janus Report on Sexual Behavior.* New York: John Wiley

Jeffreys, Sheila (2003): *Unpacking Queer Politics. A Lesbian Feminist Perspective.* Cambridge, Oxford & Malden: Polity

Johnson, Patrick E. & Mae G. Henderson, eds. (2005): *Black Queer Studies. A Critical Anthology.* Durham/London: Duke University Press

Julien, Isaac (1994): Confessions of a Snow Queen. Notes on the Making of *The Attendant. Critical Quarterly* 36(1): 120–126

Kaldera, Raven, ed. (2006): *Dark Moon Rising. Pagan BDSM and the Ordeal Path.* Hubbardston: Asphodel Press

Kaldera, Raven (2009): *Double Edge. The Intersections of Transgender and BDSM.* Hubbardston, MA: Alfred Press

Kaldera, Raven (2010): *Power Circuits. Polyamory in a Power Dynamic.* Hubbardston, MA: Alfred Press

Katz, Jonathan Ned (1996): *The Invention of Heterosexuality.* New York, London, Victoria, Toronto & Auckland: Plume

Keres, Jad (1994): *Violence Against SM Women Within the Lesbian Community. A Nationwide Survey.* Philadelphia: Self-published

Khan, Ummni (2009): A Woman's Right to Be Spanked. Testing the Limits of Tolerance of SM in the Socio-Legal Imaginary. *Law & Sexuality: A Review of Lesbian, Gay, Bisexual & Transgender Legal Issues* 18: 79–119

Kleinplatz, Peggy J. & Charles Moser (2007): Is SM Pathological? In: Darren Langdridge & Meg Barker, eds. *Safe, Sane and Consensual. Contemporary Perspectives on Sadomasochism.* Houndmills: Palgrave, 55–62

Klesse, Christian (2005): Bisexual Women, Non-Monogamy and Differentialist Anti-Promiscuity Discourses. *Sexualities* 8(4): 445–464

Klesse, Christian (2006): Polyamory and Its 'Others'. Contesting the Terms of Non-Monogamy. *Sexualities* 9(5): 565–583

Klesse, Christian (2007): *The Spectre of Promiscuity. Gay Male and Bisexual Non-Monogamies and Polyamories.* London: Ashgate

Klesse, Christian (2010): Paradoxes in Gender Relations. [Post] Feminism and Bisexual Polyamory. In: Meg Barker & Darren Langdridge, eds. *Understanding Non-Monogamies.* London: Routledge, 109–120

Kolmes, Keely, Wendy Stock & Charles Moser (2006): Investigating Bias in Psychotherapy with BDSM Clients. In: Peggy Kleinplatz & Charles Moser, eds. *Sadomasochism. Powerful Pleasures.* Binghamton: Harrington Park Press, 301–324

Koone (2008): Nigger Sex. More Than Black and White. Exploring the Boundaries of Race Play. *Instigator Magazine* Issue (19): 49–54

Kristeva, Julia (1982): *Power of Horror. An Essay on Abjection.* New York: Columbia University Press

Kuhn, Thomas (1962): *The Structure of Scientific Revolutions.* Chicago: University of Chicago Press

Labriola, Kathy (1999): Models of Open Relationships. In: Marcia Munson & Judith P. Stelboum, eds. *The Lesbian Polyamory Reader. Open Relationships, Non-Monogamy, and Casual Sex.* Binghamton: Harrington Park Press: 217–225

Lacan, Jacques (1977): *Ecrits. A Selection.* New York: Norton

Langdridge, Darren (2006): Voices From the Margins. Sadomasochism and Sexual Citizenship. *Citizenship Studies* 10(4): 373–389

Langdridge, Darren & Trevor Butt (2004): A Hermeneutic Phenomenological Investigation of the Construction of Sadomasochistic Identities. *Sexualities* 7(1): 31–53

Lapovsky Kennedy, Elizabeth & Madeline D. Davis (1993): *Boots of Leather, Slippers of Gold. The History of a Lesbian Community*. New York: Penguin Books

Leap, William L. (1999): Introduction. In: William L. Leap, ed. *Public Sex/Gay Space*. New York: Columbia University Press, 1–21

Leatherweb (n.d.): Leather/Fetish of All Colors. Accessed 15 October 2009, http://www.leatherweb.com/colors.htm

LeBesco, Kathleen (2004): *Revolting Bodies? The Struggle to Redefine Fat Identity*. Amherst, MA: University of Massachusetts Press

Lee, JeeYeun (1996): Why Suzie Wong is not a Lesbian. Asian and Asian American Lesbian and Bisexual Women and Femme/Butch/Gender Identities. In: Brett Beemyn & Mickey Eliason, eds. *Queer Studies – A Lesbian, Gay, Bisexual and Transgender Anthology*. New York/London: Routledge, 115–132

Lee, John Alan (1979): The Social Organization of Sexual Risk. *Alternative Lifestyles* 2(1): 69–100

Lewis, J. David & Andrew Weigert (1985): Trust as a Social Reality. *Social Forces* 63(4): 967–85

Lindemann, Danielle (2011): BDSM as Therapy? *Sexualities* 14(2): 151–172

Lindemann, Gesa (1997): Wieviel Ordnung muß sein? *Zeitschrift für Sexualforschung* 10(4): 324–331

Linden, Robin Ruth (1982): Introduction. Against Sadomasochism. In: Robin Ruth Linden, Darlene R. Pagano, Diana E.H. Russell & Susan Leigh Star, eds. *Against Sadomasochism*. Palo Alto, CA: Frog in the Well, 1–15

Linden, Robin Ruth, Darlene R. Pagano, Diana E.H. Russell & Susan Leigh Star, eds. (1982): *Against Sadomasochism*. Palo Alto, CA: Frog in the Well

Link, Jürgen (1999): *Versuch über Normalismus. Wie Normalität produziert wird*. Opladen: Westdeutscher Verlag

Livingston, Frank B. (1993): On the Nonexistence of Human Races. In: Sandra Harding, ed. *The 'Racial' Economy of Science. Toward A Democratic Future*. Bloomington/Indianapolis: Indiana University Press, 133–141

LLC (n.d.): SM vs. Abuse Policy Statement. Accessed 16 January 2011, http://www.leatherleadership.org/library/diffsmabuse.htm

Loeb, Elizabeth (2008): Cutting It Off. Bodily Integrity, Identity Disorders, and the Sovereign Stakes of Corporeal Desire in U.S. Law. *WSQ* 36(3/4): 44–63

Lorde, Audre (1998): *Sister Outsider*. Freedom, CA: The Crossing Press

Lorenz, Renate (2009): *Aufwändige Durchquerungen. Subjektivität als sexuelle Arbeit*. Bielefeld: Transcript-Verlag

Luczak, Raymond, ed. (1993): *Eyes of Desire. A Deaf Gay and Lesbian Reader*. Boston: Alyson

Luhmann, Niklas (1979): *Trust and Power. Two Works by Niklas Luhmann*. Chichester: John Wiley

Lukes, Steven (2005): *Power. A Radical View*. 2nd Edition. London: Macmillan

Lyng, Stephen (1990): Edgework. A Social Psychological Analysis of Voluntary Risk Taking. *American Journal of Sociology* 95(4): 851–886

MacKendrick, Karmen (1999): *Counterpleasures*. Albany: State University Press of New York

Magister, Thom (1997): Einer von vielen. Verführung und Erziehung eines Ledermanns. In: Mark Thompson, ed. *Lederlust. Berichte und Erfahrungen*. Berlin: Bruno Gmünder, 117–134

Mains, Geoff (2002): *Urban Aboriginals. A Celebration of Leathersexuality*. 20th Anniversary Edition with an Introduction by Mark Thompson. Los Angeles: Daedalus

Mattilda a.k.a. Matt Bernstein Sycamore, ed. (2004): *That's Revolting! Queer Strategies for Resisting Assimilation*. Brooklyn, NY: Soft Scull Press

Mayer, Gesa (2006): *Mono-normative Anrufungen. Eine Analyse der diskursiven Produktion von Monogamie*. Institut für Soziologie, Universität Hamburg: Diplomarbeit

Mayer, Gesa (2013): Monogame Mangel-Erscheinungen. Zur mono-normativen Logik des Mangels und ihrer Dekonstruktion. In: Ilse Nagelschmidt, Britta Borrego & Uta Beyer, eds. *Interdisziplinäre Dispute um Methoden der Geschlechterforschung II*. Frankfurt/Main: Peter Lang, 169–195

McCarthy, Michelle & David Thompson (2004): People With Learning Disabilities. Sex, the Law and Consent. In: Mark Cowling & Paul Reynolds, eds. *Making Sense of Sexual Consent*. Aldershot & Burlington: Ashgate, 227–242

McClintock, Anne (1995): *Imperial Leather. Race, Gender and Sexuality in the Colonial Contest*. New York/London: Routledge

McClintock, Anne (2004): Maid to Order: Commercial S/M and Gender Power. In: Pamela Church Gibson, ed. *More Dirty Looks. Gender, Pornography and Power*. London: BFI Publishing, 237–253

McDonald, Dee (2010): Swinging. Pushing the Boundaries of Monogamy? In: Meg Barker & Darren Langdridge, eds. *Understanding Non-Monogamies*. London: Routledge, 70–81

McRuer, Robert (2006): *Crip Theory. Cultural Signs of Queerness and Disability*. New York/London: New York University Press

McRuer, Robert & Abby L. Wilkerson, eds. (2003): *Desiring Disability. Queer Theory Meets Disability Studies*. Durham: Duke University Press

Merriam-Webster (2012): *Dictionary. Exuberance*. Accessed 21 February 2012, http://www.merriam-webster.com/dictionary/exuberance

Merrill, Gregory S. (1996): Ruling the Exceptions. Same-Sex Battering and Domestic Violence Theory. *Journal of Gay and Lesbian Social Services* 4(1): 9–21

Messman, Terri L. & Patricia S. Long (1996): Child Sexual Abuse and Its Relationship to Revictimization in Adult Women: A Review. *Clinical Psychology Review* 16(5): 397–420

Millett, Kate (1992): Beyond Politics? Children and Sexuality. In: Carole S. Vance, ed. *Pleasure and Danger. Exploring Female Sexuality*. London: Pandora Press, 217–224

Minh-ha, Trinh T. (1986/87): Difference: 'A Special Third World Women Issue'. *Discourse* 8(Fall–Winter): 11–38

Mitra, Pushpa (2005): Kink Therapy and Me. Outing Myself as a 'Kinky Client'. *Lesbian and Gay Psychology Review* 6(3): 274–278

Möllering, Guido (2001): The Nature of Trust. From Georg Simmel to a Theory of Expectation, Interpretation and Suspicion. *Sociology* 35(2): 403–420

Monro, Surya & Lorna Warren (2004): Transgendering Citizenship. *Sexualities* 7(3): 345–362

Moore, Alison (2009): The Invention of Sadism? The Limits of Neologisms in the History of Sexuality. *Sexualities* 12(4): 486–502

Moore, Alison M. (2005): Visions of Sadomasochism as a Nazi Erotic. *Lesbian & Gay Psychology Review* 6(3): 163–176

Moran, Leslie J. (1995): Violence and the Law. The Case of Sado-Masochism. *Social Legal Studies* 4: 225–251

Morrison, Toni (1992): *Playing in the Dark. Whiteness and Literary Imagination*. Cambridge/London: Harvard University Press

Moser, Charles & J.J. Madeson (1996): *Bound to Be Free. The SM Experience*. New York/London: Continuum

Moser, Charles & Peggy J. Kleinplatz (2005): DSM-IV-TR and the Paraphilias: An argument for removal. *Journal of Psychology and Human Sexuality* 17(3/4): 91–109

Muñoz, José Esteban (1999): *Disidentifications. Queers of Color and the Performance of Politics*. Minneapolis/London: University of Minnesota Press

Munson, Marcia & Judith P. Stelboum, eds. (1999): *The Lesbian Polyamory Reader. Open Relationships, Non-Monogamy, and Casual Sex*. Binghamton: Harrington Park Press

Murray, Samantha (2004): Locating Aesthetics. Sexing the Fat Woman. *Social Semiotics* 14(3): 237–247

Nägele, Barbara (1998): *Von 'Mädchen' und 'Kollegen'. Zum Geschlechterverhältnis am Fachbereich Chemie*. Mössingen, Talheim: talheimer

Namaste, Ki (1996): 'Tragic Misreadings'. Queer Theory's Erasure of Transgender Subjectivity. In: Brett Beemyn & Mickey Eliason, eds. *Queer Studies. A Lesbian, Gay, Bisexual and Transgender Anthology*. New York: Routledge, 183–203

Namaste, Vivian K. (2000): *Invisible Lives. The Erasure of Transsexual and Transgender People*. Chicago/London: University of Chicago Press

Nataf, Zachary I. (1996): *Lesbians Talk Transgender*. London: Scarlet

Nestle, Joan, ed. (1992): *The Persistent Desire. A Femme-Butch Reader*. Boston: Alyson Publications

Nestle, Joan, Clare Howell & Riki Wilchins, eds. (2002): *Genderqueer. Voices From Beyond the Sexual Binary*. Los Angeles: Alyson Publications

Newmahr, Staci (2006): Experiences of Power in SM. A Challenge to Power Theory. *Berkeley Journal of Sociology* 50: 37–60

Newmahr, Staci (2010): Rethinking Kink. Sadomasochism as Serious Leisure. *Qualitative Sociology* 33(3): 313–331

Newmahr, Staci (2011): *Playing on the Edge. Sadomasochism, Risk, and Intimacy*. Bloomington: Indiana University Press

Nichols, Jeanette, Darlene Pagano & Margaret Rossoff (1982): Is Sadomasochism Feminist? A Critique of the Samois Position. In: Robin Ruth Linden, Darlene R. Pagano, Diana E.H. Russell & Susan Leigh Star, eds. *Against Sadomasochism*. Palo Alto, CA: Frog in the Well, 137–146

Noble, Bobby Jean (2013): Our Bodies Are Not Ourselves. Tranny Guys and the Racialized Class Politics of Incoherence. In: Susan Stryker & Aren Z. Aizura, eds. *The Transgender Studies Reader 2*. New York/London: Routledge, 248–257

Nordling, Niklas, N. Kenneth Sandnabba & Pekka Santtila (2000): The Prevalence and Effects of Self-reported Childhood Sexual Abuse Among Sadomasochistically Oriented Males and Females. *Journal of Child Sex Abuse* 9(1): 53–63

O'Malley, Pat (2000): Uncertain Subjects. Risks, Liberalism and Contract. *Economy & Society* 29(4): 460–484

Pa, Monica (2001): Beyond the Pleasure Principle. The Criminalization of Consensual Sadomasochistic Sex. *Texas Journal of Women and the Law* 11(1): 51–92

Passig, Kathrin & Wolf Deunan (2002): *Datenschlag Chronik des Sadomasochismus (DACHS)*. Accessed 28 September 2009, http://www.datenschlag.org/dachs/

Petrella, Serena (2007): Ethical Sluts and Closet Polyamorists: Dissident Eroticism, Abject Subjects and the Normative Cycle in Self-Help Books on Free Love. In: Alejandra Cervantes-Carson & Nick Rumsfeld, eds. *Sex and Sexuality*. Tijnmuiden: Inter-disciplinary Press. Accessed 30 June 2014, http://www.inter-disciplinary.net/ci/transformations/sexualities/s2/petrella%20001.pdf

Phelan, Shane (2001): *Sexual Strangers. Gays, Lesbians and Dilemmas of Citizenship*. Philadelphia: Temple University Press

Pieper, Marianne (2003): Regierung der Armen oder Regierung von Armut als Selbstsorge. In: Marianne Pieper & Encarnación Gutiérrez Rodríguez, eds. *Gouvernementalität. Ein sozialwissenschaftliches Konzept in Anschluss an Foucault.* Frankfurt/Main: Campus, 136–160

Pieper, Marianne (2007): Biopolitik – Die Umwendung eines Machtparadigmas. Immaterielle Arbeit und Prekarisierung. In: Pieper, Marianne, Thomas Atzert, Serhat Karakayali & Vassilis Tsianos eds. *Empire und die biopolitische Wende.* Frankfurt/Main: Campus, 215–244

Pieper, Marianne & Robin Bauer (2005): Polyamory und Mono-Normativität. Ergebnisse einer empirischen Studie über nicht-monogame Lebensformen. In: Laura Méritt, Traude Bührmann & Najda Boris Schefzig, eds. *Mehr als eine Liebe – Polyamouröse Beziehungen.* Berlin: Orlanda, 59–69

Pieper, Marianne & Robin Bauer (2014): Polyamorie. Mono-Normativität – Dissidente Mikropolitik – Begehren als transformative Kraft? *Journal für Psychologie* 22(1): 1-35

Pieper, Marianne, Thomas Atzert, Serhat Karakayali & Vassilis Tsianos, eds. (2007): *Empire und die biopolitische Wende.* Frankfurt/Main: Campus

Pines, Ayla & Elliott Aronson (1981): Polyfidelity. An Alternative Lifestyle Without Jealousy? *Alternative Lifestyles* 4(3): 373–339

Plaid, Andrea (2009): Interview With the Perverted Negress. Racialicious Blog. Accessed 7 April 2012, http://www.racialicious.com/2009/07/10/interview-with-the-perverted-negress/

Plant, Bob (2007): Playing Games/ Playing Us. Foucault on Sadomasochism. *Philosophy & Social Criticism* 33(5): 531–561

Plato (2006): *Symposium.* Stuttgart: Reclam

Prosser, Jay (1998): *Second Skins. The Body Narratives of Transsexuality.* New York: Columbia University Press

Rambukkana, Nathan (2010): Sex, Space and Discourse. Non/Monogamy and Intimate Privilege in the Public Sphere. In: Meg Barker & Darren Langdridge, eds. *Understanding Non-Monogamies.* New York/London: Routledge, 237–242

Ramey, James W. (1976): *Intimate Friendships.* Englewood Cliffs, NJ: Prentice-Hall

Raymond, Katherine (1997): Confessions of a Second Generation.... Dyke? Reflections on Sexual Non-Identity. In: Carol Queen & Lawrence Schimel, eds. *PoMoSexuals. Challenging Assumptions About Gender and Sexuality.* San Francisco: Cleis Press, 53–61

Reid-Pharr, Robert (2001): *Black Gay Man. Essays.* New York: New York University Press

Reiersøl, Odd & Svein Skeid (2006): The ICD Diagnoses of Fetishism and Sadomasochism. In: Peggy J. Kleinplatz & Charles Moser, eds. *Sadomasochism. Powerful Pleasures.* Binghamton: Harrington Park Press, 243–262

Reindal, Solveig Magnus (1999): Independence, Dependence, Interdependence. Some Reflections on the Subject and Personal Autonomy. *Disability & Society* 14(3): 353–367

Reinisch, June M. with Ruth Beasly (1990): *The Kinsey Institute New Report on Sex. What You Must Know to be Sexually Literate.* New York: St. Martin's

Reiter, Birgit-Michel (1998): Genitale Korrekturen an intersexuellen Menschen. 'It's easier to make a hole than to build a pole'. In: *kassiber 34.* Accessed 14 May 2009, http://www.nadir.org/nadir/initiativ/kombo/k_34isar.htm

Renzetti, Claire M. (1996): The Poverty of Services for Battered Lesbians. *Journal of Gay and Lesbian Social Services* 4(1): 61–68

Reti, Irene (1993): Remember the Fire: Lesbian Sadomasochism in a Post Nazi Holocaust World. In: Irene Reti, ed. *Unleashing Feminism. Critiquing Lesbian Sadomasochism in the Gay Nineties.* Santa Cruz: HerBooks, 79–99

Revise F65 (n.d.): 2005–2010. *About the Revise F65 Project. Revise F65 Efforts for the Leather/Fetish/BDSM Community.* Accessed 17 October 2009, http://www.revisef65.org/about3.html

Reynolds, Dawn (2007): Disability and BDSM: Bob Flanagan and the Case for Sexual Rights. *Sexuality Research and Social Policy: Journal of NSRC* 4(1): 40–51

Rian, Karen (1982): Sadomasochism and the Social Construction of Desire. In: Linden, Darlene R. Pagano, Diana E.H. Russell & Susan Leigh Star, eds. *Against Sadomasochism.* Palo Alto, CA: Frog in the Well, 45–50

Rice, Carla (2007): Becoming 'the Fat Girl'. Acquisition of an Unfit Identity. *Women's Studies International Forum* 30: 158–174

Rich, Adrienne (1980): Compulsory Heterosexuality and Lesbian Existence. *Signs* 5(4): 631–660

Richards, Arlene K. (1992): Bisexuality, Perversion and Childhood Sexual Abuse. *Issues in Ego Psychology* 15(1): 33–43

Richards, Christina (2010): Trans and Non-Monogamies. In: Meg Barker & Darren Langdridge, eds. *Understanding Non-Monogamies.* New York/London: Routledge, 121–133

Richters, Juliet, Richard O. de Visser, Chris E. Rissel, Andrew E. Grulich & Anthony M.A. Smith (2008): Demographic and Psychosocial Features of Participants in Bondage and Discipline, 'Sadomasochism' or Dominance and Submission (BDSM). Data from a National Survey. *Journal of Sexual Medicine* 5(7): 1660–1668

Rick, Andrea (2007): Femmes, Fans, Freundinnen. Femininitäten nur in Nebenrollen? Konstruktionen von Cross-Maskulinitäten/-Männlichkeiten durch den Ausschluss von Femininitäten/Weiblichkeiten. In: Robin Bauer, Josch Hoenes & Volker Woltersdorff, eds. *Unbeschreiblich männlich. Heteronormativitätskritische Perspektiven.* Hamburg: Männerschwarm, 291–305

Riddell, Carol (2006): Divided Sisterhood. A Critical Review of Janice Raymond's *The Transsexual Empire.* In: Susan Stryker & Stephen Whittle, eds. *The Transgender Studies Reader.* New York/London: Routledge, 144–158

Riggs, Damien W. (2006): *Priscilla, (White) Queen of the Desert. Queer Rights/Race Privilege.* New York: Peter Lang

Ritchie, Ani & Meg Barker (2005): Feminist SM: A Contradiction in Terms or a Way of Challenging Traditional Gendered Dynamics Through Sexual Practice? *Lesbian & Gay Psychology Review* 6(3): 227–239

Ritchie, Ani & Meg Barker (2006): 'There Aren't Words for What We Do or How We Feel So We Have to Make Them Up': Constructing Polyamorous Languages in a Culture of Compulsory Monogamy. *Sexualities* 9(5): 584–601

Ritchie, Ani & Meg Barker (2007): Hot Bi Babes and Feminist Families: Polyamorous Women Speak Out. *Lesbian and Gay Psychology Review* 8(2): 141–151

Roesch Wagner, Sally (1982): Pornography and the Sexual Revolution. The Backlash of Sadomasochism. In: Robin Ruth Linden, Darlene R. Pagano, Diana E.H. Russell & Susan Leigh Star, eds. *Against Sadomasochism.* Palo Alto, CA: Frog in the Well, 23–44

Rose, Nikolas (1996): Governing 'Advanced' Liberal Democracies. In: Andrew Barry, Thomas Osborne & Nikolas Rose, eds. *Foucault and Political Reason. Liberalism, Neoliberalism and Rationalities of Government.* Chicago: University of Chicago Press, 37–64

Rubin, Gayle (1992a): Thinking Sex. Notes for a Radical Theory of the Politics of Sexuality. In: Carole S. Vance, ed. *Pleasure and Danger. Exploring Female Sexuality.* London: Pandora Press, 267–319

Rubin, Gayle (1992b): Of Catamites and Kings. Reflections on Butch, Gender, and Boundaries. In: Joan Nestle, ed. *The Persistent Desire. A Femme-Butch Reader.* Boston: Alyson, 466–482

Rubin, Gayle (2003): The Leather Menace. Comments on Politics and SM. In: Jeffrey Escoffier, ed. *Sexual Revolution.* New York: Thunder Mouth's Press, 266–299

Rubin, Henry (2003): *Self-Made Men. Identity and Embodiment Among Transsexual Men.* Nashville: Vanderbilt University Press

Rust, Paula C. (1996): Monogamy and Polyamory: Relationship Issues for Bisexuals. In: Beth A. Firestein, ed. *Bisexuality: The Psychology and Politics of an Invisible Minority.* Thousand Oaks, CA: Sage, 127–148

Rüster, Daniel (2010): Leder-Transmann im Rollstuhl ist neuer International Mr. Leather. *Blu* 15 June 2010. Accessed 3 July 2010, http://www.blu.fm/subsites/detail.php?kat=gesellschaft&id=4007

Rye, B.J. & Glenn J. Meaney (2007): The Pursuit of Sexual Pleasure. *Sexuality & Culture* 11(1): 28–51

Said, Edward (1978): *Orientalism.* New York: Vintage

Salamon, Gayle (2010): *Assuming a Body. Transgender and Rhetorics of Materiality.* New York: Columbia University Press

Samuels, Andrew (2010): Promiscuities. Politics, Imagination, Spirituality and Hypocrisy. In: Meg Barker & Darren Langdridge, eds. *Understanding Non-Monogamies.* London: Routledge, 212–221

Sassen, Saskia (2007): Die Re-Positionierung von Bürgerschaft. In: Marianne Pieper et al., eds. *Empire und die biopolitische Wende.* Frankfurt/Main: Campus, 143–168

Savran, David (1998): *Taking It Like a Man. White Masculinity, Masochism, and Contemporary American Culture.* Princeton: Princeton University Press

Schenk, Herrad (1987): *Freie Liebe – wilde Ehe. Über die allmähliche Auflösung der Ehe durch die Liebe.* München: Beck

Schiebinger, Londa (1993): *Nature's Body. Gender in the Making of Modern Science.* Boston: Beacon

Schmidt, Gunter (1998): *Sexuelle Verhältnisse. Über das Verschwinden der Sexualmoral.* Reinbek: Rowohlt

Schmidt, Gunter, Silja Matthiesen, Arne Dekker & Kurt Starke (2006): *Spätmoderne Beziehungswelten. Report über Partnerschaft und Sexualität in drei Generationen.* Wiesbaden: VS Verlag

Schütz, Alfred & Thomas Luckmann (2003): *Strukturen der Lebenswelt.* Konstanz: UVK

Sedgwick, Eve Kosofsky (1990): *Epistemology of the Closet.* Berkeley: University of California Press

Serano, Julia (2008): Why Nice Guys Finish Last. In: Jaclyn Friedman & Jessica Valenti, eds. *Yes Means Yes! Visions of Female Sexual Power & a World Without Rape.* Berkeley, CA: Seal Press, 227–240

Shannon, Deric & Abbey Willis (2010): Theoretical Polyamory. Some Thoughts on Loving, Thinking and Queering Anarchism. *Sexualities* 13(4): 433–443

Sheff, Elisabeth (2005): Polyamorous Women, Sexual Subjectivity, and Power. *Journal of Contemporary Ethnography* 34(3): 251–283

Sheff, Elisabeth & Corie Hammers (2011): The Privilege of Perversities. Race, Class and Education Among Polyamorists and Kinksters. *Psychology & Sexuality* 2(3): 198–223

Simmel, Georg (1950): *The Sociology of Georg Simmel.* Glencoe, IL: Free Press

Simmel, Georg (1990): *The Philosophy of Money.* London: Routledge

Sims, Karen & Rose Mason with Darlene Pagano (1982): Racism and Sadomasochism. A Conversation With Two Black Lesbians. In: Robin Ruth Linden, Darlene

R. Pagano, Diana E.H. Russell & Susan Leigh Star, eds. *Against Sadomasochism*. Palo Alto, CA: Frog in the Well, 99–105

Singer, T. Benjamin (2006): From the Medical Gaze to Sublime Mutations. The Ethics of (Re)Viewing Non-Normative Body Images. In: Susan Stryker & Stephen Whittle, eds. *The Transgender Studies Reader*. New York/London: Routledge, 601–620

Sisson, Kathy (2007): The Cultural Formation of S/M. History and Analysis. In: Darren Langdridge & Meg Barker, eds. *Safe, Sane and Consensual. Contemporary Perspectives on Sadomasochism*. Houndmills: Palgrave, 10–34

Smith, Sarah A. (2005): Unleashing Gender. Dependency, Subjectivity and Recognition in Dominant/Submissive Relationships. *Lesbian & Gay Psychology Review* 6(3): 177–188

Snorton, C. Riley & Jin Haritaworn (2013): Trans Necropolitics. A Transnational Reflection on Violence, Death, and the Trans of Color Afterlife. In: Susan Stryker & Aren Z. Aizura, eds. *The Transgender Studies Reader 2*. New York/London: Routledge, 66–76

Sontag, Susan (1975): Fascinating Fascism. *The New York Review of Books* 22(1). Accessed 4 July 2009, http://www.nybooks.com/articles/9280

Spengler, Andreas (1979): *Sadomasochisten und ihre Subkulturen*. Frankfurt/Main: Campus

Springer, Kimberly (2008): Queering Black Female Heterosexuality. In: Jaclyn Friedman & Jessica Valenti, eds. *Yes Means Yes! Visions of Female Sexual Power & A World Without Rape*. Berkeley, CA: Seal Press, 77–91

Stanko, Elizabeth A. (1987): Typical Violence, Normal Precaution. Men, Women and Interpersonal Violence in England, Wales, Scotland, and the USA. In: Jalna Hanmer & Mary Maynard, eds. *Women, Violence and Social Control*. London: Macmillan, 121–134

Stear, Nils-Hennes (2009): Sadomasochism as Make-Believe. *Hypatia* 24(2): 21–38

stein, david & David Schachter (2009): *Ask the Man Who Owns Him. The Real Lives of Gay Masters and Slaves*. New York: Perfectbound Press

stein, slave david (2002): *'Safe Sane Consensual'. The Making of a Shibboleth*. Accessed 17 May 2009, http://www.nla-okc.com/Files/SSC.pdf

Steinbugler, Amy C. (2005): Visibility as Privilege and Danger. Heterosexual and Same-Sex Interracial Intimacy in the 21st Century. *Sexualities* 8(4): 425–443

Stephenson, Niamh & Dimitris Papadopoulos (2006): *Analysing Everyday Experience. Social Research and Political Change*. Houndmills: Palgrave

Stokes, Mason (2001): *Whiteness, Heterosexuality, and the Fictions of White Supremacy*. Durham & London: Duke University Press

Stone, Sharon Dale (1995): The Myth of Bodily Perfection. *Disability & Society* 10(4): 413–424

Strauss, Anselm L. & Juliet Corbin (1990): *Basics of Qualitative Research. Grounded Theory Procedures and Techniques*. Newbury Park: Sage

Stryker, Susan (1994): My Words to Victor Frankenstein Above the Village of Chamounix: Performing Transgender Rage. *GLQ* 1(1): 237–254

Stryker, Susan (2006a): (De)Subjugated Knowledges. An Introduction to Transgender Studies. In: Susan Stryker & Stephen Whittle, eds. *The Transgender Studies Reader*. New York/London: Routledge, 1–17

Stryker, Susan & Stephen Whittle, eds. (2006): *The Transgender Studies Reader*. New York/London: Routledge

Sullivan, Barbara (2004): Prostitution and Consent. Beyond the Liberal Dichotomy of 'Free or Forced'. In: Mark Cowling & Paul Reynolds, eds. *Making Sense of Sexual Consent*. Aldershot & Burlington: Ashgate, 127–140

Sullivan, Nikki (2003): *A Critical Introduction to Queer Theory*. New York: New York University Press

Sullivan, Nikki (2006): Transmogrification. (Un)becoming Other(s). In: Susan Stryker & Stephen Whittle, eds. *The Transgender Studies Reader*. New York/London: Routledge, 552–564

Swann, Brian, ed. (1996): *Coming to Light. Contemporary Translations of the Native Literatures of North America*. New York: Vintage

Switch, Gary (2001): *The Origin of RACK/ RACK vs. SSC*. Accessed 30 June 2014, http://www.leathernroses.com/generalbdsm/garyswitchrack.htm

Taylor, Gary W. (1997): The Discursive Construction and Regulation of Dissident Sexualities. The Case of SM. In: Jane M. Ussher, ed. *Body Talk. The Material and Discursive Regulation of Sexuality, Madness and Reproduction*. London: Routledge, 106–30

The Experiment (n.d.). Accessed 11 May 2011, http://www.experiment-berlin.de/english.htm

Thompson, Mark (1997): Einleitung. In: Mark Thompson, ed. *Lederlust. Berichte und Erfahrungen*. Berlin: Bruno Gmünder, 9–20

Tremain, Shelley (1996): We're Here. We're Disabled and Queer. Get Used to It. In: Shelley Tremain, ed. *Pushing the Limits. Disabled Dykes Produce Culture*. Toronto: Women's Press, 15–24

Troost, Hazel/Cedar (2008): Reclaiming Touch. Rape Culture, Explicit Verbal Consent, and Body Sovereignty. In: Jaclyn Friedman & Jessica Valenti, eds. *Yes Means Yes! Visions of Female Sexual Power & a World Without Rape*. Berkeley, CA: Seal Press, 171–177

Tucker, Naomi, ed. (1995): *Bisexual Politics. Theories, Queries, & Visions*. Binghampton: Harrington Park Press

Turner, Victor (2000): *Das Ritual. Struktur und Anti-Struktur*. Frankfurt/Main: Campus

Tyrell, Hartmann (1987): Romantische Liebe. Überlegungen zu ihrer 'quantitativen Bestimmtheit'. In: Dirk Baecker, Jürgen Markowitz, Rudolf Stichweh, Hartmann Tyrell & Helmut Willke, eds. *Theorie als Passion. Niklas Luhmann zum 60. Geburtstag*. Frankfurt/Main: Suhrkamp, 570–599

Valentine, David (2006): 'I Went to Bed With My Own Kind Once': The Erasure of Desire in the Name of Identity. In: Susan Stryker & Stephen Whittle, eds. *The Transgender Studies Reader*. New York/London: Routledge, 407–419

Valentine, Gill (1995): Out and About. Geographies of Lesbian Landscapes. *International Journal of Urban and Regional Research* 19: 96–112

Valentine, Gill (1996): (Re)negotiating the 'Heterosexual Street': Lesbian Productions of Space. In: Nancy Duncan, ed. *Body Space: Destabilizing Geographies of Gender and Sexuality*. New York/London: Routledge, 146–155

Van Lieshout, Maurice (1995): Leather Nights in the Woods. Homosexual Encounters in a Dutch Highway Rest Area. *Journal of Homosexuality* 29(1): 19–39

Vance, Carole S. (1992a): Pleasure and Danger. Towards a Politics of Sexuality. In: Carole S. Vance, ed. *Pleasure and Danger. Exploring Female Sexuality*. London: Pandora Press, 1–27

Vance, Carole S. (1992b): More Danger, More Pleasure. A Decade After the Barnard Sexuality Conference. In: Carole S. Vance, ed. *Pleasure and Danger. Exploring Female Sexuality*. London: Pandora Press, xvi–xxxix

WALP (2009): *Women at Amsterdam Leatherpride. General Info*. Accessed 18 October 2009, http://www.walp.dds.nl/page1/page1.html

Walton, Kendall (2004): Fearing Fictionally. In: Eileen John & Dominic McIver Lopes, eds. *Philosophy of Literature. Contemporary and Classic Readings. An Anthology.* Malden, MA: Blackwell, 177–184

Ward, Jane (2010): Gender Labor: Transmen, Femmes and Collective Work of Transgression. *Sexualities* 13(2): 236–254

Warner, Michael (1993): Introduction. In: Michael Warner, ed. *Fear of a Queer Planet. Queer Politics and Social Theory.* Minneapolis/London: University of Minnesota Press, viii–xxxi

Weait, Matthew (2004): The Age of Consent and Sexual Consent. In: Mark Cowling & Paul Reynolds, eds. *Making Sense of Sexual Consent.* Aldershot & Burlington: Ashgate, 73–92

Weinberg, Thomas S., ed. (1995): *S&M. Studies in Dominance and Submission.* Amherst, NY: Prometheus

Weiss, Margot D. (2006a): Mainstreaming Kink. The Politics of BDSM Representation. In: Peggy J. Kleinplatz & Charles Moser, eds. *Sadomasochism. Powerful Pleasures.* Binghamton: Harrington Park Press, 103–132

Weiss, Margot D. (2006b): Working at Play. BDSM Sexuality in the San Francisco Bay Area. *Division II Faculty Publications,* Paper 47. Accessed 30 June 2014, http://wesscholar.wesleyan.edu/cgi/viewcontent.cgi?article=1045&context=div2facpubs

Weiss, Margot D. (2007): Rumsfeld! Consensual BDSM and 'Sadomasochistic Torture' at Abu Ghraib. *Unpublished manuscript*

Weiss, Margot D. (2008): Gay Shame and BDSM Pride. Neoliberalism, Privacy, and Sexual Politics. *Radical History Review* 100: 86–101

Weiss, Margot D. (2011): *Techniques of Pleasure. BDSM and the Circuits of Sexuality.* Durham: Duke University Press

Wetzstein, Thomas A., Linda Steinmetz, Christa Reis & Roland Eckert (1993): *Sadomasochismus. Szenen und Rituale.* Hamburg: Rowohlt

White, Chris (2006): The Spanner Trials and the Changing Law on Sadomasochism in the UK. In: Peggy J. Kleinplatz & Charles Moser, eds. *Sadomasochism. Powerful Pleasures.* Binghamton: Harrington Park Press, 167–187

Wilkinson, Eleanor (2009): Perverting Visual Pleasure. Representing Sadomasochism. *Sexualities* 12(2): 181–198

Wilkinson, Eleanor (2010): What's Queer About Non-Monogamy Now? In: Meg Barker & Darren Langdridge, eds. *Understanding Non-Monogamies.* London: Routledge, 243–254

Willey, Angela (2006): 'Christian Nations', 'Polygamic Races' and Women's Rights: Toward a Genealogy of Non/Monogamy and Whiteness. *Sexualities* 9(5): 530–546

Williams, Christine L. (2002): Sexual Harassment and Sadomasochism. *Hypatia* 17(2): 99–117

Williams, D. J. (2006): Different (Painful!) Strokes for Different Folks. A General Overview of Sexual Sadomasochism (SM) and Its Diversity. *Sexual Addiction & Compulsion* 13: 333–346

Williams, D. J. (2009): Deviant Leisure: Rethinking 'The Good, the Bad and the Ugly'. *Leisure Sciences* 31(2): 207–213

Winant, Howard (1997): Behind Blue Eyes. Whiteness and Contemporary U.S. Racial Politics. In: Michelle Fine, Lois Weis, Linda Powell Pruitt & April Burns, eds. *Off White. Readings on Race, Power, and Society.* New York: Routledge, 40–53

Winnicott, Donald Woods (1971): *Playing and Reality.* New York: Basic Books

Wolfe, Leanna (2003): *Jealousy and Transformation in Polyamorous Relationships*. Unpublished doctoral dissertation, Institute for Advanced Study of Human Sexuality, San Francisco, CA. Accessed 11 September 2007, http://drleannawolfe.com/Dissertation.pdf

Wollrad, Eske (2005): *Weißsein im Widerspruch*. Königstein/Taunus: Ulrike Helmer Verlag

Woltersdorff, Volker (2010): Sexual Politics in Neoliberalism. Managing Precarious Selves. In: Stefanie Ernst & Andrea Bührmann, eds. *Control or Care of the Self? The Sociology of the Subject in the 21st Century*. Newcastle: Cambridge Scholars Publishing, 210–222

Woltersdorff, Volker (2011a): 'Let's Play Master and Servant!' Spielformen des paradoxen Selbst in sadomasochistischen Subkulturen. In: Regine Strätling, ed. *Spielformen des Selbst. Subjektivität und Spiel zwischen Ethik und Ästhetik*. Bielefeld: transcript, 289–301

Woltersdorff, Volker (2011b): Paradoxes of Precarious Sexualities. Sexual Subcultures Under Neoliberalism. *Cultural Studies* 25(2): 164–182

Woltersdorff, Volker (2011c): The Pleasures of Compliance. Domination and Compromise Within BDSM Practice. In: María do Mar Castro Varela, Nikita Dhawan & Antke Engel, eds. *Hegemony and Heteronormativity. Revisiting 'The Political' in Queer Politics*. Farnham: Ashgate, 169–188

Woods, William J. & Diane Binson, eds. (2003): *Gay Bathhouses and Public Health Policy*. Binghamton: Harrington Park Press

World Health Organization (2010): ICD-10. International Statistical Classification of Diseases and Related Health Problems, 10th Revision. Accessed 19 December 2011, http://apps.who.int/classifications/icd10/browse/2010/en

Wright, Susan (2006): Discrimination of SM-Identified Individuals. In: Peggy J. Kleinplatz & Charles Moser, eds. *Sadomasochism. Powerful Pleasures*. Binghamton: Harrington Park Press, 217–232

Wright, Susan (2008): Second National Survey of Violence & Discrimination Against Sexual Minorities. Accessed 13 June 2012, https://ncsfreedom.org/resources/bdsm-survey.html

Young, Iris (1990): *Justice and the Politics of Difference*. Princeton: Princeton University Press

Young, Iris (1992): Five Faces of Oppression. In: Thomas Wartenberg, ed. *Rethinking Power*. Albany, NY: SUNY Press, 174–95

Zell-Ravenheart, Morning Glory (1990): A Bouquet of Lovers. Strategies for Responsible Open Relationships. *Green Egg: The Journal of CAW* (#89, Beltane 1990). Accessed 14 August 2012, http://www.patheos.com/Resources/Additional-Resources/Bouquet-of-Lovers.html

Žižek, Slavoj (2001): *Die Tücke des Subjekts*. Frankfurt/Main: Suhrkamp

Zussman, Mira & Anne Pierce (1998): Shifts of Consciousness in Consensual S/M, Bondage, and Fetish Play. *Anthropology of Consciousness* 4(9): 15–38

Index

Printed and bound by CPI Group (UK) Ltd, Croydon, CR0 4YY